# SAKDALISTAS' STRUGGLE
# FOR PHILIPPINE INDEPENDENCE,
# 1930–1945

# SAKDALISTAS' STRUGGLE FOR PHILIPPINE INDEPENDENCE, 1930–1945

Motoe Terami-Wada

ATENEO DE MANILA
UNIVERSITY PRESS

ATENEO DE MANILA UNIVERSITY PRESS
Bellarmine Hall, Katipunan Avenue
Loyola Heights, Quezon City
P.O. Box 154, 1099 Manila, Philippines
Tel.: (632) 426-59-84 / Fax (632) 426-59-09
E-mail: unipress@admu.edu.ph
Website: www.ateneopress.org

Cover design by Faith Aldaba
Book design by Paolo Tiausas

The National Library of the Philippines CIP Data

Recommended entry:

Terami-Wada, Motoe
    Sakdalistas' struggle for Philippine independence,
1930–1945 / Motoe Terami-Wada. — Quezon City :
Ateneo de Manila University Press, c2014.
    p. ; cm.

    ISBN 978-971-550-679-3

    1. Lapiang Sakdalista sa Pilipinas—History—Sources.
2. Philippines—History—1898–1946—Sources. 3. Philippines
Politics and government—1935–1946.  I. Title.

DS685  959.903  2014  P320130739

# CONTENTS

# ACKNOWLEDGMENTS

T hough only vaguely, I knew of the Japanese military's atrocities in China, especially in Nanjin, during the second Sino-Japanese War (1937–1945) and in Southeast Asian regions (1942–1945.) When my daughter and I arrived in Manila in January 1973, shortly after President Marcos declared martial law, to follow my husband who was invited to teach at the University of the Philippines, I felt I should know more about the Japanese occupation of the Philippines. I tried reading as many books as I could on this subject whenever I found the time.

When my knowledge of the local language became sufficient, I began enjoying watching movies and stage dramas. One of the performances by Philippine Educational Theater Association (PETA) at Fort Santiago was about a martial law during the early American occupation of the Philippines circa 1900. The play was about an ordinary citizen named Juan de la Cruz who fought against the new conqueror and died, but another Juan de la Cruz picked up where the former left off. This play was obviously criticizing Marcos' martial law and urging people to fight against it. At that time, people often drew an analogy between the oppressive Marcos regime and the Japanese occupation period. I became interested in how the Filipinos expressed a critical attitude and resistance against the Japanese military occupation through indirect and non-violent means, just like in this PETA play. This inquiry led to a Master's thesis, "Cultural Front in the Philippines: 1942–1945," in 1985. My interest in the Japanese occupation continued. Now I became interested in those Filipinos who supported or collaborated with the Japanese when Japan was not a particularly popular country among Filipinos after forty some years of American occupation. As a colonized people, all the Filipinos had to pledge allegiance to the United States.

In 1984, Dr. Setsuho Ikehata, then professor at Tokyo University of Foreign Languages and Cultures, invited me to join the three-year project, "Historical and Anthropological Study on the Philippine Folk Catholicism" funded by the Mitsubishi Foundation. For this project, I decided to look into the so-called Rizalista cults in and around Manila.

In the meantime, Professor Shizuo Suzuki, then with the Center of Southeast Asian Studies of Kyoto University, who was researching the history of the Communist movement in the Philippines, asked me to attend the interviews he was conducting with Luis Taruc, one of the leaders of the Huks, an anti-Japanese guerrilla outfit during the Japanese occupation and the anti-government liberation army in the postwar era. Prof. Suzuki was particularly interested in the postwar alliance of the Communist party and the former Ganap party, considered to be a pro-Japanese group during the occupation. I found it interesting to see how Mr. Taruc's group and the members of the Ganap forged, or tried to forge, an alliance.

I do not remember exactly how the meeting took place, but a group of former Ganap/Makapili members (members, hereafter) gathered in a house in Alabang, Metro Manila, to meet with Mr. Taruc and the Japanese "guests," Prof. Suzuki and me. The members seemed to be more interested in talking to us rather than to Mr. Taruc. When the meeting was almost over, one of them handed us a letter addressed to the Japanese government, asking for compensation for the service they rendered to the Japanese military during the occupation. Prof. Suzuki accepted the letter and promised to forward it to the Japanese Embassy in Manila, which he did a few days later.

As we were leaving, an elderly man approached me and said that he was not interested in asking any compensation from anybody because his supporting the Japanese military was based on his conviction. He assisted the Japanese because he believed the Philippines would become independent from the United States. I was intrigued by his words, and later on I paid him a visit to know more about his life and activities in the prewar and occupation time.

His name was Mr. Jeremias Adia, and he was the secretary of the Ganap party during the Japanese occupation. In the first meeting at his residence in Cabuayo, Laguna, I discovered that he was the president of a Rizalista cult called "Iglesia Sagrada ng Lahi (The Church of the Sacred Race)." I could not help but thank this luck that I could study his church for Dr. Ikehata's project and learn more about the members' activities at the same time. From then on, my visit to Cabuyao and Silang, Cavite, where the church's headquarters stood, became more regular and frequent.

In the meantime, Mr. Adia took me to the site of the 1935 Sakdal Uprising and arranged meetings with other members. I still remember vividly my first meeting with those who gathered at Mr. Adia's residence. Five or six men and a woman, most of them in their seventies, were seated in the living room. Some of them were barefooted, and their ankles were caked with half-dried mud. Obviously they were working in the rice field just before they came. The woman said to me, "So you are interested in our revolution" (sa aming rebolusyon). In many get-togethers to come, they always referred to the 1935 Uprising as the "revolution." One of them showed me an undershirt that he wore when he joined the "revolution"; he wore it to invoke protection from the Higher Being. The sleeveless white shirt had Latin prayers and figures of angels and other symbols.

These people tried to speak to me in some Japanese they had learned from the soldiers and related to me fond memories they had of some individual Japanese. They shared their excitement and expectations of achieving independence because independence meant better lives for them and their children. They also shared what they went through at the end of the occupation and right after the war: some family members were lynched by anti-Japanese guerrillas or villagers; they had hardly anything to eat in mountain hideouts at the end of the occupation where many died of starvation; some were imprisoned for a period of time and most of them had been treated like outcasts in their respective towns in the postwar era.

They vehemently denied they were traitors to the country as the government and other Filipinos labeled them. Mr. Adia and others used to say that because I was Japanese, they felt very comfortable and relaxed talking to me freely what they had kept to themselves for a long time. Once a member asked me whether I knew of a good ophthalmologist in Manila. I gave him the name and address of a Filipino specialist I used to go to. He said, "No, no. Give me the name of a Japanese ophthalmologist. I do not trust the Filipino doctor. He might blind me." Their mistrust and fear of other Filipinos were still very strong.

In 1990, the Forum for the Survey of Records Concerning the Japanese Occupation of the Philippines was formed, led by Dr. Setsuho Ikehata and funded by the Toyota Foundation. I was fortunate to be invited to this forum which gave me an opportunity to develop the subject I had been pursuing. The fund made it possible for me to do research in archives and libraries, not only in Metro Manila but also in Washington D.C. and Tokyo. Finally my research took shape as a Ph. D. dissertation in 1992, entitled "Ang Kilusang Sakdal" (Sakdal Movement), and I submitted it to the History Department of the University of the Philippines. I was encouraged to publish it as a book, but the same year, my husband was assigned to work in New Delhi, India, and I followed him with three children.

My book on Sakdal had to be put off during our four-year stay in India because I was busy, not only adjusting to a new life and learning about the fascinating culture of India but also playing the role expected of the wife of a representative of an international organization. We came back to Manila in 1996. We had barely unpacked what we had shipped from India when my husband announced that he wanted to retire early, in a year's time, and live in Washington state where we had a summer house. I was devastated because I thought he had at least ten years before his retirement. Leaving Manila was very difficult for me. I felt as if I were forced to leave my mother country, because after all, I lived there for more than twenty years and all my children had grown up, two of them being born in Manila.

After settling in at our summer house, now our American residence, I had to face another difficult challenge. Within barely a year, my husband passed away from lung cancer. Perhaps he knew of his impending death, and that was the reason he wanted to retire earlier so that he could enjoy his retirement life of playing golf and fishing, which he did for a few months.

Writing a book on Sakdal was not on my mind for some time until one day in 2003, Dr. Alfred McCoy of the University of Wisconsin encouraged me to do so. With his encouragement, I finally began organizing the dissertation into a book, but it has been a slow process. First of all, I had to adjust emotionally to the new situation after losing someone so dear. Other adjustments included learning how to drive, to write check, and to pay bills, all of which my husband used to do.

Now the book is finally here. It was impossible to reach this stage without the assistance of so many people: my family, friends, and colleagues. I would like to extend my deepest gratitude by citing their names below.

First and foremost, I thank Jeremias Adia who not only spent many hours patiently answering my questions, but also helped me reach other members. Equally important support came from Setsuho Ikehata, who gave me impetus to conduct research by inviting me to various forums and sending me encouraging words. In the final stage of the manuscript, she also gave me valuable advice. In the beginning of my research work, Reynaldo Ileto, who was leaving for Australia, generously shared with me some material he had gathered for his own research. He also read my dissertation and gave me useful comments. I would like to thank the members of the Forum of the Japanese Occupation who inspired me and broadened my view: Shinzo Hayase, Yoshiko Nagano, Satoshi Nakano, Takefumi Terada, Hitoshi Nagai, Midori Kawashima, and Ricardo T. Jose. Ma. Terresa Guia Padilla and Loida Reyes, my research assistants, helped me with reading and cataloguing the *Sakdal* and *Ganap* weekly newspapers from 1932-39. Reading all available *Sakdal/Ganap* newspapers was a daunting task, and their assistance was invaluable. I would also like to thank Lydia Yu-Jose for reading my dissertation, commenting on it, and sharing some materials. Others who supplied me with or suggested Sakdal-related materials include Brian Fegan, Jim Richardson, and Florentino Rodao. My special thanks goes to Bernardita Churchill who obtained pertinent material at the National Archives in Washington D.C.; in addition, Daniel Doeppers supplied me with some *Ganap* issues which were not available at the Philippine National Library.

When I began writing this book, I realized some materials and books were missing due to the numerous moves we made: from Manila to New Delhi and back; from Manila to Kobe, Japan; and from Kobe to Washington state. Within the state I moved one more time to my present home after my husband's passing. It is a small town close to the Canadian border, with no university or academic institution nearby. Many friends and colleagues came to my rescue by supplying me with pertinent books and materials. Especially I thank Thomas Walsh, Shinzo Hayase, and Chizuko

Otsuka-Gooding. I also have a debt of gratitude to Pamela Causgove and Fred and Machrina Mesch, who went through much of the manuscript and gave me precious editorial advice.

Finally my gratitude goes to my family members: my husband and children who had to spend numerous "motherless" weekends. My daughter, Megumi who was at the University of California, San Diego, at that time helped me secure some pertinent dissertations and books. One day I came home after spending a weekend in Atimonan, Quezon, for interviews with the members. When I announced my return at the front entrance, my husband and son, Roy, rushed down from upstairs and hugged me very tightly, as if they had not seen me for months. I learned from them that there had been a shoot-out between the Constabulary soldiers and the members of the New People's Army in the township of Atimonan early that day. I must have passed the town right after the shooting because I did see sand bags piled up in front of the city hall when I was driving through, and hardly anybody was seen on the streets.

I would also like to thank the staff of ADMU press as well as the readers who gave me valuable suggestions and comments.

Before the completion of this book, some had already died, including Jeremias Adia. Others were William Henry Scott, who often wrote me encouraging letters from his "mountain hide out"; Morton J. Netzorg, who shared with me some rare materials related to the Sakdal movement; Doreen Fernandez, who offered to read the whole manuscript when it was completed; and Shizuo Suzuki, with whom I shared a number of interviews with the members.

Finally, most of all, my profound and heartfelt gratitude goes to my late husband, Richard Osamu Wada, to whom this book is dedicated.

And lastly I would like to thank Clint Kolyer who have patiently observed and supported my slow paced work.

# PROLOGUE

The Japanese Occupation of the Philippines (1942–1945) drove a deep wedge of animosity between the Filipino people in general and those who organized paramilitary groups to assist the Japanese military and fight against the returning Americans. Immediately after the war, the People's Court was established to try Filipino collaborators. The court described the members of one such paramilitary group, the Makapilis, as those who "willfully, unlawfully, feloniously, and traitorously adhered to their enemy, the Empire of Japan." Such feelings toward them continue to exist even today among many Filipinos in southern and central Luzon.

The typical image of a Makapili would be a man hooded with *bayong* (bag made of woven palm leaves) pointing out certain men in a group suspected of being anti-Japanese guerrillas. In many cases the motivation for this was based on his personal grudge against certain people or to obtain a sack of rice from the Japanese. Many innocent people were executed as a result of this action. Even in academic circles, as late as 2008, such collaborators were still described as "those who joined the enemy and became the loathsome members of the Makapili."[1]

On the other hand, most Filipinos have been more forgiving toward their former enemy, the Japanese, who were responsible for three years of such hardship and misery. This may be due to the tolerant nature of the Filipino people as well as the Japanese recognition and acknowledgment of their brutal and inhumane acts. In the 1980s, high-ranking Japanese officials belatedly expressed deep repentance for the Japanese atrocities that had been perpetrated during the Japanese Occupation.[2] Moreover, reconciliation efforts by the nongovernment sector began in the early 2000s. One such project, Bridge for Peace, organized by Japanese youth, has been promoting dialogue between Japanese war veterans who were sent to the Philippines and Filipinos who lived through the hardship. They have been exchanging their experiences through videotape memoirs.[3] These efforts are commendable. However, war reconciliation between Japan and the Philippines cannot be complete without reconciliation within the Philippines—between those who were accused of military collaboration with the Japanese and the rest of the Filipino people.

In 2005, a conference was held in Manila to initiate dialogue between the former Makapilis and the USAFFE (United Stated Army Forces in the Far East) guerrillas.[4] It was organized by a Japanese TV production company to be televised on the government-owned HHK. The producer's motive may have been to show the Japanese audience the plight of the Filipino collaborators. The former Makapilis and the USAFFE guerrillas were seated facing each other. The Makapili side held a Pro-Japanese sign and the guerrilla side, USAFFE Guerillas. The former guerrillas aired their sufferings and sadness over losing loved ones at the hands of the Makapilis and the Japanese. Some of them even refused to join the dialogue. The Makapili side tried to explain their motives for siding with the Japanese military; however, being simple barrio folks, they lacked sufficient persuasiveness. The conference ended without much dialogue, hence, without much understanding.

Sadly, to label the Makapili soldiers simply as Pro-Japanese exhibits a lack of understanding on the part of the organizers. To accord them equal treatment, the sign should have read Makapili soldiers, which would have been the equivalent term. Or, alternatively, since the Makipilis were labeled Pro-Japanese, then the USAFFE guerillas should have been labeled Pro-American. A couple of questions come to mind. Were the Makapilis simply a tool of the Japanese military? Why did they fight the one-sided war against the overwhelmingly superior American forces when the

Japanese defeat was obvious to everyone, even to the Japanese? The first step toward understanding the Makapilis' intentions and actions is to look into their past, tracing their history back to the Sakdalista movement in 1930. Only then can the dialogue between the two camps be more fruitful; and when understanding is obtained, hopefully the scars of war may be healed.

This book is a humble attempt to bring about such understanding.

**CHAPTER 1**

# INTRODUCTION

O N THE SULTRY morning of 3 May 1935, Manila residents awakened
to the news that the city was on the verge of riot and in some parts
of the city, telephone and telegraph lines had been cut. In Bulacan and
Laguna, provinces adjacent to Manila, and some towns were under siege
by armed groups who were declaring the independence of the Philippines.
People from these towns were pouring into Manila to escape the chaos,
and by evening, major hotels in Manila had been fully booked by well-
to-do refugees.[1] Some Manila residents old enough to remember were
reminded of a similar incident that had taken place about twenty years
earlier.

On 24 December 1914, at midnight, about two hundred people
assembled in the Botanical Gardens in Manila. Some were dressed in
uniforms modeled after the soldiers of the anti-Spanish 1896 Revolution
led by the revolutionary organization called the Katipunan. Another two
hundred armed men carrying Katipunan banners attacked and captured
the municipal hall in Navotas, Rizal, shouting "Viva Filipinas" (Long Live
the Philippines)."[2] Other gatherings were taking place at various locations in Manila. In Pasay district, a proclamation written in Tagalog in

1

the name of the Revolutionary Army of the Philippines was posted on the wall of a shop. This army was organized by Gen. Artemio Ricarte, who was a veteran of the 1896 Revolution and the Philippine-American War (more on the army and Ricarte later). He was exiled in Hong Kong at the time. The proclamation said: "For a long time, the Philippines had lain in slavery but now it is her desire to get up again and draw once more the bolos (machetes) of revolution because the U.S. did not know how to fulfill its promises (of independence)." The participants, followers of General Ricarte, or Ricartistas, planned to stage a revolution simultane-ously in Manila, Navotas, and nearby places including Laguna.[3] Authorities disdainfully called this failed attempt the "Christmas Eve Fiasco." The Manila residents of 1935 realized that what was happening in the city and the surrounding provinces was yet another attempt at establishing independence.

On the afternoon of 2 May 1935, in the town of Cabuyao, Laguna, 45 kilometers (km) south of Manila, Salud Algabre Generalla (Salud Algabre) was putting on a white long-sleeved *camiseta* (blouse) and a red skirt with a blue tapis (a piece of cloth wrapped around the skirt at the waist) and was getting ready to join other revolutionaries who were assembling near the railway station. Algabre was a 42-year-old mother of five, the youngest only five months old. Most of the revolutionaries were barefoot and wore red bands across their shoulders to distinguish themselves from nonpar-ticipants. They were armed only with shotguns, bolos, double-edged knives, daggers, *balisongs* (knives with folding blades), and big sticks. Some wore *anting-anting* (amulets) around their necks. They cut telegraph wires and, at the railway station, blocked the rails with tires. They then proceeded to the Cabuyao Municipal Hall where they joined with others to make a combined force of between 300 and 400. Forming a line in front of the municipal hall, they lowered the American flag and raised the flags of the Philippine Republic and the Sakdalista Party (Lapiang Sakdalista), proclaiming independence in the name of the Philippine Republic.[4]

At around six in the evening, Algabre led another group to the highway. By this time, the number of participants had grown to nearly one thousand.[5] They cut down several trees, laying them across the road to stop traffic. Whenever traffic slowed because of the felled trees, the revo-lutionaries stopped the cars and demanded any ammunition they might be carrying. They confiscated all guns, revolvers, and ammunition from the drivers and passengers. Algabre took this opportunity to explain their demand for immediate independence to any Americans, including U.S. Navy men, who were stopped.

As the revolutionaries took the passengers' guns and ammunition, Algabre issued receipts for the confiscated items. These receipts, however, were given only to Filipinos. Americans, Chinese, and other foreigners had to give up their weapons without such acknowledgment. Algabre borrowed a fountain pen from one of the Filipino passengers to write receipts for the confiscated items. When one passenger requested the pen be returned, she said somebody else had borrowed it. Then she cut a piece from her red skirt and told him, "This dress that I am wearing represents the Filipino flag. You see it is red, white, and blue. Now take this piece of cloth as a receipt for your fountain pen and as soon as the war is over, just show me this receipt and you can have your pen back."[6]

Algabre's detachment remained on the highway all night. At dawn of May 3, she and the others returned to the town plaza of Cabuyao. They were in a jubilant mood, and the women began preparing food to feed all the revolutionaries. Since they did not have enough, Algabre returned to her house at around eight to get more rice.[7]

While she was away, Laguna Gov. Juan Cailles, a former anti-American revolutionary, and the constabulary came onto the scene. As they approached, some of the rebels abandoned the municipal building and ran across the street toward the churchyard. Even before reaching the churchyard, some of them raised the war cry, "Humanda na Kayo!" (Be ready!). The constabulary responded by firing their rifles. An exchange of gunfire began, and the rebels fled for cover behind the churchyard wall, hoping that the stone wall would protect them. Governor Cailles ordered the soldiers to cease firing and called on the revolutionaries to surrender or leave the area. He shouted that they would not fire on anyone who ran away. After half an hour of negotiations, a volley was fired from the wall and the shooting resumed. As the situation heated up, the soldiers closed in on them and the trapped combatants fell one by one. The outcome of the battle was fifty-three revolutionaries shot dead and nineteen wounded. The constabulary suffered only four wounded.[8] Around the same time, five km down the road, about one thousand revolutionaries were approaching the scene. After hearing of the incident in the churchyard, they quickly dispersed.[9]

Similar uprisings were taking place simultaneously in at least fourteen more towns and villages in the provinces of Laguna, Bulacan, Cavite,

Rizal, Nueva Ecija, and Tarlac. The revolutionaries assembled with the intent of taking control of the local municipalities. Afterwards, they were to march into Manila to replace the existing colonial government with an independent republic government. The takeover was to be proclaimed either in Kawit, Cavite, or Malolos, Bulacan.[10] In addition to Cabuyao, two more municipal halls were successfully captured: Santa Rosa, Cabuyao's neighboring town, and San Ildefonso in Bulacan Province.[11] Attempts in other towns included Biñan, Calamba, and Santa Cruz in Laguna; Tanza, Silang, and Maragondon in Cavite; Muntinlupa in Rizal; San Miguel in Bulacan; and Gapan in Nueva Ecija. The rebels were also said to have poured into the municipal halls of the Rizal towns of Marikina, Pateros, Pasig, and Malabon. If those who joined but soon dispersed were included, the number of participants could have easily reached more than ten thousand. In the four towns where the main actions took place, the number of participants and casualties can be summarized as follows. Cabuyao, Laguna: participants (1,000), constabulary (37); casualties: rebels (53 dead, 19 wounded), constabulary (4 wounded). Santa Rosa, Laguna: participants (500), constabulary (8); casualties: rebels (4 dead, 6 wounded), constabulary (3 dead, 5 wounded). San Ildefonso, Bulacan: participants (150), constabulary (17); casualties: rebels (2 dead, 11 wounded), constabulary (1 dead, 2 wounded). Tanza, Cavite: participants (600), policemen (2); casualties: rebels (1 wounded), bystanders (1 wounded). Total: participants (2,250), constabulary (62), policemen (2); casualties: rebels (59 dead, 37 wounded), constabulary (4 dead, 11 wounded), bystanders (1 wounded).[12]

Most participants were members and supporters of the Sakdalista Party, which had started as a movement in mid-1930 and formed into a political party in October 1933. Those who participated in the uprising were only a fraction of the Sakdalistas. The chief of the constabulary Guillermo Francisco estimated the total number to be 68,000 at the time of the uprising. The provincial numbers were broken down as follows: Manila, 1,000; Bulacan, 8,000; Cavite, 6,000; Laguna, 20,000; Pampanga, 500; Rizal, 21,000; Tayabas, 10,000; Nueva Ecija, 1,500.[13]

This incident was later called the Sakdalista uprising of May 1935, which was the largest popular uprising since the completion of American pacification of the Philippines three decades earlier. As seen in their attempts to raise the Philippine flag with the shout "Mabuhay ang Republika Filipina" (Long Live the Philippine Republic), the uprising was an attempt to establish independence from the U.S. occupation. It was indeed a "War of Independence," and similar to what the Ricartistas had attempted in 1914 in the Christmas Eve Fiasco.

Faced with the biggest antigovernment show of force under American colonial rule, American officials and Filipino lawmakers, journalists, and scholars were stunned, and they solemnly reflected on the cause of the uprising. While some dismissed the Sakdalistas' actions as foolish and alleged that their leaders had taken advantage of the gullible masses, the majority acknowledged the socioeconomic problems in Philippine society as the basic cause. They emphasized high taxation, social disparity, tenancy problems, and the decline of local industries due to the importation of American goods.[14] Others cited the elite-dominated political system. Even some government officials acknowledged that they had been out of touch with the masses, lacking sympathy for the plight of the poor while unemployment increased. They admitted it was understandable under those circumstances why many peasants would eventually become Communists or Sakdalistas. Some journalists emphasized that the Sakdalista Party was the party of the dispossessed. One of the journalists compared the Sakdalista uprising to the Katipunan-led 1896 Revolution by highlighting their similar conditions.[15]

U.S. colonial officials took immediate action by forming an investigative committee. They were puzzled as to the causes of the uprising and assumed it was a reaction to poverty, yet it had occurred in some of the most prosperous areas, namely, the rich rice and sugar districts of central and southern Luzon. Official records showed that tax collections in the districts affected by the revolt were higher than in districts where the uprising did not take place. Furthermore, the majority of those who had been arrested and investigated had jobs and none appeared to be in real want or hunger.[16] While economic disparity between classes was noted and the difficulty in separating economic, social, and political domains was acknowledged, the committee concluded that the main cause of the uprising was an ardent desire to establish an independent Philippine republic by foiling the coming plebiscite. The committee's conclusion came closest to understanding the Sakdalistas' true motive.

The effort to understand the May uprising of 1935 continued to illustrate agrarian problems, lopsided social development, and dominance of the oligarchy class over the majority in prewar Philippine society. One of the first in-depth studies of the Sakdalista uprising was produced in 1942 by former vice-governor general and political scientist Ralston Hayden, who organized the investigative committee. The study concluded that the participants in the uprising were those who had been left behind in the march of progress and that they were victims of local landlords and usury practices. They were economically deprived and relatively ignorant people from rural areas.[17]

Later studies in the 1950s and 1960s also emphasize the economic misery and discontent of the peasants stemming from the abuses of landlords and high usury rates as the causes of the uprising. One of the studies places the Sakdalista uprising in the same category as the politico-religious uprisings, such as the Colorum uprisings that had occurred in central Luzon in the 1920s and 1930s. It concluded that the participants in the uprising were convinced that if a commonwealth government were established in 1935, as stipulated in the Tydings-McDuffie Act (T-M Act), it would keep the landlord class in power. This thinking led the peasants to rise up to establish the kind of independence that would enable them to end exploitation by the landlords and solve all their social and economic problems.[18]

In the mid-1970s, an anthropological study looking into major popular uprisings that took place in the Philippines was produced. It covered a span of 100 years, starting from the 1840s and ending with the Sakdalista uprising. This study goes beyond earlier studies, noting that the participants' aspirations for independence were based on rational political agenda dedicated to social change. The study concludes that while still holding traditional mistaken notions, such as expecting armed assistance from Japan, the Sakdalista movement paved the way for the rational mass movements of Socialism and Communism.[19]

All of these studies amply discuss the social-economic causes of the uprising. Furthermore, they all maintain that the participants were the economically distressed and uneducated victims of an exploitative feudal agrarian society; therefore, the participants were not only credulous but also irrational. The uprising was the only way to express the discontent. These academic studies echo the way in which journalists and other intellectuals described the uprising incident at that time.

While it is true that significant numbers of the participants of the May 1935 uprising were economically deprived peasants and urban poor, as will be seen in this book, some members were prosperous, well-educated professionals, such as landlords, town proprietors, lawyers, medical doctors, writers, schoolteachers, and office workers. Furthermore, the towns in Laguna, where the Sakdalistas were successful in establishing a "republic," suffered less tenancy problems and were a relatively prosperous area compared to central Luzon, as noted by the Investigative Committee.

What is entirely missing from past studies is an examination of the movement's ideology that united the poor, the rich, the uneducated, and the intellectuals. If these studies pay any attention to the Sakdalista ideology, they simply dismiss it as utopian, unrealistic, and irrational, labeling the Sakdalista movement as a politico-religious movement. The colonial government's investigative committee as well as some academic works noted that the primary purpose of the May uprising was to establish an independent republic, but none of them elaborated on it.

Until recently, no study has connected the Sakdalista uprising of May 1935 to the 1896 Revolution. This connection has been noted by two keen observers of the anticolonial wars in Luzon at the turn of the twentieth century: Milagros C. Guerrero and Reynaldo C. Ileto.[20] Guerrero, focusing on economic and social issues, demonstrates that the peasants' struggle for independence against the Americans continued under the colonial government. The revolutionary government set up in 1898 was soon filled with graft and corruption and neglected to solve the peasants' grievances on tenancy issues. Consequently, the peasants were disillusioned and found ways to continue their struggle against the Filipino elite and the new foreign power. Guerrero suggests that their struggle finally culminated in the Sakdalista uprising.[21]

Ileto, who explored the philosophical underpinnings that motivated the participants of the revolution, states that the decision of some of the masses in Luzon to participate in the 1896 Revolution was shaped by their religious experiences and the influence of their own unique versions of Catholicism.[22] Moreover, after the failed attempt, the spirit of this revolution was carried on into the 1930s by the masses, particularly the poor and uneducated segments of society, and the Sakdalista movement was one such organization. Ileto further suggests that its tradition continued even into the 1960s, citing the Lapiang Malaya (Freedom Party), a politico-religious society.[23]

This book builds on the above observations: the Sakdalista uprising was an attempt to fulfill the aims of the 1896 Revolution and the subsequent Philippine-American War of 1899. These wars were fought not only by the peasants but also by a broad range of Filipinos. Those who refused to become members of the nation-state of American power had been trying to establish independence throughout the entire American period. During the Japanese Occupation, the same types of people, although fewer in number, grouped together, and with the Japanese military they waged the fight against the returning American forces. Even after World War II, some continued to fulfill their wishes for true independence, disguised in the form of religious organizations, such as Lapiang Malaya.

To substantiate these assertions, I shall trace the chronological development of the entire Sakdalista movement from its start in 1930 to its demise in 1945, at the end of the Japanese Occupation. Since the socio-economic aspect of the movement has been amply treated by previous studies, particular attention will be paid to participants' backgrounds, the leadership of the founder Benigno Ramos, and most importantly, the movement's guiding principle of Sakdalism.

Fortunately, the Sakdalista movement left a record of its activities and ideology in the pages of its organs, such as the *Sakdal*, *Ganap*, *The Filipino Freedom*, and *Hirang*. Many issues of these periodicals have been lost but those that remain allow us to draw heavily on the Sakdalistas' own voices. The Sakdalista Party that was formed in 1933 and its successor, the Ganap Party (Lapiang Ganap), established in 1938, also left records, such as party platforms, manifestos, memorandums, and other documents that have not been fully utilized in previous studies. Ramos's writings, including his poems, give us insight into the movement's political thought along with its ideology and orientation.

Also available are records of interviews collected by the U.S. colonial authorities during their investigation immediately after the May uprising. More recently, some fifty years later, I personally interviewed more than forty surviving Sakdalistas, most of whom resided in the towns of Laguna, Quezon (formerly Tayabas), and Bulacan and in Muntinlupa and Pasig, now part of Metro Manila. I also interviewed some family members of leading but deceased figures, such as Benigno Ramos, Celerino Tiongco, and Salud Algabre.

Efforts to establish a Philippine Republic against the American colonial regime were seen throughout the occupation period. The most significant attempt came mainly from the Ricartistas, as seen in the Christmas Eve Fiasco. Armed struggle against the American colonial government was treason, and organizations that aimed to overthrow it were immediately disbanded; their leaders and the participants arrested and imprisoned. Despite this crackdown and the manipulation of the covert operation by the government authorities, violent attempts to overthrow American sovereignty continued because the armed struggle was supported by a wide range of people coming from seemingly nonviolent "legitimate" sectors, including religious organizations, such as Iglesia Filipina Independiente, IFI (the Philippine Independent Church; also known as Aglipayan Church), and mutual-aid and civic societies.

The Ricartistas and those who supported their activities accused the former Malolos *ilustrados*-turned-politicians of being more interested in profiting personally from colonial political-economic arrangements than in bringing about immediate independence. They charged that these politicians' pro-independence politics were no more than rhetoric and equated their politics with deceit.[24] They also demanded social justice by distributing wealth and alleviating poverty. They had been critical of both Filipino and American officials and believed the only remedy was another revolution, another anti-American war.

One law enforcement official considered the participants and supporters in the armed revolts to be ignorant followers, "a class wholly without education or intelligence, or the capacity to comprehend public affairs." However, this same official also observed that the reason their struggle had been sustained even after the establishment of the American civil government was due to their cleverness and strength: giving "harmless" information when the members were investigated, letting the authorities believe they had merely been ignorant dupes of their leaders. Upon their release, they would immediately rejoin the old group or help organize new ones, and whenever the leaders were arrested or executed, someone else would revive the group under a different name.[25]

This observation aptly describes the tenaciousness of the independence movement that unfolded under the American colonial regime. While these followers might not have been educated, they had the wisdom and courage to pursue the betterment of society. As of the mid-1920s, there were about two hundred fraternal organizations and secret societies in the Philippines, nearly 70 percent of them in Manila and many secretly supported Ricarte's Revolutionary Army. The authorities considered the Legionarios del Trabajo (Legionnaires of Labor, based in Manila), Katipunan Mipanampun (Society of Adopted Sons, based in Pampanga and Manila), and Kapatirang Magsasaka (Peasant Brotherhood, based in Bulacan, Pampanga, Tarlac, and Nueva Ecija) to be the most popular fraternal societies.[26]

To avoid detection by military and police surveillance, the organizers of these societies claimed to be a mutual aid society of peasants or laborers or to have organized to promote Philippine products and traditional culture. For instance, Ang Labi ng Katipunan (Survivors of the Katipunan), the majority of whom were former Katipuneros, secretly granted military ranks to its members. When the Katipunan Mipanampun (created in 1923) was split, 60,000 members shifted to the military organization Magtanggol, and the rest joined another group called Palihan ng Bayan (Anvil of the Nation, more on this later). Dimas Alang (Touch Me Not, from the title of Rizal's anti-Spanish novel), another civic organization with an estimated forty thousand members, had a large number of known former Katipuneros and had been collecting money to aid Ricarte in Hong Kong. The group was arranging appointments to the Viper Battalion of Ricarte's Revolutionary Army. Many other civic organizations were said to have been a "smoke-screen" for the Ricarte-inspired armies. [27]

There was overlapping membership of Dimas Alang, Ricarte's Revolutionary Army, and the IFI. Therefore, it was not surprising that some Dimas Alang committees were organized by Aglipayan priests who held military ranks in the Revolutionary Army. The authorities were fearful of fusing these organizations, which would then become formidable opponent forces. Because of this, Manuel Quezon went to Hong Kong to confer with Ricarte at the end of December 1912. He persuaded Ricarte to suspend his troop organization activities and collection of money while he was negotiating independence with America. Quezon allegedly promised that he would return to Hong Kong to join Ricarte if peaceful means failed and then the two of them would begin the revolution.[28]

Ironically, the very freedom of speech and freedom to organize that the new colonial government allowed also contributed to the existence and activities of the above societies and organizations.[29] Thus, throughout the early decades of American colonial rule, the fiery yearning for "absolute, immediate, and complete independence" surfaced and was erupting or attempting to erupt here and there in the form of uprisings. In the 1930s, a group of such people initiated yet another new movement called the Sakdalista movement in an attempt to overthrow the colonial government.

CHAPTER 2

# THE EARLY YEARS OF
# THE SAKDALISTA MOVEMENT,
# 1930–1933

I N THE EARLY months of 1930, a series of racial incidents occurred that are directly connected to the birth of the Sakdalista movement. The first incident occurred in Watsonville, California, when a young Filipino migrant worker was shot to death during a race riot. In a second incident, an American high school teacher insulted and denigrated her Filipino students. A third involved violent conflicts between U.S. Navy sailors and local Filipinos. These last two incidents occurred in Manila.

By the mid-1920s, Japanese and Chinese immigration to the U.S. had been greatly restricted by the Gentlemen's Agreement (1907) and the Immigration Act (1924), and America faced an acute shortage of casual agricultural labor as a result. To address this crisis, Filipinos, as subjects of a U.S. colony, were encouraged to immigrate to America. By 1930, about 65,000 Filipinos were residing in the continental U.S., with 35,000 in California.[1] Caucasian workers on the West Coast harbored antagonistic feelings toward Asian immigrants who were willing to work for lower wages. When the Great Depression hit, the Caucasian workers' frustrations and anger increased. For instance, the Chamber of Commerce in Pajaro, a town adjoining Watsonville, California, passed public resolutions in early January 1930 filled with racist anti-Filipino comments, calling the Filipino immigrants undesirable and describing them as having unhealthy habits.[2] Shortly after that, bloody racial riots raged for five nights in Watsonville after several hundred Caucasian men attacked some of the Filipino residents. One night, a mob of 500–700 locals went on a rampage, destroying Filipino homes and property.[3] During one of these attacks, about fifty Filipinos were beaten, and a young Filipino man was shot to death. The slain worker was 22-year-old Fermin Tobera, who had come to the U.S. in 1928 and worked as a lettuce picker. Although eight Caucasian youths were immediately arrested, Tobera's murderer was never charged, as the trial judge was none other than the head of the Pajaro Chamber of Commerce.[4]

News of the Watsonville incident quickly reached the Philippines. The Filipino government demanded that Washington protect the Filipinos against further attacks anywhere in the U.S.[5] Leading Filipinos and the Manila municipal board members responded by planning a protest rally and a memorial service for the slain Filipino man. In the planning meeting, a manifesto was drafted, which stated in part, "We must protest peacefully within the Constitution....Our honor and self-respect render such action immediate and imperative." The manifesto concluded by urging every Filipino to undertake personal sacrifice at this time of racial degradation. The resolution called for setting aside 2 February 1930 to honor Tobera, naming the observance "National Humiliation Day."[6]

The University of the Philippines (UP) was an additional center of protest. More than a thousand students and faculty members partici-pated in a protest rally, demanding "the immediate political emancipation of the Philippine Islands."[7] On 2 February 1930, a "National Humiliation Day" rally was held at the foot of the Rizal Monument in Luneta Park and attended by around fifteen thousand people. The essence of this rally was captured in a Manila newspaper headline reading: "Tears Flow at Luneta."[8] Speakers included the prominent Filipino poet Jose Corazon de Jesus, who moved many to tears with his impassioned speech and patriotic lyrics delivered in Tagalog. The gathering was marked by repeated calls for imme-diate Philippine independence from the U.S. One of the speakers, Rep. Francisco Varona, said that Filipinos knew how to "shed their own blood to color the dawn of their liberty," reminiscent of Rizal's poem "The Last Farewell."[9] That same day, protest rallies were being held elsewhere, most notably in the towns in the provinces of Rizal, Laguna, Cavite, Batangas,

Bulacan, Nueva Ecija, and Pampanga. In Cabanatuan, Nueva Ecija, more than two thousand people gathered in the town plaza for a rally organized under the auspices of the province's bar association. National Humiliation Day was observed simultaneously in California, where a march of 1,000 sympathizers took place.[10]

The racial tension between the Americans and Filipinos at this time was described as acute. Even before the protest rallies took place, Gov. Gen. Dwight F. Davis had expressed concern that his American appointees were consistently rejected by Filipino lawmakers simply because they were Americans.[11] The racial violence and prejudice that had occurred in Watsonville only strengthened the Filipinos' anti-American sentiment of the time.

In the midst of these heightened racial tensions, the students of Manila North High School staged a walkout. They held several rallies seeking the dismissal of an American teacher, Mabel Brummitt, who was accused of insulting her Filipino students.

Historian and writer Teodoro Agoncillo had been one of Ms. Brummitt's students. He recalls that with a sinister smile on her face, she told a student, "You Filipinos do not take baths. You look like savages." Feeling the deep sting of this insult, Agoncillo decided to organize a secret meeting of his classmates to discuss this incident. Many others shared the same feelings of indignation, and the meeting quickly accelerated into a mini-protest rally in which they decided to boycott Ms. Brummitt's class. The following day, the streets near the school became the "classrooms" of students who refused to attend their regular classes. Students from other high schools in Manila soon joined the strike.[12]

As the protest gained momentum, daily meetings and mass demonstrations were held. The students passed a resolution charging that the American teacher readily directed a barrage of derogatory remarks at her Filipino students, such as: Filipinos were only fit to be *cocheros* (drivers of horse-drawn vehicles); it would be better if the Filipino students went back to their nipa huts (dwellings whose roofs are made of palm leaves) and ate *camotes* (sweet potatoes); and it was a great mistake for the U.S. government to spend so much money trying to educate the Filipinos for they would never learn English. The students' resolution concluded with a demand for her dismissal. By mid-February, nearly half of Manila North High School's 3,000 students had signed the petition.[13]

At some of these protest rallies, politicians and other luminaries, such as the poet Jose Corazon de Jesus, were invited to speak. Agoncillo recalled that the students, who seemed to be carried away by the fire of de Jesus's lyricism, refused to return to their classes until their demands had been met.[14] Finally, Director of Education Luther Bewley ordered the city's four high schools to be closed for the rest of the school year. After an investigation was held, the American teacher, Ms. Brummit, was found guilty of making derogatory remarks and was dismissed. This incident, reportedly involving 10,000 students, sympathizers and supporters, was considered to be one of the most sensational episodes the Bureau of Education ever experienced.[15]

The strike ended abruptly when the Bureau of Education expelled the student leaders and threatened not to issue academic credits if the students continued to participate in the strike. Looking back at this incident, although Agoncillo did not discount the Watsonville incident, he attributed spontaneous students' strike more to the experiences of their parents' generation in the 1896 Revolution. "Filipino students," he stated, "learning from the lessons of the 1896 Revolution, picked up the thread of nationalism that their heroes, from Rizal to Bonifacio and Mabini, had dropped along the labyrinth of history and set the pattern for future students to follow in the struggle for independence."[16]

While the "anti-American fever" was still infecting Manila and its suburbs, more racially related violence broke out in mid-March 1930. After a baseball game, around fifty U.S. Navy sailors clashed with some Filipino civilians in Manila's port area. Under the leadership of an American police captain, the local police managed to subdue the riot, which resulted in the arrest of three Filipinos. Later the same day, another Filipino-American conflict took place not far from the port area. In this incident, two U.S. sailors were severely beaten by several Filipino policemen, who then charged them with assaulting some Filipinos and resisting arrest.[17]

Around this time, Tobera's remains finally arrived in Manila from California. When the coffin was taken to the receiving hall of Pier Seven, laborers from the port area lined up to pay homage. The procession started with two to three thousand mourners, and as it progressed, hundreds of laborers left their factories, waited on street corners, and joined the march. That evening 2,000 laborers filled the hall to see the remains of Tobera, who had been declared a national hero, and to hear speeches given by politicians and labor leaders. The body was on display for two more days and then sent to Tobera's hometown of Sinait, Ilocos Sur, via the towns of San Fernando, La Union, and Vigan, Ilocos Sur.[18]

The American authorities downplayed all these incidents. Considering them to be "really of minor importance," Gov. Gen. Davis did not bother to cable immediate reports to Washington. In his writings after the events, Davis called the Manila North High School incident "a silly strike (that) was never (as) serious as the newspapers tried to make it." In his opinion, the whole racial complex was bound up with the agitation for independence.[19] His opinion as to the importance of these incidents was mistaken, but his notion of their grounding in independence sentiment was right on target, as revealed in the subsequent career of Benigno Ramos and the birth of the Sakdalista movement.

## The Birth of the Sakdalista Movement
### The Sakdal Weekly

When the protesting students of Manila North High School invited their parents and sympathizers to join the cause, a young government official, Benigno Ramos, attended their events. He had been profoundly touched by the recent series of incidents and found himself drawn into the strike. With his oratorical skills, he reportedly became a prominent leader of the ensuing protest rallies and strikes. Ramos allegedly told the students not to listen to Davis, Quezon, or Osmeña, who were all pleading with the students to return to classes. He also advocated a boycott of foreign-made goods, especially cigarettes.[20]

At the time, Ramos was working as director of the Senate Clipping Division. His connection with the Senate had started fourteen years earlier when Manuel Quezon and his Nacionalista Party entourage came to the town of Bulacan to campaign, and Ramos skillfully translated his speech into Tagalog.[21] As a result, he was hired at the Senate's Clipping Division, and in 1930, he was promoted to division director. Soon, Ramos became one of the best campaign orators working for Quezon and the Nacionalista Party, often speaking at party functions and rallies.[22]

However, Ramos and his mentor, Quezon, clashed over the Manila North High School incident. Quezon, who was then the Senate president, wanted to keep the issue under wraps as much as possible. This could have been because he did not want to alienate the U.S. government or perhaps he did not want Ramos to become a champion of the cause. Quezon was indignant that Ramos told the students not to listen to him. Whatever the reason might have been, Quezon was not pleased with Ramos's active involvement in the strike and asked him to withdraw from such activities. Ramos refused and, as expected, he was told to resign from his government job, which he did in mid-June 1930.[23] With this, his promising political career in the Nacionalista Party, the majority party of the time, abruptly ended.

Soon after his resignation, on 28 June 1930, Ramos formally launched an anti-Quezon, anti-Nacionalista campaign with the initial publication of the weekly *Sakdal* (To Accuse). The paper's funding came partly from Ramos's own savings and partly from the support of his friends Guillermo Masangkay and Francisco Varona. The former held the rank of colonel in Aguinaldo's revolutionary army and had been financially supporting Ricarte in Hong Kong. The latter was a well-known labor organizer who had become a representative in the National Assembly.[24] In the succeeding months, Patricio Dionisio and the members of his organization, Kapatiran Tanggulan ng Malayang Mamamayan (Brotherhood of Defense of Free Citizens or Tanggulan Society), which will be discussed below, extended their aid and cooperation.[25]

The format of the *Sakdal* weekly was the same as that of the daily newspapers. Below the masthead SAKDAL was the paper's motto: "Malaya, Walang Panginoon Kundi ang Bayan" (Independent, with No Master but the People). The paper bore a variety of slogans, including: "SAKDAL, ang bibig ng aping mamamayan" (SAKDAL, the mouth of the oppressed citizen) and "ang tagapagpahayag ng mga katotohanan" (the newspaper of the truth). In addition, beginning 5 September 1931, portraits of Jose Rizal and Marcelo H. del Pilar were positioned on either side of the masthead. The *Sakdal* weekly was published mostly in Tagalog although it occasionally carried articles in English and Spanish. Its pages were filled with articles attacking Quezon and other Nacionalista politicians. The paper frequently published detailed lists of the salaries, properties, and expenses of the politicians, especially those who were on Quezon's staff. In the paper, Ramos repeatedly expounded the importance of Philippine independence and criticized the people's tendency to base voting decisions on friendship or debts of gratitude, thus sending unworthy politicians to the legislature. He urged his readers to stop this practice.[26]

As of April 1931, less than a year later, the print run had grown to about 18,500 issues, but in October, it had decreased to about 15,200.[27] Still the *Sakdal* had a respectably large circulation compared with the well-established commercial newspapers with strong financial backing, such as the *Taliba* (Tagalog daily, 24,845) and *The Tribune* (English daily, 16,426).[28] As soon as the copies were delivered from the printing press, Ramos's whole family helped prepare them for distribution. When the newspapers were folded at around 6:00 A.M., the newspaper boys waiting just outside the office would rush in to get copies, which "sold like hotcakes." By 8:00 A.M., they would all be gone.[29]

Readers were urged to pass their copies around, especially in the provinces, where one copy was read by at least ten or more people. For the benefit of illiterate people, the paper was often read aloud before groups of listeners. Thus, the number of readers and listeners may have been as high as 200,000–400,000. Observers eventually noted that the *Sakdal* publication was the first serious attempt to reach the masses.[30]

Enthusiastic subscribers and readers sent letters to the editor, saying that the *Sakdal* was valuable and necessary because it did not flinch from exposing the truth regarding current events. The writers of these letters also stated that the paper was trusted by the "small soldiers" (lower echelons) of manufacturers and laborers, that the farmers eagerly awaited the newspaper's arrival every week, and they would usually buy a copy before spending money on daily necessities.[31] Eventually, the authorities came to consider the *Sakdal* subversive because of its firm antigovernment stance. For instance, the constabulary in Pasig, Rizal, told people not to read it, and reading the *Sakdal* was banned in the Senate, where many clerks and messengers were ardent readers of it.[32]

The most encouraging news, with strong propaganda value for the paper, was a supportive message received from Gen. Artemio Ricarte in Japan. By October 1930, his followers had sent him copies of the newspaper. He sent messages saying Ramos should not be afraid in his defense of the people's rights, the *Sakdal* was needed to awaken the people, and the paper and Ramos were truly fulfilling the wishes of the heroes of the 1896 Revolution. On another occasion, Ricarte praised the newspaper's ceaseless criticism and exposition of whatever damage was being done to "the honor, progress, and most importantly (serve as) the expression of the 'Great Vehement Wish' (for independence) of the whole Filipino people" (*dangal, kaunlaran at lalo na sa Dakilang Mithi ng Sambayanang Pilipino*).[33] Ricarte's support and encouragement further inspired the readers, and they spontaneously transformed themselves into members of a loosely organized movement called Malayang Bayan (Free Nation). For instance, a certain *Sakdal* subscriber who was impressed with Ramos's political principles began organizing a "secret society," as the constabulary called it, in Talavera, Nueva Ecija.[34] In Santo Domingo, Luisiana, in Laguna a hat merchant who sympathized with Ramos's ideals organized the local people. With the exception of three families, the whole barrio joined in the movement. Eventually, it spread to neighboring barrios and even to the town of Luisiana. In this quasi-independent manner, the Malayang Bayan movement gradually spread and was formally organized toward the end of October 1931. This movement quickly spread into the provinces of central and southern Luzon.[35]

The series of anti-Filipino racial conflicts that occurred in the early months of 1930 greatly wounded the Filipinos' pride and rekindled the people's desire for independence. The Manila North High School strike produced the future leader of the movement, Benigno Ramos, who voiced their aspirations. The Sakdalista movement would not have gained such strong support were it not for these incidents.

## Forming the Movement

One of the meanings of "Sakdal" is "to accuse." The choice of this name for the paper was appropriate since Ramos and his followers were bent on "accusing" the Quezon-dominated administration and the U.S. government of perpetuating the colonial status of the Philippines. According to Ramos, this name was inspired by the French phrase "J'Accuse" (I Accuse) from Emile Zola's article exposing corruption in the military and judicial system of France at the end of the nineteenth century. Another time, the *Sakdal* paper claimed that the name was derived from Sanskrit and meant, "to stop or end hardship and all the duties" (*hantungan o katapusan ng mga hirap at lahat na gawain*). By naming his paper "Sakdal," Ramos was calling for an end to the hardship and forced duties of the oppressed and colonized Filipino people.[36]

Not all Sakdalistas agreed on the origins of the name. Some rank-and-file members believed that the name was taken from the Bible, specifically from the Epistle (Letters) of James. The Tagalog version read: "At iyong pabayaan na ang pagtitiis ay magkaroon ng sakdal na gawa, upang kayo'y maging sakdal at ganap, na walang anomang kakulangan" (Make sure that your endurance carries you all the way without failing, so you may be *perfect* and complete, lacking nothing).[37] Yet another group of Sakdalistas understood the word "Sakdal" within the context of "maging *sakdal* ang pananampalataya mo sa Dios" (let your faith in God be *absolute*). This meaning of Sakdal was defined by Agapito Illustrisimo, who founded the

Samahan ng Tatlong Persona Solo Dios (Association of Three Persons in One God or *Samahan ng Tatlong Persona*), a politico-religious organization in Mount Banahaw on the boarder of Tayabas and Laguna Provinces.[38]

In effect, these rank-and-file members were assigning religious and spiritual meanings to the name "Sakdal" and its movement. Perhaps that was the reason the constabulary branded the supporters of the Sakdalista cause in Mount Banahaw and Atimonan in Tayabas Province the "Colorum" of Benigno Ramos.[39]

As the Malayang Bayan-turned-Sakdalista movement caught on, more and more people invited Ramos to visit their towns and give speeches. The invitations started in towns surrounding Manila and then came from other parts of Luzon and even as far south as the Visayas.[40]

### Activities of the First Year, 1930–1931
*Boycott*

In August, less than two months after the initial publication of the *Sakdal*, the paper urged a boycott of foreign-made articles, such as automobiles, men's suits, and cigarettes; foreign-owned restaurants and noodle houses (mostly targeting Chinese-owned businesses); American movies; and schools in which English was used as the medium of instruction. The goal of the movement was for the Filipino people to become kings of their own nation and to return the country to a "pure" Filipino culture, emphasizing that this was what Rizal and Bonifacio had planned and hoped for. The fact that the Filipino businesses were being taken over by foreigners was expressed in a rather emotional tone: "Hindi kaya ikagalak ng ating sarili kung maturang ang buong Eskolta ay ari ng mga Pilipino, ang Rosario ay hindi sa intsik kundi sa kababayan din natin, ang Ave[nida] Rizal ay hindi sa mga hapon kundi sa mga kabalat din natin?" (Would it not gladden us if it could be said that the whole stretch of Escolta is owned by Filipinos, that Rosario is not for the Chinese but for our countrymen that Rizal Avenue is not for the Japanese but for our own race?). At the same time, the *Sakdal* stressed that the enemy was not so much the Americans as the inclination of the Filipinos to unwittingly give money to the foreign powers by buying their goods, thereby supporting the colonial mentality.[41]

The Sakdalistas also advocated boycotting the upcoming 1931 national elections. Their rationale was that by refusing to vote, the people would be upholding the country's honor and integrity because the election would surely bring in old politicians who would perpetuate foreign domination.[42] Both the boycott of foreign goods and the elections were considered instruments to support the independence issue.

## Comments on the Tayug Uprising

In the early hours of a mid-January morning in 1931, about four hundred and fifty people with rifles and pistols attacked the constabulary headquarters, the municipal building, and the post office in Tayug, Pangasinan. At least ten civilians and thirteen constabulary officers and soldiers were killed. As for the rebels, six died (two of them women) and fifty-seven were arrested and jailed. The major dailies in the Philippines and the U.S. described the rebels as "Colorums" because they were suspected of being members of a religious group. This was perhaps due to the fact that the women, who comprised one-third of the rebels, had carried charms in the form of small prayer books, stones (possibly flints), and medals while the men wore *anting-anting* (amulets).[43]

The aims of the Tayug uprising were identical to those of the Kabola uprising, which had taken place six years earlier. In March 1925, Pedro Kabola and his followers, numbering about two hundred, entered the town of San Jose, Nueva Ecija, to proclaim independence and retrieve land from abusive landlords and distribute their property among the organization's members. His followers were mostly Ilocano and Pangasinan migrants and homesteaders.[44]

The leader of the Tayug attack was Pedro Tolosa, alias Calosa, who had established an underground society called the Philippine National Association (PNA) in 1928. He was not involved in the Sakdalista movement but some of his followers subsequently joined it, as we shall see. Constabulary investigation of the Tayug uprising revealed that many of the participants were relatively well educated and some had participated in the 1925 Kabola uprising.[45]

The Sakdalistas reacted strongly to the newspapers' branding the rebels "Colorums," which suggested they were either uneducated fools or fanatics. The *Sakdal* pointed out that many of the participants were high school graduates or dropouts, and some of them had even been to Hawaii and the U.S. mainland. The *Sakdal* criticized the authorities for branding anyone opposing the government, including the Sakdalistas, as a "Colorum." The paper pointed out that by engaging in such name-calling, the authorities failed to see the core of the problem.[46]

## Threat from the Authorities

The *Sakdal* issue of 17 January containing comments on the Tayug incident was the first publication for 1931. Issues for the first two weeks had not been published because Ramos had been warned to either stop publishing articles that severely criticized the government or risk imprisonment. Nevertheless, the 17 January issue resumed the attack.[47] In the following issues, the *Sakdal* continued exposing the ills and corrupt practices of the government; it reported that the beneficiaries of the vast lands and rich natural resources were the elite who controlled the government, American businesses, and the friars.[48]

The desire for independence was not limited to the Sakdalistas. It was widely popular, as seen in a huge demonstration of 200,000 people held in July 1931 when Sen. Harry B. Hawes, the co-author of the Hawes-Cutting Act, visited. Two months later, in September, Sec. of War Patrick J. Hurley and his party visited Manila and were met with yet another enthusiastic reception with banners reading: "Give us liberty!"[49]

Debate over how to establish eventual independence within U.S.-dominated Philippine politics characterized the political scene for the next several years. The general thrust of the American proposals was to change the Philippines' status to a commonwealth for an interim period, during which the country would have a greater degree of autonomy in preparation for independence. The Sakdalistas and other radical groups were opposed to these proposals. They charged that the Philippine government's willingness to consider and negotiate the temporary status of autonomy rather than demanding immediate independence violated the principles for which they should actually have been fighting. The role of the Sakdalistas in these debates will be discussed in detail as this chapter proceeds.

## Donations for General Ricarte

In August 1931, the Sakdalista movement started to collect donations for Gen. Artemio Ricarte, who was in Japan at that time. When Bishop Gregorio Aglipay, the head of IFI, passed through Yokohama on his way to the U.S., he learned that Ricarte was gravely ill. He immediately informed the *Sakdal*, which started a collection campaign. The newspaper emphasized that Ricarte had not asked for contributions and it was the *Sakdal*'s own initiative to collect the funds for him. Ricarte's biography and his ideals for a future independent Philippines were featured on the front pages of the *Sakdal*. Readers of the paper sent in poems and essays praising Ricarte, who was the only one who had never changed his oath of allegiance to the Republic.[50] Here is an example of how the campaign unfolded: a town meeting was held in which a *Sakdal* article about Ricarte's patriotism was read aloud. The audience was deeply moved, some even wept, and many reached into their pockets to donate whatever they could spare. Among them were poor *sakateros* (people who sell fodder), farmers, and animal herders who only had a couple of centavos in their pockets.[51]

The names of the donors and the amounts contributed were meticulously recorded and published under the title "Ambagan kay Hen. Ricarte" (Contributions for General Ricarte). Among the first donors were Tanggulan members (more on the Tanggulan Society later) and Bishop Aglipay of IFI.[52] The paper forwarded the donations either directly to Ricarte or through Narciso Lapus, then Ramos's right-hand man, who was in charge of the campaign. Ricarte expressed his "deep debt of gratitude" (*malaking utang na loob*) to the *Sakdal* paper and affirmed that he had received P2,000 so far. He mentioned in the letter that he was in favor of the nonviolent boycott movement that the Sakdalistas were undertaking, but he also emphasized that the following idea should not be abandoned: "Liberty should not be asked for but should be taken by way of the most precious treasure that a man possesses; namely, blood and one's own life." Simply collecting donations for Ricarte was enough to make the *Sakdal* subversive in the eyes of the authorities, and one donor from Gapan, Nueva Ecija, was arrested.[53]

## The Union Civica Filipina and the Malayang Bayan Movement

When the fundraising campaign for Ricarte ended, the Sakdalista movement undertook a new activity in conjunction with the Union Civica Filipina. This newly formed organization believed that the country's leaders, including Quezon, Osmeña, and Roxas, were not performing their duties to secure independence from the U.S. and criticized the economic elite who had been backing Quezon and the Nacionalista Party. The organization insisted that political freedom rested on economic independence, which should be obtained through love, sacrifice, action, and education. The Union Civica promoted Filipino-made products, which would revitalize livelihoods and commerce, and advocated the value of the native language and a frugal lifestyle.[54]

The Union Civica was headed by prominent lawyers, businessmen, and medical doctors, drawing mainly from the Democrata Party and outspoken nationalists. Other organizations, in addition to the Sakdalista group, were also invited to join the Union, including civic organizations such as Palihan ng Bayan, the Tanggulan Society, and the Communist Party.[55]

The Union Civica planned a big public meeting that was dubbed as "Miting ng Pagtutuus" (Meeting of Confrontation). As the name implies, the meeting was a gathering of citizens intent on exposing the current administration, which had neglected to secure independence and had become wealthy through "treachery, conspiracy, and cover-ups."[56]

On 22 November 1931, the "Miting," sponsored by the Union Civica, was held at the Olympic Stadium and attended by 7,000 people who came mainly from Manila and neighboring provinces. Quite a few representatives of the Filipino Veterans Association were present. At the Miting, the formation of the Radical Party, headed by Atty. Alfonso Mendoza was announced.[57] The Miting passed a resolution calling on the U.S. Congress to immediately grant independence, without granting trade concessions to the Philippines, as this was the only solution to the Philippines' problems. The Miting also drafted a resolution to be sent to the U.S. Congress. Benigno Ramos read the resolution aloud in Spanish. In part, it read:

> That we protest against any decision on Filipino problems that deviates from immediate and complete independence, which is the fervent desire of our people. We also protest against any conspiracy that has the aim of destroying the true will and sentiment of our country, which hopes for complete power over her destiny.[58]

At the end of the Miting, more resolutions were added for lowering the high taxes and abolishing the Independent Mission to Washington, D.C. Miting participants also criticized schools that used English as the medium of instruction.[59] While Vicente Sotto urged the adoption of Tagalog as the national language, Benigno Ramos criticized the government officials for being more concerned about losing their wealth than gaining independence. Ramos charged that the government officials made the Filipinos believe that without free trade, they would die. He pointed out, "We did not have free trade before and we were able to live. We still could live and probably be better off in the long run without free trade."[60]

Although the Miting had been called by the Union Civica, many of the active organizers were from the Malayang Bayan (Sakdalista movement).[61]

The Malayang Bayan favored a united radical opposition and, consequently, advocated that people join their organization, the Tanggulan Society, the Palihan, or the Katipunan ng mga Anak-pawis sa Pilipinas (KAP, Proletarian Labor Congress of the Philippines), a labor federation.[62] In the aftermath of the successful rally at the Olympic Stadium, the Malayang Bayan organized their supporters into a more structured movement, which became the base for the Sakdalista movement and, later, the Sakdal political party.

Shortly before the Miting took place, the Eighth Independence Mission to the U.S. was organized. Prior to departure, the mission participants met with Quezon and agreed that they would propose a bill based on the Fairfield bill of 1924. This bill provided for a 20-year commonwealth period, or independence in 1944. The organizers of the Miting alleged that since the mission sought only autonomy and not complete independence, they considered it to be a waste of public funds. The participants agreed to hold a torch parade the night before the mission was to depart. To show their defiance, on 4 December, members and sympathizers of the newly organized Radical Party marched from Rizal Avenue to Plaza Moriones, in Tondo, where 2,000 participants gathered despite a torrential rain.[63]

## Peaceful Disobedience

At the end of 1931, the Sakdalista movement, having been greatly inspired by Gandhi's nonviolent civil disobedience movement in India, launched its own "Mapayapang Pagsuway" (Peaceful Disobedience). This boycott campaign was similar to the one the year before but was pursued with more vigor and with a broader array of measures emphasizing that this campaign was the Sakdalistas' weapon to achieve independence. It included the boycott of foreign goods, particularly automobiles, most of which came from the U.S.; the boycott of stores owned by "the enemies of Independence"; nonpayment of taxes, including the cedula tax (community tax, its payment certificate was used as identification); and refusal to send their children to schools in which English was used as the medium of instruction.[64] Reviving the boycott movement reflected the members' strong sentiments for economic and cultural independence, expressed in the Sakdal as "Stop asking the U.S. for loans. It is more honorable for a person to live in a hut or small house and to be free from debt than to live in a palace and have all living expenses funded by debt. Without sacrifice, there is no patriotism."[65]

It is hard to know how successful this campaign was, but there is evidence that it had some impact in the field of education. For example, in his annual report, a division superintendent of schools in Bulacan stated:

> This is the province of a political organization known as Sakdal....The propaganda of this organization has greatly influenced enrollment in at least two municipalities—San Ildefonso and San Jose del Monte.[66]

By mid-1932, the Sakdalista leaders' convictions began to sway. It was difficult to boycott foreign-made goods, especially since the *Sakdal* paper could not be published without using imported goods, such as paper, ink, typewriters, and a printing press. In the same manner, the Sakdal leaders began to doubt whether the election boycott was practical because even if the Sakdalistas did not vote, elected officials would still be running the country.[67]

At this time, the tax-cut issue received top billing on a list of issues important to the Sakdalistas. They urged Gov. Gen. Theodore Roosevelt, Jr. to abolish the cedula tax and lower other taxes. Their next priority was to lower the large salaries of top government officials, increase the salaries of lower-ranking government employees, and sell friar-owned lands to the tenants.[68] These demands became an enduring part of the Sakdalista political agenda, as we shall see.

## The Tanggulan Uprising

At the start of 1931, the *Sakdal* was defending the rebels in the Tayug uprising. At the end of the year, the movement was linked to a new uprising planned by the Tanggulan Society. Toward the end of 1931, a rumor spread that some Tanggulan members were going to stage an uprising on Christmas Eve. When the Tanggulan leaders converged on the city for a meeting on 9 December 1931, the authorities mistook this as the rumored offensive and arrested around a hundred and fifty Tanggulan members. Interrogation of the arrested members revealed that indeed they had been planning to cut the power lines in Manila, seize government buildings, and declare independence on Christmas Eve. Patricio Dionisio, the founder, had been trying unsuccessfully for months to restrain the radical faction of the Tanggulan Society.[69] In the aftermath of the foiled uprising, the authorities suppressed the society, and Dionisio was imprisoned. Thereafter, quite a few Tanggulan members shifted their allegiance to the Sakdalista movement.[70] Acting Gov. Gen. George Butte enumerated the causes of Tanggulan unrest, which included the lack of satisfactory and constructive relations between the rural landlords and tenants; delays and probable abuses affecting disposition of public lands, and problems with the settlement of land titles in general.[71] As always, the analysis of the uprising was focused solely on the economic aspect, which was definitely one of the causes but not the sole cause.

The Tanggulan Society had its start as Katipunan ng Bayan (Brotherhood of the People), which was organized by Patricio Dionisio in 1927. It was a Ricarte-inspired secret society, and its primary objective was to propagate the radical ideas of Andres Bonifacio, the leader of the 1896 Revolution, with regard to the plight of small farmers and city laborers.[72] The new organization aspired to the patriotic goals of social, economic, and political change, with the foremost objective being national independence. By December 1928, the organization's membership had reached more than forty thousand, and provincial and municipal chapters had been established in Manila and surrounding provinces. As the movement grew, constabulary and police surveillance intensified. Consequently, Dionisio registered the association as a mutual-aid organization, and in 1929 changed its name to Kapatiran Tanggulan ng Malayang Mamamayan to emphasize that it was a mutual-aid organization. The real aim of overthrowing the colonial government by force was concealed. On the surface, the Tanggulan Society kept promoting and patronizing locally made goods, calling on members to practice the principles of cooperation and giving aid to fellow members in need.[73]

Shortly after the *Sakdal* paper began publication, membership in the Tanggulan Society swelled to about ninety-seven thousand. The larger numbers were due partly to the supportive articles the paper had published as well as to the fusion with other organizations, such the Kapatirang Magsasaka. The Kapatirang Magsasaka was the most influential peasant organization in central Luzon, having about one hundred twenty thousand members as of 1927. This fusion, which occurred in November 1930, was a significant addition to the Tanggulan Society.[74]

Dionisio, who was a lawyer, used to be a member of the communist-inspired labor federation, KAP, organized by Crisanto Evangelista in 1929. Dionisio was elected to the executive committee of the KAP but resigned a year later. When the Communist Party of the Philippines was formed in August 1930, and Dionisio saw that many KAP members had become Central Committee members of the Communist Party, he left the organization. Although Dionisio agreed with the Communist Party line opposing American imperialism, he believed that the Communists were agents of the Soviet Union and that "the Orient must be for the Orientals." As the Tanggulan Society grew, many members of the KAP, particularly cigar workers, joined the Tanggulan Society. Moreover, some Communist Party members who saw a basis for cooperation against American imperialism attended various Tanggulan meetings.[75]

The peasants in central Luzon, especially those in Nueva Ecija, understood that the purpose of the Tanggulan Society was to defend peasants against the unfair practices of landlords and to make relations between tenants and landowners better.[76] Some peasants in Bulacan considered the Tanggulan Society to be a secret nationalist organization of which the Kapatirang Magsasaka was the outer movement. They also regarded the Tanggulan Society as a version of the Ricartista movement, and some members ordered uniforms modeled after those of the Katipunan's. The society's network spread to the whole Tagalog-speaking area of central Luzon. The Ilocano-speaking area also had its counterparts.[77]

The authorities were aware of the Sakdalista movement's affiliation with the Tanggulan Society and the close relationship between Ramos and Dionisio. Ramos had often invited Dionisio to write articles for the *Sakdal* regarding Tanggulan activities and his criticism of government injustices. Ramos and Dionisio attended each other's meetings. In September and October 1931, the two held mass meetings in the central and southern Luzon, gaining thousands of new supporters and they relied on each other for advice. Furthermore, when Ramos was arrested in March 1931, for reasons that were never stated (but perhaps for his radical opinions expressed in the *Sakdal*), Dionisio was one of the half-dozen lawyers who volunteered to defend him.[78]

Ramos and Dionisio had much in common. They came from the same province of Bulacan. Both were skillful and strongly nationalist Tagalog-language writers, orators, and poets. The two were also members of the Aklatang Bayan (National Library), a prestigious literary organization that encouraged people to write in Tagalog, the national language. Also, Dionisio lived in Ramos's neighborhood in Tondo, and he was the *compadre* (godfather) of one of Ramos's children.[79] However, they soon parted ways, as Dionisio disapproved, for unknown reasons, of Ramos's taking part in the Union Civica activities of late 1931. The rift between them deepened further when Dionisio was freed from jail at the end of 1932 and became a member of Quezon's unofficial staff.[80]

Considering the close association of the two groups, it is not surprising to see that when Tanggulan members were arrested that night, some of them were also Sakdalista leaders. Consequently, the *Sakdal* was charged with agitating the rebellious sentiment of the Tanggulan members.[81] The paper continued to print articles containing inflammatory antigovernment and anti-U.S. sentiments far into December. Finally, in order to keep the *Sakdal* from reaching a wider readership, the Bureau of Posts ordered a mailing ban, claiming that the paper was libelous and seditious. The ban took effect sometime in early February 1932, and remained in place until June. As a protest, the *Sakdal* kept publishing defiant articles, one of which announced that it was not intimidated by this high-handed treatment and vowed to continue fighting against the nepotism and favoritism (*sistemang tayo-tayo lamang*) prevalent in the administration.[82]

## Campaigns, 1932–1933
### Purchasing a Printing Press

In May 1932, the Sakdalista leaders decided that it would be more practical to purchase their own printing machine rather than to continue sharing a press with other organizations, such as the Communist Party and the now-defunct Tanggulan Society. A new campaign to collect donations was launched utilizing methods similar to the collection campaign for Gen. Ricarte the previous year. As in the earlier campaign, donors' names and the amounts given were meticulously recorded and then printed in the newspaper. One of the first donors to this new collection drive was Gen. Artemio Ricarte.[83]

The shared printing arrangement had facilitated interaction among the leaders of the radical organizations at least once a week to exchange opinions and ideas. Sometimes, the *Sakdal* invited the Communist Party leaders to publish in its pages. Although the Communists had their own newspaper, they utilized the better-circulated *Sakdal* to reach the remote rural areas.[84] While it is not certain why the Sakdalista leaders decided to operate their own printing press, perhaps events in the previous year had influenced their decision. In May 1931, the Communists' national convention was raided by law enforcement. In September, the Manila Court of First Instance declared the Communist Party an illegal organization.[85] After the party was ruled illegal, the *Sakdal* became one of the Communists' outlets. As suggested by these arrangements, the Sakdalistas' relations with the Communists were cordial throughout 1931 up to early 1932. Although the Sakdalistas did not agree with the Communists on certain issues, and while the Sakdalistas emphasized they themselves were not Communists, they recognized and admired the Communists' sacrificial commitment to fight for the poor. They also defended some Communists who had been sentenced and said, "We (the Sakdalistas and the Communists) are one in search of (a) remedy for the condition that the poor have been placed (in)."[86] However, around mid-1932, the Sakdalistas and the Communists became hostile toward each other and began publishing articles attacking one another (more on the hostile relationship later). Perhaps this rift explains why the Sakdalistas no longer wanted to share the printing press.

In June 1932, after the postal ban had been lifted, the *Sakdal* celebrated its second anniversary of publication with an editorial describing the past two years as full of sorrow, doubt, and many lessons learned about the country's problems. The *Sakdal* declared that it had no shield other than the best interests of the people, and it had no capital other than the legacy left by the heroes of the 1896 Revolution and their ancestors. A part of that legacy was the cry of the Filipinos to rid themselves of oppression and slavery and to establish an affluent, honorable, and stable Republic of which their children could be proud.[87]

## The Sakdalistas' Own Independent Mission

In December 1932, after much discussion in Washington, a combined bill, now called the Hare-Hawes-Cutting (H-H-C) Act, was passed in Congress. It became a law in January 1933, overriding President Hoover's veto. The provisions of this law included limited independence, which would be granted after ten years, and limits on duty-free sugar, coconuts, coconut oil, and cordage. Beginning in the sixth year of the ten-year transition period, an export tax would gradually be imposed. After the transition period, full U.S. tariffs would apply. The United States would retain military and naval bases in the Philippines and it would still control finances, currency and foreign affairs.[88]

In the Philippines, opposition and support for the bill came from several directions. The radical nationalists, such as the Sakdalistas and members of the Union Civica, opposed it because it did not grant independence quickly enough. The sugar interests, which preferred a longer transition, opposed the bill's trade provisions. Supporters of the bill included known advocates of independence who were not fully in agreement with its provisions yet considered them the most favorable that could be had under the circumstances. Also supporting the act were several Sakdalista leaders, including Narciso Lapus. These leaders were later dismissed from the Sakdalista movement and accused of having gone over to the Nacionalista side.[89]

When the approved act came to the Philippines for consideration, Quezon and his supporters, later to be called the "Antis," opposed it on the grounds that it would imperil the country's economic, social, and political institutions.[90] Frustrated with the work of Osmeña and Roxas, who had led the Independence Mission, Quezon announced early in February 1933 that he planned to sail to Washington to obtain a better independence bill. By early April, he had joined them in Washington.

The Sakdalistas, who were also very much against the act, believed it to be a U.S. deception, disguising an attempt to make the Philippines a permanent colonial state.[91] The Sakdalista leaders decided that Ramos should go to the U.S. to protest the act in Congress and to rally the American people to the cause of Philippine independence. In October 1932, an appeal was sent to the U.S. Congress in the name of the Malayang Bayan, demanding immediate independence for the Philippines "without any qualifications whatsoever" now that the Filipino people had already established a stable government."[92]

The fundraising campaign to send Ramos to Washington, D.C., was launched at the end of 1932, and the mission was called "Misyon ng Bayang Api" (Mission of the Oppressed Nation). In their fundraising efforts, the Sakdalistas stressed that it was a very different mission from the one sent by the legislature because it was funded by voluntary donations rather than forced tax payments. The Sakdalista leaders announced that if the total donations did not reach P4,000, the money would be returned to the donors. They felt that a poor showing would mean that the people did not want the Sakdalistas' assistance in obtaining independence, and the movement leaders did not want to jeopardize the integrity of the organization over such a small amount since the only capital it possessed was honor and integrity.[93]

As in the past, donations poured in. To further boost this campaign, a "Miting ng Bayang Malaya" (Meeting of the Free Nation) was held on 11 December 1932, at the Olympic Stadium.[94] Representatives from the central Luzon provinces as well as the Visayan region participated. The meeting ended with an outpouring of "Sigaw ng Bayan" (Cries of the People); "Mabuhay ang Bayang Ayaw Paalipin" (Long Live the Nation Who Refuses to Be Enslaved); "Mabuhay ang Bayang Pinagpala ng mga Bayani" (Long Live the Nation Blessed with Heroes); and "Lubos at Kagyat na Kasarinlan Lamang ang Aming Kailangan" (Absolute and Immediate Independence is Our Only Need).[95]

In one of the general meetings held in February 1933, it was decided that Celerino Tiongco, a wealthy landlord, would become the acting editor of the *Sakdal* while Ramos was away. Tiongco had participated in the 1896 Revolution and was a former municipal mayor of Santa Rosa, Laguna. He was introduced to rank-and-file members as one of the "recognized pillars of intelligence and dignity, respected in the province where Dr. Rizal was born." Around the first week of March 1933, Tiongco took over the paper's editorship and also became its publisher and business manager.[96]

## Mission to the U.S.

Ramos and company finally left for the U.S. in March 1933. As Ramos's plans to negotiate directly with the American leaders heightened the Sakdalistas' hope, donations for the mission kept pouring in even after he had left.[97] The Sakdalistas' expectations and hopes were expressed in the paper. Some contributors said that they should offer everlasting gratitude, first to God and second to Ramos, the great editor of the *Sakdal*, because he offered light in the midst of their dark explorations and was leading their race from misfortune to the land of independence. Other contributors said that the incumbent politicians were obeying the wishes of the colonizer, but Ramos was rushing forward and expressing the true sentiment of the people. Admiring his courage, some said that at a time of fear and terror, in Ramos the spirit of heroism was being brought into life. For his part, Ramos had declared in advance of the trip that he would never be dazzled by money or favor and promised that he would try to return to the Mother Country her pearls that had been lost in the sea of the Orient.[98]

Ramos and his party arrived in Yokohama via Shanghai at the end of March. Later, Ramos wrote home describing the hardships of the colored race (Chinese) under white oppression.[99] In Yokohama, Ramos was the guest of Gen. Ricarte at his restaurant Karihan Luvimin, and the two chatted until midnight, exchanging much news. Ramos left for Honolulu

**Welcome Meeting in Stockton, California** (18 April 1933)
*Source: Jeremias Adia*

the following day. Most of the Filipino residents in Yokohama and Tokyo, including Ricarte's whole family, came to the pier to wish Ramos a safe and successful trip to the U.S. Ricarte called Ramos "mahal na kapatid" (beloved brother) and at the time, the relationship between the two was full of warmth and mutual respect.[100]

In early April, Ramos and his companions arrived in Honolulu. A concert and a dance in his honor were held under the auspices of the Filipino Labor Union.[101] Ramos reached San Francisco in the latter part of April, staying there until the middle of June. While there, he went on speaking tour in California cities, such as Stockton, Pasadena, and Los Angeles, appealing to the American public for Philippine independence to be granted immediately on the basis of the existing Jones Law, which provided for independence as soon as the Philippines had a stable government. This was the same message in the appeal that had been sent earlier by the Malayang Bayan to the U.S. Congress, as we saw above.[102]

Ramos also propagated the principles of the Sakdalista movement among the Filipinos in America by publishing a four-page *Sakdal* issue in English called *Manila Sakdal's Supplement* with the help of Tomas D. Española. The paper urged its readers to buy as many copies of the issue as possible and give them to their American friends, including every governor and state legislator, every U.S. senator and representative in Washington, and the president and his cabinet. Thousands of copies were likewise sent to the principal European and Asian countries as well as to the countries in Central and South America. Inspired by the paper, the *Sakdal* supporters in the U.S. eventually published their own newspapers, including the *Three Stars*, *Los Angeles Examiner*, and *Filipino Tao* (The Filipino People).[103]

Tomas Española, who looked after Ramos in California, was born in 1873 in Antique and joined Aguinaldo's revolution in 1898. After the war, he managed a hacienda in Antique until leaving for Hawaii in 1913. Later, he moved to California, where he worked on a sugar beet plantation and asparagus farms. He eventually settled in Stockton and opened a recreation parlor in 1924. He joined the American branch of the Caballeros de Dimas Alang (Knights of Dimas Alang) and later, he joined the Mga Anak ng Bukid, Incorporated (The Children of the Rice Field, Incorporated) with the understanding that these organizations would work for Philippine independence. He became strongly attracted to the Sakdalista movement when he read its organ, and he immediately joined the organization. Ramos described him as "ama-amahan ng lahat ng mga naninirahang pilipino dine sa Amerika" (like a father to all the Filipinos living here in America).[104]

During Ramos's visit, Española established the Central Independence Campaign Committee and urged people to form independence committees in their own localities. He emphasized that this was the ultimate campaign for complete and absolute emancipation and the Filipinos' last stand for their God-given right to live free so that they could shape their own destiny.[105]

From California, Ramos proceeded to Washington, D.C., passing through Utah and Colorado. His party arrived in the U.S. capital on the first week of July. According to a telegram sent by Ramos from Washington, D.C., dated 9 July, some Filipino politicians tried to block his entry into the U.S. capital. When he arrived, he found that the U.S. Congress was in recess; therefore, nothing much could be accomplished with regard to lobbying against the H-H-C Act. However, he was said to have met and held discussions with some U.S. senators, including Millard Tydings and William King. These two senators allegedly advised Ramos that if he wished to wrest power from Quezon, then he should do so by means of the ballot. Ramos had also requested a meeting with Pres. Franklin D. Roosevelt, who had replaced Hoover in March, but was told that the president was out of town on vacation.[106]

In June, while Ramos was in the U.S., Quezon, Osmeña, and Roxas, the Filipino leaders of the Independence Mission, returned to Manila. Between July and mid-October, debate over the H-H-C Act continued. The Filipino leadership was split into two opposing sides: the "Pros," who accepted the act, and the "Antis," who opposed it, as mentioned earlier. Quezon took action against the "Pros," who had formerly been his allies, removing Osmeña, vice president of the Nacionalista Party and president pro tempore of the Senate, and Roxas, Speaker of the House of Representatives, from their positions. As the struggle continued, Osmeña and Roxas solicited the support of Rafael Palma and Maximo M. Kalaw, president and dean, respectively, of UP. Quezon rallied around himself such figures as Gen. Aguinaldo, Bishop Aglipay, Sumulong, and even some Communists.[107] Eventually, the "Pros" became the minority in the legislature and acted as an opposition party. On 17 October 1933, the "Antis" gained victory when the Philippine Legislature declined to accept the measure. Subsequently, the legislature appointed Quezon to head another mission to the U.S. to seek a better independence bill, later to be called Tydings-McDuffie (T-M) Law. The legislature also discussed the possibility of holding general elections in June 1934, so the Filipinos could express their wishes at the polls.

After Ramos returned to the Philippines, the Sakdalistas began transforming the Sakdalista movement (the Malayang Bayan movement, to be precise) into a political party, as had allegedly been advised by the American lawmakers.

## CHAPTER 3

# THE SAKDALISTA PARTY AND ITS ACTIVITIES, 1933–1935

A T THE END of September 1933, a huge crowd of Sakdalistas assembled in Luneta Park to welcome Ramos home from the U.S. Speaking at the foot of the Rizal statue, Ramos declared the Sakdalistas should establish a political party that would embody the spirit of their principles, which called for immediate, absolute, and complete independence.[1] A month later, on 29 October 1933, the Sakdalista Party was formally proclaimed. The timing was opportune as the Democrata Party was losing ground as an opposition party while the Nacionalista Party was still split into "Pro" and "Anti" factions. Since the Communists were still absent from the field, the Supreme Court having declared the party illegal, the Sakdalista Party was well-positioned to serve as a genuinely radical opposition party in the coming election.

## The Sakdalista Party (Lapiang Sakdalista)
### Establishment of the Party

In late 1933, the Sakdalista Party announced its platform in a 60-page publication, entitled *Pamahayag at Patakaran ng Lapiang Sakdalista* (Proclamation and Principles of the Sakdalista Party or simply *Pamahayag*) written mostly in Tagalog. The preface describes the reasons the Sakdalista movement had changed its policy from electoral boycotts to participation. At first, the movement aimed to expose the prevailing conditions in an attempt to open the eyes of erring officials and unaware citizens to the truth (*katotohanan*). The movement also hoped to facilitate the understanding of the reasons (*katuwiran*) for independence.[2] Now, the Sakdalista leaders felt they had succeeded in these attempts; however, they realized that no politician had ever worked for Philippine independence solely under the terms set out in the Jones Law, so they called the incumbent politicians the "new Federalists." Thus, they thought it was time to put their own representatives into electoral offices, national as well as local, to work for true independence. The preface declared this with the birth of the Sakdalista Party, "narito na ang '96 ng ating Kalayaan, hindi sa digmaan, kundi sa halalan!" (Our Freedom of '96 is here, not through war but through elections).[3]

This explanation resonated well with Sakdalista followers. The president of a newly organized local Sakdalista Party chapter sent an emotional letter to the *Sakdal* expressing his determination to fight for the party's cause:

> If we wish to be free, we must keep it alive. Whatever comes out of our lips should be turned into reality. We must make the respectable ideas come alive, for today they are slowly disappearing. I am reminding you of the heavy cross that we have been forced to carry. The path is thorny, with many hindrances and steep ravines. But whatever hardship and suffering (*hirap at pasakit*) come, we are following the genuine beat of our heart(s), with a genuine love for the country where we were born. Our journey (*lakad*) will not be in vain. In front of us are hindrances, yet the holy ideals with which our parents entrusted us are waiting. We must turn them over to the people following us so that when we are quiet in rest (death), they can stand up and continue. Long live the holy ideals! Long live the real hero! Death to the immoral, selfish (*ganid*), and greedy (*sakim*)! Long live the Philippines![4]

## Party Emblem

The Sakdalista Party's emblem was an extended right hand holding a heart with flames. Above this was a shining star from which multiple rays radiated. Underneath the open hand were the letters: "L. x B. A.-S. F.,"

**Photo 1. Sakdalista Emblem** (1933)
*Source: Pamahayag at Patakaran ng Lapiang Sakdalista*

an abbreviation of "Lapian ng Bayan Api, Sangkapuluang Filipinas" (Party of the Oppressed Nation, the Whole Philippine Archipelago). The star symbolized the guiding light that led the three Magi Kings to the newborn Jesus, and it conveyed the message that Filipinos could depend on the party just as the Magi had depended on the star. In other words, the party would lead them to independence and a free Philippines. The multiple rays radiating from the star represented light from heaven, which, along with the sacred spirits of the heroes of the 1896 Revolution, would help the Sakdalistas in their quest for independence. This light also symbolized the truth (*katotohanan*) that would guide the people to the great path (*dakilang landas*). The right hand symbolized the Sakdalista's fight for the freedom of their motherland. The heart expressed everlasting love and devotion and the noble duty of citizens to help their fellow countrymen who were being oppressed.[5] The emblem (see photo 1) represented what the Sakdalistas held sacred: Christianity and the spirits of the heroes of the 1896 Revolution.

These values can be gleaned on the cover page of the Sakdalista Party's *Pamahayag*, along with various quotations: from Jesus Christ, "Know the truth, and the truth will set you free"; from Andres Bonifacio, "To a man with a sense of shame, his word is inviolate"; and from Jose Rizal, "Before we will be able to help others as we wish, we must first have our independence" (his response to Padre Pastells).[6] The words from these revered martyrs and other 1896 revolutionaries can be found in the pages of the *Pamahayag*. Jose Rizal received special attention; one entire page was devoted to Rizal and included his portrait with the caption: "One Who Suffered and Offered His Death so that the Mother Country Could Live."[7]

## Party Platform

As an introductory remark, the party declared that it would fight within the law to achieve its goal of immediate and complete independence, which the party believed was also the desire of the U.S. The party asserted that America was not the enemy: "Let us help the great America in fulfilling our independence." To achieve this end, all Filipinos, rich or poor, literate or illiterate, should unite. The party activities were going to be open rather than secret and its aims would be spread through the newspapers, public speeches, and campaigns. The party wished to establish a government that would be neither capitalist nor communist but fully and wholly Filipino in its origins and objectives. It would bring happiness and peace to all of the country's children as well as resident foreigners.[8]

The party platform began by addressing the sorry conditions the country was facing as a result of the politicians' failure to gain independence during the past 26 years, ever since the establishment of the National Assembly. While pretending to fight, the politicians had made themselves wealthy at the expense of the people, who were being buried deeper in poverty. The politicians imposed many types of taxes to keep the people poor so that they would be preoccupied with making ends meet and thus forget about independence. The politicians also tried to hinder "the good aims" of the U.S. by emphasizing the "Japanese menace" and falsely predicting that even higher taxes would follow when the U.S. departed from the islands.[9]

These politicians also utilized public institutions, such as the schools, to indoctrinate the minds of the Filipino youth. The laws they created favored the rich and ignored the poor, and the elections that put them in positions of power were full of corruption and graft. Worse, these laws were enforced by the constabulary, police, and the judicial system, through which the people often suffered injustices. The Sakdalista Party also charged the politicians with having brought in a decadent culture from foreign lands, including vulgar dances, such as the Rag and the Shimmy, which did not fit in with the traditional Filipino customs. Furthermore, because of the corrupt administration (*salaulang pamamalakad*), the people's money was being wasted and the culprits responsible escaped punishment while citizens who could not pay their taxes were persecuted. As a result, the people were heavily burdened by high taxes, and their children were suffering from hunger and illness due to lack of nourishment. Destitution was widespread, and the traditional means of livelihood had been rendered useless by imported items (the document mentions *cocheros* or rig drivers being displaced by imported automobiles as an example).

Another method the politicians used to rule the country was to create divisions among the people based on differences in language, social class, and organizational affiliation, which made unity difficult. Furthermore, they sent constables to Moroland (*Kamorohan*) to fight the Muslims, which created deep resentment in the Muslim community toward not only the constables but also the Christian Filipinos.

Meanwhile, the politicians extended ready hands toward the rich. For instance, when the Filipinos in California telephoned then Resident Commissioner Guevara to ask him to look into the death of Fermin Tobera, their calls were ignored (or so the Sakdalistas alleged). Likewise, the constabulary, sanitary department, police, and similar institutions became enemies of the "little people" because they neglected to serve them. The greatness of the schools, the courts, and the civil service had been also destroyed. These politicians wished to continue using their government positions to acquire more wealth and believed their power was secure as long as the U.S. remained in the Philippines.[10]

In view of these sorry social conditions, the party proposed thirty-five concrete objectives, which can be organized into the following nine sections: (1) Government and Its Officials and Employees; (2) Industry and Commerce; (3) Justice; (4) Land and Tenancy Arrangements; (5) Labor Issues; (6) Education, Culture, and Religion; (7) Defense and Military; (8) Social Welfare; and (9) Taxation. The section on Government and Its Officials and Employees contains the longest list of grievances and proposed reforms, reflecting the deep resentment and criticism against the incumbent politicians and high government officials. Other sections that were given attention included land and social justice issues to address the problems of the large number of peasant members. Since one of the major problems the rural folks faced was the high occurrence of usury, the Sakdalista Party gave especially detailed instructions on how loans should be handled. As for landownership, in the Sakdalistas' view, the land had been unjustly taken away by the friars and big hacienda owners, who manipulated the law in their favor; therefore, the land should be returned to the rightful owners. The party proposed that landlords would once again show a benevolent and paternalistic attitude toward their tenants, lamenting the withering of traditional patron-client relationships.[11]

Having introduced concrete reforms, the party described the future independent Philippines under the Sakdalistas' administration. They would have a strong regular and reserve military force of Filipino youths for the defense of the country. Instead of the cedula tax and taxes on land and agriculture, new taxes would be imposed on guns, which everyone would be free to own. Filipinos would have their own factories for producing weapons and ammunition for military use. They would also manufacture their own commodities, develop their own industries, rather than depend on imported goods, and generate exports. Even luxury items would be manufactured locally, so more people would be able to indulge in luxuries, and the money spent on them would go to fellow Filipinos instead of foreigners. The party envisioned a truly Filipino society in which the unique Filipino culture and language would flourish. The educated would use their talents for the good of the country rather than for political agendas or personal gain. The poor would own land and have fair access to credit. The party wished to establish a society in which the status of the poor would be elevated and their rights respected so they could lead honorable and dignified lives even as the rich continued to prosper. Although the focus was on the underprivileged, here we see that the party would not neglect the welfare of the rich or the landlords. Oppression, crime, vice, and indolence would diminish because people would have their own sustainable livelihoods. As a result, patriotism would increase, brotherly love would abound, and resentment toward others would lessen. Under an independent Philippines, the people would become prosperous and powerful.

The party firmly believed in the ability of the Filipino people to govern themselves. After all, they had experienced the anti-Spanish and anti-American wars; they had produced Rizal and thousands of other heroes; and they had their own unique history, civilization, and culture—all of which was proof they were capable of governing themselves as an independent country. Furthermore, the country would become a worldwide model of stability with harmony and love among the people, thus creating a peaceful life for both Filipinos and foreigners. Lastly, the party asked people to vote for Sakdalista candidates because they were truly of the people and could therefore understand the people's suffering. The party declared that it would obtain independence once and for all by the end of 1935. If independence were not achieved, the Sakdalista legislators would voluntarily resign from their government positions, thus being the first to acknowledge their failure.

The *Pamahayag* closed by emphasizing that only the teachings and deeds of the 1896 heroes, Rizal, del Pilar, and Lopez Jaena, could lead the way to independence. This task would require sacrifice, pure hearts, and complete unity among all Filipinos. Therefore, all those who wanted to join the party—rich or poor, educated or uneducated—should have a strong heart, determination, a firm understanding of the struggle, and not be afraid of the outcome, whatever it might be (*matibay na puso, buong-loob at matatag na kaisipan ukol sa paglalaban nito at di lilingon sa anumang kasasapitan*).

## Organizational Structure

At the party's founding congress on 29 October 1933, the following officers were elected: Atty. Felino Cajucom (president), Simeon de Sena (secretary), Benigno Ramos (sugo ng Bayang Api, representative of the Oppressed Nation), and Ramon Crespo (Ramos's private secretary). Felino Cajucom was a seventy-nine-year-old veteran of the Philippine Revolution, who was said to have been Jose Rizal's roommate in Paris. He served briefly as governor of Nueva Ecija during the short-lived Philippine Republic.[12]

At the initial congress meeting, the following provinces were represented on the *Sanggunian* (Council): Laguna (9 councilors), Bulacan (7), Rizal (6), Nueva Ecija (5), Tarlac (5), Tayabas (4), Batangas (2), Cavite (2), Marinduque (2), Capiz (2), Cebu (2), Iloilo (1), Panay (1), Cagayan (1), Antique (1), and Misamis (1). Many of the representatives were urban intellectuals, including lawyers, medical doctors, small-scale businessmen, and landowners, who were native to these provinces.[13]

The party was to be headed by a National Committee composed of the presidents of the Provincial Committees. The Provincial Committee would consist of the heads of the Municipal Committees within the province. Under the Municipal Committees were the Barrio Committees, each with 12 members.[14]

Owing to an enlistment campaign called "Sacred Enlistment," party chapters were quickly established all over the islands. From the end of 1933 to the early months of 1934, chapters were found in almost all the provinces of central and southern Luzon and in the regions of Ilocos, Bicol, and the Visayas.[15]

## The Election of 1934
### The Election Results

With the party structure in place and its grassroots presence expanding, the Sakdalistas were set to campaign for the coming election in June 1934. In an appeal to the members, the party again emphasized that its movement was law-abiding and the election was an effective weapon for changing the present situation and achieving independence. Accordingly, the party advised members to avoid doing anything against the law. The appeal further stressed that each party member should disseminate the following points to potential voters: (1) Voting for the old politicians, be they "Antis" or "Pros," Democrata or Nacionalista, will only lead to continuation of the people's suffering, especially with regard to taxes. (2) Votes should not be given in the name of friendship or to pay debts of gratitude. (3) One of the most effective ways to spread the seeds of the Sakdalista principles is to sell more *Sakdal* newspapers.[16] The party members were also encouraged to repeat, "I, too, am (like) Benigno Ramos and have an obligation to finally change this situation. We need to have independence for the sake of our country and our own dignity."[17]

With the election campaign underway, the Sakdalista Party announced its existence to the international community by sending a cablegram to Pres. Roosevelt in January 1934, declaring that the Jones Act, sponsored by the Democratic Party, could not be exchanged for anything but independence.[18] In May 1934, on the eve of the election, Ramos declared that some might criticize the Sakdalista Party as being foolish for having such utopian ideals, but time would prove whether their criticisms were right. Ramos also declared that he had faith in his fellow Sakdalistas, who were true to the principles of the party, for they held in their hearts the legacy of the 1896 Revolution heroes.[19]

In the June election, the Sakdalista Party made a noteworthy showing, especially in the provinces of Tayabas and Laguna. In Quezon's home province of Tayabas, voters sent Sakdalista candidate Antonio Argosino (second district) to the House. Dionisio C. Mayor (first district) also did well, only 800 votes behind the winning candidate of the "Anti." In the town of Atimonan, also in Tayabas, Sakdalista senatorial candidate Jose

T. Timog garnered more votes than Senate Pres. Manuel Quezon although Timog did not do well enough elsewhere to be elected.[20]

In Laguna, two Sakdalista candidates, Aurelio Almazan and Mariano Untivero, were elected to the House. In the Senate race, Celerino Tiongco pulled more votes than Rafael Palma, the former UP president, although he did not get enough votes to overcome Democrata leader Juan Sumulong.[21] But in Tiongco's town, Santa Rosa, the majority of municipal councilors were Sakdalista Party members. Also in Laguna, two party members were elected to the Provincial Board and five were elected presidents (mayors) of towns. In Nagcarlan, Untivero's hometown, eight out of the ten new members of the Municipal Council were from the party, including the president and vice president. Most of those elected from the party had little formal schooling beyond the primary grades. Other victories included the governor of Marinduque province and a score of municipal officers in the provinces of Bulacan, Nueva Ecija, Rizal, and Cavite.[22] This was the first time that the urban and provincial poor had spoken their own interest via organized party politics.

Many of the Sakdalista Party supporters, however, could not vote because they did not meet the literacy qualifications for voter registration. For instance, as late as 1931, in Barrio Baliti of San Fernando, Pampanga, 98 percent of the barrio residents were reported to be illiterate.[23] When we think of this, the fact that voters had managed to send three Sakdalista representatives to the elite-dominated national legislature while electing one governor and numerous local-level politicians is phenomenal.

## Reactions to the Sakdalista Showing

These unexpected victories at the polls thrust the Sakdalista Party into the limelight. Gov. Gen. Frank Murphy welcomed the Sakdalista Party's victory as the emergence of a true opposition party although he also expressed concern that the party might become dangerous, perhaps because of its strong support from the peasants and laborers.[24] Most journalists did not fully understand the party's positions. Some newspapers called the Sakdalista representatives from Laguna "semi-communists" due to the party policy of not paying taxes to the government.[25] An editorial in *The Tribune* called them an essentially communistic left-wing party and stated that this was the first time the nation's lawmaking body would have an extremely radical faction in its halls. The editorial went on to say that the election of the Sakdalista members stood as refutation of the charge that the little man could always be herded to the polls to vote as he was told, refusing to stay forgotten by using the weapon democracy had given him, namely, the ballot. The paper sincerely congratulated the party on its victories, saying it was a sign of new awakening in the political conscious-ness of the masses.[26] Conrado Benitez of UP held the same opinion, saying that the Sakdalista Party's successes proved that the people were no longer satisfied with "parlor socialism." He warned that the masses might resort to drastic measures if the government failed to deliver better service.[27]

The party's ability to elect relatively inexperienced candidates drew special attention. The newly elected Aurelio Almazan was a native of Los Baños and an American-educated attorney. The other, Mariano Untivero, was also an attorney and came from a well-to-do family. Both were said to have spent almost nothing on their election campaigns, unlike their opponents, and did not utilize expensive placards or bodyguards. All they had were volunteer party member inspectors who kept watch at the vote-counting centers.[28] Although it was only one town, the ability of an unknown Sakdalista candidate to outpoll Quezon's home province of Tayabas was also noted.[29]

The newspapermen and the opinion leaders tried to further analyze what had brought the party to this spectacular victory. They cited one factor as the economic depression of the coconut industry due to govern-mental neglect since most of the Sakdalista Party's success at the polls had occurred in the coconut-producing areas of Laguna and Tayabas. Coconut oil exports had fallen nearly 30 percent in 1930, leading to a marked drop in employment in the Manila milling industry. Indeed, the local price of coconut oil started to fall in the middle of 1931 and by the first half of 1932, raw copra exports had dwindled by 60 percent. In 1933, there was almost no foreign (American) demand for copra. By mid-1934, the lower demand for coconut had brought severe economic hardship to Laguna and Tayabas. Small landowners and middle-class peasants who had cultivated cash crops also experienced a decline in their standard of living since the post-World War I boom.[30]

In the cities, especially in Manila, jobs were not easy to find because the depression brought layoffs of workers engaged in export processing industries as well as those who handled export goods at the port. There were bankruptcies of smaller commercial establishments, especially textile businesses, as competition from imported Japanese textiles, coupled with the reduced purchasing power of the citizens, produced heavy unemployment in that industry. By contrast, cigar production, which had been on the decline since the early 1920s, increased in the mid-1930s due to the production of cheap cigars. Although the boom was a brief one, it was strong enough to enable the cigar workers at La Minerva Cigar Factory, for instance, to stage a strike in 1934 that lasted nearly a month and a half. [31] No doubt these people could have cast votes for the newly established party in the hope of economic betterment. However, when we look at Manila, the people voted for traditional labor or radical leaders, such as Francisco Varona of the "Pros" and Alfonso Mendoza of the "Antis," both of whom garnered around eleven thousand votes while Sakdalista Party candidate Antonio Velisario garnered a little over five hundred.[32] In Manila, where labor movement was strong, the Sakdalista Party did not attract city labors, the majority of whom had been already members of the labor unions. Many who were suffering severely from the economic depression, especially in the rural areas, were illiterate and therefore had no franchise. Moreover, as an editor of *The Sunday Tribune* reported, the party had also been supported by small landowners, industrialists, shopkeepers, and urban professionals who were not necessarily in dire economic situations.[33]

Those who voted for the Sakdalista Party did so with a desire for a clean, corruption-free administration that would truly serve the people and earnestly pursue the long-awaited independence. An independent society, so eloquently portrayed by Ramos, meant different things to different voters. Independence would alleviate the distressing social and economic conditions. Filipinos would be treated with dignity as citizens of an independent country, and they would enjoy their own culture and proudly speak their native language. This sentiment, as validated by the preceding events, could have been a significant factor in the Sakdalista Party's popularity, which led to the phenomenal results at the polls.

Despite the Sakdalista Party's victories, the election was an overwhelming success for Quezon. With the passage of the T-M Act in the Philippine Assembly just before the election, Quezon's "Antis" occupied a big majority in the Lower Houses.[34] Perhaps in recognition of Quezon's continued ascendancy, the Sakdalista Party quickly repositioned itself. Now that it had entered the center stage of national politics, it wanted to sever its links with the "subversive secret organization" of the disbanded Tanggulan Society, despite having derived strength from it in the past.

Likewise, the Sakdalistas wanted to disassociate themselves from the outlawed "godless Soviet agent" of the Communist Party, with which they had had a cordial relationship for a period of time. Shortly after the election, the Sakdalista Party declared that it was neither pro-Communist nor pro-Tanggulan Society in creed, faith, or deed.[35] The party wanted to impress upon the authorities and the people in general that its actions were carried out in compliance with the laws of the country. With a feeling of euphoria, the party continued its activities with increasing power and energy.

## Post-Election Activities

The Sakdalista Party organized Thanksgiving rallies in various towns to celebrate its election victory. Ramos, who spoke at all these celebration rallies, stated that while the party's three elected representatives might not be able to accomplish much in the legislature, their electoral victories showed that the party was recognized by a good number of voters and that in time, it would become the party in power.[36]

In these rallies, strong protests against the T-M Act were expressed. The speakers urged a boycott of the 10 July election for delegates to the upcoming convention that was to draft a constitution for the Commonwealth. They said that the Act was like a leech sucking the Filipinos' blood.[37] The Sakdalistas viewed the T-M Act as immoral. They believed there were two paths—one was the path of love of wealth and the other was the path of love of justice. The former path was wide and easy to find but would lead to death since the love of money was the root of all evil. The latter path was narrow and hard to find but would lead to goodness, justice, and truth. The metaphor of the wide and narrow path is clearly a rhetorical allusion to the New Testament.[38] According to the Sakdalistas, the T-M Act was a step along the first path. Being devoted solely to money and business, this Act was considered to be a law for people preoccupied with *sikmura* (the stomach). The Sakdalistas feared the T-M Act would completely destroy any hope of the country's independence. In rather emotional tones, the Sakdalistas said that if the T-M Act were ratified, the sacrifices made by their heroes in the past wars would have been in vain.[39] Hence, the celebration rallies turned into anti-T-M campaigns.

In these rallies, a hint of disagreement surfaced over how to achieve the party's objectives. For the most part, the speakers advocated nonviolence and emphasized that Sakdalistas believed in a philosophy that encouraged followers to live like Rizal, selfless and dedicated to social, economic, and political justice for the people. They proclaimed that independence should be obtained "through diplomacy, boycott, and bloodless revolution." However, some speakers advocated remaining open to less peaceful methods. Comparing the independence campaign to courtship, one speaker argued that if the lady (independence) could not be won through good ideas, then force might be necessary, alluding to the common Tagalog saying, "Kung hindi makuha sa santong dasalan ay dadaanin sa santong paspasan" (If it [what you need] cannot be taken by praying to the saint, then take it by force).[40] As time went on, this difference in methods became increasingly evident. At that time, however, the party was relatively united and it remained devoted to the goal of absolute independence by the end of 1935. Party members vowed to establish clean, corruption-free, democratic legislative bodies at all levels, local to national. Meanwhile, the party branches continued to expand into other regions and now included Mindanao.[41]

In order to strengthen party unity, moral guidelines for the members were further emphasized. Children were expected to love and respect their parents and to help the aged; men were expected to show respect to women; young girls were expected to be modest (*mahinhin*); and everyone was expected to keep the traditional Filipino customs. The members were asked to show reverence toward one another (*magkamapitagan*) and to give sympathetic aid (*pagdadamayan*) to their neighbors and fellow countrymen.[42]

As the party's new delegates to the legislature, the two representatives-elect, Untivero and Almazan planned to present seventeen bills outlining a range of reforms based on the Sakdalista Party platform we have just examined. Sakdalista proposals included an independence bill based on the promises made in the preamble of the Jones Law; rejection of the T-M Act; abolition of the cedula tax; investigation into ownership of all friar lands; promotion of native industries and reduction of dependence on imports; development of a national military force; establishment of factories to manufacture arms; and teaching of native dialects in all public schools and the use of these dialects in the Courts of First Instance.[43]

The proposals of the Sakdalista representatives were not well-received and they were criticized, especially since Almazan advocated for a salary reduction for lawmakers. This proposal so offended the other legislators that members of the majority party drew up a petition to oust the Sakdalistas from any committee chairmanships they held.[44]

## Activities in the Provinces

When the party was preparing for the June 1934 elections, many newly created Sakdalista committees (Lupong Sakdalista) sprang up in the towns and villages of the central and southern Luzon provinces, especially in the provinces of Bulacan, Tayabas, and Laguna.[45] These committees gathered around the local leaders in their respective locations and were rather autonomous, having their own programs and agendas. Some of these committees organized the local youth and provided them with information about farming and agriculture, local industries, and how to earn a livelihood in general. The committees urged the youth to be patriotic and participate in the country's decision-making processes.[46] Although the movement already had ten basic principles, called "Ang Tuntunin ng Umiibig sa Simulain ng 'Sakdal'" (Rules for Love of the *Sakdal* [weekly] Principles, more on this in Ch. 7), some *Lupon* members created their own *Sampong* (sic) *Tuntunin* (Ten Basic Rules). For instance, Ciriaco V. Campomanes of Tayabas created his own *Tuntunin* (Rules), which had the following rules: love your country like you love your God; work for the oppressed country (*bayang api*) to attain her freedom (*kalayaan*) so that all will be delivered from slavery; protect Philippine traditions by using indigenous products; and help your brothers, companions, and fellow believers who are working and sacrificing for the attainment of absolute and genuine independence of the Mother Country.[47] Going beyond a mere political statement, the principles were guidelines for daily life that endeavored to teach the party members how to live honorably, how to unite to work together, and how to protect Philippine traditions. The Pasig members of the Sakdalista Party in Rizal developed their own set of statements, passing resolutions that were signed by over one hundred local party members. These resolutions included the following rules: protest any law like the T-M law (Act); protest the establishment of the government of the Commonwealth; and ask the government of the United Sates to fulfill the promises contained in the Jones Law as soon as possible.[48] A similar resolution passed by the Sakdalistas of Imus, Cavite, said that the people's current leaders were nationalists in word only and that their hearts and deeds were devoted to materialism.[49] The independent nature of the local committees shaped the future activities of the party, as we shall see later.

## Ramos's Travel to Japan

In early November 1934, Ramos announced that he was going to the U.S. again to pressure Congress to reconsider the T-M Act and to lobby for the fulfillment of the Jones Law. A few weeks later, he and his attendants, valet Ricardo Enrile and personal secretary Ramon Crespo, left the Philippines for the U.S. via Japan.[50] Soon after arriving in Japan in the first week of December, as if he had had a sudden change of mind, Ramos made it known that they would be staying in Japan indefinitely as the time for pleading with the U.S. had come to an end. In actuality, Japan had been his final destination from the beginning.[51] Back home, except for a few leaders, the news was a total surprise to the Sakdalistas as well as to the people in general.

Ramos had two specific goals to achieve in Japan. The first goal was to publish a newspaper so as to gain international support by informing people of the purpose and ideology of the Sakdalista Party. The second goal, which was more important, was to obtain concrete assistance from the Japanese in the form of arms and ammunition. This contradicted the Sakdalista Party's prior advocacy of achieving independence through peaceful means. The party continued to proclaim this message of peaceful means in the early months of 1935, even as Ramos was attempting to obtain arms.

Ramos began his work as soon as he arrived in Tokyo, where he and his party were initially accommodated at the residence of Masao Maruyama.[52] Ramos was provided with an interpreter, Tomoji Kageyama, who had spent some ten years in Buenos Aires working as a plantation contractor and spoke fluent Spanish. Kageyama introduced Ramos to Diet member Kumpei Matsumoto, who had studied at the University of Pennsylvania. Matsumoto was the head of Ajia Seinen Kyodan, or The Congress of Young Asia, which advocated an ideology of Asian unity. He was an ultranationalist and had close contact with well-known extremists, such as Shumei Okawa and Ikki Kita. Ramos and Matsumoto immediately became close friends, meeting an average of three times per month. Matsumoto introduced Ramos to other ultranationalists such as Mitsuru Toyama, an influential figure in the ultranationalist organization Kokuryukai (Black Dragon Society). Later, Ramos met with military leaders, such as Gens. Iwane Matsui, Sadao Araki, and Senjuro Hayashi, and the members of the Dai Nippon Seisan Party (Great Japan Production Party), a political party with ultranationalist leanings.[53] The Japanese people Ramos met sympathized with his goal of independence for the Philippines and helped pay his expenses in Tokyo. They also gave him a Japanese name, Sakurada as family name and Mosuke as first name (Sakurada sounds like Sakdal, and Mosuke is part of his name, [Ra]mos, "suke" being popular name-ending for males).[54]

Ramos also had frequent contact with a group of young Japanese. One of them, Uzuhiko Ashizu, wrote a supportive article that was published in a Japanese magazine. Ashizu was impressed with Ramos's fighting spirit and heroic traits and considered him a comrade in the task of liberating Asia from Western imperialism. However, he objected to Japanese military adventurism, such as the Japanese occupation of Manchuria, because it was the same path taken by Western imperialism. He was willing to dedicate his life to the war of liberation, but he would not allow himself to be used to fulfill Japanese imperialistic desires. He believed that Japan should liberate Asia not through military conquest but by uniting all the Asian anti-imperialists. For that reason, he warned Ramos against seeking aid from the Japanese government or military, which had hidden imperialistic motives. Efforts to secure arms and ammunition from them would clearly be futile anyway, Ashizu insisted. Instead, he suggested that Ramos approach nongovernment private supporters or groups.[55] We shall return to Ramos's activities in Japan in Ch.5. In the meantime, let us examine what was taking place in the Philippine political scene.

## Campaign for Anti-Tydings-McDuffie Act

After Quezon showed his strength in the June election, his "Antis" and Osmeña's "Pros" slowly regrouped. Quezon's move was enthusiastically welcomed by his opponents, the "Pros," because both parties realized that harmonious interparty relations were necessary to meet the challenge of the Commonwealth. The Sakdalistas criticized this move as a dirty trick, for it only reinforced Quezon's political influence.[56]

Meanwhile, in early December 1934, Millard Tydings, one of the authors of the T-M Act, visited the Philippines as chairman of a congressional mission. When the Philippine legislature accepted the T-M Act in May 1934, it also requested the formation of a committee to conduct an investigation to determine whether the independence law contained "imperfections and inequalities." This was done as a way to secure revisions of the trade provisions of the independence law. Subsequently, five American senators were appointed to the Committee of the Congressional Mission.[57]

To coincide with their visit, Sakdalista representatives decided to produce a pamphlet entitled *Memorial*, a short appeal for immediate, absolute, and complete independence, written in both Tagalog and English. They decided to present a copy to the U.S. President, members of Cabinet and Congress through the Congressional Mission.[58] Five Sakdalista representatives took the *Memorial* to the Manila Hotel, where Tydings and his group were staying. They also invited the mission's members to be guest speakers at a public meeting under their sponsorship, but the invitation was turned down. Undaunted, the Sakdalistas sought additional ways to convey their views and decided to print 1,000 copies of the *Memorial* and distribute them to all the foreign consuls in Manila.[59]

When Tydings spoke to the Philippine Constitutional Convention in late December, he declared that the Filipinos were not ready for independence because they were still economically dependent and that economic independence should have priority over political independence. The Sakdalistas refuted this and asserted that if this principle had been applied at the time of the American Revolution against Great Britain, the U.S. would never have become an independent country. Their protests were of no avail since the 202-member Constitutional Convention had finished its work drafting the Constitution, which was signed at the end of February 1935. A plebiscite confirming the T-M Act and the Commonwealth was scheduled for 14 May 1935.[60]

The Sakdalista Party leaders planned an all-out campaign against the T-M Act. They decided to take the following steps:

1.  The barrio-level committees should meet every weekend to propagate Sakdalista principles.
2.  The leadership should give lectures once a month to train members on how to explain the Sakdalistas' stand on independence to the people.
3.  Each Sakdalista should recruit others into the movement.[61]

As part of the campaign against the T-M Act, the Sakdalistas began accepting invitations to public debates. One such gathering was in the cockfighting arena in San Pablo, Laguna. The topic was "Is There Complete Independence with the T-M Act?" The panel of judges consisted of three "Antis," three Sakdalistas, and one Independent, yet the result was five to two in favor of the Sakdalista orator.[62] Other gatherings included one in Santa Rosa, Laguna, which was attended by more than three thousand people. Another in Intramuros, Manila, near the Colegio de San Juan de Letran, was said to have an audience of 6,000. The Sakdalista flag was hoisted on a stage made especially for the occasion.[63]

Toward the end of March, the Sakdalista Party intensified its campaign against the T-M Act. All Sakdalista speakers were asked to end their individual speaking engagements by 20 March to enable the regional committees to coordinate the campaign efforts.[64] Campaign fever caught on even in the far-off island of Leyte, and daily meetings were held from the end of March to the first week of April.[65] One of the final actions of the campaign was a debate between the Sakdalistas and students from the UP Debate Club, held at the end of April. The topic was "The Teachings of the Sakdalista Party: Are They Detrimental to Independence or Not?"[66] Meanwhile, the date of the referendum was fast approaching.

## Renewed Determination of the Sakdalistas

Despite Ramos's absence from the Philippines, the rest of the Sakdalista leaders and members tried to build a strong unified political party and movement. The Sakdalista leadership appealed to the members, invoking *damay* (sympathy) by describing the country's status as one of slavery and suffering and linked independence with economic improvement. In one poem that appeared in the *Sakdal*, the country's pitiful condition was illustrated in emotional images: hungry children all skin and bones; thin and pale mothers; and poor people whose lands and houses had been confiscated and who had been thrown into jail for unpaid taxes.[67]

The Sakdalista Party members were reminded of their duty to take on responsibilities and tasks to obtain independence:

It is our important duty, therefore, to place ourselves under the SAKDAL flag, which is the true picture and symbol of our loyalty to the responsibilities and tasks we have sworn to. Then let us pray fervently to our Merciful Creator that somehow, through the peaceful means being undertaken by the SAKDALISTAS, a new day will again dawn, a day lit by the golden rays of our country's freedom, for which our loyal and brave Rajahs, Rizal, Bonifacio, Luna, del Pilar, and many other countless heroes of our race all offered their valuable lives in the historical revolutions of 1896 and 1898 (should be '99).[68]

As is evident in this passage and in numerous other articles, the Sakdalistas continued to see themselves as heirs to the heritage of Rizal and other revolutionary heroes. It was not clear, though, whether the writer of this article sincerely believed in using peaceful means to achieve independence and did not know the real purpose of Ramos's visit to Japan, or if he actually knew but didn't say so because he wanted to avoid a government crackdown.

To further strengthen unity, the Sakdalistas continued to hold ceremonies. The most important ones were the annual Rizal Day celebration on 19 June and the anniversary of Rizal's death on 30 December.[69] During these gatherings, the National Anthem was sung, but with these different lyrics:

> Bayang magiting/Na ayaw mapaalipin/Bituing maningning/Ng aming paggiliw/
>
> Kaming iyong kawal/Ay handang makilaban/Sa ganid na pakay ng mga dayuhan/
>
> Sa bayan mo't kabukiran/Sa ilog mo't kaparangan/Ama nami'y nangamatay/Dahil sa iyong Kalayaan/Ang lahat ng Pilipino/ Nakikidigma dahil sa iyo/Kaming anak mo'y narito/Babawiin ang Laya mo/Pilipinas naming pinakamamahal/Di ka namin pababayaan/Manglulupig ay dapat na mamatay (Mamatay!)/ Mabuhay ka aming Bayan (Mabuhay!) [70]

> (Brave country/Which does not want to be enslaved/Shining star/Of our love/
>
> We, your soldiers/Are ready to fight/ Against the greedy intentions/ Of the foreigners/In your towns and fields/In your rivers and plains/Our fathers died/For your Freedom/All the Filipinos/Are fighting for your cause/We, your children, are here/To recover your Freedom/Our most beloved Philippines/We will never forsake you/The invaders should die (Die!)/Long may you live, our Country [Long may you live!])

## Movements within the Movement

Despite continued calls for unity in 1934 and 1935, the Sakdalistas began showing signs of divergence within the movement, with some members becoming involved in secret societies and revolutionary plots. This phenomenon was noted right after the June election, as mentioned earlier. For instance, in three villages located in Nagcarlan, Laguna, the very municipality where the Sakdalistas elected a majority to the council, a society called the Sakdalistang Lihim (Secret Sakdalistas), the term the party leaders used, was formed. In four villages in Lucena, Tayabas, similar organizations were seen. The motive of these secret movements was said to establish a "Republica Filipina" (Philippine Republic). The Sakdalista leadership declared that this movement could be harmful to the party because it was collecting money from the poor, most probably to be used for purchasing arms and ammunitions to achieve its goals. The party disowned these groups and announced that it would not be held responsible for anything they might do and emphasized that its goal was to obtain complete independence peacefully, based on the Jones Law.[71]

The party leaders were also concerned that some of the members might try to organize a Ricartista revolution in the name of the Sakdalista Party. Persistent rumors circulated, alleging that Gen. Artemio Ricarte had been arranging the purchase of arms and ammunition in Japan and that a cargo of guns would soon be delivered to the Philippines. In mid-July 1934, the Cavite Provincial Committee received reports that some members, alleged Ricartistas, were collecting signatures of people who wanted to join the uprising and claimed they were doing so on orders of the Sakdalista Provincial Committee. The committee flatly denied having given any such orders and accused those involved of smearing the name of the Sakdalista Party.[72] In April 1935, the Sakdalista headquarters received an unverified report that Gen. Ricarte had returned to the Philippines to lead an uprising. Concerned that the Sakdalista Party's name might be used to attract followers to this rumored uprising, the Sakdalista leadership continued to vehemently deny involvement in any secret movement or planned uprising.[73]

The party leadership's criticism and denial of the above-mentioned unauthorized societies and activities could be interpreted as strategies designed to mislead and conceal their real motives. However, it was also true that some leaders did believe in peaceful means to obtain independence and were not aware of Ramos's hidden motives. They simply believed that Ramos was trying to influence the Japanese government and private citizens to obtain their support.

Those who were ready to rise up must have come from Ricarte-inspired societies before they rallied around the Sakdalista flag. What gave them more justification for their armed uprising was the ever-increasing harassment by the authorities against Sakdalistas, who were vigorously campaigning against the T-M Act. As the months passed leading up to May 1935, tension between Sakdalistas and government authorities continued to grow.

## Harassment of the Sakdalista Party

As 1935 progressed, the *Sakdal* weekly faced a dramatic drop in circulation. While circulation had been about 18,500 in October 1931, by March 1935, subscriptions had dwindled to about 6,400.[74] The diminishing readership could have been due to the harassment and effective anti-Sakdalista propaganda on the part of Quezon and his supporters, who, after the June 1934 elections, focused attention on the Sakdalista activities in a way they had not done before.

Quezon quickly mounted a personal attack on Ramos. He accused Ramos of smearing his reputation out of bitterness over Ramos's dismissal in 1930. He also accused Ramos of squandering the money donated by members and criticized him for not having *utang na loob* (a debt of gratitude) toward Quezon, who had arranged his job in the government. Ramos and the Sakdalistas responded swiftly to all these accusations. To the charge that he lacked utang na loob, Ramos replied that the value of his service to the country was far greater than the paychecks received from Quezon. Besides, the money had come not from Quezon himself but from the people's taxes. Ramos charged that it was Quezon who lacked *utang na loob*, having failed to show proper gratitude to Osmeña for making him a name in politics.[75] Against the accusation of embezzlement, the Sakdalistas declared that every centavo they received had been announced in the *Sakdal* and that an auditor ensured the money was used solely for Sakdalista activities. Ramos argued that the government missions to the U.S. were the ones that should be investigated, as these junkets, or *excursiones* (excursions, or pleasure trips), were an expensive *konsumisyon* (problem, or cause for exasperation).[76] The strongest response to Quezon was Ramos's open letter phrased in the strongest possible terms, calling him the real enemy of independence: "All you have done is cause the death of Filipinos, preparing them for total slavery, filling the hands of the greedy, and stealing money that should rightfully go to the people."[77]

Quezon did not content himself solely with accusations and rhetoric. He ordered the Philippine Constabulary to closely monitor the Sakdalistas' meetings, speeches, and other functions. Consequently, from June 1934 onward, Quezon was well informed of the activities of the Sakdalistas and Ramos, as seen in the reports compiled by the local constabulary and municipal presidents.[78]

Criticism of the Sakdalista movement continued. The Sakdalista Party platform was ridiculed as utopian promises of betterment for the poor, thus sowing the seeds of discontent among the poor by means of this unrealistic utopian vision. The Sakdalistas answered these charges by agreeing that the popularity of the Sakdalista Party was due to the distressing conditions throughout the Philippines, and refuted the accusation that Ramos was the one sowing these seeds of discontent. Rather, the flames of discontent were being fanned by the failure of the party in power. The governing politicians had betrayed the national honor by abandoning the cause of independence for the sake of personal pleasure and self-aggrandizement.[79]

Another form of harassment took place in the Assembly. The two Sakdalista representatives were finally removed from their committee chairmanships only three months after they had been nominated. The Sakdalistas speculated that the majority had hoped that the two Sakdalista representatives could be bribed into silence by being given the chairmanships; however, they remained firm in their opposition to the T-M Act.[80]

At the provincial level, some repressive moves were seen in Santa Rosa, Laguna. On New Year's Eve 1934, the provincial governor imposed a ban on local dance parties and other New Year's Eve celebrations. The Sakdalistas were warned not to leave their homes because it was alleged that they were planning to take over the town.[81] The Santa Rosa Sakdalistas were targeted again in March 1935. Five Sakdalista councilors and the vice president of the town were suspended by the provincial authorities because they defied the authorities' order. The Sakdalista-dominated municipal council passed an ordinance permanently closing a cabaret where a murder had taken place. The provincial board of Laguna disapproved of this action, as the cabaret brought in Pl,000 a year to the town. But when the board ordered a repeal of the ordinance, the Santa Rosa council refused to comply, saying that the loss of income was more than compensated for by reductions in the expenses of the municipal government. The provincial board dismissed this reasoning and ordered the suspension of the recalcitrant Sakdalista councilors.[82] The lawmakers and the administration now moved to block the legal political avenues available to the Sakdalista legislators, national as well as local.

Another form of harassment by local authorities was the refusal to issue meeting permits and to disrupt meetings.[83] As a means of avoiding this kind of harassment, the Sakdalistas began holding meetings and discussions in private homes. However, this didn't provide any guarantee of security either. In Manila, a special meeting at a private residence was interrupted by an American policeman asking for a permit. When he was told a permit was not needed, he left only to return with a truckload of policemen who stopped the meeting.[84]

In Gapan, Nueva Ecija, a local parish priest claimed that he had been given orders by Archbishop O'Doherty to prevent the Sakdalistas from holding meetings in his town unless they first secured the archbishop's permission. The Sakdalistas figured out that the archbishop had been offended when they said that Catholic prayer was for the benefit of the foreigners. As usual, the Sakdalistas took this opportunity to criticize the Roman Catholic Church, pointing out that the head of the Roman Catholic Church was a foreigner, an Irish American to be specific, and that the Jesuit, Franciscan, and Dominican Orders were all headed by foreigners who still owned big haciendas in the Philippines. The Sakdalistas were not against Christianity. In fact, they wanted Christianity to be taught in schools alongside teachings about the lives of the Filipino revolutionary heroes and love for the country; however, they called attention to the foreign and oppressive nature of the Catholic Church, which should not be overlooked.[85]

As the early months of 1935 passed, it became extremely difficult for the Sakdalistas to hold meetings in many parts of central and southern Luzon. Again, Gapan was a flashpoint of tensions. In March, three truck-loads of constabulary soldiers showed up at a place where a Sakdalista meeting was scheduled. The soldiers in one of the trucks were armed with machine guns. Despite this attempt to intimidate, the meeting was started but there were very few participants.[86] In Cavite, in the early months of 1935, four Sakdalistas were charged with sedition before the Court of First Instance.[87]

Reflecting on this situation, the *Sakdal* began printing articles toward the end of 1934, hinting that violent means could be employed if other avenues were closed to them. For example, one article claimed that the only peaceful solution was to fulfill the Jones Law; however, if these legislators allowed themselves to be intimidated by the pro-U.S. groups, the country would never obtain independence peacefully and armed revolution would

**Photo 2. The Filipino Freedom** (March 1937)
*Source: National Library of Australia*

be unavoidable. The article claimed that the number of Filipinos ready to die for the cause of independence was greater than the number who wanted the U.S. to stay.[88]

### The Filipino Freedom—The New Organ

Another form of harassment was the placing of a mailing ban on the *Sakdal* weekly. At the end of March in 1935, newspapers in Manila printed a copy of a letter purportedly written by a Japanese commander in Taipei, Taiwan, which was part of the Japanese Empire. This letter urged Filipinos not to be misled by Japanese-American enmity because the Japanese were actually friends of Philippine independence. The letter also attacked Quezon as a traitor to the cause of true independence. Director of Posts Juan Ruiz questioned the letter's authenticity, claiming that it had actually been written by Ramos. Citing the letter's insults aimed at Quezon, he banned the *Sakdal* newspaper from the postal service in April.[89]

In response to the mailing ban, the *Sakdal* headquarters initiated another weekly newspaper, *The Filipino Freedom: Ang Tinig ng Bayang Api* (Voice of the Oppressed Nation) while the *Sakdal* continued its publication. The maiden issue of *The Filipino Freedom* came out sometime in April 1935. The format was the same as the *Sakdal*'s, usually six to eight pages and included several articles in English, which were soon replaced by Tagalog.[90] The masthead of *The Filipino Freedom* had a picture of the rising sun with the word "kasarinlan" (independence) written across the ten rays. The sun was rising behind three mountains representing Luzon, the Visayas, and Mindanao. On each side of the picture were slogans such as: "We are for immediate, absolute, and complete independence. Democracy can survive only in an independent country." Later, these slogans were replaced by quotations from the Bible such as: "Tell the truth (and) perfection (will) find all the people lying; Only God is truth"; and M. H. del Pilar's words, "Love this country, which embodies our characteristics and our greatness. Neglecting her means submitting to our and our children's oppression"[91] (see photo 2).

### Mounting Tensions

As the 14 May 1935 plebiscite neared, the government intensified its own campaigns on behalf of the plebiscite while the Sakdalistas continued their opposition to it. Upon Quezon's request, House Speaker Quintin Paredes toured nearby provinces and even the Visayan Islands.

When Paredes and his party arrived at Gapan, Nueva Ecija, the Sakdalistas staged a protest demonstration. A big banner bearing the words "Paredes, go back. We want independence, not a Commonwealth" had been hung on a building owned by the local Sakdalista leader. Meanwhile, the protesters were shouting slogans in Tagalog such as "Down with the traitors of immediate independence" and "We are against the law providing for the Commonwealth." Several Sakdalistas were arrested and their protest signs were removed. They were permitted to attend the rally; however, they were instructed not to ask questions or chant anti-Commonwealth slogans. Similar protests were encountered in the Visayas (including Tacloban). In response to these protests, the government representatives began directly criticizing the Sakdalista Party in their speeches, departing from their original plan of simply informing the people about the plebiscite and provisions of the Constitution.[92]

Meanwhile, the government campaign in favor of the Commonwealth began showing some success, even among the Sakdalistas. Sakdalista Rep. Antonio Argosino from Tayabas, who supported Quezon's "Anti," now openly defected to the Nacionalista camp. Other organizations, such as the Katipunan Mipanampun, an organization of 50,000 peasants and laborers centered in Pampanga, as mentioned earlier, also decided to campaign in favor of the Constitution. The Palihan ng Bayan, with whom the Sakdalistas had a close association, seemed to be shying away from the "communistic" Sakdalista ideas and was becoming more compatible with the government campaign.[93]

Speaker Paredes was somewhat alarmed by the Sakdalista Party's strength, which he had encountered in his speaking tours in the provinces. Upon his return, he conferred with other government officials regarding a new campaign against the discontented elements, especially the Sakdalistas. As a result, the provincial executives of nearby provinces were asked to redouble their efforts against the revolutionary rhetoric being preached by the "disgruntled groups."[94]

In view of the tense situation, Sec. of the Interior Teofilo Sison issued a circular ordering all government and constabulary commanders in the central Luzon provinces to conduct personal investigations of the widespread activities of radical groups, mainly those of the Sakdalistas. Apparently, a number of these reports were eventually forwarded to acting Gov. Gen. Hayden. Finally, the secretary called for a special conference that urged the suppression of all radical activities.[95]

An additional expression of the government's stance appeared in a memorandum and a departmental order, both issued by Sec. of Agriculture Eulogio Rodriguez in early April 1935. The first one was addressed to acting Gov. Gen. Hayden, and in it Rodriguez expressed his concern about the intense antigovernment propaganda campaign being waged by the Sakdalistas, "Reds," and other radical groups. He claimed that some of these orators were declaring that complete independence by the end of the year could only be achieved through blood. Rodriguez urged that these "irresponsible" orators be arrested, and he recommended that the Department of Labor mobilize its agents to track every movement of the Sakdalistas and other radicals. He also urged the provincial governors, constabulary, municipal presidents, and police force to work together to devise a system to monitor the movements of these radicals.[96] The second document was issued to all Agriculture Department employees, particularly provincial field men. They were ordered to counteract Sakdalista propaganda by means of an intensive educational campaign of "enlightenment."[97]

In response to the government's oppressive stance, criticism was aired in some intellectual sectors, saying the strong-arm approach would probably be counterproductive because forbidding the Sakdalistas to hold meetings would not solve the problems but would instead contribute to the Sakdalistas' strength. The intellectuals cautioned that laborers should be given a more equitable share of the goods they produced and more attention should be paid to their interests.[98] Unfortunately, this caution fell on deaf ears. Armed with Rodriguez's circular, Laguna Gov. Cailles now renewed his campaign against the Sakdalistas. The same approach was seen in other provinces, including Bulacan and Tayabas. The *Sakdal* reporter who reported the suppression of these meetings stated that the Sakdalistas' frustration might "create a big fire all over the country."[99]

Despite the mounting suppression and harassment by the authorities, party members continued their fierce fight against the T-M Act and the May referendum, even coming up with a different organ, *The Filipino Freedom*, which could bypass the postal ban.

### The People's Image of the Sakdalistas

The uncompromising attitude of the Sakdalistas was capturing the people's imaginations. It became rather common to use the word "Sakdalista" to describe somebody as an incorruptible and uncompromising dissenter. For instance, S. R. Barros, an editor of the *Mabuhay*

*Journal* and a founding member of the rebel literary group Kapisanang Panitikan (Literary Association, established in 1935), described the newly established society as: "siyang sakdalista at aristokrata sa panulatang tagalog" (it is [the association of] Sakdalistas [uncompromising dissidents] and aristocrats in Tagalog writing). Jose Laurel, who respected the Sakdalistas' courage for resisting the status quo, delivered a speech about freedom of the press by saying, "We need more of that vigor and the courage of an independent and free press in the country. In this sense, I welcome more 'Sakdalistas' of the press."[100] An example of the view of Sakdalistas as fierce pursuers of justice and incorruptible dissidents, who were protectors of the poor and the powerless, can be seen in the following verse:

> Once there was a *presidente* (town/city mayor) who wouldn't give a
>     permit
> To men who'd hold a little meeting when they badly wanted it;
> The governor saw his wisdom, and the judges thought him wise,
> And the Department Secretaries praised him to the skies,
> But when they sought to honor him with a raise of salary,
> He had completely vanished in a cloud of mystery:
> And then they found his body completely flattened out.
>
> (Refrain: And the Sakdal will git [*sic*] you if you don't watch out!)
>
> And one time a bad policeman who'd shout *cocheros* down
> With many a wicked cuss-word and many a wicked frown
> He never stopped the limousines nor shouted at rich men,
> Only at the lowly poor he scowled (at) again and again
> And just as he was strolling once with usual power and pride,
> There were two Sakdalistas a-strolling by his side,
> And they hacked him with their *bolos* 'fore he knew what t'was about.
> (Refrain)
>
> And there was a tax collector who called himself quite tough
> He said: "Be nice to *hacenderos* (plantation owners), but the *taos*
>     (common people), treat 'em rough."
> And he used to walk and swagger with a highly tilted nose,
> And with a snarl and word went forth, that dreadful word "foreclose."
> One day, for being unable to pay a little tax,

He tried to oust a man from home—when lo! A gleaming ax
Nipped head from tough man's shoulders: and he bit the dust, poor
    scout.
(Refrain) [101]

## Calls for Patience, Calls for Revolt

In the midst of the harassment and increasing tensions, Sakdalista leaders continued to urge their followers to be patient. They made an analogy to Christ's sufferings as being similar to what the Sakdalistas were going through, overcoming the oppression of colonialism and recalling the lives that Rizal and del Pilar had led. The members were reminded that only in the midst of grief and misfortune would true independence arise.[102]

Still, some Sakdalistas were clearly unwilling to be content with peaceful means and openly argued that armed struggle was the only way out of the situation. From their perspective, armed revolution was necessary to awaken those who had become comfortable and complacent in their present lives. By taking a more radical approach, these Sakdalistas believed they were carrying out the unfinished work of Rizal, Bonifacio, and del Pilar. They believed that misfortune and even death would be satisfying if the drawing of their own blood would bring people to their senses. They argued that the day of the 14 May plebiscite would be a day of death and the subjugation of freedom and that it must therefore be stopped by any means.[103]

Serafin C. Guinigundo of San Miguel, Bulacan, a well-known Tagalog poet and writer, wrote a poem encouraging the Sakdalistas to continue their struggle:

Tayong mga maliliit ay magyakap
Sa atin ang di sumama'y mawiwikang lilo't sukab
Hindi mahal ang Paglaya't inuuna pa ang pilak
(Oh! ang hanayang mga tao'y nararapat na mautas
Ang taguring kayumanggi sa kanila'y hindi dapat).

We, the small ones, should embrace
Those who do not join us will be called traitorous and treacherous
That they do not love Freedom and put money first
(Oh! those kinds of people should be terminated.
They do not deserve to be members of the brown race).[104]

The Sakdalistas' views, as described above, and this poem, which appeared in the *Sakdal*, could indeed be a reflection of the sentiment of the radical members. Officially, the only means for stopping the referendum was a boycott. In late April, acting Sakdalista Party Pres. Celerino Tiongco was still imploring members not to participate in the referendum, emphasizing that the proposed Commonwealth would not only deny the country independence but also add to its state of slavery.[105]

The following incident indicates that the radical faction was indeed planning an armed uprising. In April, a month before the referendum, seven Sakdalistas in Tayabas were accused of sedition in a criminal complaint. They were charged with plotting a conspiracy against the government and the life of Sen. Pres. Quezon. The complaint alleged that they had been working since October 1934 to enlist people in an army that would rise up in revolt on 15 December 1935, under the leadership of Ciriaco Campomanes, the Tayabas regional representative of the party, who had written the "Ten Basic Rules" discussed earlier. Once Pres. Quezon had been killed, said the official document, the Sakdalistas would govern the Philippines, and their soldiers would be given salaries out of funds confiscated from the government. Campomanes had allegedly ordered uniforms for the officers and soldiers of this army. Most of the arrested Sakdalistas were former Tanggulan members who had taken on a Sakdalista identity to avoid harassment by the authorities. According to the authorities, the money they had collected was to be sent to Japan and Germany to purchase more firearms.[106]

The Sakdalistas in Tayabas interpreted the arrests as harassment by the local government in retaliation for their campaign against the 14 May referendum. Hundreds of Sakdalistas reportedly went to see Campomanes in the municipal jail in Sariaya. While responding to reporters' questions, Campomanes said that the present government was totally corrupted by *pulitikos* (politicians out for personal advantage) and that the coming plebiscite would do more harm than good for the country.[107] He neither denied nor admitted the charges that he was organizing a revolt. Considering the fact that the May Uprising was yet to occur, he most likely belonged to the radical faction of the Sakdalista Party and was indeed preparing for a revolt.

There were other Sakdalistas in Tayabas, however, who chose nonviolent means to obtain independence. They sent a letter to Acting Gov. Gen. Hayden on 30 April, complaining that the Sakdalistas in their province were continually being threatened with prosecution for sedition. They questioned whether working to defeat approval of the Constitution should be considered sedition and requested that Hayden protect their rights to freely express their opinions and ideas, hold public meetings, and denounce corruption in the government.[108]

Hayden's response, written about a week later, explained that his policy was intended to protect the Sakdalista Party's legal rights to freedom of speech and assembly. He noted that he had received a similar complaint earlier on 9 April from the secretary of the Sakdalista Party committee in San Pedro, Laguna, and he had affirmed this same principle to Sec. of the Interior Teofilo Sison. Nevertheless, in tense situations, it was up to the local authorities to determine whether to issue permits, according to Hayden.[109] As seen in the Tayabas case, as of late 1934, two different factions coexisted in the Sakdalista Party: one vowed to obtain independence through violent means and the other through political means.

By April 1935, the constabulary was taking the possibility of Sakdalista-planned violence very seriously. Since September 1934, the Intelligence Division of the constabulary had been receiving information on a prospective Sakdalista uprising and since January 1935, the reports had become increasingly specific, saying that the Sakdalistas were planning to take up arms against the government in some towns in Bulacan and Cavite.[110]

On 29 April 1935, the Intelligence Division of the constabulary received a report that the Sakdalistas were planning to stage a disturbance on the day of the plebiscite. Should this uprising fail, they would stage another one in August or September, by which time Benigno Ramos should have been able to obtain help from Japan and would send firearms, ammunition, airplanes, and soldiers. On the basis of these reports, Brig. Gen. Basilio Valdez, the Constabulary chief, canceled his plans for an inspection tour of Northern Mindanao, replacing the tour with a shorter trip to Romblon, which would enable him to be back in Manila by 10 May to prepare for the expected trouble.[111] Confident of his information, he assured acting Gov. Gen. Hayden that he anticipated no disorder before the plebiscite. In the early morning of 2 May, Constabulary Chief Valdez received another report that the Sakdalistas were preparing for uprisings to be held simultaneously that very night in Manila, Rizal, Bulacan, Cavite, Laguna, and Tayabas.[112]

However, Valdez chose to believe his earlier information that 14 May was the day of trouble. He did not consider the new report to be of great urgency because he had been receiving numerous reports nearly every day. Nevertheless, he forwarded the information to Colonel F. W. Manley, who was in Baguio accompanying Hayden on a visit to the North. The report was also sent to Teofilo Sison, Sec. of the Interior and Labor. In addition, Valdez briefed the various provincial constabulary commanders on where the uprisings were expected to take place so they would be prepared to send detachments should the need arise. He also left orders for Col. Guillermo Francisco, his immediate assistant, to be on the alert, especially in the province of Bulacan. Valdez then went ahead with his scheduled trip to Romblon to inspect the constabulary in the Visayas.[113]

## CHAPTER 4

# SAKDALISTA ACTIVITIES AND ANOTHER ATTEMPTED UPRISING, 1935–1936

T HE INFORMATION ABOUT an uprising on 2 May, which Valdez had ignored, turned out to be true. At a press conference in Tokyo, immediately after the uprising, Benigno Ramos admitted to taking a leading role in the preparations for the uprising. It was originally planned as a way to foil the 14 May plebiscite and to establish the Philippine Republic. However, the outbreak came prematurely because the local leaders could not hold their members in check.[1]

**Preparation for the Uprising**

Contrary to the party platform, Ramos had believed in armed struggle. As we recall, the leaders of the Sakdalista movement, the Communist Party, the Tanggulan Society, and the Palihan ng Bayan used to meet frequently and exchange opinions at the shared printing press where they printed their respective organs. On one such occasion, Ramos pointed out that it would be hard for them to agree on how to carry out their objectives because Anto (Crisanto Evangelista of the Communist Party) was an internationalist who regarded workers and peasants as the only "authentic" Filipinos and looked to Russia for help. Godoy (Eusebio A. Godoy) was using the Palihan as a means of bargaining with the government. Dionisio (of the Tanggulan Society) wanted to revolt despite the lack of ready arms. Therefore, Ramos suggested that they should first form an organization or movement. After one was firmly established, they could then rise up and ask for help from any country opposed to the U.S. imperialists. That country, he stressed, should be close to the Philippines, strongly insinuating Japan. On another occasion, Ramos allegedly told Dionisio that he endorsed the idea of carefully organized local insurrections because violence of a highly dramatic nature would set off a general uprising throughout the Philippines.[2] All these incidents point to Ramos's belief in violence as an effective means to overthrow the colonial government. As the Sakdalista movement was being organized, Ramos and some of the leaders close to him were contemplating an armed revolt as a future course of action. This can be detected in the emphasis they placed on Gen. Artemio Ricarte's letter, which had been printed in the *Sakdal*. As we recall, the revealing sentence was in boldface, "We should not totally forsake the idea that liberty should be taken by blood and life" (see Ch. 2). When the June 1934 elections proved to be a phenomenal success, and the Sakdalistas' image as incorruptible fighters was becoming popular, Ramos and the radical faction saw this as an opportune time to shift to violent means. Accordingly, Ramos left for Japan to obtain arms and ammunitions.

To prepare his followers for the coming uprising in May, Ramos sent out copies of a four-page tabloid newspaper called *Free Filipinos* (also known as *Filipinos Libres* and *Malayang Tao*) at the end of April. The copies were secretly circulated among some of the Sakdalista leaders. The newspaper articles were written in English, Spanish, Tagalog, and Japanese to give the Sakdalistas at home the impression that their movement had captured international attention.[3] Although readers could not have understood the Japanese language, the inclusion of a Japanese section strongly suggested that Ramos had a powerful connection to the Japanese government or influential Japanese and that Japan's assistance could be expected. In fact, one of the Japanese articles, "Nihon Kokumin ni Uttau" (Appeal to the Japanese Nation), pleaded for Japanese assistance by saying: "The Philippine struggle has failed due to the lack of arms, and Japanese arms would mean liberty for the Filipinos."[4]

Ramos declared that the *Free Filipinos* had been published by the Junta Patriotica de Filipinas Libres (Patriotic Junta for Free Philippines) and printed in the Philippines; then his secretary had brought copies to

Japan.[5] The reason for making such a claim may have been to avoid police surveillance in Japan while Ramos was secretly attempting to secure arms from whatever sources were available. It was also possible that Ramos wanted to authenticate the *Free Filipinos* as a Filipino paper in the eyes of foreign readers. According to Ramos's personal secretary, Ramon Crespo, the papers were being printed in Japan and the copies were mailed to the U.S. as well as England and countries in Europe and Latin America, but Ramos was able to publish only four issues due to lack of funds.[6] Crespo's claim seems to be valid, as evidenced in a Japanese police report in 1936:

> Recently, five hundred copies of the maiden issue of a newspaper called *Tagalog Malaya* (Free Tagalog) were secretly printed at the Nippon Press in Tokyo in place of the *Sakdal*, the organ of the Sakdalista Party. They were shipped through Capt. Katsubei Mori of a regular liner of the Osaka Shipping Company that travels between Japan and the Philippines.[7]

Other indications that the *Free Filipinos* was being printed in Japan include the fact that the paper seemed to have been circulated much more widely in Japan than in the Philippines. The papers were distributed not only to the ultranationalist Japanese and military authorities that Ramos was trying to influence but were also found among some ordinary Japanese citizens, such as a hotel clerk in Tokyo.[8] Another indication of the paper's being printed in Japan was that the articles were being written solely by Ramos. The names listed as the editorial staff were either fictitious or pseudonyms of Ramos, such as Regidor Bernardo (Regidor was the name of Ramos's son), L. Gagalangin (the street where Ramos lived in Manila and where the Sakdalista Party had its headquarters), R. Enrile (Ramos's valet in Tokyo), and Eugenio Salazar and Wistano Biroy, which were Ramos's pen names.[9] If the paper had been published in Manila, other Sakdalista leaders would have contributed articles.

The articles in the *Free Filipinos* criticized the U.S. for failing to honor its word on the fulfillment of the 1916 Jones Law. Even though independence had not yet been granted under the Jones Law as promised, the U.S. was negotiating a new form of the colonial government called Commonwealth. Filipino politicians, especially Quezon, and American colonial officials were criticized. The former were called the "Number One Slave of U.S. Interests."[10] The paper reiterated the idea that the Sakdalistas were against Communism and stood for the revival of Filipino family traditions along with Oriental culture and civilization. To appeal to the Japanese people and their government's political aspirations, the paper stated the Sakdalistas also aimed to develop a strong and lasting union among all the countries of the Far East.

The *Free Filipinos* included several photographs. One was a montage of twenty-five Filipino patriots and heroes with Jose Rizal in the center. The caption read: "These Filipinos gave their lives for the Freedom of their Country. The independence movement of the Filipinos is a series of long, unceasing struggles, hardships, sacrifices, tears, and bloodshed." There were also photos from the Tayug Uprising of 1931, portraying the aftermath of dead bodies lying on the ground. The captions below these photos read: "Land-Grabbing Pauperization-System are (*sic*) Striking Characteristics of American Domination in the Philippines...Women assumed the leadership in this people's revolt...they preferred death rather than seeing their country still agonizing under American domination...Their bravery and courage opened the eyes of the people."

The paper also carried strongly worded attacks on the T-M Act and the cedula tax. These criticisms and the description of the Filipinos' struggle for independence had been published repeatedly in the *Sakdal* weekly and were not new to Filipino readers. However, the inclusion of Japanese characters must have given them the strong impression that the Japanese were somehow involved and that their rendering aid was imminent.

Around the same time the *Free Filipinos* was circulating, the manifesto and Ramos's writings were smuggled into Manila. Ramos's manifesto, written in Tagalog and dated 7 April 1935, appealed to the constabulary soldiers, the Scouts, and all of the police forces, asking them not to harass but to protect the Sakdalistas in case they tried to overthrow the government.[11] Ramos's writings were printed in the 4 May issue of the *Sakdal*. In one of them, entitled "Sukdulan na ang pang-uulol sa atin" (Madness Had Reached Its Height in Us), Ramos implored the Sakdalista followers to love their country more than their lives, especially now that it was confronted with the great danger of the U.S. refusing to set them free by establishing the Commonwealth. The Filipinos would become free only when they were ready to offer their lives, following in the footsteps of their heroes.[12]

After reading the *Free Filipinos*, Ramos's manifesto and the articles appeared in the *Sakdal*, the Sakdalistas felt the uprising was near at hand and were confident of Japanese assistance in terms of arms and ammunition, and they expected that the constabulary and police force would not oppose them. That was the reason most of the Sakdalista revolutionaries carried only machetes and clubs as weapons.

The original uprising had been planned for 14 May; however, the local leaders moved the date up to 2 May. The following telegrams exchanged between Ramos and the leaders at home illustrate the course of events: One sent to Ramos, dated 22 April 1935, reads: "CONGRESS 3 SATURDAY DOUBLE AGREED CHAIR WITH US SEND WEAK [*sic*] ADVICE QUICK." This meant "Revolution ready three weeks ago; now advise us what to do." Another telegram to Ramos, dated 30 April, states: "YOU WILL RECEIVE ONE HUNDRED PESOS CONGRESS BEGINNING ANSWER," which meant, "You will receive P100. Revolution about to begin." To this Ramos replied on 1 May, "CONGRESS DAPAT CATORCE DARATING CAMI SAGUITIN KUNG MAPAGAANTAY CONTESTACION PAGADA," meaning "Revolution should be on 14 May; we will arrive there; answer if it can wait." The following day, the Sakdalista leaders answered "CANNOT WAIT CONGRESS TODAY" (Revolution can no longer wait. [It is] today). Ramos answered: "FOUND MARNE GRAND POMADE" (Found many big guns already made).[13] Again, one of the telegrams sent by Ramos explains why some believed in Ramos's arrival with arms and ammunitions.

Shortly before the uprising, Ramos allegedly wrote a letter addressed to his brother Marcos, instructing him to burn Manila. He wanted his followers in Manila to bomb government buildings, invade Chinese and Japanese stores, attack Malacañan Palace (governor general's official residence) and capture the governor general, seize firearms and ammunitions from gun stores, loot the Philippine National Bank and government treasury, and cut all telephone and power lines in the city. In the meantime, the Sakdalistas in the neighboring provinces, after seizing the local governments, would invade Manila.[14]

The evening before leaving the Philippines for Japan, Ramos called aside some of the Sakdalista leaders, including Celerino Tiongco, Elpidio Santos, Simeon de Sena, and Salud Algabre, and told them that he had lost confidence in the desire and ability of the politicians to secure independence and that their only recourse was a revolution. In the first week of February 1935, two months after arriving in Japan, Ramos was joined by Tiongco and Santos, along with Ramos's wife, mother-in-law, and two children. After conferring with Ramos, Tiongco and Santos returned to Manila in mid-March and reported the results of their conference with

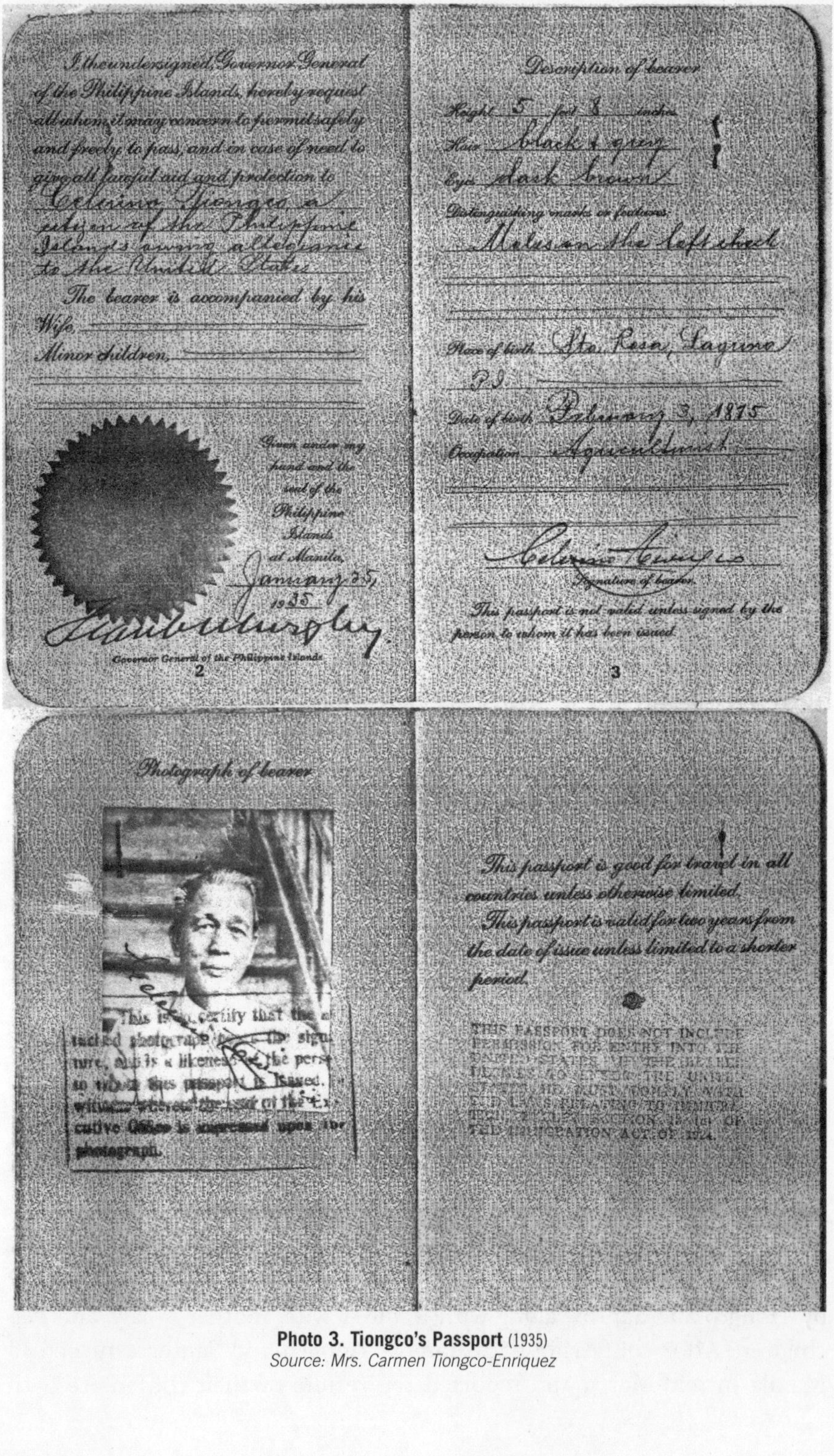

I the undersigned, Governor General of the Philippine Islands, hereby request all whom it may concern to permit safely and freely to pass, and in case of need to give all lawful aid and protection to Celerino Tiongco a citizen of the Philippine Islands owing allegiance to the United States

The bearer is accompanied by his

Wife,

Minor children,

Given under my hand and the seal of the Philippine Islands at Manila, January 25, 1935

Frank Murphy

Governor General of the Philippine Islands

2

Description of bearer

Height 5 feet 8 inches

Hair black & grey

Eyes dark brown

Distinguishing marks or features:

Moles on the left cheek

Place of birth Sta. Rosa, Laguna P. I.

Date of birth February 3, 1875

Occupation Agriculturist

Celerino Tiongco

Signature of bearer.

This passport is not valid unless signed by the person to whom it has been issued

3

Photograph of bearer

This is to certify that the attached photograph bears the signature, and is a likeness of the person to whom this passport is issued. In witness whereof the seal of the Executive Office is impressed upon the photograph.

This passport is good for travel in all countries unless otherwise limited.

This passport is valid for two years from the date of issue unless limited to a shorter period.

THIS PASSPORT DOES NOT INCLUDE PERMISSION FOR ENTRY INTO THE UNITED STATES. IF THE BEARER DESIRES TO ENTER THE UNITED STATES HE MUST COMPLY WITH THE LAWS RELATING TO IMMIGRATION. SEE SECTION 13 (c) OF THE IMMIGRATION ACT OF 1924.

**Photo 3. Tiongco's Passport** (1935)
*Source: Mrs. Carmen Tiongco-Enriquez*

Ramos[15] (Tiongco's passport, see photo 3). It is not surprising that the plan of uprising was leaked to the constabulary intelligence since informers had been planted among the ranks of the Sakdalista Party by the authorities. Although Santos knew of Ramos's original plan for 14 May, he could not contain the others and agreed with Algabre, the Cabuyao leader of the uprising, to go ahead and stage the uprising, using Ramos's last telegram as an excuse.[16] These clandestine activities of the Sakdalista leaders would explain the rampant rumors prior to the actual uprising.

The Sakdalista leaders were not all in agreement about starting the revolution. For instance, Tiongco voted against the idea of an uprising after finding out that armed assistance from Japan was not a certainty. His appeal to the Sakdalista members, as late as 22 April, was to boycott the plebiscite indicated his decision.[17] Instead, Tiongco's plan was to organize mass demonstrations on 13 and 14 May, and induce the voters to turn down the T-M Act. He would also ask the American government to annul the plebiscite returns if they showed less than two million votes in favor of the Constitution. However, Tiongco's plan was interrupted by the report that Ramos had given instructions to Elpidio Santos and others who allegedly had direct communication with him to go ahead and stage an uprising. Upon hearing this, Tiongco decided to go into hiding so as not to be implicated.[18]

Celerino Tiongco, a graduate of San Juan de Letran College and a landlord from Santa Rosa, had been the mayor of the town during the Spanish period and eventually joined the anti-Spanish revolution. He respected Quezon and thought that he had both the qualities and the opportunity to be held next to Rizal in greatness. However, Tiongco opined that Quezon's association with all the "big shots" of industry and business made him think first of money rather than independence.

Tiongco's son Felix once asked him what good independence would be if they had to undergo miseries caused by the revolution. Tiongco replied that independence demanded sacrifice. He illustrated his point by giving an example of Jose Rizal, who, in spite of his outstanding qualifications and promising future, had willingly sacrificed everything for the cause of freedom, even to the extent of giving up his life. Tiongco criticized American influence on the Filipino youth, who were content to lead comfortable lives under American colonization and called his son a product of American institutions. "The longer America stays here, the greater will be the number of people with ideas like yours. Then we shall never have our independence." Responding to the argument that Japan would take over the Philippines as soon as it was granted independence, Tiongco said, "Japan will always be there, and if we are afraid of her, then we shall never become independent."[19]

For those Filipinos who tried to overthrow the colonial government, Japan seemed to be the perfect place to purchase arms and ammunition because she was geographically close and was growing strong through her rising military. Moreover, Filipinos remembered the Japanese involvement in the 1896 Revolution and the subsequent Philippine-American War. (This aspect will be discussed in Ch. 8) Even after the failed uprising, Ramos's efforts in securing ammunition in Japan continued.

**Rumors of Another Uprising**

Immediately after the 2–3 May Uprising, Sakdalista Party members in various towns sought to hold public meetings to explain what had taken place. However, the authorities cancelled the meeting permits because rumors of another uprising were starting to spread.[20] On the night of 13 May, the Sakdalistas were to attack the Japanese in Manila in order to compel the Japanese Consul to request help from the Japanese Navy. Then Benigno Ramos and his party would enter the Philippines along with the Japanese troops. On 14 May, the Sakdalistas were to seize the ballot boxes in order to nullify the plebiscite. From 12 to 16 May, a big Sakdalista flag would be hoisted on the mountain above Susong Dalaga, Gapan, in Nueva Ecija to help the Japanese airplanes locate the Sakdalistas. Then the planes would drop firearms and ammunition in the provinces of Bulacan and Nueva Ecija. Celerino Tiongco and Elpidio Santos would use these planes to escape, if necessary, in which case a plane would drop them off on a Japanese war ship near the Pacific coast of Tayabas. Some people, believing these rumors to be true, evacuated to nearby towns.[21]

Japanese Consul Gen. Atsushi Kimura categorically denied the persistent rumors of Japanese assistance, saying that nothing could be more ridiculous. He also clarified the Japanese government's stand on Ramos. The government would accord Ramos the same protection extended to other political refugees in Japan, just as the Filipino patriots who had sought refuge in Japan during the anti-Spanish revolution had been protected. However, the Japanese government would deport any political refugee, including Ramos, the moment he took advantage of his privileged status to conduct propaganda against any government, domestic or foreign. He added that the authorities would be closely watching Ramos's activities in Japan.[22]

## The Government's Countermeasures

Although the Philippine authorities had managed to quell the bloody uprising, they thought they could have avoided it altogether had they been more alert and prepared. As rumors of another revolt circulated, officials felt that utmost caution had to be taken to ensure that the 14 May plebiscite would be successful. In the aftermath of the uprising, more than a thousand Sakdalistas were arrested.[23] At the same time, the government appealed to Sakdalista fugitives in the mountains to surrender, saying that it had no intention of arresting the rank-and-file members, only the leaders, and those who did not surrender would be considered highway robbers or bandits.[24]

In the meantime, many municipal officials gave the Sakdalistas the opportunity to avoid arrest by signing affidavits stating that they were separating from the organization.[25] In Cavite town, 3,000 Sakdalistas were reported to have sworn allegiance to the authorities. Meanwhile, a decision of the Philippine Cabinet on 10 May affirmed that Sakdalista officials in municipal, provincial, and insular offices would be allowed to remain in office on the basis of pledges to the Department of the Interior to cooperate in preserving peace and order. The authorities also took steps to restrain the campaigning for the plebiscite since the situation in the provinces where the Sakdalistas had risen in arms was still alarming. As the day of the plebiscite approached, Sec. of the Interior Teofilo Sison ordered that severe penalties be dealt on anyone who sought to intimidate or prevent any voter from exercising his right of suffrage. Sison had good reason for concern as he had received a report that the popular peasant organization Kalipunang Pangbansa ng mga Magbubukid sa Pilipinas (National Peasants' Confederation in the Philippines or KPMP) had joined the Sakdalistas in order to foil the plebiscite.[26] The plebiscite took place as scheduled, and despite the persistent rumors of Sakdalista attacks, most places experienced an orderly vote. Nevertheless, at least in Laguna, many women stayed away from the polls out of fear of possible violence.[27]

After the 14 May plebiscite, trials of Sakdalistas commenced in the places where the major uprisings had taken place. Benigno Ramos, Celerino Tiongco, and 100 other leaders were charged with sedition at the Santa Rosa court in Laguna as well as in the court in Bulacan. In the province of Bulacan, no fewer than ten lawyers defended the accused. Rep.

Alfonso Mendoza of the Radical Party and Rep. Isauro Gabaldon, former resident commissioner to Washington, D.C., were part of the legal team.[28] One of the accused was Salud Algabre, who turned herself in to the police. She was charged with rebellion and robbery but was released in July after posting a bond of P4,000 raised by the local Sakdalista leaders, most of them proprietors in the barrios and towns.[29]

The accused Sakdalistas were tried and the May Uprising seemed to have become a thing of the past. However, the local authorities continued to be vigilant. One of their strategies was to organize citizen bands and arm them with shotguns so they could make night patrols to protect themselves and intimidate the Sakdalistas at the same time.[30]

## Sakdalistas' Efforts to Reestablish the Party

The May Uprising divided the party. Some members were dismayed by its failure and, in shame, just lay low while others left the party altogether. Those who remained attempted to assess and reestablish the party. About two weeks after the uprising, a caucus of some one hundred representatives who had not participated in the uprising was held in a village in Laguna. They discussed the reorganization of the party, reformation of its platform, and restoration of its good name. Although the general public called the participants of the Sakdalista uprising "irresponsible elements," the prevailing belief within the party was that they were heroes who had offered their lives for the independence of their country.[31]

As a result of this meeting, the Sakdalistas planned a mass meeting for June 1 to explain the party's attitude toward the uprising. This would be followed by a national convention on June 2 at the Opera House. The government officials were in a quandary as to whether they should issue the necessary permits.[32] After agreeing with the authorities' request not to carry any arms into their meetings or to make any inflammatory speeches, permission was granted. However, the meeting was transferred to the Sakdalista Party headquarters instead, and around three hundred members attended.[33]

A different approach toward the authorities was taken in Tayabas. The Sakdalistas led by Jose Timog, who had garnered more votes than Manuel Quezon at the 1934 elections, made an agreement with the government. This agreement was called the Pact of Lucena and was finalized barely one week after the uprising without the sanction of the party's central headquarters. The governor of Tayabas, the undersecretary of the

Interior, and some constabulary officers represented the government in the negotiations. This showed the government authorities' efforts to solve the problem amicably as they recognized the Sakdalistas' strength in the locality. During the conference, Timog pointed out that the government had failed in protecting the rights of the poor. He stressed that most of the Sakdalistas in Tayabas were not cognizant of the plans of their fellow members in other places and that the members who had participated in the uprising were only a radical faction of the party. The conference agreed that the government and the Sakdalistas would jointly maintain the peace and order, for the good of all. Those who wanted to follow in the footsteps of their brothers in Laguna, Cavite, and Bulacan would automatically be expelled from the party chapter in Tayabas.[34] Eventually, some members in this area temporarily left the party to organize a quasi-religious organization called Kapatiran (A)ng Litaw na Katalinuhan (KLK) (Brotherhood of Outstanding Intelligence).[35]

**Defending the Sakdalistas' Actions**

In the meantime, those who remained in the party defended their comrades' actions and asked the members to keep faith in the movement by invoking the experiences of Christ and the "Martyr of Bagong-Bayan" (Jose Rizal). The Sakdalista leadership pleaded with members to persevere and go against self-interest in order to reach the victory for which their brave heroes and parents had died.[36] One of the members stated that the Sakdalista movement had only been in existence for five years, yet no other political party in the Philippines displayed so much zeal and determination to accomplish the ideals of curing all the economic, moral, and political maladies, in addition to their willingness to encounter hardship for the sake of a common cause. Independence could be obtained only through the efforts of these forgotten masses, who possessed genuine and pure patriotism.[37]

The oral pleadings of the four accused Sakdalista leaders charged with sedition in the Cavite Court of First Instance further demonstrate the virtue of sacrifice. Before they were sentenced to not less than two years and not more than four years, one of them faced the judge and criticized the shooting of the defenseless Sakdalistas in Cabuyao. He said that if they were still thirsty for the blood of Sakdalistas, "I am ready to offer my life to the bosom of the Mother Country if it is forbidden by law to show heroism and love for freedom and independence." He claimed that they had simply tried to sow the seeds of Rizal, Mabini, del Pilar, and other true children of the country. The accused emphasized that if there were no suffering, there would be no holiness; and if there were no holiness, then there would be no redemption. Christ would not have been fully revealed as the Son of God if he had not died. So, to fully become the children of the country, they had to bear countless punishments.[38] These four Cavite Sakdalistas were praised by fellow members as the real heroes of redemption of the Mother County because they readily accepted the consequences of their actions. Moved by their determination, some wrote to the *Sakdal* saying that there was nothing more glorious in life than to fight against oppression, to protect the rights of one's race (countrymen) and to die for principles and for the sake of the country.[39]

Meanwhile, Ramos in Tokyo sent a letter, dated 30 May, to the *Sakdal* showing respect for and acknowledging the courage and heroism displayed by the Sakdalistas, especially those from Cabuyao, Santa Rosa, and San Ildefonso, as well as the other "Soldiers of Freedom." Ramos wrote that beyond the mistakes and confusion of those who had launched the uprising, their acts of offering their lives should be praised all the more because they had only followed the light of heroism. Ramos's final appeal was that they not lose hope because "the Father of Sakdal" (Amang Sakdal) would return.[40]

### The First Election under the Commonwealth

The 14 May plebiscite resulted in the overwhelming approval of the Constitution and the T-M Act. The next step was to hold the first election under the Commonwealth to elect the president, which was set for mid-September. At the end of July, the Sakdalista Party's National Assembly was held and 200 delegates attended. A debate on the upcoming election regarding whether to participate or not was included in the schedule. While Representatives Almazan, Untivero, and their supporters insisted on participation, the majority followed Ramos's plea to boycott the election, and the assembly voted not to participate.[41] Nevertheless, the debate continued. A *Sakdal* editorial explained the ineffectiveness of boycotting the election to bring down Quezon, because defeating him without destroying the Commonwealth would bring greater hardship to the people. A boycott would be counterproductive as long as the Commonwealth government existed. Finally in mid-September, the acting president of the Sakdalista Party, Jose Timog, announced that the party had resolved not to participate in the election after all. However, he later changed his mind and said that those who had previously given their word to vote before the decision had been made were allowed to vote.[42]

If the May Uprising had not taken place, the Sakdalista Party could have assumed the role of a genuine opposition party, like the one in 1934. In the meantime, two old revolutionaries, Emilio Aguinaldo, the Philippine-American War veteran, and Gregorio Aglipay, one of the founders of the IFI, ran for the presidency against a coalition ticket of candidates headed by Manuel Quezon and Sergio Osmeña, as president and vice president, respectively. Gen. Aguinaldo invited the Sakdalistas to join his forces, although he strongly condemned the May Uprising. Celerino Tiongco was with Aguinaldo's Nationalist Socialist Party when his candidacy was proclaimed.[43] Those Sakdalistas who did participate must have voted either for Aguinaldo or Aglipay since their platforms were in favor of acquiring complete and absolute independence within three years or sooner.[44]

The election results were: Quezon, 69 percent of the 1,021,445 votes; Aguinaldo, 17 percent; and Aglipay, 14 percent.[45] This meant that more than 30 percent of the electorate showed resentment toward Quezon and Osmeña's newly formed coalition. The voters knew that neither Aguinaldo nor Aglipay had a chance of winning, yet they voted for them to show their frustration, disillusionment, and disappointment with the Nacionalista-dominated government. If the disenfranchised masses had been included, the percentage of antigovernment sentiment could have been much higher.

### Persistent Rumors and Harassment

After the differences had been set aside, the Sakdalista Party continued its activities. One of its first moves was to prepare a "Memorial" to be submitted to U.S. Sec. of War George Dean and members of the congressional delegation, who were arriving in mid-November 1935 for the inauguration of the Commonwealth Government.

The *Memorial* stated that the 14 May plebiscite was not legal for a number of reasons. The people were not given enough time and opportunity to understand the real meaning of the Commonwealth Law and its government and Constitution. Many did not vote in the plebiscite, and the poll clerks and inspectors had voted in their stead. The *Memorial* also stressed that it was useless to strive for political and economic freedom if the souls of the people remained under alien rule and that the development of a uniquely Philippine culture was the key to Philippine independence.[46]

As the inaugural day approached, the authorities decided to be more vigilant and tighten their control because they had obtained information that this time the Sakdalistas planned to prevent the inauguration of the Commonwealth. The officials were eager to hold the most important national ceremony in recent years without untoward incidents. To achieve this, even the signatories of the *Memorial* were arrested and later charged with the crime of illicit association despite the fact that a typewritten copy of the *Memorial* was sent to Gen. Valdez and Capt. Guido of the constabulary for their approval. Some of the Sakdalista orators were also arrested. In addition, the Sakdalistas were allowed to hold meetings, but a permit was required and their meetings had to be open to the public, even to the agents of the law. Furthermore, personal mail was intercepted and censored, and speaking against the Commonwealth government was not allowed.[47]

In the midst of the rumors of another uprising, the inaugural ceremony took place on 15 November 1935. It started with the declaration of the Commonwealth of the Philippines by Sec. of War George H. Dean, who represented Pres. Franklin D. Roosevelt. This was followed by the administration of the oaths of office in front of 250,000 spectators. The first to be sworn in was Manuel Quezon. His address as the first president of the Commonwealth was followed by colorful military and civic parades, which were attended by 20,000. For this occasion, Quezon conditionally pardoned thirty-two prisoners, the majority of them Sakdalistas. Thirteen of them were from San Ildefonso and eleven were from Santa Rosa.[48]

However, events in the town of Atimonan, Tayabas, where Sakdalista candidate Jose Timog had defeated Quezon in the 1934 election, took a different turn. On that day, the constabulary soldiers collected bolos and other weapons from anyone who entered the town. They patrolled the streets, and the crowds that usually milled about in the main streets were nowhere to be seen. Not only was there no festive air but there were no tricolored Philippine flags either, no bursting firecrackers nor ringing bells. Normally, when a civic parade took place in that town, it was half a kilometer long, but that day none of the local organizations took part; a few of the members of the Municipal Council attended, and only schoolteachers and students were seen. After the parade, a speech was given in the municipal hall but the audience was sparse. An observer noted that no one seemed to be enthusiastic about the Commonwealth in the town of Atimonan.[49] This was quite a contrast to the celebration that took place in Manila.

While the authorities breathed a sigh of relief over the inauguration ceremony, the constabulary authorities were again on alert because they had received a report that another uprising would occur on 31 December, the deadline set by the Sakdalistas to obtain independence. The rumors suggested that Benigno Ramos would come back from Japan with arms and ammunition, several squadrons of Japanese bombers, and a similar number of battleships. The rumors became more credible when Ramos's wife Liboria returned from Japan on 10 December. The Sakdalistas assumed she was bringing orders from Ramos regarding the planned uprising.[50] As the rumors became widespread, the law enforcers were kept busy arresting anyone who uttered remarks considered seditious. In mid-December, Salud Algabre was arrested again at a meeting in Tondo and charged with sedition for allegedly uttering words inciting the crowd. While her case for sedition of the 1935 Uprising was appealed to a higher court, she came to Manila and directed the Sakdalista activities in their headquarters in Gagalangin, Tondo. On 29 December, some thirty Sakdalista leaders, including Celerino Tiongco and Elpidio Santos, were arrested on charges of sedition.[51]

The authorities were relieved when 1935 ended without any more trouble, only to face a report/rumor of two possible uprisings in 1936—one on 1 May, and another on 12 May, both pending instructions from Ramos in Japan.[52] Despite these rampant rumors, during the observance of his 58th birthday, President Quezon granted conditional pardons to several hundred prisoners, including thirty-one Sakdalistas (twenty-nine from Cabuyao and two from Bulacan) on 18 August 1936.[53]

## Separating and Merging

As mentioned earlier, in Tayabas some Sakdalistas left the party to organize the KLK immediately after the failed May Uprising. Later that year, the supreme head of this organization, Angel Lorenzo, was arrested because the authorities believed the KLK had the same principles and teachings as the Sakdalista Party.[54] In other places, several new organizations similar to the Sakdalista Party had sprung up under different names since the uprising. One established in Santa Cruz, Marinduque, had more than a hundred people. They arrived from Tayabas at the end of April of 1936, carrying a big flag with the word "Sakdalistas." Although they appeared to be a religious group, their hymns and the principles of their religious beliefs manifested strong antigovernment, proindependence sentiment. They had been living in a cave and were being led by a man the members believed to be the successor of Jose Rizal. They paraded through the town with the necessary permit.[55] Other organizations included Tagumpay (Victory), formed in Tayabas and the Samahan ng Tatlong Persona in Mount Banahaw in Laguna/Tayabas. These associations were said to be gaining adherents in the provinces of Southern Luzon, a Sakdalista stronghold. The Sakdalista leaders considered these groups to be religious societies and denied any connection with them.[56] Although the Sakdalista officials might not have recognized them as members, the members of these quasi-religious organizations considered themselves Sakdalistas. Considering the fact that they were organized after the crushing of the May Uprising, we can assume that those who longed for more spiritual fulfillment were the force behind these organizations.

With the party relatively inactive and lacking in unity, its temporary president, Felicisimo Lauson, took charge of the labor movement's campaign to demand higher wages. He stated that only independence could ultimately end workers' problems, but meanwhile, the welfare of the laborers and the poor should be addressed.[57] Lauson's activities showed the link between the Sakdalista Party and the labor organizations in that each supported the others.

## Holding the Party Together

The Sakdalistas were faced not only with harassment but also with uncertainty borne of a lack of information as to when their leader, Ramos, was returning. They were getting restless, and some were losing faith in the party. In view of this, and to boost members' morale, the leaders published a list of books in the organ and encouraged the members to read them. It included *Noli me tangere* and *El Filibusterismo*, by Jose Rizal, and memoirs of the past revolution, such as *Himagsikan ng mga Pilipino Laban sa Kastila* (Filipino's Revolution against Spain) by Artemio Ricarte. They hoped that by reading these books, the members would be filled with humane thoughts (*maka-taong isip*), a pro-Filipino spirit (*maka-Pilipinong kaluluwa*), and pro-Sakdal behavior (*maka-Sakdal na gawain*). Some readers responded positively; one of them said that he was dedicated to the task of improving the lot of the downtrodden, defenseless peasants and that Sakdalism had taught him to hold righteous convictions, to the extent of dying for them.[58]

In an attempt to hold the members together, the *Sakdal* published guidelines on how the Sakdalistas were expected to behave in everyday life. Good Sakdalistas were expected to avoid engaging in quarrels and useless gossip, be helpful to the oppressed and the unfortunate, study and observe closely all that they saw and felt so that their movements and actions were always proper, and pray to God so that independence would soon be granted. The guidelines warned against the divisiveness within the party that had been initiated by the anti-Ramos faction, which was planning to inaugurate a new president.[59]

Despite these efforts, a number of Sakdalistas decided to leave the party because they were disenchanted with the party leadership. Some joined forces with the National Socialist Party of Gen. Aguinaldo. Others established a new movement in San Ildefonso and San Rafael, Bulacan, advocating that the government purchase the Hacienda Buenavista.[60]

Faced with numerous rumors of Sakdalista disturbances, the party leadership finally issued a manifesto at the end of May 1936, declaring that they were not pro-Japan, didn't have plans to seize power from the government, and should therefore not be harassed.[61] Shortly thereafter, in the middle of July 1936, the Sakdalista Party formally decided to cease its activities altogether until Ramos's return. It was a unanimous decision made by the representatives during a meeting of the party leadership, stressing that the party was not by any means dissolving itself. Members who wished to extend financial assistance to Ramos were still encouraged to do so.[62]

### Another Attempt at Uprising

At the end of September 1936, Sec. of the Interior Elpidio Quirino ordered all provincial governors and municipal presidents to be alert to the activities of radical elements, mainly the Sakdalistas, and instructed the agents of the law to suppress them.[63] This must have been based on information and rumors they obtained regarding another "revolution" to be staged by the radical faction of the Sakdalista Party. The information this time proved to be true.

On 2 October 1936, Pablo Penullar, owner of a big tract of sugarcane and rice fields in Bayambang, Pangasinan, called a meeting of the party in the town. His aim was to prepare for a local Sakdalista "revolution," as he was told similar actions would take place in Manila and other parts of the country. Around eighty members gathered at Penullar's house, all armed only with bolos, having been informed that Japanese airplanes would come to their aid. Since no Japanese planes came and no uprising in Manila occurred, they all returned home without incident.[64]

Pablo Penullar was the leader who had been arrested in January 1915, right after the Christmas Eve Fiasco, for organizing an uprising. He was imprisoned for the crime of sedition and spent two years at hard labor in Corregidor. He became a Methodist-Episcopalian preacher and was later expelled from the church for allegedly engaging in the immoral conduct of adultery. He left for Hawaii but was brought back to answer to the charge. He was eventually acquitted since the plaintiff in the case refused to testify against him. In 1931, he reemerged as one of the leaders of the Tayug Uprising of Pangasinan. At the time of this most recent uprising, Penullar held the rank of field marshal in the Sakdalista "military" and his aide was a veteran of the Philippine Revolution.[65]

The following day, 3 October, a series of bombings occurred in at least eleven different places in Manila and a fire broke out at an American-owned hardware store and adjoining warehouse. The fire raged for several hours because a large section of Manila had no water supply, the main water pipe at the Santa Mesa railroad crossing having burst. Several houses and four rooms in a hotel were destroyed. It turned out that the Sakdalistas in Manila had set this fire as signal that could be seen from Laguna, Cavite, and other places nearby. Upon seeing the fire, other Sakdalistas were expected to join the uprising.[66] The signal came one day later than Penullar's planned uprising in Pangasinan.

The police authorities traced the arson to a man who had checked in at the hotel and left a suitcase containing a crude bomb. That morning, a suspicious-looking young man had been spotted at the Santa Mesa Crossing, and the authorities suspected the culprit had probably broken the water pipe as part of the plan. Two Sakdalistas, Teodoro Navarro and Lorenzo Galang, were arrested on 5 October, on suspicion of involvement in this incident.[67] These occurrences showed that another general uprising had indeed been planned, although it was not well coordinated. From early to mid-October, police had located bombs in several Manila buildings, leading to the arrest of three more Sakdalista leaders. One of them was Fruto Ramos Santos, the staunch octogenarian Sakdalista, who had been arrested for sedition in December the previous year.[68] At age 18, he entered into a mountain to try living the life of a hermit but realized that the country's independence could not be achieved by prayer. When he was 22 years old, he had the chance to personally meet with Jose Rizal. Inspired by Rizal, he decided to dedicate his life to attaining freedom for the country. Eventually he fought in the anti-Spanish War of 1896. He was trained in the law and he had been appointed as associate judge in the past.[69] His activities as a Sakdalista continued into the Japanese Occupation, as we shall see later.

The staging of the uprising on 3 October had been in preparation for a long time by three groups; mainly one in Manila, in Rizal, and in Pangasinan. After setting the fire in Manila as a signal, their plan was to burn the Japanese Consulate and some Japanese businesses in order to force Japanese intervention.[70] The Sakdalistas in the provinces were to come into the city and take over; then sweep through the nearby provinces to assume control of all the municipalities. They all believed that Ramos was arriving on board a Japanese plane to provide aid to carry out this plot. When Fruto Santos and his comrades arrived in Manila, they saw that several places in the city were already on fire and police and armed men were everywhere. In order to avoid arrest, they had to leave their explosives, bombs, dynamite, bolos, and Sakdalista flags in the nearby town of Malabon. Some Sakdalistas in the provinces of Pangasinan, Nueva Ecija, Cavite, and Rizal were reportedly engaged in activities connected to this second uprising.[71]

The Sakdalista members' houses were searched immediately and any Sakdalista-related materials, such as flags and publications, were confiscated. Felicisimo Lauson, temporary president of the Sakdalista Party, announced that the party had never officially or unofficially sanctioned violent activities, much less the bombing and arson incidents. They all disclaimed any knowledge of this incident, saying the party should not be blamed for these individuals' actions, and they protested the authorities' actions as tromping on human rights.[72]

Despite their denial, a rumor immediately spread that the Sakdalistas planned to burn or blow up public buildings and churches in the provinces. The constabulary soldiers were placed on red alert at all vital points in towns close to Manila.[73] This rumor was not groundless. On the night of 24 October, about five hundred Sakdalistas from all over the province of Pangasinan (two hundred from Bayambang alone) gathered in the outskirts of the town in an attempt to bomb the municipal building. Around one hundred and forty were arrested, including Pablo Penullar, and charged with sedition.[74]

In reporting these events, most of the journalists connected the bombing incident to the social and economic hardship brought about by a recent typhoon. Filipino journalist Leon Ma. Guerrero, however, placed emphasis on the continuity of maintaining the fighting spirit for the country's independence. He said that if Andres Bonifacio, one of the leaders of the 1896 Revolution, had been still alive at the time of the May Uprising, he could well have been one of the plotters of this uprising. Guerrero speculated that Bonifacio's name would have appeared in the newspaper like this: "Among those arrested, Andres Bonifacio, [age] 73." Guerrero compared the two organizations, the Sakdalista Party and the Katipunan, and he concluded that both doctrines were the same in that they expressed the dreams of poor Filipinos, who were yearning for national as well as individual liberty. Both organizations made similar accusations about the prevailing conditions: "Bonifacio's Spain was the Sakdalistas' America. The former's landlords and politicians that the Katipuneros had fought against are still living." Guerrero asserted that the "Cry of Cabuyao" might well have been the "Cry of Balintawak."[75]

The attempted uprisings in Manila and Pangasinan had been planned by Frisco D. Villanueva, one of the representatives from Capiz at the time the party was established and a candidate for representative for the city of Manila in the 1934 elections.[76] Villanueva believed that the destruction of Manila would demonstrate their power and that American and other foreign business interests would crumble and disappear, thus forcing the U.S. to give them independence immediately, not ten years later. Villanueva was of the opinion that only through revolution could liberty be obtained.

Villanueva was once a preparatory law student in the Philippine Law School. When the original scheme to bomb Manila in early October failed, Villanueva and his companion Amado Tejano, a former student of Far Eastern University, left for Pangasinan. With Penullar, they planned the 24 October uprising, which included killing townspeople who owned fire-arms and taking their weapons. After that, they would rush to the town center, attack municipal officials, and then take over the local government.

Villanueva emphasized that Ramos had not given them any instruc-tions, contrary to the rumor. In an interview with a *Philippines Free Press* reporter who visited him in Lingayen jail in Pangasinan, Villanueva said:

We want to be free of all American domination. Independence has been repeatedly promised to us, first by President McKinley in his instruction to the Schurman Commission and in the preamble of the Jones Law, which promised that as soon as a stable situation prevailed in the Islands, independence would be granted. The U.S. knew there had been established a stable government. But what did it do but to give us the Tydings-McDuffie Act. We have lost faith in America. Will that same government keep its word at the end of the Commonwealth? We don't think so. That is why we tried to overthrow the government by force. There is no such thing as a Filipino government. Today is Quezon's government, which is an instrument of the Americans. Even the Philippine Army is such an instrument, because the U.S. President has the power to summon the Philippine Army in case the U.S. is at war.[77]

Villanueva declared that even after he and his comrades were imprisoned, others would continue the fight. He confided to the reporter that he was dedicated to the Sakdalista cause and was ready to give his life if necessary. Villanueva and Tejano were charged with conspiracy to commit rebellion, arson, and illegal possession of explosives and other types of deadly weapons.[78]

Villanueva was transferred from Lingayen Jail to Bilibid Prison in Manila, on 1 December 1937, to serve the rest of his sentence that would end in April 1943. In January 1938, he was placed in *bartolina* (solitary confinement) for refusing to honor the American flag. However, on 24 June, President Quezon granted him absolute pardon but Villanueva refused it. His reasons were that accepting the pardon might imply that he had surrendered to the American colonial system and he did not want to be free if it meant leaving his comrades, including Penullar and Tejano, behind.[79]

The reporter decided to interview Pablo Penullar as well. When it was suggested to Penullar that he had not learned his lesson after spending two years at hard labor in Corregidor in relation to the 1914 uprising, he responded, "Oh, yes, I learned a lot from that experience. I learned that nothing can be accomplished unless you work for it. For twenty years, I worked and labored for myself and my family. But I am not satisfied. I feel selfish working only for my own self and doing nothing for my country." Penullar firmly believed that after the government had been entirely Filipinized, destitution and hardship would vanish because the Americans and other foreigners who had dominated commerce and industry would cease to enjoy the privileges they now had. He emphasized to the interviewer that he and his comrades would continue fighting for complete independence. "Some of us—myself and my comrades—may go to prison, but others will take up the work where we leave off. We are not doing this for our own good. We are doing this for everyone, even the current government officials who so strongly disapprove of our work and aim to destroy it." Looking straight at the interviewer, Penullar said: "Let me remind you that the first few drops of water are not enough to corrode or wear out a rock. It will take hundreds, thousands of drops to do that, and the drops must be continuous."[80]

Meanwhile, rumors of another uprising continued to circulate.[81] In the first week of December, the Sakdalista Party leaders dismissed these rumors and called on members to refuse to participate in any violent actions. Pres. Lauson urged the members to cooperate with the government for the time being.[82] Later, in April 1937, he tried to oust Ramos from the Sakdalista Party leadership and to establish an alternative National Directorate. Lauson's attempts met strong opposition from the members, who regarded his actions to be "against the clean and sacred principles of the Sakdalista Party." Some members called Lauson's actions shameful and urged Lauson's followers to return from the path taken by Judas and Satan.[83] The party faced the possibility of disintegration because of the absence of their leader, the attempted uprising of 1936, and manipulation by some members; however, the loyal Sakdalistas held the party together.

## CHAPTER 5

# SAKDALISTA ACTIVITIES AND RAMOS IN JAPAN, 1937–1938

A FTER RAMOS'S WIFE Liboria left for Manila, Ramos was quite worried about her health and planned to return to the Philippines. However, the directorate of the party and Ramos's two children were vehemently opposed to his decision to come home while the rumors of another uprising were circulating. They feared that Ramos would be arrested as soon as he set foot on Philippine soil. While he was contemplating possible ways to return home, Liboria passed away at the end of May 1937.

Many Sakdalistas and other sympathizers attended the funeral. Signatures of the mourners revealed that the Sakdalista Party members came from more than twenty provinces. Even the representatives from the Communist and Socialist Parties participated.[1] The queue to the cemetery was long; a funeral procession of about a hundred automobiles followed behind the coffin. After that came a procession of people four km long, some carrying placards of condolence and others carrying placards demanding independence. While the Sakdalistas said that eighty to one hundred thousand people attended the funeral, a confidential report by the authorities estimated attendance to be about fifteen thousand.

Whatever the numbers might have been, it was one of the most impressive funeral processions in Manila.[2]

Benigno Ramos sent a short poem along with hundreds of roses. The poem said in part: "Wala akong sapat na luha upang itangis ang maagang pagpanaw sa gitna ng ganitong aping kalagayan" (I have not enough tears to shed on your early demise in this enslaved condition).[3] For some Sakdalistas, this was also the day to challenge the city mayor, who had imposed difficulties and restrictions on Sakdalista activities. Indeed, through attendance at this funeral, the Sakdalistas showed their strength in numbers in terms of membership and supporters, which substantiated their claim of being one of the biggest and best-organized political associations in the country.[4]

Before the close of 1937, more rumors regarding the outbreak of uprisings swept through seven provinces of central Luzon.[5] For instance, in Sariaya, Tayabas, a secret society called the Andres Bonifacio had been organizing a Sakdalista army, and military ranks had been conferred on several hundred members. Its plan was to seize the Sariaya municipal headquarters to signal a general uprising. The Sakdalistas' renewed activities and the rampant rumors of uprising may have been fanned by the strong support for the Sakdalista Party shown at Liboria Ramos's funeral and the brief visit from Japan by Ramos's valet, Ricardo Enrile, in mid-June. Although Enrile's sole purpose in coming back was to check on Ramos's children and to see how the party was being run, the rank-and-file members interpreted his visit as a sign that the plan of sending arms and ammunition from Japan was being arranged.[6] The only things Enrile brought home with him were Ramos's writings in the form of essays and an appeal to the Sakdalista members, which appeared on the pages of the *Sakdal* and *The Filipino Freedom*.[7] At any rate, Ramos's being in Japan was the strongest cause for the rumors to circulate continuously.

Despite Ramos's absence and the second failed uprising, the leaders loyal to Ramos carried on the Sakdalista Party activities. The party encouraged its members to continue supporting Ramos because he had been working hard towards the eventual establishment of the republic and had declared that the Sakdalistas would not use violence again.[8] It was a contradictory statement and hardly convincing to the authorities or to the public in general because the very fact that Ramos was in Japan was interpreted to mean that he was securing arms and ammunition. This chapter will end with Ramos's activities in Japan leading up to his return in 1938.

During this rather dormant period of 1937, some noteworthy activities brought the Sakdalista Party into the national political arena. These activities included the formation of a united opposition, the participation in the Joint Preparatory Commission on Philippine Affairs and in the provincial and municipal elections.

**Forming a United Opposition**

Despite the Sakdalistas' legitimate activities, the authorities did not lower their guard against them because they feared there might be a follow-up attempt to bomb the city, as had happened in the previous year. As if to confirm this fear, in mid-September 1937, it was reported that eleven Sakdalistas allegedly tried to bomb the Malacañang Palace, the government buildings, and the water mains and power plants in Manila. The alleged bombing proved to be only a rumor but this kind of rumor continued to circulate in Manila and its neighboring provinces for the rest of the year.[9] New Year 1938 started with yet another rumor of Sakdalista uprising, sending law enforcement agents to the designated area every time they obtained such information. Several policemen armed with riot gear were detailed to their respective municipal buildings in the towns of Laguna and Rizal Provinces. Finally at the end of January 1938, the Laguna governor was obliged to order a freeze on issuing permits for meetings and demonstrations by the Sakdalistas.[10]

In the midst of myriad rumors, the organization remained fluid, with new people coming in when the old ones left. At the end of April 1938, a merger between a peasant group and the Sakdalista Party took place. This peasant group, known as Dumating Na (The Time Has Come), had around three thousand members, and among them were tenants of the Hacienda Buenavista in San Jose, Bulacan.[11] Behind the merger and the persistent rumors of Sakdalista violence lay the unsolved agrarian problem in central Luzon and the Sakdalistas' efforts to alleviate the landlord-tenant dispute.

In some towns in Bulacan, Pampanga, and Nueva Ecija, the situation had become almost critical due to a rice crisis and food shortage, as the price of rice had been soaring since the end of October 1935. In fact, the peasant unrest due to eviction even increased after the 1935 Sakdalista uprising.[12] The Sakdalistas, especially the peasant members, were involved in the landlord-tenant disputes. The authorities had all the more reason to cancel the permit for the Sakdalista meetings, fearing that violence might blow up at any time, especially in central Luzon.[13] Filipino politicians and opinion leaders, especially the delegates to the Constitutional

Convention of 1935, were acutely aware of the need for a social justice program to establish a stable society by eliminating rural discontent. Thus, the Constitution contained the promotion of such a program. In an effort not to repeat the May Uprising of 1935, President Quezon ordered a survey on the agrarian and economic conditions in central Luzon where large church-owned estates existed. The survey report revealed that the common economic problems in these areas arose from tenancy issues. The report strongly suggested the necessity of radical changes in relations between the landowners and the peasantry, who were reduced to being no better than slaves under the increasing commercialization of agriculture.[14] Eventually, the Assembly under the Commonwealth produced agrarian reform measures and laws establishing a minimum wage for laborers employed in public work projects, thereby guaranteeing the freedom of employees or tenants to join legitimate union organizations.[15]

At the end of August 1937, Quezon spoke over the radio and stressed that long-range programs for economic development and social services would be adopted and carried out. These included expanding public education, building more roads and hospitals, improving sanitary conditions, breaking up the few remaining big-landed estates, giving more impetus to the development of Mindanao, and establishing new industries.[16] Most of them were the same programs for which the Sakdalista Party had been advocating for years.

Quezon's program, termed a "social justice program," sounded beneficial to the peasants and laborers; however, nothing much was actually accomplished. The funds for the social justice program were often diverted to a massive program of public works, which was welcomed by the members of the Assembly since it would generate electoral support for the Nacionalista Party and its candidates.[17] It was difficult to carry out a social justice program under the Commonwealth government, which was dominated by the landowning elite and antilabor/peasant officials. In fact, many laws were rendered ineffective. Eventually, Quezon's program came to mean "techniques for reducing unrest without fundamentally changing the system."[18]

Quezon's program was a result of the mounting unrest of the people, whose voices were given concrete form by the opposition forces, which eventually formed a united opposition against the Quezon government. In early November 1936, an open letter was published in an English daily, explaining why the people were resorting to violence. The letter severely criticized the oligarchic Quezon administration and the U.S. government, which had been supporting it. The letter was signed by thirteen different leaders who represented antigovernment groups, such as various labor unions and political parties, including the Communist, Socialist, and Sakdalista Parties. The letter began by saying that the people would not expose themselves to losing their lives or rotting in prison for frivolous causes. They were doing so because political and social injustices, not just economic deprivation, have been committed against them, and this created intense discontentment. They asked, "Have we and our forefathers fought in the past revolutions only to obtain the present sultanesque [*sic*] (dictatorial) form of government?" The letter ended with an address to High Commissioner Frank Murphy and other American officials, stating that the unreasonable support and unbroken favoritism given to Quezon over the past thirty years had shaken their belief that the U.S. was genuinely interested in establishing and maintaining a responsible and democratic government in the Islands.[19] Soon after this open letter was published, the same thirteen signatories organized a united opposition against the Quezon administration.

In early February 1937, the signatories organized the second convention at the Opera House, the first having been held in early December 1936. One of the hottest issues debated on was the neutralization of the Philippines. The united opposition strongly supported this idea, as the American naval stations in the Philippines could not save the Philippines, nor was the U.S. legally bound to protect the Philippines since protection was only a promise, not a binding agreement.[20] Among these opposition groups, the Sakdalista Party was considered the most influential, having a significant peasant following. As a result of this meeting, the Popular Front was organized in preparation for the local elections in December 1937. The moving force behind this united opposition came mainly from the Communist Party members. In around 1933, the Comintern in Moscow launched the United Front movement worldwide. This new Comintern line defined the main enemy of Communism as not the bourgeoisie but the rising world fascism.[21] Although the Sakdalistas still held a stereotyped image of the Communists, by this time, no anticommunist articles appeared in the pages of the *Sakdal*, as used to occur in 1934.

## The Communists and the Sakdalistas

Initially, relationships between the two groups had been rather cordial. Sometime in the early 1930s, probably before the communist members' mass arrests in late May and the crackdown on the Tanggulan

Society in December 1931, the leaders of various radical groups—such as the Communist Party, the Palihan ng Bayan, the Tanggulan Society, and the Sakdalista Party—used to meet frequently at the printing press they shared, as mentioned earlier. They exchanged opinions or argued over certain issues on U.S. colonialism, Filipino landlords, capitalists, Nacionalistas, and the oligarchy. In one of the meetings, Ramos called for cooperation, saying something like: "We (addressing Evangelista and Dioniso) are all from Bulacan, like Plaridel (M. H. del Pilar), Ponce (Mariano Ponce), and other heroes. We all love our native land. Whichever succeeds among the movements that we lead, it will be an honor to our Province of Bulacan and to Mother Philippines."[22]

However, around mid-1932, the Sakdalistas and the Communists became hostile towards each other and began publishing articles attacking the other. The split appeared to have arisen from Ramos's efforts to distance himself from the Communists in the wake of their mass arrests (in May 1931) and the eventual judgment that the party was an illegal organization, as we saw earlier.[23] The rift must have widened further when the Communist Party, opposing the H-H-C bill, unwittingly supported Quezon in mid-1933 during the split between the "Pros" and "Antis," while the Sakdalistas opposed both groups. The breakdown of cooperation, however, did not entirely end the relationship between the Communists and the Sakdalistas. For example, in October 1934, at the height of the dispute, and in the midst of the mutual polemics and name-calling, the Communist Party invited the Sakdalistas to join the National Independence Conference, a united front, which was organizing on the issue of independence. However, the Sakdalistas declined.[24]

During this dispute, the Communists accused the Sakdalistas of being the puppets of the imperialists and capitalists. They characterized the *Sakdal* as "a mouthpiece of the bourgeoisie."[25] The Communist Party published a pamphlet in the form of an open letter to Benigno Ramos written by Severo Dava, the party's foremost propagandist. Dava criticized the Sakdalistas for being ignorant people. He argued that the Sakdalista Party policy was not truly revolutionary because it was not class-based, and exhibited backward-looking xenophobia, and its activities had been a money-spinning racket.[26]

In response to this attack, the Sakdalistas said that they wished to see neither a communist nor a capitalistic government in the Philippines. What they wanted was a truly Philippine government that would embody the Filipinos' own customs, thoughts, sentiment, knowledge, and history, along with all the great qualities that had been passed down from generation to generation.[27] One of the Sakdalistas' criticisms of the Communists was that instead of truly loving Philippine independence, the Communists planned to allow the Soviet Union to dominate the Philippines. Although the Communists seemed outwardly to be working to save the oppressed from the powerful capitalists, their victory would once again place the Philippines under the "white" race. As proof, the Sakdalistas noted that when the Communists had their convention, they displayed the red banner of the Soviet Union instead of the Philippine flag and a bust of Lenin instead of Rizal or Bonifacio, and they sang the "Internationale" instead of the Philippine national anthem.[28] Instead of respecting Rizal, Mabini, Bonifacio, and the other heroes of the 1896 Revolution, the Communists respected the foreign heroes of the Soviet Union and hoped to someday raise a red flag, not a Philippine flag, on Philippine soil. The Sakdalistas also took issue with the Communists' denial of the existence of God and the divinity of Jesus Christ, and for this, the Sakdalistas ranked Communists with the Jews. The Sakdalistas said the Communists could not succeed in a country like the Philippines, where the people were religious.[29]

These differences notwithstanding, some rank-and-file Communist Party members seemed to have joined the Sakdalista uprising, as there was no official decision not to participate. When the Sakdalistas' plan of uprising was leaked to the Communist members, the Central Committee called for an emergency meeting to discuss whether the party should support it. During the all-night discussion, some members reminded the participants of their earlier self-criticism for failing to support the Tayug uprising of 1931 because it considered the Tayug members religious fanatics. This time, there was also an opposition. While they recognized the Sakdalistas' opposition to American imperialism, the Communists argued that the Sakdalistas were the tools of the Japanese imperialists/militarists/fascists. However, the party did not reach any conclusive decisions on whether they should support the Sakdalistas' actions or not.[30] Therefore, it is assumed that some of the Communists joined the Sakdalista uprising.

Furthermore, after the Sakdalistas' failed revolution of 1935, the Communist Party praised the participants as "sincere and heroic" patriots who were fighting for "true liberation." The Communist Party asked its supporters to show solidarity with detained Sakdalistas by campaigning for their release and offering assistance to their families.[31] By 1937, the

Sakdalistas showed a more conciliatory attitude toward them by publishing Communist members' articles in their organ.[32]

## The Joint Preparatory Committee on Philippine Affairs

In June 1937, news reached the Sakdalista Party that the members of the Joint Preparatory Committee on Philippine Affairs and Manuel Quezon, who had been away for a little over half a year, were expected to arrive from the U.S. in August. The committee wanted to visit the provinces to survey the economic conditions, particularly the sugar-producing region of Negros. Based on confidence gained at Liboria Ramos's funeral, the Sakdalistas decided to hold a big public meeting on the occasion of the committee's visit to counter the administration's claim that the Sakdalista Party was comprised of only a small portion of the Filipino people.[33]

Celerino Tiongco declared that more than three hundred thousand Sakdalistas would attend the meeting. In spite of the Sakdalista leaders' assurances that they had no intention of using violence, some followers were determined to engage in violent methods. Due to the Sakdalista scare, all the roads leading into Manila were closely guarded, and anyone deemed suspicious was arrested. In view of this, the law enforcement agents decided to conduct an educational campaign among the local Sakdalistas.[34] In an effort to contain the Sakdalistas' activities, they arrested some members for allegedly possessing bombs. In most cases, permits for the local Sakdalista meetings were not issued, and if they were granted, the attendees were harassed. Moreover, registered letters addressed to several Sakdalista leaders were censored. Twenty-four hours before the scheduled arrival of Quezon and the Preparatory Committee members, all the national-level Sakdalista leaders were detained.[35] On the day of their arrival, the city police and fire department personnel were on duty around the clock. They intended to use water for the dispersal of demonstrators as well as to extinguish any fires that might result from bomb explosions.[36]

Just before the hearing, the Sakdalista Party prepared a *Memorial* to be submitted to the committee. Major points included: (1) The Philippines must first be endowed with full capacity to enter into a binding agreement with any foreign country; (2) The Philippines needs industrial development of its own; (3) The Philippines must be at liberty to dispose of its revenues in any way that suits its needs; (4) The Philippines opposes further investment of American capital in the exploitation of the natural

resources; (5) Independence is the only solution to the many serious problems and the only way to secure true cooperation between the Philippines
and the U.S.; (6) The U.S. naval bases are prejudicial to the country's
economic interests; and (7) The Sakdalistas are in favor of neutrality for
the Philippine Islands.[37]

The hearings of the Joint Preparatory Committee took place in Manila
in September 1937. Most of the attendees were Filipinos but a small
number of local American businessmen were seen. Among the Filipinos
who gave testimonies were four Sakdalistas, including Elpidio Santos.
Except for Santos, they all spoke in Tagalog with English interpreters.[38]
Perhaps it was their way of showing that they should merit independence
since they were citizens of a country that had a distinctive culture and
language.

Santos noted that the representatives of Philippine industrial and
commercial organizations were emphasizing the loss of duty-free access
to American markets, which would mean the death of the Philippine
economy, and claimed that the Philippines should be given ample time to
readjust its economic condition. When the transition period ended, these
same Filipino delegates would ask for another extension. Thus, the result
would be perpetual retention of the Islands. However, Santos declared
that his party had no desire to ask for such a concession from the U.S. and
stressed that the Philippines should be given liberty to seek markets in
foreign countries for their own products.

As for the military issue, Santos believed that defense should be
undertaken by the citizens of each country without help from foreign
powers. One reason for this was that after the transition period, he was
sure those Filipino delegates would again say that the U.S. must continue
to retain the Philippines since she was not yet prepared to defend herself.
Another reason he cited was that if the president of the United States
could mobilize all the armed forces of the Islands by a single proclamation, then it would be possible that the military could be used to kill fellow
Filipinos who were considered enemies of the Philippine government.
After all, he said, military preparation would not guarantee the safety of
the Philippines. In fact, the presence of American naval bases might invite
outside intervention whenever it was considered to be a menace to the
security of other foreign countries. In concluding his speech, Santos stated
that real cooperation would only be possible between two peoples who
were enjoying equal rights and privileges.

The next speaker, Fernando Manuzon, the president of the Cavite branch of the Sakdalista Party, began his statement by thanking the U.S. government for forming the committee to explore the issue of independence for the Philippines. Chairman J. Van A. MacMurray, perhaps slightly annoyed by the stress on independence made by Santos, immediately reiterated that the committee had not been requested to recommend a date for political independence either earlier or later than that fixed in the Independence Act (T-M Act). MacMurray reminded Manuzon that his statement should be confined to the consideration of economic problems. Since Manuzon was not allowed to deliver his prepared speech, he quoted from the *Memorial* on trade relations by simply saying, "A free Philippines, even without the American markets, or whosoever, can live, can stand alone firm, and maintain her dignity among other nations."[39]

The third speaker, Ignacio Martinez, vice president of the Cavite Sakdalista Party, believed that no economic stability could be obtained unless the political situation was first adjusted and that under the T-M Act, the Philippines would never be economically or politically independent. He likened the Filipino poor masses to a water buffalo that had to go wherever its master, the agents of Wall Street, would steer it unless independence from the U.S. were achieved. The last speaker, Tomasa Ortiz, simply stated that she had nothing to say about trade relations except: "The Filipino people are earnestly asking for independence right now and not tomorrow." Along with their statements, the speakers submitted both a memorandum and *Memorial* to the committee.[40] The Sakdalistas reiterated their stand on independence to the members of the committee and accused the Nacionalista-dominated Commonwealth government of abandoning the aim they once so fervently appealed to the American lawmakers to grant.

Indeed, the T-M Act was, as the Sakdalistas insisted, the major obstacle to economic adjustment because as long as the U.S. controlled the tariffs, the Philippines could not protect or develop its own products. This meant further dependence on the U.S. market and underdevelopment of Philippine industry.[41]

Two other groups presented similar points of view: the Popular Front and the Communist Party of the Philippines, the latter being allowed some limited activities. These two organizations pointed out that the free-trade arrangement encouraged the establishment of new industries that had attained a certain degree of prosperity and raised the standard of living among the wealthy and middle classes. However, this prosperity had not reached the majority of the people. For the common Filipino industrial and agricultural laborers, free trade only meant a high cost of living without adequate improvement in wages and income.[42] The Sakdalistas could not have agreed more with the Popular Front's assessment on this point. The only difference was that while the Popular Front wanted liquidation of free trade to be gradual and not abrupt, the Sakdalistas desired this immediately and were ready to face the economic hardship that would accompany such a move.

For this occasion, each provincial Sakdalista Party chapter sent representatives to witness the hearing. This included the Sakdalista chapter in Baguio, which consisted only of Igorot men and women.[43] Participating in the Joint Preparatory Committee gave the Sakdalistas an opportunity to express their views in the official political arena.

### The 1937 Elections

In December 1937, the first elections under the Commonwealth were held to elect city, provincial, and municipal officials. It was also the first time that women were given the right to vote and run for public office. The Sakdalistas joined as part of the Popular Front, which consisted of members of the National Socialist (of Aguinaldo); the Republican (of Aglipay), the Democrata, the Young Philippines, the Radical Party (of Mendoza), the Communists, the National Labor Party, the New Philippines Party (dissidents from the Young Philippines), the Bloque Popular (those who dissented the Nacionalista Party), and the Nuclio Totalitario Filipino (a fascist group). Celerino Tiongco was one of the opposition gubernatorial candidates for Laguna.[44]

The Popular Front was against the establishment of naval bases in the Philippines. It was in favor of neutralization and the definite termination of free trade, but, at this time, against a sudden liquidation. The Front insisted on the restoration of the provisions of the Constitution that had been violated by President Quezon and wanted to reduce his authority to exercise power.

Since those who joined the Popular Front had little in common, they sometimes held contradictory stands. For instance, the Sakdalista Party desired definite liquidation of free trade, and the Nuclio Totaritario Filipino exhibited fascist ideas; therefore, unity was not maintained. In the case of Lucban, Tayabas, the Sakdalista Party put up its own candidate apart from the Popular Front.[45] They were "united" only in their criticism of the Quezon administration. Moreover, the members of each organization or party were not well informed on the program of the Popular Front. Therefore, their campaign lacked a persuasive program for the future and did little except point out the negative aspects of the incumbent government. The majority party candidates, on the other hand, campaigned on the issue of social justice and pointed out concrete achievements, though exaggerated, on behalf of the underprivileged in contrast to the mere promises of the opposition groups.[46] In preparation for this election, the "Pros" and "Antis" merged and became the solid Nacionalista Party in September 1937. As predicted, the party won by a landslide, sweeping many Nacionalista candidates into provincial and municipal administration posts.[47] The election was a dismal failure for the Popular Front, to which the Sakdalista Party belonged.

## Patriotic League of the Filipino Women

Undaunted by the 1937-election defeat, the Sakdalista activities continued. In April 1938, the Sakdalista women organized themselves into the Samahang Makabayan ng mga Babaing Pilipina (Patriotic League of the Filipino Women, or Samahang Makabayan). The League was established to commemorate the one-year anniversary of Liboria Ramos's death. Chapters were organized, for instance, in places such as San Isidro, Cavite, and Marikina in Rizal.[48] The League's primary objective, needless to say, was to achieve complete independence. The members believed that in working toward this goal, there should not be any discrimination between men and women. They also claimed that there had not been any comprehensive women's movement in the country that was dedicated to the welfare and freedom of the whole Archipelago. The membership of Samahang Makabayan included a wide range of social strata, just as the Sakdalista Party did, and was probably the only women's organization that focused on national independence. It had its own rules and regulations as well as publications.[49]

The Samahang Makabayan's main ideas included living honorably, sacrificing for the sake of the country, and abandoning individualist tendencies. There is a picture on the League's *Pamahayag* (Proclamation) of an angel-like Filipina with wings dressed in the *baro at saya* (traditional loose blouse and long skirt). She is blowing a horn and pointing to the rising sun, from which emanates multiple rays of light (see photo 4).

**Photo 4. Makabayan Emblem** (ca April 1938)
*Source: Pamahayag at Patakaran ng Samahang Makabayan ng mga Babaing Pilipina*

Underneath this image was a poem summarized as follows: The Mother Country should rejoice because the day of freedom is nearing, as an angel has been sent to help. She has gone beyond the clouds of sadness and oppression in order to show the honorable way. The poem ends thus: "She is pointing out to everyone the east/So that there they may see the day of redemption/And to the rhythm of the birds' singing in the fields/She tells everyone to go on and search for independence."[50]

The Sakdalistas believed that a woman's main duties were motherhood and contributions to the home. They thought women should not get directly involved in politics since becoming politically active would take their attention away from the home and might result in the breakup of the family. The Filipino women were urged to shed Western (American) influences and emulate historical Filipino female figures, such as Maria Clara, Teodora Alonzo (Rizal's mother), del Pilar's wife, and Tandang Sora, a revolutionary of the 1896 Revolution.[51]

The Samahang Makabayan reiterated the familiar Sakdalista call for the necessity of enduring hardships for the sake of the country's welfare in addition to the need for the Filipinos to help and love one another instead of oppressing their fellow countrymen. The Filipino language, spirit, and thought were held in high regard. The League was not against borrowing from other cultures but advocated the selection of aspects that were not in conflict with Filipino culture. A picture of the four leaders of the organization and quotations attributed to them were printed on the *Pamahayag*.

Not much information regarding these women leaders can be found. One of them, Bibiana Tuazon (secretary and assistant treasurer), was born in 1917 in Gapan, Nueva Ecija, and was the eldest of eight children. The family owned a small dry goods store in town. Since her mother was disabled due to an automobile accident, Tuazon had to drop out of school after the sixth grade to help run the household. However, she continued to educate herself at home. She had been a member of the Sakdalista Party since 1935, and was a regular contributor to *The Filipino Freedom*. One of her poems, "Gumising Ka, Bayan," appeared in the paper. In part, it went like this: It was the time to wake up, for the country that had been enslaved and put to sleep by foreigners for such a long time/All the difficulties they are facing today were created by betrayers/They were the agents of the Americans and the friars, who sucked the blood of the poor, who stole the wealth and brought death to the Philippines/They had honorable titles (college diplomas) but caused fellow countrymen to rot/ They were honorable "oily-mannered" (*langisero*) people who knelt down to foreigners, selling their honor without hesitation/They have all become millionaires today, projecting a noble political career, all bootlickers are great politicians/ All the brave people should join the (Sakdalista) movement/It is indeed a pleasure to be buried in the grave of one's beloved Mother."[52] Later, during the Japanese Occupation, Bibiana Tuazon worked for the Japanese Propaganda Corps.

The Sakdalistas' views on women were traditional and conservative. They believed that a woman's role was confined to the home, and women were expected to serve the movement through their husbands or fathers. However, there were some women who were exceptions to the prevailing view within the Sakdalista movement, such as Salud Algabre, who led the uprising, and a handful of active women such as Candida Gomez (Ch. 4., fn 51) and Bibiana Tuazon. When Bibiana Tuazon joined the Propaganda Corps, the Corps leader, Capt. Junsuke Hitomi, thought Tuazon was just like a Japanese woman, demure and modest. At the gatherings sponsored by the Propaganda Corps, she conveyed the need for Filipino women to shed Western influences and return to their traditional roles as simple, diligent Asian women. She told one of the Japanese Propaganda Corps members that she would not marry and have children as long as the Philippines was under the U.S. colonial regime because her children might suffer the status of slaves of the white race.[53] In the Sakdalista women's perspective, fulfilling this traditional role and also being active in the movement were not contradictory.

### Quezon's Attack and the Sakdalistas' Counterattack

If the Social Justice Program was a carrot, the attack on the anti-Quezon radicals was a stick. After the establishment of the Commonwealth, Quezon had virtually eliminated the political opposition parties and now turned to the radical oppositionists who had been a constant irritation to him. Persistent rumors of Sakdalista uprisings had not only been damaging to the country's peace and order but also personally embarrassing to Quezon. The fact that a sizeable group of people looked up to Ramos as the leader who would bring final independence to the Philippines was humiliating to him. One of the methods utilized to suppress all the radical movements was to control the information network, which included exercising censorship of radio broadcasts by creating a National Information Board. To further suppress radical dissent, the Assembly extended the scope of the Sedition Law. Under this broader scope, speeches, proclamations, writings, emblems, cartoons, banners, and other methods that expressed antigovernment sentiment were considered seditious and would be punishable with imprisonment and/or fines.[54]

While suppressing the radicals, Quezon managed to enlist the support of his oppositionists, especially radical peasant/labor organizers and orators, by showing a conciliatory attitude toward them as the labor movement grew stronger. One such move was to create a labor federation in 1937, and through this federation Quezon practically controlled the labor movement.[55] Quezon proclaimed amnesty for the exiled and imprisoned Communist members on New Year's Day of 1937, in the hope of winning them over to his side. This action, however, was prompted by the American Communists, who emphasized that an independent Philippines should be founded on democracy and that this would be the best way to counter the rising fascism.[56]

Around this time, perhaps prompted by the government, the *Philippines Free Press* attacked several editors/writers of radical newspapers and magazines, dismissing them as "the weak voices in the huge ocean of Quezon's government." Included here were Pedro Abad Santos of *Socialism Today*, Severo Dava of the *Kalayaan* (Communist Party), Celerino Tiongco of the *Sakdalista*, Antonio Velisario of *The Filipino Freedom*, Braulio Abad of the *Sakdal*, among others.[57] As we know, the last three were the organs of the Sakdalista Party.

This anti-Sakdalista campaign on the part of the Quezon administration became more conspicuous. Numerous accusations were hurled at the Sakdalistas, and their request to hold meetings continued to be denied. While the Sakdalistas charged that Quezon was a new type of dictator, Quezon and his supporters singled out Ramos and denigrated him as a person who had no college degree and had been fired from the Senate. They argued that Ramos was not capable of bringing independence to the country while Quezon was the right person to perform that job. They warned the people not to attend Sakdalista meetings or they would go hungry and suffer shame. Quezon even called the Sakdalistas "enemies of the government."[58]

To counter this attack, Ramos sent a lengthy essay from Japan, entitled *Quezon is the Real Enemy of the Government in the Philippines*, which was later published in Manila in booklet form. This forty-page booklet in English, along with its Tagalog translation, declared that the Sakdalistas might be opposed to Pres. Quezon's policies but they were not enemies of the constituted authority. Ramos accused Quezon of making the Filipinos starve to death and making the foreigners rich, terrorizing and continuously monitoring the people by using spies, prohibiting public meetings, seizing the letters of the Sakdalista Party president, and depriving the Filipinos of their livelihood and then overburdening them with taxes.

Ramos lamented the fact that the Philippines had no Navy or Air Force to protect the country against an invading power. At the same time, the people had been suffering deprivations because Quezon had squandered the people's money on luxurious trips abroad, beautifying his royal yacht, and bulletproofing his car. If only he had put that money into munitions plants and factories for land, sea, and air armaments, a national defense could have been realized, and at the same time, provided jobs to thousands of Filipinos. Therefore, Quezon was the real enemy of the government, yet he was trying to blame the Sakdalistas for all his sins. Ramos ridiculed Quezon by saying: "To Quezon, the attacks of Benigno Ramos are painful and worse than the Japanese inroads into Davao and the treacherous piracy of the friars who have already accumulated a fertile portion of the best lands of the Islands...."[59]

Infuriated by Ramos's frontal attack, Quezon took an uncompromising stand against the Sakdalistas. During a weekly press conference held in September 1937, Quezon announced that he believed the Sakdalista Party was unlawful because of the recent outbreaks of violence. He claimed that their leaders were out to make money on the poor people and alleged that Ramos was having a good time in Tokyo:

> I do not think that Sakdalism is going to grow. The time for them is gone. Fusion may have a favorable effect on the popular front, but even this will not be able to grow to be minority in the National Assembly.[60]

While declaring the Sakdalista leaders to be crafty agitators who deserved punishment, Quezon showed a patronizing attitude toward the Sakdalista followers by saying that they were nothing less than Ramos's victims; therefore, instead of punishment, they needed education.[61] While publicly declaring that the Sakdalista movement and Ramos did not mean much to him, in private Quezon had been contemplating a way to bring Ramos home. On the eve of the establishment of the Commonwealth government, he tried to expedite Ramos from Japan, using him as a bargaining chip in negotiations with the Japanese Consul General. Quezon promised the consul general that he would disallow the cancellation policy of all illegal Japanese land leases in Davao if the Sakdalista leader were expelled.[62] For his part, Ramos was also contemplating a way to come home.

### Ramos in Japan

Ramos's earlier activities in Japan were discussed in Ch. 3. Let us now briefly view Ramos's activities from the post-May Uprising period to his return home in August 1938. As part of his efforts to obtain arms and ammunition in Japan, Ramos visited various places to give speeches and held discussions with whoever was willing to assist him in his endeavor. He usually spoke in Spanish or English through a Japanese interpreter, and after the speech, he collected donations from the audience. In his

Photo 5. Ramos giving a speech in Japan in June 1936
Source: *Sakdal* weekly, 5 August 1936 issue

speeches, Ramos praised the Japanese Empire, from which he believed support and help could be expected [63] (see photo 5).

In addition to his speeches, Ramos had his essays published for the Japanese readership. In these, he discussed the pitiful Philippine situation under U.S. control and the Sakdalistas' struggle for change. He portrayed the Commonwealth government as a robot of American imperialism whose purpose was to destroy Filipino freedom, traditional customs, industry, language, unity, and race. He said that the Commonwealth government was a mestizo government, whose representative, Manuel Quezon, was a typical mestizo, and the Sakdalistas, who were pure native Filipinos, would never compromise with these half-breeds.[64] It seems Ramos was emphasizing the "purity of blood" to appeal to the Japanese readership. "Purity of blood" was also important in the Philippines, and it was associated with patriotism. In 1907, when the Nacionalista Party was deciding on the party candidates, some candidates were criticized for being mestizo when, in fact, "pure-blooded Filipinos" were preferred. Quezon was disdainfully called "Tisoy" among the Sakdalistas. This discrimination might be contradictory, however, because if he had been a fellow Sakdalista, it would not have mattered. For instance, Tiongco, a Chinese mestizo, was fondly called "Don Sili" (Mr. Hot Pepper, i.e., small and thin) by the Sakdalistas because of his small slanted eyes.[65]

The failed May Uprising of 1935 became the focus of international attention, at least among the Japanese and the Americans. Ramos suddenly became a cause célèbre in Japan. Those Japanese who supported him were determined to protect him from rumored deportation. Immediately after the failed uprising, Uzuhiko Ashizu, the young nationalist mentioned in Ch. 3, wrote a statement entitled "Philippine Independence War and Our Party's Attitude: Don't Hand Over the Freedom Fighter to American Authorities." He emphasized that the Sakdalista uprising was a war of independence, which was not only for the Filipinos but also for all the Asian nations. His statement ended with: "If the Japanese government yields to the wish of the American government and hands over Mr. Ramos, it would betray the expectations of a thousand million Asian peoples who rose up to rebuild the Orient. Their trust in Japan would be greatly damaged. We cannot allow this to happen. We wish the Japanese government would show moral authority and not betray their freedom fighters' faith. We demand the safety of the Filipino freedom fighter."[66]

The statement was personally handed to the minister of Foreign Affairs who, after reading it, allegedly commented, "I will not allow Ramos to be deported, as Japan's prestige is at stake."[67] The minister's order must have been transmitted to the Japanese Consulate in Manila, which declared that extradition proceedings against Ramos would be of no avail, as we saw earlier.

Ashizu wrote several articles based on a lengthy interview with Ramos. One of them, *Introducing the Sakdalista Party*, written under the pen name Hokuba Nansen, was published in the form of a pamphlet. It portrays Philippine society under enslavement conditions enforced by the U.S. The Sakdalistas only wished to regain what was rightfully theirs. Nacionalista and Democrata politicians tried to obtain independence as well; however, they were eventually bought off by the Americans and lost their fighting spirit. The article ended with Ramos's appeal to the Japanese youth: "It is only the Sakdalistas, not the Nacionalistas or Democratas, who have the pride as an Oriental people. We wish to establish a united front with the

Japanese and to rebuild the Orient under the leadership of Japan. We, the Sakdalistas, have been pursued and killed brutally by the authorities. Is there any way the Japanese, especially those who respect the chivalrous spirit, could assist us?"[68]

A group of Japanese supporters belonging to the Dai Nippon Seisan Party not only protected and supported Ramos but also took up his cause. Shortly before the inauguration of the Philippine Commonwealth in November 1935, the party's representatives brought a petition addressed to the president of the United States to the American Embassy in Tokyo. It urged the American government to grant immediate and complete independence to the Philippines and said that the Japanese people were determined to oppose "these aggressive and unlawful acts of the U.S. against the Philippines." On the same day of their visit, a cablegram signed by Ryohei Uchida, president of the party, was sent to the American President in Washington.[69]

It was not only the politically aware Japanese who showed interest in Ramos. The ordinary Japanese, who learned about the Sakdalista uprising through the newspapers, also held Ramos in high regard and called him "the gallant liberator of the Philippines." A hotel reception clerk in Tokyo who read the *Free Filipinos* was eager to talk to Filipino guest Leon Ma. Guerrero about the uprising. Guerrero's impression was that while high Japanese officials were publicly disclaiming any knowledge of Ramos or even condemning him, in private they approved of him and his fight for independence. In truth, both the Japanese "big shots" and the people in the streets admired Ramos, Guerrero opined.[70]

While admiration of Ramos as an independent fighter was still high, a meeting took place in Tokyo in early October 1935. Around thirty people attended the meeting, including some well-known ultranationalists as well as a navy commander and an attorney. The attendees were affiliated with certain political leanings, particularly those of the ultranationalists who were concerned about the southern regions. Perhaps as a result of this meeting, one of the participants, Diet member Shiro Koike, eventually visited Manila at the end of November.[71] There is a strong possibility that he conferred with some Sakdalista leaders through Ramos's introduction. If so, it must have given the Sakdalista members the impression that the Japanese government was ready to assist their cause. Koike's visit could have contributed to the numerous rumors of Japanese assistance that circulated at the end of 1935.

In the meeting in Tokyo, it was suggested that Ramos should approach the military in Taiwan about obtaining weapons. Two months later, in December 1935, Ramos took a trip to Taiwan to pay a visit to the Chief of Staff of the Japanese Army. After a month's stay, at the end of January 1936, he returned to Tokyo empty-handed. While he was in Taiwan, he was apparently advised by a major general to get in touch with the Dai Ajia Kyokai (The Great Asia Society), which he did immediately upon his return. The ultimate aim of the Dai Ajia Kyokai was to propagate Japanese culture and to establish an Asian League to unite all the Asian nations. Many Asian pro-independence nationalists from colonized South and Southeast Asia had been invited to attend and speak at the association's regular meetings.[72] Ramos met with Koreshige Inuzuka, who was a board member of the association. Inuzuka became Ramos's protégé in Japan, and later, when the Japanese forces invaded the Philippines, he connected with Ramos and continued his support (more on this in Ch. 8).

In September 1936, Ramos tried to go to Manchuria to get in touch with the Japanese military to obtain weapons confiscated from the Chinese during the Japanese invasion. While Ramos and his valet, Ricardo Enrile, were in Kobe to take a ship to China, they were advised by the Japanese police to carry residence certificates and to bring along a Japanese interpreter. While they were considering this, they had to spend the night in Kobe police custody. Ramos decided not to proceed to Manchuria since it would take some time to obtain the resident certificate and he did not have enough funds to hire an interpreter. They returned to Tokyo the following day.[73] However, Ramos decided to capitalize on this incident and sent two telegrams to the Sakdalista headquarters, saying that he and his staff had been arrested and detained in Kobe.

The Sakdalistas at home were shocked and immediately published an extra *Sakdal* issue, displaying deep disappointment: "But now we cannot help but entertain the notion that the Japanese people are bound to display, if they are not displaying it now, a double-faced international program, the very purpose of which is to profit out of the honest, sincere, and Godly ideals of the justice- and liberty-loving peoples of the neighboring countries."[74] They decided to hold a public demonstration to express their indignation over Ramos's arrest. They likewise agreed to send a note of protest to the Japanese Consul General in Manila.[75] However, since Ramos had been "released immediately," these plans were not carried out.

Ricardo Enrile's short visit to the Philippines was mentioned earlier.

When Enrile returned to Japan in early October of 1937, Ramos was encouraged by the news that the party was continuing its activities and that an impressive number of people had attended his wife's funeral. Inspired by the report, he again tried to go to China to discuss the issue of weapons with military and naval authorities there. However, this trip never materialized.[76]

While Ramos managed to get some Japanese, especially the members of the Dai Nippon Seisan Party and Dai Ajia Kyokai, to rally around him, some ultranationalist Japanese were disappointed in Ramos. In one of the meetings with them, Ramos, perhaps out of frustration and desperation for not getting what he wished, solicited their help by saying, "When I win the war and become the president, I will build a villa for you on a beautiful mountain in Luzon." The Japanese supporters were appalled and told him, "There should be no talk of a luxurious gift among us freedom fighters." After that, they did not want to have anything to do with Ramos, branding him a spiteful, worldly man who would try to get their support by promising material rewards. Furthermore, the Japanese criticized him for his big showy gestures, gold ring, and big gold watch and chain, which they considered earmarks of Western influence.[77] Ramos was no more successful in obtaining arms and ammunitions from other sources and did not produce any concrete results.

During Ramos's stay in Japan, the target of his activities was not limited to the Japanese. He sent a cablegram to Pres. Roosevelt shortly after the May Uprising, demanding the withdrawal of the American government from the Philippines. Later the same year Ramos sent a ten-page printed pamphlet to the U.S. President and Congress, entitled *The American Government Does Not Like Peace in the Philippines.*[78] In the pamphlet, Ramos warned that the acceptance of the T-M Act by the Filipino legislature, the plebiscite of 14 May 1935, and the Commonwealth presidential election of September 1935 should not be considered the will of the Filipino people for three reasons: (1) the Filipino legislature was part of the American Government; (2) the voters in the Philippines derived their right of suffrage from the laws of Congress; and (3) the election was conducted by the American government in conformity with its laws. Ramos concluded that the nonfulfillment of the Jones Law meant that the American government did not regard the Filipinos worthy of consideration and respect, thereby soiling their self-respect, honor, and dignity.[79]

However, Ramos's tone began to change after 1937. His argument now centered on Japan. He sent telegrams to the U.S. Senate and Pres. Quezon, criticizing them for permitting the Japanese to enter the Philippines without regulation and urging them to apply a strict law against the Japanese to restrict their activities before they became a danger, referring to Japanese economic activities and inflow of immigration, especially in Davao.[80] With these telegrams, Ramos tried to show there was some distance between himself and Japan. At the same time, Ramos had softened his stand against the U.S.

While Ramos still held the opinion that whoever dared to damage the Filipinos' liberty, life, livelihood, and unity should be considered the Filipinos' enemy, he stated in a letter to the Sakdalista Party members in August 1937 that not all foreigners, insinuating Americans, were necessarily enemies. He urged the people to act with self-control and in moderation (*gumamit ng kahinahunan at pagtitimpi*) now that the war was raging in China.[81] This change could be attributed to several factors: Ramos's stay in Tokyo had not produced any notable results, much less any military assistance from Japan whether government, military, or civilian sectors. After working hard with the ultranationalist Japanese for four years, Ramos realized that their influence on the government and military was not as strong as he had anticipated. As far as the Japanese government was concerned, it had been following the Taft-Katsura agreement of 1905, though not legally bound by it since it was simply a memorandum. The agreement recognized U.S. colonial possession of the Philippines in exchange for U.S. recognition of the Japanese protectorate in Korea. By the time the Philippines had obtained commonwealth status, the Japanese government was focusing on economic pursuits and maintaining a relationship of goodwill with the goal of enjoying smooth economic activities with the Philippines. Minister of Foreign Affairs Hachiro Arita assured Pres. Quezon on his visit to Japan in February 1937 that Japan had no territorial interest in the Philippines.[82] Ramos had begun to concede to the fact that the Commonwealth government was going to stay in power for at least the next ten years. At the same time, Ramos began anticipating that the flame of Japanese aggression in China might leap to the Philippines despite the assurance of the Japanese Ministry of Foreign Affairs. With these views in mind, Ramos decided to change his tactics and planned to take a new approach.

## CHAPTER 6

# RAMOS'S RETURN AND THE GANAP PARTY, 1938–1941

R AMOS'S CHANGE OF tactics can be seen around February 1937, when he confided to his Japanese friends that Philippine independence should not be achieved by force.[1] He began to think it was wise to reconcile with Quezon and return home. Since he still had quite a force behind him that was keeping the Sakdalista cause alive, he realized he could lead an opposition party at home. Toward the end of 1937, he approached Nagakage Okabe, a lawmaker from the House of Peers and the Vice Pres. of the Hiripin Kyokai (the Philippine Society of Japan) to serve as the go-between in this endeavor.[2] However, nothing seemed to have come from this.

Earlier in April 1937, a letter written by Eugenio Salazar as Vice Chairman of the Sakdalista Overseas Affairs Committee was sent to Gen. Senjuro Hayashi. It alleged that Japan, having created vested interests, was establishing grounds for sending warships and armies to the Philippines under the pretext of protecting her citizens in the Islands. Salazar reiterated that the Filipinos wanted a friendly relationship; they did not, however, wish to be conquered.[3] Written under one of Ramos's pen names, this letter showed Quezon and U.S. officials that Ramos was critical of Japan.

It may also have been intended to pave the way for his next move. In mid-1937, Ramos wrote a lengthy open letter, "Mungkahi sa Pamahalaan ng Commonwealth" (Suggestions to the Commonwealth Government). In this letter, he told the government officials that they should treat their fellow countrymen well, at least better than the foreigners; nurture in the hearts of the Philippine soldiers the idea that they are serving the people and not their enemy; compel the Japanese in Davao to follow Philippine law and not allow foreigners (Japanese) to build exclusive schools and hospitals; buy rice and handicrafts from the Filipino people; open more land for cultivation; and build toilets everywhere so that the environment would not be polluted.[4] Instead of frontally attacking the government, Ramos's open letter made reasonable requests and suggestions. At the same time, he tried to convince the Filipino authorities that he and the Sakdalistas were not in any way "tools" of the Japanese.

At the end of October 1937, Ramos launched a test balloon in the form of written advice addressed to the Sec. of State. Later the same content was conveyed to Pres. Quezon and High Commissioner McNutt, titled "Philippines for the Filipinos." In this, he declared that the Philippines was the land of the Filipinos as well as the Americans; for the former, due to birthright, and for the latter, the right of conquest. Therefore, the Philippine government should not assist or protect any foreigners other than Filipinos and Americans. He criticized the landholdings of the Japanese and religious organizations and urged the Commonwealth government to confiscate their land and distribute it among the labor class.[5] In this statement, he virtually accepted the Commonwealth government and American presence in the Philippines. Several months later, the bait was taken. At the end of February 1938, the former acting secretary general of the Sakdalista National Assembly, Gaudencio Bautista, arrived in Japan. He tried to see Ramos but was refused because Ramos's son had warned Ramos that Bautista was not to be trusted. Instead, Ramos's valet and Japanese advisor met with him. Bautista told them there was no other way to obtain independence in the Philippines except to use violence and that Gens. Alejandrino and Aguinaldo (both Philippine-American War veterans), Dr. Sotto (most likely Vicente Sotto), and Monsignor Aglipay were willing to shoulder the expense if Ramos would purchase arms in Japan. Ramos answered Bautista through the two emissaries that the most important thing for Philippine independence was the unity of the people and that the use of violence to fight one another was foolish. If the

Filipinos fought among themselves, the American authorities would use the unstable situation in the country as an excuse to prolong the withholding of independence.[6] Bautista had indeed been sent by Quezon to see where Ramos stood on the independence issue and whether he was still pursuing an armed revolution.[7] Quezon had been trying to bring Ramos back to the Philippines for a long time. At the same time, Quezon was faced with the possibility of Japanese invasion of the Philippines, which he wanted to avoid at all costs.

Earlier in July 1937, a fight between the Japanese and Chinese forces erupted at the Marco Polo Bridge on the outskirts of Beijing. It signaled an all-out attack of the Japanese military in northern China. In August, a large Japanese force landed in Shanghai to launch a war against China. Immediately, an evacuation operation commenced. As a result, 1,500 American and Filipino evacuees were brought to Manila. At the end of the year, in mid-December, the American and British gunboats on the Yangtze River were bombed by the Japanese. This was followed by the fall of Nanjing, where the "Nanking Massacre," one of the most atrocious and inhumane military actions ever committed, took place. Naturally, people in the Philippines were talking about an impending Japanese invasion.[8]

Faced with this reality, Quezon suddenly left for Japan in June 1938. Since foreign policy was still in the hands of the Americans, the purpose of his visit was announced as a private pleasure trip. However, one purpose of his trip was to confer with Minister of Foreign Affairs Kazushige Ugaki to obtain Japan's reassurance that she would not invade the Philippines. Minister Ugaki stated that Japan had no territorial ambitions in the Philippines and that Japan's sole interests were economic cooperation and cultural exchange. When the Philippines became independent, Japan would consider neutrality in the most friendly and favorable way, Ugaki promised.[9] The events that unfolded in December of 1941 were far from what he had assured.

Another purpose of Quezon's visit to Japan was to meet with Ramos to persuade him to come back to the Philippines. Quezon vehemently denied the second purpose to the reporters who had interviewed him when he landed in Kobe. He declared, "Ramos is nothing to me and I have no desire to talk to him."[10] However, following his carefully laid-out plan, Quezon did meet with Ramos the day he sailed home and left him with these cautiously selected words, "If you come back to the Philippines, dispense with all formalities and come directly to my Palace at once."[11]

Quezon could always claim that this was just a diplomatic invitation; however, it was Ramos's understanding that Quezon had the intention of pardoning him. There must have been some kind of agreement reached between the two. Just before Ramos left Japan, a Japanese journalist interviewed him. When asked about his future plans in the Philippines, Ramos answered that he would reorganize the Sakdalista Party and cooperate with Pres. Quezon. He emphasized that he would do his best for the sake of the country through proper political channels such as the Assembly. Ramos further said that the 200 Sakdalistas still in prison would soon be released.[12] Ramos issued a public statement firmly denying any rumor that the Philippine court had issued an order for his arrest. He claimed he had been innocent of inciting the May Uprising, as evidenced in the telegrams he sent just before the incident. He declared that he was returning home full of confidence and righteousness, wanting to dedicate his efforts to the welfare of the Filipino people.[13]

For his part, Quezon was desperate to bring Ramos home. He recognized Ramos's ability as a leader and knew that the Sakdalista Party still constituted a powerful opposition force. As long as Ramos remained in Japan, the Sakdalistas would continue to expect Japan's support in their struggle, believing that Japan was ready to extend assistance once the revolution was declared. Quezon wanted to crush this delusion and also wanted Ramos to stop criticizing him and the Commonwealth government. Besides, Quezon did not want to see a sizeable number of Filipinos collaborating with Japanese military forces in the event of possible invasion. Before Quezon met with Ramos to discuss his return, he wanted to make sure exactly where Ramos stood on how to achieve independence. That was the reason Bautista had been sent to Japan to confer with Ramos. It was finally confirmed that Ramos had forsaken the violent overthrow of the government, and only then did Quezon decide to see Ramos in person. After a four-year sojourn in Japan, Ramos finally returned to the Philippines at the end of August 1938.[14]

When Benigno Ramos arrived at Pier Seven, about twenty thousand loyal Sakdalistas were waiting for him. When the ship neared the pier, the crowd shouted greetings, such as "Mabuhay si Ramos!" (Long live Ramos) and "Palitan si Quezon!" (Remove Quezon [and let us have Ramos]).[15] To the Sakdalista followers' great disappointment, instead of landing there to greet his welcome party, Ramos was whisked directly to Bilibid Prison by a special motorcade.[16]

Ramos was indicted for insurrection and sedition as a result of the May 1935 Uprising. However, he was later released upon posting bail of P36,000. The bail money had been collected from his welcoming party of supporters, who passed the hat around as soon as they realized Ramos had been arrested. During a press interview held in prison, Ramos said that Quezon had advised him to return and "face the music." Ramos announced that he had given up his opposition to Quezon and would support the Commonwealth government. He explained that his decision was made in the face of "the brewing danger in the Far East." [17] Ramos's return signaled the start of a new phase in the Sakdalista movement.

### The Ganap Party

The day following his arrival, a caucus of Sakdalista Party leaders was held at party headquarters. During this meeting, Ramos announced, "Quezon's politics now coincide with my idea of what is best for the people. It is my duty to support him, especially his social justice program." [18] After the meeting, he showed the gifts he had received in Japan and some photographs featuring him with Japanese government officials and the members of the Dai Nippon Seisan Party. To further emphasize his supposedly strong connections with high-ranking Japanese military personnel and politicians, Ramos sent telegrams thanking them for the courtesy and kindness they had accorded him while he was in Tokyo. [19]

While Ramos tried to give the impression to Quezon and the U.S. officials that he was not in any way the tool of the Japanese, he purposely displayed his close relations with the influential Japanese to his followers. Perhaps, he wanted to show them that he had worked hard while in Tokyo and that he would be in a good position to negotiate with the Japanese should the need arise.

After the caucus, Ramos met with Filipino journalists for an interview session. Ramos praised the Japanese policy of "Asia for the Asians," as well as the one-language policy. He stated that the Japanese people were firmly behind their army and navy and they were ready to defend the country. He was impressed by the age-old tradition that the head of the country, the Emperor, joined the farmers in planting rice. [20] The Japan Ramos had lived in was in the midst of war with China, and individual freedom of speech and assembly had been suppressed under a mobilization policy for the war effort. He had seen only the Japanese people's "selfless dedication" to their country, and he was impressed.

In a general assembly of the Sakdalista Party held in mid-September 1938, the party's name was changed to Lapiang Ganap (Ganap Party).[21] The main reason for the change was to distinguish the majority group from the anti-Ramos faction in his party, which still carried the name "Sakdalista Party." Another reason may have been to circumvent the legal issue because the question of the Sakdalista Party's legality was still pending in various Philippine courts, and therefore, the order of the Department of the Interior barring the Sakdalistas from holding public meetings was being enforced. The only way for them to immediately become politically active was to change the party's name. Anyone wanting to become a Ganap Party member had to take the following oath: "For the country in which I was born, the God I owe my life to, for the poor everywhere, I will fight for the rights and duties given me by the laws and will make use of every proper means in order to uphold the purpose or ends to bring about freedom. May the spirit of our ancestors and heroes guide me."[22]

The six-page manifesto of the Ganap Party, which was written in English with Tagalog version, was prepared in a rather hasty manner. Much more conciliatory to the U.S.-sponsored Commonwealth government, the Ganap manifesto emphasized that under the present regime, the "forgotten men" could secure their prosperity and advancement and that American sovereignty was not a hindrance to their social and economic improvement. It also said that the Ganap Party would support the Quezon administration in its social justice program. At the same time, the party was concerned about Quezon's accumulation of personal power, and urged the revival of the Senate, which had been abolished when the Commonwealth government was established. The party also advocated for a more compact and solid Filipino nation, along with the need to set aside personal dissension and partisanship in light of the current conflict in the Far East. [23] In order to repel a possible invasion by a foreign country, insinuating Japan, the Filipinos had no alternative but to unite. This point was stressed by Ramos in the first press conferences that had been held immediately after his arrival.[24]

Regarding national defense, the Ganap Party proposed the following measures: establishing safe places of refuge in case of an invasion, increasing Army enlistment, strengthening the Armed Forces, creating a Philippine Navy to defend the coastal areas, and manufacturing arms and implements of war. It also suggested that all natural resources should be under state control. In addition, the party called for increased cooperation between the government and the people.[25] Other suggestions in the manifesto called for a wider scope of health activities; strict teaching of Filipino customs, etiquette, and right conduct in all public and private schools; greater Filipino emigration; development of Philippine foreign trade; reduction of land taxes; and implementation of the social justice program.[26]

To prove that the Ganap Party was no longer antagonistic toward Quezon, Gregorio Tobias, the president of the newly formed party, sent a telegram to the U.S. Sec. of War so as to avoid involvement in a clash between the U.S. and Japan:

> We are grateful and respectfully beseech America Philippine separa-
> tion for benefit of both, especially Filipinos under President Quezon's
> wise leadership with the help of (the) whole Ganap people. [27]

As Ramos and Quezon had presumably agreed, the Ganap Party showed a supportive attitude toward the Quezon administration.[28] Besides, by that time, Ramos was convinced that the U.S. would indeed grant independence in 1946 and that the Japanese invasion was imminent. But Ramos's criticism of Quezon and Quezon's antagonism toward Ramos was very much alive beneath the surface.

As we saw earlier, there had been an anti-Ramos faction within the party while he was away. This anti-Ramos faction was further divided into two groups: one group accusing him of having turned into Quezon's henchman, and the other suspecting him of having fascist militaristic ideas. Both groups had attempted to seek his ousting, and they blamed Ramos for the "slaughter of our brothers in Cabuyao and Santa Rosa." While Ramos supporters automatically became members of the Ganap Party, the anti-Ramos faction claimed that the old Sakdalista Party was not dead and its principles were very much alive.[29] Refuting this claim, Ramos's supporters asserted that the anti-Ramos faction had tried to destroy the Sakdalista Party while he was away, and yet they were still calling themselves Sakdalistas.[30]

The Sakdalista Party remained in the Popular Front and joined a coalition called the Allied Minorities, led by Juan Sumulong. The Allied Minorities included the Radical Party, the Young Philippines, and the Popular Front. The Popular Front, in turn, consisted of the Democrata Party, the Republican Party, the Socialist Party of the Philippines (of

Aglipay and Aguinaldo), and the United Workers of the Philippines in addition to the (old) Sakdalista Party.[31] The close alliance between the Socialist Party (of Abad Santos) and the old Sakdalista Party was seen when Narciso Lapuz delivered a speech at the huge gathering of ten thousand peasants in Angeles, Pampanga, which had been organized by Pedro Abad Santos.[32]

One of the first activities of the Ganap Party was to participate in the elections for the second National Assembly on November 8, barely two months after Ramos's return. This time, the party decided to support some Nacionalista candidates such as Gregorio Perfecto of the north district of Manila and Felipe Buencamino Jr. of Nueva Ecija.[33] The decision was based on the fact that the platforms of the Nacionalista Party and those of the Ganap were substantially the same as the one Ramos had declared upon his arrival, that is, his politics and that of Quezon's coincided, and he felt it was his duty to support Quezon's social justice program.

Ramos did not run because he did not meet the residency requirements.[34] Instead, he vigorously campaigned for the party candidates and others the party supported. Before going off on the campaign trail, he announced that he would not merely engage in the election campaign but would preach about the need for promoting brotherhood and unity among the Filipinos in view of coming independence. He emphasized that the government should pay greater attention to the people's welfare, lamenting that nothing had improved in his hometown of Bulacan during his four-year absence.[35] At the same time, Ramos emphasized the imminent Japanese invasion of the Philippines and advocated for the Philippines to strengthen its defenses so that she would not be placed under the control of any foreign power. He also said that whether or not the U.S. would abandon the Philippines depended on the Japanese military power in the Far East. When Ramos's speech was reported in Japan, some Japanese criticized him for being anti-Japanese.[36]

In the meantime, some five thousand oppositionists (including the old Sakdalista Party members) gathered at the Manila Grand Opera House on 6 October, and proclaimed their own candidates. These candidates—including Jose T. Nueno, Rosa Sevilla-Alvero, and Wenceslao Vinzons—represented an alliance of the Popular Front and the Young Philippines, consisting of fifteen men and women. They took turns delivering speeches criticizing the majority party, the city, and the national officials who did nothing to alleviate the people's plight. They accused Quezon of creating a dictatorship in the country, reducing freedom of speech, and restricting freedom of the press, interfering with the courts, and turning the National Assembly into a rubber stamp.[37]

During the election campaign, Gen. Jose Alejandrino, a veteran of the 1896 Revolution, who represented the Popular Front, declared that their platform was for obtaining independence as soon as possible and was opposed to the dominion form of government. He emphasized that the role of the Front was to create a strong opposition, as this was the only means to avoid a dictatorship. However, he said that the Front was willing to side with the party in power in case of emergency and cooperate if the Nacionalista Party would materialize what it promised the people.[38] The Ganap Party was not alone in showing a more conciliatory attitude toward the majority party in view of the Japanese aggression unfolding in China.

The Ganap candidates were defeated on all election fronts. The voters were confused by the lack of differences between the Nacionalista Party and the Ganap Party. This lack of differentiation was evidenced by the Ganap Party's support for some of the Nacionalista candidates. Furthermore, the Ganap Party did not support the opposition candidates of the Popular Front in this election because the opposition candidates included the old Sakdalistas who had renounced Ramos and the Ganap Party. For example, in Laguna, the Ganapistas supported Crisanto Guysayko, the Nacionalista Party candidate for assemblyman, who was running against the Popular Front candidate.[39] In the case of Nueva Ecija, the Ganap Party put up its own candidate, Vicente M. Sison, while supporting the Nacionalista candidate Assemblyman Felipe Buencamino Jr. who was running for re-election. He won in every town of the fourteen municipalities.[40] The Ganap candidates' emphasis on supporting Quezon's social justice program and working for the general improvement of their respective districts was not attractive enough to motivate voters to cast their votes for the Ganap candidates.[41] Another reason for the defeat was that the party had had less than two months to prepare and it still lacked leadership, which made it rather weak. The 1938 election results were a sweeping victory for the incumbent majority party, the Nacionalista Party, taking every one of the ninety-eight Assembly districts. Election fraud and harassment against the Ganap Party were reported. In Tayabas, Ganap members claimed that half of the barrio residents around Lucena were not able to vote because their names were not on the registers; also, some laborers were required to vote openly or else they would lose their jobs.[42] Despite all these problems, the Ganap members had to concede that their standard bearers were not

**Photo 6. Inang Filipina** (ca July 1939)
*Source: Mga Patak ng Luha ng Bayang Api*

as popular as they once were. As time went on, however, this would prove to be a hasty conclusion.

**Renewed Popularity**

With the New Year of 1939 came the news that Benigno Ramos and twenty other Sakdalistas were to be charged with illegal association before the Manila Court of First Instance.[43] The Commonwealth authorities continued to press charges against Ramos, and in May, he finally broke off with Quezon. This was partly because he did not see a conciliatory attitude demonstrated by Quezon, which was an assumed agreement between the two when they had met in Japan. More importantly, Ramos felt confident that he was regaining his following through election campaigning and frequent trips to the countryside. The Ganap Party's increasing popularity was noted by government officials, who observed that the party was "rapidly sinking roots into numerous fertile spots of the Islands" and that "the new movement threatens to result at some future date in another upheaval, the nature of which only time will tell."[44] This report indicated that after the elections, people, especially the rural areas of central and southern Luzon, began rallying around the new banner the Ganap Party had hoisted. It is difficult to ascertain exactly how many people became supporters since no *Ganap* subscription records were available. However, the increased number of supporters was large enough to attract the authorities' attention.

This resurgence of popularity could be attributed to what Ramos tried to convey to the people, part of which was gleaned in the party's publication, *Mga Patak ng Luha ng Bayang Api* or *Mga Patak* (Teardrops of the Oppressed Nation).[45] In comparison to a four-page party manifesto that was written hastily, the new publication was forty pages long and dwelt on Ramos's political, social, and moral views, which were to serve as a guide for the party members.

The cover of the booklet has a picture of Inang Bayan (Mother Country) in traditional *baro at saya* (blouse and skirt) with long hair. Her hands are tied with chains and tears are trickling down her cheeks, as if seeking *damay* (sympathy) from her beloved children (see photo 6). This picture reminds us of one of the Katipunan's initiation rites in which the leader imitated a woman in chains who beseeched compassion from her sons.[46] To indicate that the Ganap Party cherished Jesus Christ and Jose Rizal, their quotations were placed on the cover page, the same ones that had appeared in the *Pamahayag* of 1934.

The Ganap Party's role was described as that of a mediator between the government and the people, holding the intention of settling things peacefully and fairly within the bounds of reason (*katuwiran*). The people were not to blame the foreigners (Americans) for all the mistakes of the present administration. In fact, the government leaders were all Filipinos who had been elected by the people. Therefore, they should refrain from blindly placing the blame on those in power. Everyone had the responsibility of helping his leaders, obeying laws, and paying taxes. If there were something to be fought for, it should be brought to the attention of those in power through the means provided for by law. If violence were used, it would lead to the destruction of the race.

According to Ramos, there were two types of people in the country: the rich and powerful people (*mga malaki*) and the poor people (*mga maralita*). The former included American, Chinese, Japanese, English, and Spanish businessmen, mestizos, priests, and those in government; the latter included tenants, servants (*alila*), and the "big people's helpers" (*bataan lamang ng mga malaki*). As Ramos stressed, these two camps had to come closer: "Everyone is a child of this country and they should all be rich. As America has promised independence to be on 4 July 1946, we should prepare for it and not fall into the hands of another country. What we should do is build the strength of the country by improving the lives of the poor. We are still under America; therefore, no one, aside from the Americans and Filipinos, should benefit from the wealth and livelihood in this country. To entertain other foreigners (Japanese and Chinese) is already a violation of reason. It is a fact that since we are the colony of America, it is the duty for the government to be obedient to the colonizing country and people must respect that government."[47] Since his return from Japan, Ramos had taken every opportunity to stress the importance of unity for the coming independence as well as possible war.[48] By this time, Ramos, like most Filipinos, expected an imminent Japanese invasion, considering the situation in China; therefore, his appeal for the unity of the people must have been sincere.

Besides these points, the central Luzon peasants and the masses were once more attracted to Ramos's organization because of his moral teachings—the teachings that the members were to bear in mind while carrying out their task of achieving independence. Ramos reminded them that love for one's country was equated to one's love for God and, therefore, he who worked for the redemption of his country worked for God. All redemption and the well-being of the people could be achieved only through suffering with God-given clear thinking that knew real reason. "It is the duty of the people to pray to the Lord, the source of our heroes' spirits, for our freedom, our heroes, and (our) parents." Ramos appealed to the members to be morally upright, generous, and compassionate so they could carry on the noble tasks that the Ganap Party was undertaking. The Ganap members were to emulate the characteristics of a person who strives to help himself, plants but does not expect to enjoy the fruit, and is concerned for the welfare of others. Ramos also encouraged them to unite through obedience and mutual aid. He stressed that the Ganap member should be a debt-free person because being in debt was the root of all trouble. In order to avoid debt, one should strive for a clean and noble way of living and refrain from engaging in any vices. If a Ganap member slapped, beat, struck, threatened, or wreaked vengeance upon his opponent, he should be dismissed immediately. Ganap members were encouraged to create a happy family wherein husband and wife love each other, and the children respect and obey their parents. Good hygiene was considered important and so were good manners such as respecting one's neighbors' privacy. Ramos gave specific instructions to the Ganap members on how to behave at meetings. For instance, he cautioned the members to avoid arguments and to refrain from using words that might hurt other's feelings. He urged every member to meet at least once a month and make the meetings a venue for reading, studying, and discussing the party platform and articles published in the *Ganap*.[49]

Religion, morality, and philosophy of everyday life were interwoven into the Ganap Party's political activities. One is again hit by the striking similarities to the writings of the Katipunan leaders, who wrote moral guidance for the members. Ramos, like his predecessors, wanted to instill in his people high moral standards, self-reliance, and a sense of compassion. Without these qualities, independence would not mean much; the people must reach a certain level of consciousness to deserve independence, as Rizal had said. Ramos spoke to the people about how to raise their morality to deserve the coming independence. His preaching once again hit a chord with the people of central and southern Luzon.

### Ramos's Arrest and Trials

As the ranks of the Ganap Party supporters swelled, the authorities' Ganap-bashing commenced. A piece of information collected by the Intelligence Division of the constabulary was used to attack Ramos. He had allegedly organized two separate cabinets, calling one secret and the other popular. The secret group consisted of loyal Ramos supporters.[50] Another allegation was that Ramos had said the country's next logical ally would be Japan and strongly advocated for an alliance with her. In order to prove to Japan that the Filipinos could maintain their independence, Ramos strongly suggested creating a reserve fund to guarantee that independence. According to the constabulary, the amount should be between P2 million and P6 million to be raised from members and sympathizers of the Ganap Party. This reserve fund was called the *Pangsagot sa Kasarinlan* (Guarantee of Independence).[51]

The creation of a reserve fund was indeed true. Since his return from Japan, Ramos had been saying: "Without the cooperation of Japan, the stability of our peace, security, prosperity, and even political freedom shall never be achieved."[52] Ramos's reasoning for the "Guarantee for Independence" was based on his apprehension about what would happen after the U.S. left and independence was obtained: "We are thankful if (the U.S.) does not leave, but if (she) does, what will be the condition (of our country)?"[53] He was afraid that the value of the peso would depreciate and that there would be no effective government, no fighting ships, and no arms and ammunition. Ramos explained that besides the money they had been collecting, they could also borrow money from outside creditors and spend it on the people's needs, using their lands as collateral. America could no longer guarantee the Filipinos' independence because the U.S. was so far away. The only country they could seek a guarantee of security from would be Japan, which was geographically close to the Philippines. However, this did not mean that the Ganap members were pro-Japanese. Ramos strongly reiterated that they could not possibly be "pro-any country" since their hearts and spirits, their wholehearted love and affection were for the whole archipelago of their very own, the only land of their birth. They would not allow themselves to be ruled by another country or to be enslaved. As far-fetched as it seemed, Ramos seemed sincere in his appeal for a guarantee of independence so that the Philippines would not be under Japanese rule. The contributions, which started to come in around January of 1939, took the form of a subscription fee or donation to the party organ, *Ganap*.[54]

Around this time, members were urged to have their pictures taken and placed on their membership cards, called ladaw, to make the Ganap Party appear more official. Ramos was reported to have told his followers that the holders of the ladaw would be entitled to certain privileges should the Japanese finally come, while nonholders might suffer certain unpleasant consequences.[55] It was yet another preparation on the part of Ramos should Japan invade.

In early January 1939, the Court of First Instance of Manila ruled that the Sakdalista Party was an illegal association, and its twenty-nine top leaders, including Celerino Tiongco, Ciriaco V. Campomanes, Fruto Santos, and Salud Algabre, were sentenced to a number of months and ordered to pay a fine of P200.[56] In mid-May, Ramos was arrested. The charges included estafa (swindling) for the collection of voluntary contributions without a permit from the Bureau of Public Welfare and for his alleged involvement in secret plots that would create a situation that would give an alien power the opportunity to intervene. Secret Service agents disclosed that an alien military group would soon be coming to the Philippines to direct a special squad of Ganap members to assault local nationals of an alien power and to sabotage the commercial firms of such aliens starting on 15 May 1939. Through this subversive action, the alien government or its armed forces would be obliged to intervene to save their countrymen. "The alien power" was obviously Japan. This was a fantastic allegation but this kind of rumor had been circulating since the mid-1930s, and this time it was used to arrest Ramos. The arresting authorities boasted that they had nipped the alleged plot in the bud. Ramos immediately posted a bond of P1,400 for his temporary release and pleaded not guilty before the Manila Municipal Court.[57]

Ramos interpreted these arrests as systematic harassment and a sinister campaign of Quezon to discredit him. Since Ramos's return, he had not seen any evidence of a conciliatory attitude on the part Quezon, which was an expected outcome from their meeting in Japan. Therefore, Ramos renewed his fight against Quezon. In early July, Ramos announced his candidacy for the presidential election of 1941. As part of the campaign for the coming election, a huge rally was held in August in Candelaria, Tayabas, President Quezon's home province. Before an audience of more than five thousand, Ramos defended himself against the estafa and charges of rebellion that had been filed against him. The need for the money was explained as part of preparation for independence because cannons, warships, airplanes, and destroyers were the best guarantee of independent country.[58]

Ramos was arrested once again in mid-November, on the day he was scheduled to pose with the Ganap members in Gapan, Nueva Ecija, for a "March of Time" newsreel. Thousands of Ganap members who waited for Ramos's arrival were indignant upon hearing news of his arrest. This time he was charged with sedition and defamation, which were based on Ramos's "defamatory" speeches collected by the constabulary: "President Quezon was the greatest enemy of independence"; "If Quezon ever cheated the members of the Ganap Party, there would be bloodshed and death"; and "Run down the President, who has been spending the people's money for his own pleasure."[59]

On 7 December, Ramos was sentenced to an undetermined prison term ranging from four to ten years and fined P15,000 at the Laguna Court of First Instance. He was denied the right to post bail, which was said to be the first case of its kind in Philippine court history. Ramos's bail was denied because he allegedly had a plan to escape to Japan aboard a Japanese ship, according to the testimony of a constabulary officer. Ramos's supporters planned two simultaneous demonstrations to protest his imprisonment in December; however, the required permits were denied on the grounds that they might cause a public disturbance. Following several trials in courts in Manila, Laguna, and Bulacan, Ramos was given an accumulated maximum jail sentence of sixteen years. In January, he was finally sent to Bilibid Prison, where he was kept incommunicado, to serve a reduced sentence of twelve years and six months for the three offenses of rebellion, illegal association, and estafa. Throughout the first half of 1940, Ramos's trials continued and new sentences were added.[60] However, by mid-1940, Ramos seemed to have forsaken the idea of appealing to higher tribunals.[61]

## Continued Activities of the Ganap Party
### Publication of Hirang

Despite Ramos's arrest and subsequent imprisonment, his followers vowed to carry on the party's activities.[62] In mid-1939, members of the Samahang Makabayan, the league of women Ganapistas, came out with their own organ called *Hirang* (Chosen One). Most of the articles and poems were in Tagalog and a few were in English. The paper's masthead, "Hirang," was adorned with sampaguita (jasmine) flowers forming a chain. The sides had pictures of Jose Rizal's mother and M. H. del Pilar's wife (see photo 7). On both sides of the masthead were slogans expressing their beliefs:

> Man was made with the ability to stand up so that one's honor will reach as high as the sky. Animals were made to crawl so that their thoughts are sunk in the mud. If you are human, be honorable.[63]

**Photo 7. Hirang** (January 1941)
*Source: Jeremias Adia*

The *Hirang* paper lasted for only two years, or until July 1941, when it had to shut down publication due to the high cost of materials.[64]

In mid-May 1940, the National Council of the Ganap Party unanimously adopted a *Memorial* to be sent to the U.S. President and Congress. This memorial was a reiteration of the party's firm stand on independence. The Ganap Party flatly denied the allegation that the Filipino people had abandoned their stand on independence because of unsettled conditions in the Far East. Doing so was "to close one's eyes to the history of our race and to efface the memory, to us sacred, of Rizal and other Filipinos who in the past gave their lives for our liberty." The Ganap Party pleaded with the U.S. not to deviate from the policy written into the Jones Law and later included in the T-M Act.[65]

## 1940 Elections

In September 1940, as the war clouds were hanging thick and dark, the Japanese military invaded northern French Indochina. As we have seen, whenever the rumors of uprising circulated, Japan was mentioned either as a source of assistance or as the place from which Ramos or Ricarte were to re-emerge. Ramos often cited Japan as a model country to be emulated, and this led many Filipinos to believe that the party was somehow in the service of the Japanese military. The authorities pointed out the existence of the identification cards as proof. They alleged that they were to be shown to the Japanese in the event of the invasion.[66] Under such suspicion, the Ganap Party participated in the special National Assembly elections in December. This election was held to fill four vacant seats for the Assembly in the provinces of Albay, Iloilo, Leyte, and Nueva Ecija as well as provincial governors and municipal positions in all districts. Leonardo Gonzales, the lone Ganap candidate for assemblyman, ran unsuccessfully in Nueva Ecija. The party put up their own candidates for governors and municipal officials. By this time, the presidency of the party went to Celerino Tiongco and the vice presidency to Pilar J. Aglipay, the widow of Gregorio Aglipay.[67]

Three weeks before the election, Pio Duran, one of the two Nacionalista candidates running for the Assembly seats in Albay, was asked by the party to withdraw from the race on the grounds that his expressed views were prejudicial to the continuation of friendly relations between the Philippines and the U.S. The party claimed that Duran advocated aligning with an alien nation and welcomed that nation's hegemony in the Far East.

The party assailed his view, which they considered a direct challenge to the aspiration of the Filipino nation for independence and loyalty to the U.S.[68] The "alien nation" was, of course, Japan. Nevertheless, Duran ignored the request and ran in the election but he lost.

The Popular Front ran as one party; however, it was split into Sumulong and Abad Santos factions, and infighting between the two was observed. The Sumulong faction branded the Abad Santos faction as "red" and warned against the spread of communism by their candidates. Moises Nicomedes of the Abad Santos faction claimed that their faction was the real Popular Front organized in 1936 and that Sumulong had been expelled on 8 October 1939 for alleged political complicity. Guillermo Capadocia, candidate for Manila councilor, who belonged to the same faction, explained that the Popular Front was established to combat fascism because the communists and socialists believed that under their party, democracy would have a chance to survive.[69] The Sumulong faction of the Popular Front joined forces with other opposition groups called the Democrata Nacional-Popular Front.[70]

As in the election two years earlier, the Ganap Party was not pushing immediate and absolute independence since it was supposed to be granted in 1946, and the party supported Quezon's social justice program. The party's campaign slogan vaguely described the Ganap Party candidates as purely Filipino and wholeheartedly patriotic candidates who wanted freedom for the Mother Country. The party stressed that the reason it was participating in the election was to show that the Ganapistas could hold a clean campaign, unlike the Nacionalistas, and would dissipate what the old politics had created. As late as the end of November, barely two weeks before the election, the party in Biñan, Laguna, for instance, had to make an announcement to reassure the members that their party candidates were indeed running for the election. This reflected the Ganapistas' lack of enthusiasm for this election; however, they pleaded with members to exercise their right to vote and to do so wisely to honor the Mother Country. They considered Election Day the day to cleanse their feelings (*pakalinisin natin ang ating mga damdamin*) and stay clean even though others might cheat.[71]

The Ganap Party managed to select ten candidates running for Manila city councilor, among them three women, including Loreto Makalinaw, vice president of the Samahang Makabayan. Others included Antonio Velisario, the editor of The Filipino Freedom, and Ciriaco V. Campomanes, the radical Tayabas leader who expressed hopes of changing the condition of the poor and the "little people" of the city. However, none of the Ganap Party candidates was elected.[72] Although the Ganap candidates had lost, the election results of the Municipal Board showed that six out of the ten seats went to opposition groups, making the opposition a majority. This was the first triumph of the opposition in twelve years in the city government. In the provinces two minority governors, Jose Robles Jr. of Nueva Ecija and Wenceslao Vinzons of Camarines Norte, were elected.[73]

The Socialist Party had a strong showing in central Luzon, the place where serious agrarian conflicts had taken place. Pedro Abad Santos ran for the governorship of Pampanga but lost to anti-peasant reactionary incumbent governor Sotero Baluyot. When taken into consideration that half of Abad Santos's followers were illiterate, disqualified voters, it is surprising that he was behind by fewer than ten thousand votes from Baluyot. This means that Abad Santos had captured at least 40 percent of the vote. Furthermore, the Socialist Party produced eight mayors out of twenty-one municipalities in Pampanga.[74] The strong showing of opposition parties in this election could be attributed to the adult reading and writing programs designed to increase the number of new voters. The Electoral Commission's decisive actions to control election violations also contributed to the growth of the opposition parties.[75]

With the Ganap Party leader in jail and the members under strong suspicion of being Japanese sympathizers, their Ganap Party platform was not attractive enough to voters. However, the opposition groups in general were getting stronger. Slowly and gradually their growth would have been expected had it not been for the atmosphere of urgency in which unity of the nation had become the most critical matter.

## The 1941 Elections

In November of the following year, presidential, legislative, and local elections were held. A landslide victory for the Nacionalista Party was predicted since it was unwise to create a shift in the administration, which needed to conserve all its energy for national defense. Despite the repeated defeats, the Ganap Party decided to participate in the election. The Ganap candidate for president was Celerino Tiongco and for vice president, Pilar J. Aglipay, who pledged to serve all her countrymen without giving special consideration to any particular group or faction, thereby strongly denying that she would work only for Aglipayan interests.[76] The congressional candidates included Mariano Untivero and Aurelio Almazan in Laguna; Andres Pelagio and Ramon Pas Crespo in Rizal; and Sancho A. Sallvia, who ran as both Ganap and the Popular Front candidate in Tayabas. Paulo V. Capa, former president of the old Sakdalista Party, acted as campaign manager for the party.[77]

Ganap candidate Untivero stressed that his party held no subversive ideas and that its objectives were to help the government carry out President Quezon's social justice program, to introduce reforms in the government, and to realize the country's independence.[78] An unexpected Ganap Party candidate for the Assembly was Jesus Lava, a communist. He was initially reported to have been proclaimed an official candidate of the Ganap Party in Tarlac. Actually, he wanted to be an official candidate of all three groups: the Ganap Party, the Popular Front of Sumulong, and the Abad Santos faction. He eventually ran in Bulacan under the Popular Front of the Abad Santos faction.[79] Lava's initial attempt to run under the Ganap Party banner seems to be in accordance with the communists' policy of forming a united front against fascism. While they had their own candidate, the Ganap Party supported some Popular Front candidates this time. For instance, in Nueva Ecija, the Ganapistas were behind Francisco S. Bumanlag who belonged to the Abad Santos faction.[80]

Juan Sumulong, presidential candidate, issued a statement in which he said that he had no illusions as to what the results of the elections would be. He expected an overwhelming victory for Quezon and regretted the weakness of the opposition, which he thought was largely due to a lack of organization and unity. Nevertheless, he criticized the majority party and assailed its intellectual dishonesty, duplicity, lack of good faith, and abuse of power. Sumulong argued that the majority party had not done as much for the country as it should have during its thirty-five years of reign. Instead of simply opposing the majority party, this time the Popular Front presented an alternative program for the future Philippines, which included completely eliminating the practice of nepotism; placing more emphasis on national defense; making the social justice program more effective; helping build the character and genius of the Filipino race while maintaining a government of, by, and for the people; and insisting on a truly democratic form of government.[81] Indeed, democracy in the country had been threatened because Quezon had declared in mid-1939 that political parties were unnecessary in the Philippines.[82]

Despite the overwhelming victory of the Nacionalista Party, three opposition candidates managed to get elected into the House: Emigdio Nietes of Antique (Popular Front, Sumulong faction), Alfonso Mendoza of the south district of Manila (Democrata-Nacional), and Wencesslao Vinzons of Camarines Norte (Young Philippines).[83] The Ganap candidates for Laguna, Untivero (second district), and Almazan (first district), still showed some strength although both had lost. One observer even predicted that Almazan might win. Untivero did relatively well, garnering 6,325 votes while the winning Nacionalista candidate, Crisanto Guysayco, received 11,391 votes.[84]

In both elections, the Ganap Party was not as critical of the Nacionalista Party as the other opposition parties were. The Ganap Party knew that it had very little chance of winning the seat, yet it participated in the elections on principle. The Ganapistas wanted the people to know that they were still for independence that would bring prosperity to all, that they could carry on a clean and corrupt-free election, that they were not a tool of a foreign country, and that they would support Quezon's social justice program.

Although the Ganapistas had repeatedly emphasized that they were not the tool of any foreign country, their voice seemed to have been muzzled by the noisy turmoil of what was taking place in Asia and Europe. Affirmation of Quezon as president of the Philippines (winning 80 percent of the votes) showed the Filipinos' willingness to defend the country under his leadership and fight against a Japanese invasion. The U.S. said that the 1941 election result "completes United States-Philippines understanding regarding the Far Eastern problem."[85]

While recognizing Japanese power in Asia and being ready to negotiate with her, the Ganapistas were not willing to be subjected to Japanese control, as we have seen in their expressed ardent desire for independence. Unfortunately, they were already deeply involved with Japan. Their age-old expectation of Japanese assistance had sent Ramos to Japan. By the time he and the party leaders realized no such assistance was forthcoming and decided to assist the Quezon administration in uniting the people to face the Japanese, it was too late. In fact, it was impossible to reverse people's perception that the Ganapistas were Japanese allies. Both the Ganapistas and the Filipinos in general had been under the spell of "the legend of Japanese assistance." The latter, fearing the assistance of the Japanese, persecuted the Ganapistas.

## The Ganapistas as Suspected Fifth Column

After the Japanese invasion of French Indochina, the Filipinos antici-pated an imminent Japanese offensive. In order to unite the Filipinos under the American flag, "Loyalty Day" was observed at the end of June 1941 and attended by 200,000 people at Luneta Park. The whole city of Manila had been exercising blackout drills as part of their war preparations.[86]

When the news of the Pearl Harbor bombing by Japanese warplanes reached the Philippines in early December 1941, followed by news of the bombing of Davao, Camp John Hay, Clark Field, and other military bases, President Quezon assumed emergency powers. A state of total emergency was declared in mid-December. Quezon authorized the suspension of all government activities and services to divert any unexpected funds to national defense and protection of the civilian population.[87]

The average Filipino citizen suspected and feared that the Ganapistas were linked to Japan, resulting in rumors such as: "Ganap members were signaling to Japanese airplanes under blackout" or "they had been poisoning water supplies." As a result, known Ganap members, totaling one hundred and fifty, in Pampanga, Rizal, Bulacan, Nueva Ecija, and Tayabas, were arrested in mid-December. Some of them were severely tortured by the arresting detectives, perhaps to obtain information about the Ganap Party's connection to the invading Japanese forces.[88] One of the arrested Ganap Party leaders allegedly confessed that there was a plot for Ganapistas to cooperate with the Japanese Army in the conquest of the country. Immediately, the law agents raided the party headquarters and then announced they had found proof of the alleged pro-Japanese activities among the seized documents, papers, and photographs, singling out those of Japanese military officers.[89]

In Atimonan, Tayabas, the stronghold of the Sakdalista movement, the governor ordered that the Ganap Party members' registration with the Civilian Emergency Administration be revoked on the grounds that the Ganapistas were leaning toward a particular alien power.[90]

The Ganap members vehemently denied that they had ever engaged in any "fifth-column" or spying activities for the Japanese. Even before these incidents occurred, the women members had predicted this kind of fabrication was going to happen. They announced on a page of their organ *Hirang*:

The Ganapistas are law-abiding and peaceful citizens of the Philippines. They love their country and would not be treacherous enough to be advanced guards to pave the way to the conquest of the country by any foreign power.[91]

Indeed, the Ganapistas were by no means "advanced guards" of the Japanese invading forces. The Japanese military had no connection whatsoever with the Ganap members before the invasion, as historical evidence shows (see Ch. 8). However, after the occupation of the Japanese forces, the majority of the Ganap Party members, including old Sakdalista Party members, did fully cooperate with the Japanese military.

In order to gain some understanding of this seemingly contradictory action, we shall closely examine the forces behind the Sakdalista movement, its membership, leadership, principles, and philosophy, which sustained the movement for more than ten years.

## CHAPTER 7

# THE SAKDALISTA MEMBERSHIP, RAMOS, AND SAKDALISM

W HEN THE MAIDEN issue of *Sakdal* came out in June 1930, the residents of Manila and nearby provinces were still feeling the heat of anti-American sentiment stirred up by the Watsonville incident, followed by the Manila North High School strike, and other racially related violence. Those who first subscribed to the paper and eventually formed the movement came from diverse sectors of Philippine society. Discontented and critical of the current situation, they aspired for the country's independence. The members of the Sakdalista movement can be roughly classified into six groups: (1) intellectuals, professionals, landlords, and proprietors; (2) participants in the 1896 Revolution and the Philippine-American War, and subsequent Ricarte followers (Ricartistas) and members of the mutual-aid societies who supported them; (3) peasants; (4) city laborers; and (5) anti-Catholic religious organizations. After examining the membership, we shall look into their leader Benigno Ramos and Sakdalism Ramos and the members created.

## The Membership
### Intellectuals, Professionals, Landlords, and Proprietors

Benigno Ramos, publisher of the *Sakdal*, was one of the orators at the Manila North High School rallies. The articles in the *Sakdal* expressed a strong opposition voice, alleging that Quezon and his administration were abandoning the demand for complete and immediate independence and that colonial status had brought indignation to the people and the country. The initial subscribers-turned-supporters saw the Sakdalista movement as a potentially strong opposition movement to the Nacionalista-dominated politics. The publication of the *Sakdal* was made possible by the support of antigovernment politicians. Ramos fearlessly exposed corruption in the government, for which the paper was censured and often banned from mailing issues. The paper's position was attractive to opponents of Quezon and his administration, particularly those who were not identified with existing political parties. They included a number of intellectuals and professionals, students, government officials, public school teachers, rank-and-file employees of private companies, and vernacular writers, poets, and essayists.[1]

Despite its strong appeal to the poor, the movement's national and local leadership rested in the hands of well-educated middle-class professionals and people of means from the landlord and proprietor class. For example, the first president of the Sakdalista Party, Felino Cajucom, was a lawyer; Venancio R. Aznar, the vice president, was a well-known Tagalog writer and a founding member of Kapisanang Panitikan (Literary Association); and Celerino Tiongco, the party's deputy president and occasional editor of the *Sakdal* and *Ganap*, was a wealthy landlord and the former mayor as well as a judge in Santa Rosa, Laguna.[2] Other leaders included Elpidio Santos of Pasig, Rizal, an attorney, and Ciriaco Campomanes of Tayabas, a medical doctor. The Ganap Party leadership was in the hands of proprietors, industrialists, landlords, and attorneys.[3]

### Ricartistas, Members of Mutual-Aid Societies, and Veterans of the 1896 Revolution and 1899 Philippine-American War

Although the Sakdalistas declared their intent to obtain independence through peaceful and legal means, the movement no doubt attracted those who had fought in the past two wars and those belonging to various Ricartista societies or armies, some of whom formed mutual-aid associations to shield their true aim from the authorities. They had been waiting for the opportune time to rise up. In the following discussion, we shall trace Ricartistas' long, sustained independence activities.

After the U.S. takeover of the Philippines, Artemio Ricarte was the perfect person to rally around since he had refused to swear allegiance to the American colonial government. When he was captured in 1900 and refused to pledge allegiance to the U.S, he was deported to Guam the following year. In early 1903, the U.S. authorities allowed him to return to the Philippines and pressured him to pledge allegiance but he again refused. This time he was deported to Hong Kong. In December 1903, he secretly returned to the Philippines to prepare for an anti-American war. A large number of people, especially labor union members, showed enthusiastic support. However, Ricarte was captured in May 1904, and placed in solitary confinement for six years. When he was released in June 1910, he still refused to recognize American colonial authority and was sent back to Hong Kong.[4]

Supported by his followers at home, in February 1911, Ricarte formed the Consejo Revolucionario de Filipinas (Philippine Revolutionary Council), a government-in-exile with the aim of achieving immediate and complete independence, under which the recruitment of soldiers for the Revolutionary Army of the Philippines commenced. Ricarte supporters who began sending donations included Gregorio Aglipay, the head of the IFI; former revolutionaries, such as Agapito Zialcita; "Japanophiles," such as Ramon Diokno; and laborers of the Katubusan Tobacco Factory.[5]

In the meantime, Ricarte sent letters to friends and supporters at home, encouraging them to organize a general boycott against American commerce and industries and to patronize those of the Philippines instead. He repeated Kropotkin's words, "Liberties are not given; they are taken." In another letter, Ricarte encouraged people to unite and rise "with the shout of Viva la libertad! Viva la Justicia!" (Long Live Liberty! Long Live Justice!)."[6] No doubt copies of these letters circulated not only among the Ricartistas but also among others seeking immediate independence for the country.

After Ricarte's letters reached the Philippines, many military organizations were formed and pledged to serve under Ricarte's orders.[7] In Manila and surrounding towns as well as in Bulacan, more than twenty-seven thousand people were said to have pledged to the Revolutionary Army. One former revolutionary pledging his loyalty to Ricarte said, "I have spilled mine (blood) in the two past struggles but as the work is not yet terminated, there is still left in me sufficient (blood) to shed." Other former Katipuneros were heard to have said that they were ready to die like Bonifacio and his soul lived in them as a sacred redeeming soul.[8]

In April 1912, Ricartistas in Pangasinan attempted to capture the provincial capital and set up an independent government. Seven towns were involved and over five hundred arrests were made. Two months later, a plot was planned by Ricartistas for the fourth of July celebration in Manila. They were to assemble with short bolos and daggers hidden in their clothes and at a given signal, they were to attack the participating infantry to take their arms. The plan was foiled by a last-minute change of plan by the military authorities who had received the information of the possible attack.[9] In August 1914, on Balintawak Day, the Ricartistas reportedly planned a coordinated revolt; however, it was never carried out. The plan of uprising might have been motivated by Ricarte's sending a number of copies of a constitution around July 1914 (originally written in March 1913) for the future independent country, which he called the Rizaline Islands.[10] Four months later, the so-called Christmas Eve Fiasco took place.

After the "Fiasco," the U.S. authorities believed that relative peace would prevail in and around Manila. Yet two weeks later, rumor of a plot to stage a revolt circulated widely in the town of Bayambang, Pangasinan. This new uprising would coordinate with the revolutionary group in Manila to stage a general revolt in 1920, if independence had not been granted by that time. The leader of the Pangasinan group was Pablo Penullar, who led the local people in the poorly coordinated Sakdalista uprising of October 1936, as we saw in Ch. 4.[11]

Due to the failed Christmas Eve uprising, the U.S. authorities demanded extradition of Ricarte from Hong Kong. At the same time, the British authorities in Hong Kong decided to remove all political exiles from Hong Kong as World War I had broken out in Europe. The Indian independence fighters in the British colonies seized this opportunity to agitate for non-participation in the war. Ricarte was accused of aiding these Indians and was sent to Shanghai to be handed over to the American authorities. However, he escaped from his detention cell with the assistance of some Japanese whom Ricarte had associated with earlier and secretly entered Japan in June 1915.[12] When his presence in Japan became known in the Philippines, the Ricartistas believed that the shipment of arms from Japan would be only a matter of time. Thus, even one year after the "Christmas Eve Fiasco," the Ricartista movement was still quite active, and the authorities placed guards at vital points in affected districts in and around Manila.[13]

In 1922, two generals of the 1896 Revolution, Pio del Pilar and Leon Villafuerte, organized a secret military organization called Magtanggol (Defend). Del Pilar was banished to Guam along with Ricarte in 1901. Villafuerte had fought with Gen. Macario Sakay, a staunch anti-American War general, until their arrest in 1906, and he had just been released from Bilibid Prison. This organization began granting a military rank to anyone who could afford to pay for one.[14]

As late as 1929, a revolutionary army was discovered in Manila. This army planned to purchase munitions from Japan and obtain the Japanese Navy's assistance in an attack to establish independence. There was no clear evidence that the organizer was a Ricartista; however, his aim and method of securing the arms and ammunitions were similar to the Ricartista-inspired armed organization.[15] These Ricartista activities of armed uprisings were usually supported by the seemingly harmless mutual-aid civic organizations, such as Dimas Alang. They claimed to be such in order to avoid detection by the authorities, as we saw in Ch. 1.

Many elderly veterans of the anti-Spanish revolution and anti-American war lamented that the Republic they helped to establish had disappeared and that Aguinaldo had forsaken the struggle for independence.[16] No doubt, some of them became Ricartistas and eventually supported the Sakdalista movement.

## Peasants

Peasant participation was evident in the Sakdalista uprising of 1935. Before they became Sakdalistas, many of them had been members of peasant organizations, such as the Kapatirang Magsasaka.[17] Even before Ramos was involved in the Manila North High School incident, he had been active in defending the peasants' plight. For instance, he acted as one of the spokespersons representing the San Ildefonso tenants of the Buenavista Estate who wished to purchase the land from the archbishop.[18]

The peasants' predicament, especially the process of how they got buried in debt and lost their land during the American colonial period, has been amply described by scholars of peasant studies. From these studies, we learn that initially the American colonial government was keenly aware of the agrarian problem and attempted to remedy it by purchasing most of the friar lands that were for sale to lessees and undertook cadastral surveys in 1913. However, the lands were so expensive that only a handful of people could afford them and, consequently, they fell into the hands of the landed elite. In the wake of the U.S. free-tariff policy, demand for export crops, such as sugar, abaca (hemp), coconut, and tobacco, had increased, and haciendas had grown accordingly. The landlords, who were also the local elite (*principalia* class), had all the resources needed to obtain land in order to profit from cash crops. They manipulated land laws, conducted fraudulent land surveys, and sometimes grabbed land outright. Thus, a cadastral survey, which was meant to be a tool to reduce tenancy, resulted in the landed elite's further enlarging their holdings while new home-steaders and long-established small landholders eventually lost title to their lands. In the meantime, the Catholic Church still owned the biggest estate in central Luzon. Under these conditions, the tenant farmers in central Luzon were either suffering from high rent or were unable to meet sharecropping quotas. To cope, they borrowed money from landlords at outrageously high interest rates and had to live perpetually under the control and command of the landlords. Those who could not pay back their loans were eventually evicted. The condition of those peasants who joined the 1896 Revolution to improve their lot remained the same: tax burdens as well as abuse and exploitation by the landlord.[19]

Another effect of the free-trade agreement between the U.S. and the Philippines was an influx of American manufactured goods. The importa-tion of these goods destroyed small-scale local industries such as weaving and hat making, which had provided needed supplemental income to peasants. Many peasants also could not participate in local and national elections because they were illiterate or could not pay for the cedula tax certificate, which served as an identification card.[20]

Against this background, peasant unions were born in central Luzon toward the end of the 1910s. In 1922, the confederation of peasants' unions were created under the name of the Kalipunang Pangbansa ng mga Magbubukid sa Pilipinas (KPMP) and later, another association, Kapatirang Magsasaka was organized. The KPMP adopted Katipunan's Decalogue for the members' guidance.[21] This was a strong indication that some KPMP members joined the Sakdalista movement and vice versa. Many peasants were drawn to the Sakdalista movement because it exalted the 1896 Revolution, and they were encouraged to respect

Philippine tradition. Besides, it was customary to belong to more than one organization.

When the Sakdalista Party was organized, their expressed grievances were brought to the central political arena. Joining the movement allowed them to work for change. Previous studies on the May 1935 Uprising have aptly described the social and economic hardships under which the peasants had been placed.

## City Laborers

In 1927, a Bureau of Labor survey revealed that laborers' earnings were not sufficient to maintain their families and that the quality of city laborers' lives had not changed much since 1905, despite the rising economy during World War I and the early 1920s.[22]

In the early 1930s, Manila's tobacco and cigar factories were already on the decline and thousands of laborers were without work. The reduction of export activities caused massive layoffs of workers engaged in port-related jobs, such as stevedores, warehousemen, and freight transportation workers. Export-oriented processing industries, such as coconut oil factories, were also affected. The salaries and pensions of civil servants, schoolteachers, and retirees stayed the same while retail prices began to fall, so those who retained their jobs or received pensions enjoyed greater purchasing power. This accentuated the suffering of those who had lost their jobs. The Great Depression affected different people and at different times.[23]

By the 1930s, many city laborers, including servants, seamen, casual workers, and waiters and waitresses, were members of well-organized labor unions. Their objectives were to protect not only the laborers' economic interests but also racial integrity and dignity. The purpose of some unions also included "to protect the Filipino workers from abuse and maltreatment by drunken American soldiers."[24]

Hundreds of Manila laborers lined up from Pier Seven to the funeral parlor where the body of a slain victim from California was laid in state, as discussed in Ch. 2. It is not surprising that these laborers were among the first subscribers of the weekly *Sakdal*, as the movement expressed strong anti-American sentiment while devoting itself to issues of direct concern to blue-collar workers. Almost every issue of the paper included articles discussing the rise in living costs, the plight of the city laborers, and the labor movement. However, in the case of Manila, their indignation over racial violence and their aspirations for independence did not necessarily translate into electoral votes, as shown in the poor performance of the Sakdalista and Ganap Parties at the polls. The majority of the laborers had already been organized into labor unions before the Sakdalista movement was formed and they seemed to have cast their votes along the union political line. However, when it came to the provincial city laborers, it was a different story.[25]

## Members of Anti-Catholic Religious Organizations

One of the most significant areas of nationalist expressions during the 1896 Revolution can be seen in the spiritual domain. Since the Catholic Church and Spanish domination were viewed as one and the same, many Filipinos expressed their desire for independence by leaving the Catholic Church at the time of the revolution and joining other religious movements. Many joined the newly created IFI, which won over a significant portion of the population.[26] In 1903–1904, the membership of the IFI was estimated to be between 2,000,000 and 3,500,000, at least one-fourth of the total population.[27] The number of adherents gradually dwindled, partly due to the Supreme Court ruling in 1906 that the Roman Catholic Church was the legal owner of all the church buildings that the IFI had taken over. In some provinces, though, such as Ilocos Norte and Zambales, and in some Laguna towns, more than half the population still belonged to the IFI.[28]

Bishop Gregorio Aglipay—who was also the founder of the Katipunan in Tarlac—and his priests had been closely connected to independent movements. For instance, some IFI priests in Ilocos Norte were said to have been collecting contributions for Ricarte by saying they were donations for parochial fees. In the past, other priests had figured quite prominently in the revolutionary movement, such as the one staged in Nueva Vizcaya in 1910.[29]

For IFI members, the Sakdalista movement and the activities of the church became synonymous. For instance, an IFI priest would offer morning services at a Sakdalista member's residence while the meeting was held in the afternoon. The close relationship between the IFI and the Sakdalista movement was seen also in Ramos and Bishop Aglipay's joint attendance at many meetings and their participation in anti-Quezon parades.[30] Furthermore, the widow of Bishop Aglipay, Pilar J. Aglipay, became the vice-president of the Ganap Party and was a candidate for vice-president on the Ganap ticket in the 1941 national election.

It is difficult to determine just what percentage of Sakdalistas were IFI adherents; however, we can safely deduce that a high number of Sakdalistas were IFI members. My assertion is based on a recent study of Francis A. Gealogo, who informs us that church members were taught repeatedly that their sacred and inescapable duties were to obtain independence and to emulate the sacrifices of those who suffered for the cause of independence. Furthermore, they were taught that in the eyes of the church, Rizal, Mabini, and Bonifacio were considered IFI spokesmen, prophets, and evangelists. Rizal especially was held up as an example of how a patriot should sacrifice his life for the redemption of his people. One popular form of literature circulated in the church was *novenario ng Balintawak* (Novena Prayers of Balintawak), which was published in the 1920s and 1930s, and included the compilation of writings of Filipino heroes of the 1896 Revolution: the *Decalogue* of Mabini, *Kartilya* (Primer) of the Katipunan, and excerpts of Rizal's essays and letters.

Another widely circulated piece of literature within the church, the *calendariong maanghang* (spicy calendar, meaning stinging remarks), contained political satire and discussions of social issues of the time. They included criticism against the administration of Quezon and Osmeña for delaying independence in order to retain their power.[31] What was printed in the novenario and the calendario had a striking similarity to what appeared repeatedly on the pages of the *Sakdal*. It is very likely that some articles in the paper were actually written by IFI members.

The IFI had considerable influence on the development of the politico-religious organizations, such as the Rizalista cults that revered Jose Rizal. Indeed, the IFI, the Colorum societies, and the Rizalista cults had such a close relationship that they were often considered one and the same.[32] The existence of politico-religious organizations was particularly notable in the provinces of Rizal, Tarlac, Laguna, Batangas, Tayabas, and Pampanga. These societies honored and revered not only Rizal but also the 1896 revolutionary heroes.[33] Some members from the politico-religious organizations joined the Sakdalista movement because it reflected their desire for prosperity in an independent country and a society full of brotherly love under the guidance of Christ and Rizal. They interpreted "Sakdal" to mean complete faith in God instead of understanding it in the more conventional sense of "an accusation" (against the status quo). The membership included those who later founded the Samahan ng Tatlong Persona. Its leader, Agapito Illustrisimo, claimed to have been a co-founder of the Sakdalista movement. According to him, "the Voice" had commanded him and Ramos to take leadership of a movement seeking independence for the Philippines and soliciting assistance from foreign countries. The Samahan ng Tatlong Persona was registered with the government in 1935 under a different name, the Samahang Pananalangin Ukol sa Kalayaan ng Bayan, Inc. (Society for Praying for the Freedom of the Country), or SPUKB, Inc. When they participated in political activities, the members claimed to be Sakdalistas or members of SPUKB, Inc. while the Samahan ng Tatlong Persona functioned as the spiritual expression of their activities.[34]

Whether Illustrisimo actually co-organized the Sakdalista movement is irrelevant, for the record strongly indicates that his followers were active in the Sakdalista movement. Illustrisimo had traveled extensively in the central Luzon towns, meeting with members of the other politico-religious groups, including both Rizalista and Colorum groups. Given his affiliation with the Sakdalista movement, Illustrisimo's frequent travels could have helped spread the movement among these people of similar persuasion.[35]

In addition to members from the IFI and politico-religious organizations, the Sakdalista movement drew ministers and laypersons from Protestant churches. When the American occupation commenced, some Filipinos saw the Protestant churches brought by the Americans as an alternative to the Roman Catholic Church. They initially believed that belonging to a Protestant church was a way to hasten the country's independence. Eventually, some Protestants began to move their own churches away from American control. One such organization was Iglesia Evangelica Metodistas en las Islas Filipinas (Methodist Evangelical Church in the Philippine Islands) or IEMELIF. Formed in 1909, this church was firmly established among the people of the central Luzon area and has been the largest of the completely independent and indigenous Protestant groups in the islands. The IEMELIF's involvement in the Sakdalista movement was noted in the *Sakdal* issues.[36]

Many people who joined the Sakdalista movement or party had overlapping affiliations, such as being members of the IFI, the Ricartista movement, the Tanggulan Society, and the Kapatirang Magsasaka. The majority of the Sakdalistas, especially the peasants, had simple moral values and ethics, such as courtesy and hospitality. They also valued respect for elders, respect for the memory of the dead so as to perpetuate their good example, respect for the spirit of the clan, tolerance, self-control, the chastity of women, unity of the family, and valor and heroism in the face of danger. These values were found in old Filipino tales, *salawikain* (proverbs), *corido*, and *awit* (both are recited metrical romance) and were held in high regard by "the unspoiled men and women" on the rustic farms, at least among the Tagalogs.[37] These people believed that living in accordance with the universal laws of mutual respect, love, honesty, humility, and charity would bring them peace and prosperity. They were all attracted to what Benigno Ramos had to offer and eventually rallied around his leadership to create the movement.

## Benigno Ramos

Benigno Ramos was born in 1892 in Taliptip, Bulacan, in the province of Bulacan.[38] He completed the intermediate grades but did not finish high school. Nevertheless, he got a teaching position in an elementary school in the same province, qualifying for the job by passing the necessary language examination. Shortly after he began teaching, Ramos wrote a play that ridiculed the local priest, a rebellious action that sent him to the town jail for twenty-four hours. After that incident, he left for Manila to seek his fortune as a poet and writer.[39]

In Manila, Ramos was employed by the weekly magazine *Renacimiento Filipino/Muling Pagsilang* around 1911. In literary circles, Ramos quickly earned a reputation as a fiery poet. When the prestigious literary organization Aklatang Bayan was established, he was invited to be a member. Ramos quickly rose to prominence as an important literary figure of the time, having been named one of the most promising young poets of his generation. Aklatang Bayan members included Patricio Dionisio, the founder of the Tanggulan Society, who also assisted Ramos's movement in the early days, and Jose P. Laurel, whose authority Ramos would challenge during the Japanese Occupation period.[40]

Soon Ramos started to receive praise as a "revolutionary poet" from the well-known literary critics of the time because he did not dissemble and had the ability to delve into the great issues of the time. Critics predicted that eventually he would be able to bring about social change.[41] He also came to be recognized not only as a poet but also as an orator, critic, and journalist. Most of all, he was recognized as a person who stood by his convictions. Whenever Ramos's poems criticized the American colonization of the Philippines, he used pen names. It was customary to adopt more than one pseudonym in order to avoid detection by the authorities. Eventually, Ramos came to use one of his pen names, "Ruben," as his middle name, thus "Benigno R. Ramos."[42]

## His Poems and Other Literary Works

Ramos's skill as a writer and poet had a great deal to do with the Sakdalista movement's success in its formative years. By the time he published the *Sakdal* weekly, he had written more than a hundred poems.[43] Most of his poems and *balagtasan* (poetical joust; name comes from the poet Balagtas) are filled with sadness and anger at the deplorable social conditions of his time. One of his poems warns oppressors, especially the rich, to change their ways ("!Bulkan!") (Volcano!) and another encourages the peasants to fight for their land ("Asyenda") (Hacienda). We can easily detect Ramos's deep feelings for the powerless, uneducated, oppressed, and poor. In his short story on Mexican bandit Pancho Villa, Ramos implied that the desperate conditions found in Mexico also existed in the Philippines.[44]

Ramos attributes the sad plight of the poor and the desperate economic condition of the country to foreign domination, as seen in "Pilipinas" (The Philippines): "If yesterday I was oppressed by Prayer (referring to Spanish colonization)/Now I am more oppressed; my brave Rizal has died and still his enemies live on..."[45] To change this situation of social and economic inequality, Ramos advocated independence for the Philippines. Thus, he wrote a balagtasan entitled "Balagtasan ng Kalayaan" (Poetical Joust on Freedom). Five characters appear: Bathala ng Kasarinlan (the God of Independence); Huwan de la Cruz (Juan de la Cruz, the ordinary Filipino man); Diwa ni Rizal (the Spirit of Rizal); Tiyo Sam (Uncle Sam, or U.S.); and Hukumang Pandaigdig (World Court). The Spirit of Rizal comments that even George Washington would be against what Uncle Sam is doing to the Philippines. Rizal is depicted as encouraging the Filipinos to continue fighting for independence while he assists from above.[46]

In the poem "Alaala" (A Recollection), Ramos suggests that to carry out the task of gaining independence, the people should derive inspiration from the heroes of the 1896 Revolution.[47] Another poem, entitled "!Bayani!" (Hero), is dedicated to Jose Rizal, whom he calls "the Christ of the Philippines" and says that his memory would never fade even after his death.[48] Ramos's comparison of Rizal to Christ was not his only use of biblical allusions. In "Bagong Hudyo" (The New Jew), Ramos likens contemporary society to the time when "evil" Jews caused the death of Christ. Christ represents those Filipinos who suffer injustice and inequality while the Jews represent the country's rich politicians. Ramos also expressed his religious convictions in works, such as "Ang Diyos Ko" (My God).[49] According to this poem, God is not inside the temple but in the middle of the fields with the grieving ones. God is in the company of the lowly laborers and in the spirits of those who strive to awaken the nation and change its destiny. This poem shows that Ramos believes in God but does not believe in institutionalized religious organizations, such as the Roman Catholic Church.

Ramos also criticized the social and cultural climate of the twentieth century in a serialized story entitled "Talsik ng Siglo XX" (Splash of the Twentieth Century). In this story, Ramos laments that people of his day lack concern for others and attributes this sorry situation to the materialism of the time, saying that in the twentieth century, "ang salapi ay siyang puri, ay siyang buhay, siyang Dios, siyang lahat . . . Kung walang salapi ay wala" (money is honor, life, God, everything. If you have no money, you are nothing). Ramos also addressed Filipino women, vigorously advocating that they should never become imitators of the foreigners but remain genuinely Filipino in both thought and character.[50] In another short article, written in 1922, Ramos warns of the trick the U.S. introduced to the Philippines—*pulitika* (politics). He notes that while Spain used religion to make the people forget their problems, the U.S. utilized pulitika.[51]

As we have seen, Benigno Ramos's rebellious spirit and strong patriotism were already evident during his early days. Some historians attribute Ramos's establishment of the Sakdalista movement to his *amor propio* (sense of pride, or honor) and his affront at being dismissed by Quezon.[52] However, this was neither the sole nor main cause of Ramos's turning against the establishment. Rather, his commitment to social justice and independence was consistent with his literary expressions prior to his dismissal in 1930. He realized how galvanizing his oratorical skills had been at the Manila North High School rallies. Perhaps he got carried away in the heat of the nationalist sentiment. In any event, he uttered words critical of the administration for failing to obtain independence, directly criticizing his mentor Quezon. After his dismissal from the Senate, Ramos continued to write critical articles, poems, and essays in the *Sakdal*, sometimes using pen names. In one of the earliest issues of the *Sakdal*, Ramos urged poets to be instruments for the betterment of society.[53]

In one article in the *Sakdal*, Ramos talked about the legend of King Bernardo Carpio, a popular legendary figure in the nineteenth century. Ramos wrote that for a hundred years, this king, who was strong and brave, had been imprisoned in a cave in San Mateo, with both hands and feet bound in chains. People believed that if he became free, he would redeem the people and the country from their oppressive state. Carpio became the only hope of the people, especially the powerless and the poor. Andres Bonifacio once visited the cave in San Mateo (actually, he visited the Cave of Pamintinan in Montalban). When Bonifacio came back out of the cave, people believed that Carpio had emerged in the body of Bonifacio. It is for this reason why Ramos stated that people called Bonifacio "Hari ng Katagalugan" (King of the Tagalog Region). When Carpio was freed in this fashion, the first Republic of Malolos was established. But somehow one of his hands again was manacled. It would soon become free again, and King Carpio's name would continue to offer hope for relief from the sufferings of the people, "whose conscience was clean." Ramos concluded this story by urging readers to revive in their hearts new hope for independence.[54]

Another of Ramos's article drawing on folk revolutionary symbolism was entitled "Ako ang Diwa ng Kalayaan" (I am the Spirit of Freedom). The article was accompanied by a picture of a long-haired woman with tears running down her cheeks and hands in a praying position tied in chains. This picture was titled "Inang Bayan" (Mother Country) and reappeared on the page of the Ganap Party publication, *Mga Patak*. The article started with the Spirit of Freedom saying to the Filipino people, "I am talking to you as a messenger of the Holy Spirits of all our Heroes." She narrated the lamentation and sorrow of all the Filipino people, who for a long time had been searching for Freedom. She declared that Bathala (the Creator) had sent her to awaken them.

> I am your brave spirit but you did not hear me while I had been tirelessly calling to your hearts. And today again I am knocking on the door of your hearts (*kalooban*), so that you will be awakened. Freedom will come not through someone else but through you...I am the Spirit of Freedom. Follow me because I ask nothing from you except love

of your honor (*karangalan*) and purity (*kapurian*); I do not need your money but I do need your sweat and blood...

For a long time, I have sobbed because of the injuries that animals (*mga halimaw*) have inflicted upon you. I am infuriated, but now is not the time to surrender to anger. What must be done before anything else is for me to prepare you for unity so that you will be free.

She ends with:

Follow what I, the Spirit of Freedom, of the Heroes, messenger of God, have said...I am telling you to be ready for our Great Day. Be strong and firm (*magpakatibay at magpakatatag*)...Redemption is rising (*Namamanaag na ang katubusan*). Be ready. I am your Freedom; I am your dream...[55]

The readers of this article must have been struck by the similarity between this narrative and that of Emilio Jacinto's "Pahayag" (Revelation), which appeared in the *Kalayaan* in 1896.[56] In "Pahayag," a white phantom or shadow surrounded by a halo of white vapor (woman) appeared in front of a suffering youth and said, "Do you want to know who I am?...My name is Kalayaan...." She told the youth that she had felt the sufferings of the Tagalogs and had come to save them. She demanded their sacrifice and death. Jacinto's "Pahayag" had been reprinted in the *Philippine Review* in July 1918; therefore, it is most likely that Ramos was familiar with it.[57]

Ramos's story of King Carpio and use of the figure of the Spirit of Freedom showed his understanding of the traditional mindset of the masses. He used the very language and symbols that had moved people to join the 1896 Revolution. Ramos was not only well versed in the culture of the Filipino people, but he also had a clear understanding of its value within the framework of the struggle for independence.

## Images of Ramos

In addition to expressing his stand for the poor and oppressed, Ramos described the character of the ideal leader: "The leaders, particularly of a colonized country, should know how to sacrifice and to carry the burden of a deep sorrow. Nobody has ever reached Victory without going over Golgotha and being nailed to the cross of Calvary for the welfare of the people." On the one hand, Ramos presented himself as such a leader; on the other hand, he accused the leaders amassing wealth of being nothing but "despoilers."[58]

Ramos created his own image by portraying himself not only as a suffering leader but also as a strong and trustworthy political broker. In 1933, during his visit to the U.S., he promised his followers "to put an end to all this talk (negotiation with the U.S.). If I am unable to end it, I will give my life in exchange...It is unfortunate that we, the poor, are not blessed by the Creator (Bathala) with abundant wealth. But I am full of hope that the Oppressed Land that represents you will not neglect you but will rather renew its zeal in order to give you strength in your struggle for the independence of the country and the redemption of the unfortunate poor."[59]

In short, he tried to build an image of himself as a humble person lacking material wealth but blessed with unmatched passion and the strength to fight. Like Christ, he was willing to bear hardships and undertake sacrifices for the welfare of others. In this emulation of Christ, he was like the fallen heroes of the Revolution, particularly Rizal. He made the comparison explicitly when he was being harassed, stating that Rizal had had similar experiences and that history was repeating itself. Ramos, like Rizal, could have used his influence and opportunities for self-gain; instead he chose to be on the side of the masses.[60] His popularity as a charismatic leader may have been based on the Christ-like, Rizal-like persona that he appropriated for himself throughout the entire period of the Sakdalista movement.

The followers wholeheartedly accepted these images that Ramos projected. In their perception Ramos, too, had sacrificed his bright future and suffered poverty for the sake of the cause. They appreciated his willingness to be "nailed to the Cross" so that the noble Sakdalista aim might be realized.[61] One of the followers praised him as a modern-day Rizal and the Messiah for a new society. He described Ramos as:

> A white bird that is a messenger of the heroes from the highest heavens
> in order to send a written message of new life to a country prostrated
> without hope even on the very first step of her steep Calvary.[62]

Having just observed Ramos speaking in the town of Lukban, Tayabas, this same supporter said that ever since Ramos's appearance in that town, the town folk had been talking about nothing but Ben Ruben and his ideals.[63] He connected the heroes of the 1896 Revolution with Ramos as a new leader who was trying to achieve independence through peaceful means in a Gandhi-like movement that was ready to undergo "an unequalled amount of suffering and perseverance in order to reach its aim." Often the audience was moved to tears by Ramos's speeches. One follower said, "In the past, Bonifacio was granted by the Creator the power to establish the Katipunan and rescue the Mother Country from extreme slavery. Who knows but the 'Ben Ruben' of today may be the Bonifacio of yesterday." [64]

Ramos's followers contended that he was incorruptible and the only opposition leader that Quezon could not buy off. Compared with other pro-independence, pro-labor people who went to Quezon's side, Ramos was truly for the poor and would dare to serve the country despite the dangers he might face "without expecting any favors, compensation, votes, or positions, now and forever."[65]

Ramos was considered a true Filipino at heart, in his thinking and in his actions (*Pilipino sa puso, sa diwa at sa gawa*). At a time when mastery of English was becoming the way to advance one's social position, he wrote poems and published the weekly in Tagalog, protected and promoted things Filipino by calling for boycotts of foreign-made products, and advocated not sending children to English-speaking schools. Even in his physical appearance, he was genuinely Filipino, as evidenced by his dark skin.[66]

In order to make the Sakdalista movement appear the legitimate successor to the unfinished 1896 Revolution, Ramos successfully recruited the unyielding revolutionary Artemio Ricarte to his cause by orchestrating donations. He continuously mentioned the general's uncompromising struggle for Philippine independence and actually had a meeting with him in Yokohama.

At the same time, Ramos drew on the modern techniques for organizing the masses, having been thoroughly exposed to them in his work for Quezon and the Nacionalista Party. Ramos was effectively able to enter into the worlds of the educated people, the ordinary people, such as peasants and laborers, and the spiritually inclined people, speaking on the issues of the day and preaching love, dignity, and sacrifice in terms that resonated with the masses. At the same time, he was acquainted with Western radical anarchist ideas since he claimed to have taken the name "Sakdal" from Zola's "J'Accuse" (I Accuse). He also had some knowledge of communism, and he personally interacted with Filipino communists, such as Evangelista and Capadocia.

When it was judged wise and opportune, Ramos changed his strategy. Initially, he made vicious attacks on those who supported the transitional Commonwealth, considering them to be traitors. But when Ramos realized that there was not going to be any military assistance from Japan and that the U.S. was going to stay in the Philippines until the end of the Commonwealth, he changed his strategy. Moreover, Ramos considered the Japanese invasion imminent and warned his followers. He wanted to work for unity among the Filipinos by stressing the importance of developing a national spirit and culture, which in turn would sustain independence. At the same time, Ramos recognized the power and danger of the Japanese military. Based on his observations of what was taking place in China, Ramos believed that the survival of the Philippines largely depended on Japan. It was not only Ramos who felt the need to forge strong ties with Japan and emulate some of the aspects of Japanese culture that had made Japan powerful. Many Filipino intellectuals and politicians of his time, including Quezon, felt the same way and vigorously worked toward that end.[67]

Ramos was not hesitant to compromise with the people in power for the good of his organization or himself. In this regard, he turned out to be no less shrewd and seasoned politician than Quezon. His looking to Japan for armed assistance by following the Katipunan tradition could be criticized as being naïve and anachronistic since the conditions of the 1890s were different from those of the 1930s. He erred in assuming that the ultranationalists who supported him were powerful enough to influence the Japanese government and the military. His frustrated hopes of support from Japan can be equated to the hopes of some Filipino communists who believed the U.S. would not grant independence and sought Russia's assistance.[68]

## Sakdalism: Principles and Philosophy

Ramos and the other leaders gradually formulated the Sakdalista guiding principles to answer the needs of the members, who came from different social and educational backgrounds but mainly from the rural areas of central and southern Luzon. Their thoughts were expressed through language and imagery drawn from the Bible, the writings of Rizal and Katipunan revolutionaries, and the experiences in the 1896

Revolution and the Philippine-American War that followed. This assertion is based on the reading of their organs: *Sakdal, The Filipino Freedom, Ganap, Hirang*, and other party publications, such as *Pamahayag* and *Mga Patak*, as well as interviews of the participants of the May 1935 and October 1936 uprisings and court records of the trials.

## The Bible: The Old and New Testaments

In his poems and other literary works, Ramos portrayed Philippine society in the most critical way, as discussed above. He often compared these conditions with those in the Roman-occupied Israel of biblical times. Likewise, members likened Ramos to Christ and government officials to the Pharisees, Caiaphas, Pontius Pilate, or King Herod, all of whom were in one way or the other responsible for nailing Christ to the cross. Sometimes, Filipino government officials, cast as betrayers of the cause of independence, were branded "Judas Iskariote," the betrayer of Jesus. An IFI member wrote asking *Sakdal* readers to consider who the enemies of Christ were and who his genuine companions were.[69]

Frequent quotations from Exodus were printed in the *Sakdal*. For instance, when the leaders wanted to encourage their followers, they quoted Moses' promise to the children of Israel that liberation was near at hand. When Ramos wanted to stress that the people themselves were responsible for their fate, he described it this way: God had offered the people of Moses' time the strength needed to climb to victory but they had thrown that power away. Instead, they had sold their rights by allowing themselves to be enslaved; therefore, the people themselves had created that sorry situation. The Sakdalistas were often reminded of Christ as a person who criticized the misgovernment and imperialism of old Judea, and he was now revered as the Son of God and as one who died for his principles yet became the victorious enemy of the oppressors. In order to attain the desired freedom at the soonest possible time, God's assistance was often invoked in tandem with human effort.[70] With reference to Christ, all those who loved their country had to travel the thorny path to Golgotha. Sacrifice was inevitable since only by going through hardship could they achieve their goal. This message was stressed again and again in the pages of the *Sakdal*.

Tomas Patenia, an active Sakdalista member, contributed many articles to the paper. According to him, Ramos was simply following orders from God (Dios). Whoever was not a Sakdalista was God's enemy, as the foundation of the Sakdalista Party was love and God is love. Patenia encouraged the people to be unyielding because they were serving God by protesting. If they remained faithful, the independence of the country would surely come soon.[71] Patenia interpreted Ramos's independent mission to the U.S. as the realization of God's order, just as Moses had obeyed God. He asserted that the time would come when God would punish those who were thirsty for the blood of poor citizens and were oppressing the people.[72]

To Patenia and other Sakdalistas who shared his views, good and bad were obvious and clear. The good were the poor and the oppressed, and the bad were the rich betrayers of independence. In the process of seeking independence and justice, the good would be persecuted and experience hardship and suffering but they would triumph in the end because God would always be with them. Those who were faithful would be given the crown of life after death. The Sakdalistas often cited Christ's teachings on preoccupation with material wealth, which made one a slave to it, and said that the poor would ultimately be the fortunate ones because they would be saved.[73]

The Sakdalista membership abhorred the rich, especially the politically connected rich. They believed the wealthy enriched themselves while pretending to be in favor of immediate independence. Most of the rich were portrayed as heartless and selfish. In addition to citing Christian teachings on abhorrence of material wealth, Sakdalistas often quoted the traditional poems of Baltazar (Balagtas), who had criticized the greedy rich by saying, "Ang laki sa layaw karaniwa'y hubad sa bait at muni't sa hatol ay salat" (Those who grow up amidst the revelries of wealth are devoid of judgment and kindness and lacking in counsel).[74] It is in this context that the appeal of Ramos's unyielding accusations of Quezon and other Nacionalista politicians as "maka-tian" (stomach-first) should be understood. These messages must have been especially appealing to the poor peasants and laborers who had been materially deprived.

The Sakdalista Party's emblem, which is taken from the Christian symbols of devotion, the Sacred Heart of Jesus, and the Guiding Star, most succinctly illustrates members' spiritual aspirations.

## The Sacrifices of the 1896 Heroes and Rizal's Writings

In addition to likening themselves to the disciples of Jesus, some Sakdalistas drew inspiration from the anti-Spanish, anti-American war heroes. On the occasion of Andres Bonifacio's birthday celebration in 1931, Ramos rhetorically asked why the government would not allow anyone to speak about the revolution since it had recognized and praised Bonifacio's leadership. His answer was that present-day Filipinos, leaders and citizens alike, were cowards who lacked the courage to rise up in arms against their oppressors and the foreign rulers, as Andres Bonifacio had done.[75]

Articles on the revolutionary heroes' sacrifices appeared in practically every issue of the *Sakdal* weekly. In the eulogy of the 1896 heroes, sacrifice was associated with material deprivation, as all the heroes had died poor while the betrayers of the revolution led luxurious lives. Rizal chose to suffer rather than surrender his principles and lead a comfortable life.[76]

From the perspective of the Sakdalistas, nothing had changed since the times of the Spanish period; Spain and the friars of yesterday had been replaced by today's America and Filipino politicians. That was the reason why the heroes would never die in the Sakdalistas' memory. Their heroes' endurance of hardship as well as their bravery inspired today's lovers of freedom to fight for justice and for their country. When perseverance and sacrifice were asked of the Sakdalistas, the paper pleaded, "Our heroes underwent tremendous sufferings. When compared with theirs, our sacrifices are so insignificant."[77]

Among the 1896 heroes, Ramos and his followers held Jose Rizal in the highest regard, calling him "the Christ of the Philippines," or "Sugo ng Dios" (a messenger of God), equating his sacrifice with that of Christ. The *Sakdal* often reminded its readers that Rizal had not only suffered like Christ but had identified with the poor, throwing away everything for the sake of his country, thereby transcending class differences. Moved by his death, they were ready to embrace misfortune and continue the fight against the government.[78]

In addition to being inspired by the sacrifices of Rizal and the other heroes, the Sakdalistas tried to derive guiding lessons from Rizal's writings, especially his novels: *Noli me tangere* (*Noli*) and *El Filibusterismo* (*El Fili*). As early as 1892, *Noli* was translated from Spanish into Tagalog by Patricio Mariano and Rizal's brother Paciano. And in 1912, English translations of the two novels were produced. The English language books on Rizal's life written by Austin Craig were published in 1909, 1913, and 1927. Rizal's correspondence, which amounted to six volumes, was published in the 1930s.[79] The Sakdalistas, therefore, had access to the Tagalog as well as English translations of the novels and books on Rizal. Furthermore, since excerpts of Rizal's essays and letters were published in IFI's novenario, the IFI members in the Sakdalista movement were well versed in Rizal's writings, as discussed earlier. Every Sakdalista was encouraged to read, learn, and understand the messages of the novels so they could carry on the God-given task of obtaining complete independence.[80] These two novels were like a Bible to the Sakdalistas.

Ramos often relied on Rizal's work to make his points. Maria Clara's words in *Noli* were quoted to show compassion for the poor. The importance of a free mind and free thinking was stressed by quoting Kabesa Tales in *El Fili*: "There would be no master if there were no one to make masters; there would be no slaves if nobody were forced to be a slave." Therefore, Ramos concluded that a free mind is the key to ending enslavement.[81]

Rizal's letters and essays were also quoted to support the Sakdalistas' belief that people must be willing to die fighting for their beliefs. For instance, in a letter to his parents, Rizal said that while he was sorry to have brought them misfortune, he did not regret what he had done and would repeat the same actions if necessary in the future because he felt this was his duty.[82]

As stated earlier, the Sakdalistas' aversion to the rich and powerful was based on Christ's life and teachings. This idea must have been further reinforced by passages in Rizal's novels, such as the following: "The rich do not think of anything but to augment their riches; they are blinded by pride and the pomp of circumstance."[83]

Some Sakdalistas considered Rizal a pacifist, emphasizing the following words from *El Fili*: "Freedom should be won by deserving it, not by the blade of the sword." This idea was expressed through the voice of Father Florentino at the end of the novel.[84] However, a majority of Sakdalistas viewed Rizal as an advocate and supporter of armed revolution. A *Sakdal* editorial argued that the Sakdalista movement disagreed with those scholars and historians, such as Wenceslao Retana, Austin Craig, and Jose P. Santos, who contended that Rizal was against Bonifacio's revolution. In fact, the Sakdalistas believed it was Rizal who had sown the seeds of the revolution. The *Sakdal* editorial concluded that Rizal had been the brain while Bonifacio was the arm and bolo of the struggle.[85]

Certain passages and characters in Rizal's novel *El Fili* must have reinforced Ramos's position on the use of foreign language for everyday life. The hero Ibarra, disguised as Simoun, tells the Filipino student Basilio that Spanish would never be the common language in the country because there were no words in that language to express the ideas and sentiment of the Filipinos, and as long as a people conserved their language, they could preserve their liberty.[86] As we saw, Ramos was a strong advocate of using Tagalog, because he believed that culture was the soul of the people, and as long as it was not subjugated by a foreign force, the people could remain liberated.

The Sakdalistas considered the deeds and utterances of Rizal and other heroes to be national treasures and their heritage; therefore, they were urged to transmit them to the coming generations. Grandmothers and mothers were encouraged to sing of the heroes' bravery while putting the children to sleep. They were to teach their heroes' words so that the love of their race and the respect for their fellowmen would be awakened. They considered Rizal their guiding light for action because he possessed purity, honor, bravery, patriotism, and the utmost heroism.[87] The Sakdalistas succinctly stated that Rizal's principles and beliefs were the same as theirs: "Today, what the Sakdalistas are doing is simply continuing his (Rizal's) principles," and "Sakdalism is the fruit of the seeds planted by Rizal. Just as Rizal's persecution, imprisonment, and eventual execution opened the eyes of his contemporaries, so the light of Sakdalism has opened the eyes of fellow Filipinos (today)...." Many Sakdalistas viewed Ramos as simply completing what Rizal had started, reminding the members that a person who died for justice would have eternal life.[88] To encourage the members to carry out their duty, Rizal's voice called out:

> I have not departed from this place. I am here. I have been back for a long time. And perhaps I heard the news, the song of the air, and your heartbeats. My voice is my appeal. Wake up, children of the unfortunate country, and help me fulfill my work.[89]

Ramos and his followers frequently promoted the ideals of love and virtue, the central messages of the movement. They also took to heart the mission of raising people's intelligence and dignity through moral guidance by emphasizing personal responsibility for one's destiny. Their emphasis on personal responsibility for one's destiny seems to have come from Rizal's novels as well: "Our ills we owe to ourselves; let us not cast the blame on anyone...." As Rizal warned, power in the hands of ignorant men without moral education was like a weapon in the hands of a madman.[90] This explains why Ramos and other leaders stressed the importance of leading a moral and honorable life and even went so far as to create several "tuntunin" (rules) for the Sakdalistas to abide by.

## Katipunan Teachings and the Sakdalista "Rules"

Ramos's appropriation of the Katipuneros' writings (such as Jacinto's *Pahayag*) and experience (such as Bonifacio's entering the cave) is apparent. How then were the teachings and rules of the Katipunan rewritten to suit the Sakdalistas' time? Sakdalistas were expected to undergo moral purification in order to carry on the God-given sacred mission with strength and courage, making themselves worthy citizens of the future independent country. Toward this end, a list of "Ang Tuntunin ng Umiibig sa Simulain ng 'Sakdal'" (Rules for Those who Love the "Sakdal" Principles) was created. Written in a simple, easy-to-follow style, the rules can be summarized as follows:

1. Love your country above political parties, friends, and associations. Your country encompasses all that is good and great. Therefore, to love your country is to love the Creator and Reason (Bathala at Katwiran).
2. Give priority to loving your countrymen over foreigners.
3. Remember that whatever happens to you, you should sympathize only with your countrymen, not with foreigners.
4. Treat your poor fellowmen with virtue and greatness; never become rich through ill methods.
5. Never oppress others. Act with reason, because thereby one is always brave. Do not be afraid of being hit or lied to.
6, Only follow what your God (Dios) says. What is whispered into your spirit is the great law of reason, goodness, respect, and love for your fellowmen and their rights.
7. Always love and follow the lessons of your heroes (of the 1896 Revolution) because they are the first messengers of God on Earth.
8. Love all fellowmen, respect the old, and love your spouse (*asawa*) and children.
9. Before you follow foreigners, follow those of your own race. Before you serve the rich, first serve the poor; before you love the powerful, love your fellowmen. Action is more important than words.
10. To perform your duty is a holy thing. The blessings of independence are attained by those who know how to liberate themselves. The leaders of a country have a duty to God and to all men to do good to those they lead and to save them from misfortune.[91]

This list of commands bears a striking similarity to the *Decalogue* formulated by the Katipunan members.[92]

Another moral guide of the Sakdalistas was called "Ang Limang Utos ni Bathala" (Five Orders of God). The five orders include:

1. Respect your father and mother, who gave you birth into this land that God has created.
2. Do not kill. (Here, killing meant not only physical killing but also oppression of the helpless and the poor.)
3. Do not have intercourse with anyone who is not your spouse. (Here vulgar movies and objectionable places, such as cabarets, were cited as additional examples of immorality.)
4. Do not steal. (The guide described how the Roman Catholic Church had been stealing from the people.)
5. Do not appropriate things from the house of your fellowman.[93]

Sometimes, aphorisms taken from "Kartilya ng Katipunan" (Teachings of the Katipunan) and Filipino proverbs were printed in the *Sakdal* to remind members how to carry out the struggle: "A hundred kilograms of speech are lighter than one gram of action"; "Life which is not consecrated to a lofty and sacred cause is like a tree without a shadow, if not a poisonous weed"; "To a man who has a sense of shame, his words are like a vow"; "Work is more noble when done quietly"; "Thoughtless steps taken are easily snatched away"; and "There is no greater holiness than to die for a good reason."

Both groups of followers, the Katipuneros and the Sakdalistas, equated love for one's country with the love for God and they believed that they were performing a holy duty in bringing independence to the country. They were taught to be virtuous, compassionate moral exemplars, sometimes drawing inspiration from ancient wisdom.[94]

Despite the many parallels in the rules of the two groups, Sakdalista and Katipunan, there were also differences. The Sakdalista rules seem to have a strong anti-foreign element that was missing from the Katipunan teachings. This may have been an expression of the heightened racial tensions of the early 1930s. The Sakdalistas believed that one of the things that had led the upper classes astray, in addition to their love of money and lack of compassion for fellow Filipinos, was their excessive attachment to foreign ways, goods, and markets; mostly American. This was an indictment against those Filipino elites who had assimilated into the colonizer's mentality. The elites, according to the Sakdalistas, considered themselves culturally superior to their own people and looked down upon Filipino indigenous cultural values.

When the Katipunan writings were created, on the eve of the 1896 Revolution, their circulation was quite limited.[95] However, they had been popularized by IFI adherents in their novenario and in the Sakdalista movement even some thirty years after they were written and had been taken to heart among the masses of central and southern Luzon. The writers of the Katipunan literature, Bonifacio and Jacinto, were influenced by Rizal's writings. Ramos and other leaders used Katipunan-style teachings in order to disseminate the spirit of the revolution, violent or nonviolent, to the people who came from different social backgrounds.[96]

There is no other document that so succinctly expresses Sakdalista philosophy than its manifesto "Ano Ang Sakdalismo?" (What is Sakdalism?) In the aftermath of the May Uprising, the *Sakdal* published a special thirty-four-page supplemental issue. Most of the content was a repetition of articles that had been published in previous *Sakdal* issues. This special supplement was perhaps intended to explain what had led to the uprising and to clarify the Sakdalista Party's stand. One long article summarized the Sakdalista principles and ideology in three compact slogans: "The Philippines is for the Filipinos Only" (*Ang Filipinas ay para sa mga Filipino Lamang*); "All Filipinos Should be Equal in the Blissful Enjoyment of Livelihood, Equal as Individuals and Equal in Rights" (*Ang Lahat na Filipino ay Maging Pantay-pantay sa Ginhawa ng Kabuhayan, sa Pagkatao at sa Karapatan*); and "Government Personnel Should Sacrifice to Alleviate the Conditions of the People" (*Ang mga Taong Pamahalaan ay Dapat Magpakahirap upang Guminhawa ang Bayan*).[97] In connection with the last slogan, the hardships of the leader versus the relief of the people were elaborated on: if provincial leaders worked hard, the welfare of the province's residents would improve. This point was supported with a quote from a Bible verse: a person cannot serve two masters, the Devil and the Angel. In the same way, it was impossible for a politician to love both wealth and independence.[98]

The article declared that all three slogans were based on Jose Rizal's teachings and deeds. It quoted Rizal's poem Last Farewell: "If you need color with which to stain the dawn, let spill my blood, and scatter it in the good hour...." The article reiterated that Rizal was the seed of Sakdalism and that he was a true Sakdalista in deed.[99] They believed spreading Sakdalism was a way of continuing the aspirations of Rizal and they were willing to suffer the ultimate sacrifice. As seen in the Sakdalista Party manifesto published in 1933, carrying on Rizal's and other 1896 heroes' teachings and deeds was the only path that would lead to real freedom.[100]

A large number of Sakdalistas came from the economically deprived class and because of this, they perceived themselves to be noble and pure of heart, and therefore knew how to be honorable. The Sakdalista members were always reminded of cultivating clean and pure hearts that knew how to sacrifice, for the struggle depended on the purity of the fighters.[101] These moral principles appeared to hit a responsive chord among the people of central and southern Luzon, who felt they were being invited to join an organization in which an individual's worth depended on honorable conduct, not on material wealth or social standing. The country's future was not to be entrusted to the elites who, in their minds, had misled them for the past three decades. As expressed by one Sakdalista, love of country had been monopolized by those "who had high noses, fair-complexioned faces (were from) families of Kings (the rich), and (were) children of priests" (*tangos ng ilong, puti ng mukha, angkan hari, anak ng pari*). It should no longer be this way. Even a person like himself (a simple peasant), who was uncultured and had grown up in the fields (*taga-bundok at laki sa parang*), had the capacity to love his country, and it was the Sakdalista movement that had taught him how to do so.[102] The Sakdalista campaign for independence made the movement's members "tunay na anak ng bayan" (genuine children of the country) in the tradition of the glorious and honorable 1896 Revolution.

The feeling of self-worth, dignity, and sacrifice rooted in the past two wars inspired them to take up arms to establish a republic, even in the mid-1930s. Honor and dignity were the only things the poor could afford to possess, and these qualities were treasured and tightly guarded. The words "honor and dignity" appear in numerous pages of the party organs, manifestos, and memorials sent to the U.S. officials. Ramos and the radical wing of the Sakdalista movement, who were in the majority, thought that their honor must be protected with the ultimate sacrifice, the shedding of blood. It also meant repaying gratitude to Rizal and other 1896 heroes. Their May Uprising of 1935 and the October Uprising of 1936 were the times to discharge their duties, expressing a devotion to the heritage of the independence struggle. As one of the participants of the May Uprising told acting Gov. Gen. Hayden, he was willing to suffer the consequences of his actions as long as the next generation could enjoy the fruits of independence.[103] The leaders of the attempted October Uprising of 1936 believed that the series of small actions would culminate in major change, just as small raindrops can eventually make a dent in the rock. Racial dignity and the notion of freedom played a key role in keeping their struggle alive throughout the American colonial period and into the Japanese Occupation. These sentiments motivated people of means and high education to transcend elite-oriented class interests to join this mass movement. On the part of the poor, eliminating poverty was one of the ways to recover their dignity.

These people were the ones who "collaborated" with the Japanese Occupation forces. Ramos and the Sakdalista movement leaders tried their best to prepare their followers for the possible Japanese invasion and subsequent occupation. They were ready to negotiate with the Japanese in order to establish independence. Among the rank-and-file members, the legend of Japanese assistance in pursuing their cause was still very much alive.

**Sakdalista Gatherings** (ca 1934)
*Source: Jeremias Adia*

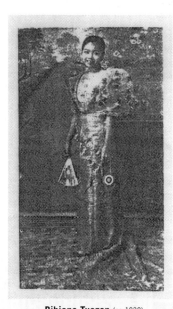

**DIRECTORIO GENERAL DEL PARTIDO "GANAP" DE FILIPINAS**
LADAW (Tarjeta de Identificación)

CERTIFICAMOS que *Felisa Anda* cuyo retrato y
Pinatitibayan namin na si .................................................. na ang larawan
firma aparecen aqui es un Correligionario adicto al Comité No. *2* del Bar-
at lagda ay kalakip dito ay Kapanalig na kasapi sa Lup. Blg. *2* ng Na-
rio *1. Por ol*, Municipio *Atimon* Prov. *Tayabas*,
yong ........., Bayang ........................., Lal. ........................,
de *32* edad, con familia compuesta de *may asawa at 7 anak*
may ........ gulang, at angkang binubuo ng ...............................................
cuyo cargo actual es *Kasapi*
na ang tungkulin ngayon ay ....................... at ipinamamanhik
todos le rindan cooperación y respeto.
namin sa lahat na pagkalooban ng tulong at pamim..... **OCT 19 1939**

Retrato        2326 Juan Luna, Manila, ...................., 19....

.............................        .............................
Presidente General        Tapdis (Jefe de Campaña)
JUAN REIS-MATEO        BENIGNO R. RAMOS

*Felisa Anda*
Firma del Afiliado—Lagda ng Kaanib

**Ladaw** (ca 1939)
*Source: Jeremias Adia*

**Bibiana Tuazon** (ca 1938)
*Source: Pamahayag at Patakaran ng Samahang Makabayan ng mga Babaing Pilipina*

## CHAPTER 8

# UNDER THE JAPANESE OCCUPATION, 1942–1945

W HEN THE FORMAL occupation by the Japanese military began on 2 January 1942, the majority of Ganapistas felt relieved, believing that they would no longer be harassed. At the same time, they felt a sense of awe and euphoria that the rumors they had been hearing for the past forty years had finally become a reality. These rumors foretold the outbreak of war between Japan and the U.S. and declared that the Philippines would obtain independence after that war. Furthermore, the rumors claimed that when the Filipinos would fight against the American occupation forces, Japan would assist them (Filipinos) by shipping arms and ammunitions. Some Ganapistas felt that the opportunity to establish independence had finally arrived. This could explain why they assisted the Japanese, at least at the beginning of the occupation.

### Japanese Assistance

The rumors of Japanese assistance began circulating in the 1890s, even before the 1896 Revolution. Earlier in 1892, Rizal's friend Blumentritt wrote to him about certain conditions needed for a successful revolution, one of which was to have a foreign power on their side.[1] Two years later in 1894, Japan started the Sino-Japanese War. Japan's subsequent military victory over China impressed Filipino freedom fighters so much that they looked toward Japan as the place to seek support or obtain arms and ammunition. During this time, many articles on Japan began appearing in *La Solidaridad*, an organ of the Propagandists, Filipino freedom fighters, in Spain.[2]

Blumentritt's advice and the Propagandists' attention to Japan must have influenced the revolutionaries at home because they took the possibility of Japanese assistance seriously. As early as mid-1895, the Cuerpo de Compromisarios—whose task was to collect funds to support the Propaganda Movement in Spain and distribute its written material in the Philippines—was discussing the possibility of purchasing arms and ammunitions from Japan. One of its members, Jose Ramos (later called Jose Ishikawa) went to Japan for that purpose.[3] In March 1896, the Katipunan distributed its first and only organ, *Kalayaan* (Freedom, dated 18 January). Although it was printed in Manila, the editor was listed as Marcelo H. del Pilar and the place of printing was listed as "Yokohama, Japan," so as to make it appear that del Pilar was in Japan actively engaged in anti-Spanish activities, presumably with the help of some Japanese supporters, if not the government.[4]

In May 1896, three months before the outbreak of the Revolution, the Japanese cruiser *Kongo* arrived in Manila Bay. The Katipunan leaders sent representatives to confer with the commander of the ship.[5] Two months later, in July, Andres Bonifacio allegedly approached a Japanese resident in Manila asking him to assist in establishing a trading company that exported goods to Japan. Revenue from sales would be used to purchase rifles from Japan.[6] In reality, the meeting of the Katipunan members with the Japanese commander was no more than a cordial social call, and Bonifacio's plan remained only a plan.[7] However, along with the *Kalayaan* appearing to be printed in Japan, these incidents were enough to cause rumor of an impending shipment of weapons from Japan and Japanese assistance to Katipunan's cause. This kind of rumor was being spread on every corner in Manila. How widespread it was can be gleaned by the fact that Japanese-owned bazaars were filled with Filipino customers who came to purchase goods even if the shop was far away, just to show respect and admiration for Japan.[8]

Another proof of how strongly people believed in the rumor lies in the testimonies of those who were investigated by Spanish authorities after the outbreak of the revolution. They included a host of people, ranging from the Guardia Civil Veterana to Katipunan members. All of their testimonies included accounts of Japanese assistance and the planned purchase of arms from Japan.[9]

These testimonies were not groundless since some Filipinos did go to Japan in an attempt to purchase arms. After the outbreak of the revolution, Gen. Emilio Aguinaldo sent some of his men—including Jose Alejandrino in 1896, and Mariano Ponce and Faustino Lichauco in 1898—to Japan to arrange a purchase of arms. In the course of negotiations with Japanese military and civilian personnel, an agreement was reached to ship arms and ammunitions and to provide some Japanese volunteers to assist Aguinaldo's revolutionary forces. In 1899, a shipload of ammunition as well as six Japanese volunteers left for the Philippines on board the *Nunobiki-maru*. However, the ship was sunk by a typhoon off the coast of southern China before it reached its destination.[10] Another group of Japanese volunteers, who arrived ahead of the *Nunobiki-maru*, reached Tarlac in mid-June 1899 and were welcomed by Gen. Aguinaldo. However, they eventually left, mainly due to the language problem. Other Japanese were reported to have joined the Filipino "rebels" in Batangas and were arrested by the Americans.[11]

After American hostility toward the Filipino revolution became obvious, the Filipinos were drawn even closer to the Japanese. There were some Japanese military personnel who stayed in the Philippines for a length of time and forged close relationships with some of the Filipino revolutionaries, such as Emilio Aguinaldo and Teodoro Sandiko. For instance, Japanese officer Capt. Tokizawa passed information on American troop movements and military strategy to Aguinaldo through Sandiko.[12] On another occasion, Capt. Tokizawa gave an informal banquet in honor of Sandiko at the Japanese Consulate. All of the Japanese residents in Manila attended, which made Sandiko feel that the Japanese desire for Filipino independence was sincere. As late as 1898, Capt. Tokizawa offered to accompany anyone who was willing to go to Japan to purchase arms.[13]

Arms and ammunition had indeed been sent from Japan but they never reached their destination. It is also true that some Japanese military officials and civilians joined the revolutionary forces but their activities hardly bore fruit. The important point was not the end result but the fact that Japanese assistance had been rendered. Although exaggerated, news of these events spread rapidly and widely. The personal association of the

Filipino revolutionaries with Japanese officers must have been known and talked about by the people, who then became further convinced of Japanese assistance. The Filipinos who actually negotiated arms purchases in Japan, such as Jose Ishikawa and Mariano Ponce, returned to the Philippines in the early 1900s. They were the concrete proof of actual arms dealing in Japan.

The rumor of Japanese involvement in the struggle for independence was further reinforced by the Japanese victory over Russia in 1905. This victory led the Filipino people, especially those who wanted independence from the U.S., to believe that war between the U.S. and Japan would soon begin and as a result, Japan would assist the Philippines in establishing independence. In fact, in 1909, the information division of the constabulary received information that Ishikawa, Sandiko, and Trias were planning a revolution with arms sent from Japan, and Vicente Lucban, a general from the Philippine-American War, left for Japan to purchase arms.[14] Although these could have been simply rumors, American colonial authorities kept close watch on Ishikawa and Ponce until around 1910, suspecting that they might still try to purchase arms from Japan.[15] The authorities even believed that the leader of one politico-religious organization, Felipe Salvador, who prophesied that the war between Japan and the U.S. would soon begin, had returned from Japan to mount a propaganda campaign.[16]

The Katipunan's minutes further promoted the rumors of Japanese assistance. Some references to events in the minutes were not trustworthy and were assumed to be a fabrication made after the revolution.[17] Whatever the motivation of the fabricator(s) might have been, the Katipunan's minutes strongly supported the notion of impending Japanese assistance. The minutes suggest that as early as April 1893, an agreement had been concluded between Japan and the Katipunan specifying that Japan would aid them in their struggle for independence against Spain.[18] Further, in December 1894, the Katipunan members allegedly visited Apolinario Mabini to solicit his advice. He urged them to send representatives to Japan to purchase arms. Accordingly, in March of the following year, four delegates were said to have been sent to Japan to confer with the Japanese government as to the method of acquiring arms and other things necessary for the revolution. On their return in June 1895, the delegates reported that as soon as the Katipunan could send P10 million to the Japanese government, Japan would start shipping the weapons to them.[19] The minutes reported that in May 1896, the Japanese cruiser *Kongo* arrived in

Manila Bay and the meeting between the Katipunan representatives and the commander was held, as mentioned above. Furthermore, the minutes stated that at the end of the meeting, a written agreement was drawn that included the stipulation that the Katipunan would submit to the Japanese Consul in Manila the sum of P300,000 as a deposit for 100,000 rifles and 150 cannons and corresponding ammunition, which would be sent and unloaded on a day and place designated by the Katipunan.[20] This was, of course, a fabrication.

The publication of Pio Valenzuela's memoirs added credence to the rumor of Japanese assistance. Shortly before the outbreak of the revolution, Valenzuela visited Dapitan to consult with Jose Rizal regarding the Katipunan resolutions for carrying on the independence struggle. Rizal allegedly told him that when he was in Japan, a Japanese Cabinet minister made available three merchant ships to be used for transporting arms to the Philippines. Rizal tried to arrange for a loan from a rich Filipino merchant in Manila to pay for the shipment but was turned down.[21] The minutes of the Katipunan and Valenzuela's memoir, whether true or not, helped sustain the notion of Japanese assistance among those who sought independence.

In the meantime the Japanese victory over Russia created fear among the colonial officials of Japanese advancement to the Philippines. Gov. Gen. Cameron Forbes linked Filipino anti-American, pro-independence activities to Japanese agitation. Fearing the worst, he launched an anti-Japanese propaganda campaign in 1909. Forbes proposed sending some Filipino journalists to Japanese-occupied Taiwan and Korea to observe conditions there and then write about the oppressive aspects in the mass media. He also suggested training school teachers to inculcate distrust of Japan in the minds of the Filipino youth and inducing at least one political party to include in its platform opposition to aggression by any foreign power, strongly insinuating Japan. His other suggestions included having colonial government control of one newspaper that would publish anti-Japanese articles and familiarizing the constabulary and the Philippine Scouts with Japanese propaganda techniques. By 1920, this propaganda seemed to have borne fruit, and Japan was portrayed as hateful, greedy, tyrannical, cruel, and fearful.[22]

Despite American propaganda, rumors of Japanese assistance continued to circulate clear into the 1930s. Even when Ricarte was in Hong Kong, people were saying that if war should break out between Japan and the U.S., Ricarte would come back to defend the Filipinos. This rumor became more convincing after Ricarte sought exile in Japan in 1915.[23] In 1934, the rumor reemerged when Ramos, acting in line with Katipunan tradition, went to Japan, thus giving the rumor further authenticity. In the eyes of the Sakdalistas, Japanese assistance was very real. Indeed, the rumors have such power to make people take action, sometimes to the extent of dedicating their own lives.

The May Uprising of 1935 erupted, partly due to the strong belief that arms and ammunition would be sent from Japan. Even after its failure, persistent rumors of uprising were heard. These rumors were manifestations of the Sakdalistas' strength, which in turn increased solidarity among them and boosted their morale. For the Sakdalista movement, these rumors played a powerful political function. Law enforcers also believed these rumors and rushed to various locations in anticipation of violence. The authorities were all at the mercy of rumors. As late as December 1939, a constabulary officer who believed in the rumor of Japanese assistance testified in the trial that Ramos planned to escape to Japan aboard a Japanese ship. Therefore, Ramos's bail was denied despite the vehement denial by the Japanese captain of the ship.[24]

Quezon's assessment of the effectiveness of rumor was correct. As long as Ramos stayed in Japan, the rumors would continue and the Sakdalistas' unity and fighting spirit would not fade away; in fact, it would continue to challenge the authorities. Finally, in 1938, in order to crush both the rumors and the Sakdalista movement, Quezon decided to have Ramos brought back to the Philippines, as we saw earlier. However, even after Ramos's return to the Philippines, the rumors did not completely die down.[25]

On 19 December 1941, Ricarte was flown to Aparri in Northern Luzon and set foot in his homeland after twenty-six years of exile in Japan.[26] The rumor that the people, including the Ganapistas, kept hearing about the general's return to the Philippines with the Japanese military had finally materialized. The Ganapistas felt further reassured of Japanese assistance when they heard what Gen. Masaharu Honma, the commanding officer of the Fourteenth Army of the invading Japanese force, had said: "The Philippines is for the Filipinos and Asia for the Asians."[27]

In the meantime, the Japanese military force freed Ramos, Tiongco, and other Ganap leaders from prison. The USAFFE surrendered soon after MacArthur and Quezon had left the Philippines. The Ganapistas were elated, thinking that soon the old Nacionalista-dominated political system would be replaced by a new one, possibly under the leadership of the Ganap Party, and an independent republic would soon be established. Then the land would be returned to those who lost it, the cedula tax and land rent would be lowered, industry would be developed, the indigenous Philippine culture would flourish, and the Filipinos' honor and dignity would be restored. In order to bring about these conditions, the Ganapistas were prepared to cooperate wholeheartedly with the Japanese military.

## Collaboration with Japanese Military

The Propaganda Corps of the Japanese Imperial Army landed in Lingayen at the end of December 1941. When they passed through the town of Gapan, Nueva Ecija, on the way to Manila, a woman Ganapista named Bibiana Tuazon joined the corps. She was the secretary of the Samahang Makabayan. Tuazon thought it was a good opportunity to proclaim that the time had come to achieve the much-awaited independence with Japanese assistance. The Japanese Army's Propaganda Corps emphasized that Japan was not the enemy and would recognize Philippine independence in due time; defeating the Anglo-U.S. powers was necessary in order to obtain real independence; and Filipino women should shed frivolous U.S. influences and become "real" Asian women with lofty morals and virtues. Tuazon wholeheartedly agreed with this and gladly joined the pacification campaign.[28]

Upon reaching Manila, the Propaganda Corps immediately dispatched goodwill missions to the provinces to obtain the people's cooperation. Initially, the provinces of Laguna, Tayabas, and Bicol were chosen because both Laguna and Tayabas produced foodstuff, such as rice and vegetables, and Bicol had rich copper and other mineral mines necessary for the war effort. Gen. Artemio Ricarte, who was considered to have high propaganda value by the Japanese Military, and rightly so, was invited to be the leading member of the Corps; however, he declined this post because, upon the request of the Japanese military, he had to visit other places that needed urgent attention. He tirelessly visited the towns in Luzon as well as Panay Island to give speeches, urging residents to cooperate with the new occupation forces. In his place, he sent his eldest granddaughter Minviluz Dominguez who spoke some Japanese, having lived in Japan for about ten years. According to Captain Hitomi, the head of the Propaganda Corps, he chose Ricarte over Aguinaldo for his propaganda value. Indeed, the choice of Ricarte and his granddaughter was effective. When Dominguez was speaking on the stage during their tour in Bicol, an old man in the audience, perhaps a cook since he was wearing a white apron, suddenly burst into tears. He said he had fought against the Americans under Gen. Ricarte and was glad to know he was still alive.[29] Perhaps similar scenes unfolded in other areas where the Propaganda Corps and Ricarte had visited.

Another Sakdalista, now a Ganapista who volunteered to work for the Propaganda Corps, was Fruto R. Santos, an aged 1896 Revolutionary veteran and one of the leaders of the planned October uprising in Manila in 1936. Willingness of Tuazon and Santos to cooperate with the Japanese military was based solely on their own volition since Ramos was still in prison at that time. The members of the Samahan ng Tatlong Persona also assisted the Japanese military's propaganda effort. Shortly before the Japanese invasion, Agapito Illustrisimo, founder of the Samahan, insinuated Japan's eventual victory by saying: "The sun of victory will rise in the East." They held a parade with dancing and sang the praises of the Japanese Army in the towns in Laguna and Tayabas. Eventually, anti-Japanese Marking's guerrillas took Illustrisimo and executed him as a Japanese collaborator.[30] Illustrisimo must have been one of those who believed the legend of Japanese assistance.

Wherever they went, the Japanese troops met Filipinos who were willing to assist them in procuring food and working as laborers for little compensation. The Japanese soldiers came to know later that many of these Filipinos were mainly the Ganapistas. To cope with the new situation and further assist the Japanese military, some of them began organizing themselves. One of the organizations was called Bagong Pagkakaisa (the New Unity or BP).[31]

## The Bagong Pagkakaisa

Formed in mid-January 1942, BP was mainly composed of Ricarte followers, 1896 Revolution veterans, and old Sakdalista Party as well as Ganap Party members. The others included some IFI adherents, middle-class citizens and professionals, and those who adhered to "Oriental principles and ideals." BP membership did not exceed a hundred. The board members included Leon Villafuerte, who was an aged veteran of the 1896 Revolution and the Philippine-American War. He was with Macario Sakay's revolutionary army during the latter war, as mentioned earlier.

Others included Alfonso Mendoza of the Radical Party; Paul Verzosa, "Japanophile" scholar; and Joaquin Galang, bishop of the IFI. The purpose of BP was "to defend and perpetuate the newly acquired freedom by driving away Anglo-Saxon imperialism." The BP's initial chief concern was to restore peace and order; therefore, one of its first activities was to make sure that basic necessities, such as rice, sugar, matches, and cigarettes, were sold and distributed fairly by government agencies.[32]

When the Japanese military faced the difficulty of bringing the USAFFE to surrender, the BP sent a letter to the Japanese military commander at the end of March, offering its members for military service. Toward the end of April, the organization passed a resolution stating its readiness to call up 1,000 informants and 50,000 soldiers for the Japanese military effort.[33] However, the Japanese military authorities ignored this offer. When the Philippine Executive Commission was established by the Japanese military's demand at the end of January, its members were all prewar Commonwealth government officials, headed by none other than Quezon's executive secretary, Jorge Vargas.

The BP members were greatly disappointed that Quezon was still in power even after the start of the Japanese Occupation, and even after he and MacArthur had left the Philippines. On 8 May, immediately after the fall of Corregidor, the BP passed a resolution severely criticizing the Executive Commission, stating that such a structure was similar to the prewar Commonwealth government and that it was rife with corruption and abuse of power.[34]

The BP strongly advocated for the dissolution of the Executive Commission and proposed the establishment of a dictatorial government headed by Gen. Ricarte. The BP members claimed that he would be the best person in that position because he led a clean and honorable life, was sincere, had suffered great hardships, and had sacrificed personal comfort for the sake of his mother country.[35] They considered the Japanese Occupation their only opportunity to realize their aspirations of obtaining independence under Japan and establishing their own political power.

However, the Japanese military authorities continued to ignore the BP's offer of all-out cooperation. This was because they were acting under the military guideline which clearly stated that in implementing military administration in occupied areas, the existing governing structure should be utilized as much as possible and with due respect. This agenda precluded the installation of Gen. Ricarte and his followers in any important government office. The military originally thought of using Ricarte to persuade Quezon to cooperate with Japan. When Quezon moved to Corregidor, Ricarte was treated as bargaining chip in the event Vargas and the others refused to cooperate. Otherwise, Ricarte was to be used solely for propaganda purposes, which was the real reason he had been brought back to the Philippines.[36] This Japanese military policy is another piece of concrete evidence that the Japanese military had no connection with the Ganap Party members in preparing for the invasion, contrary to the widespread rumors circulating just before the occupation.

In view of this situation, some BP members began to think that they could function better if they cooperated with the Executive Commission. Eventually, it was split into pro- and anti-cooperation factions and the "Antis" were expelled from the organization. The members who remained continued the BP's activities, mostly as propagandists accompanying Gen. Ricarte who urged cooperation with Japan. Their activities dwindled, and in January 1943, they were ordered by the Kenpeitai (military police) to dissolve the organization. This was because they were alleged to have been enriching themselves by selling safe-conduct passes signed by Gen. Ricarte, a charge not totally without basis.[37] These Ricarte followers would surface again in November 1944 as an armed force called Peace Army, as we shall see later.

## The Ganap Party

A day before the Japanese military entered Manila on 1 January 1942, Ramos and fifteen other Ganap members, including Celerino Tiongco, were brought to Little Baguio on Bataan Peninsula by the Commonwealth government. After the Japanese arrival, they were moved from one place to another within Bataan for fear on the part of the government that they might offer full cooperation to the Japanese. At the end of April, they, who were in Mariveles, were finally released by the Japanese military. Ramos made a courtesy call on the Japanese military commander to thank him and pledged to call upon his followers in the provinces to advocate cooperation with the Japanese military.[38]

Toward the end of December and before the Japanese landing, Ramos allegedly wrote to Pres. Quezon in the midst of Japanese air attacks. Ramos expressed his loyalty and offered his services to the U.S. and the Philippines governments, stressing the importance of unity of a people faced with war. He further said that no sane people could tolerate this hideous murder of civilians by the Japanese blind bombing and their condemnable goal to conquer the Philippines by force. Ramos allegedly claimed that he had severed all connections with the Ganap Party, but he stressed that the Ganapistas were patriotic people and they would side with the government. However, his offer was ignored.[39] Upon returning from Japan, Ramos showed a conciliatory attitude toward Quezon and even supported some Nacionalista candidates in the elections. During the election campaigns in 1938, 1940, and 1941, the Ganap Party candidates reiterated that they would support the government, especially Quezon's social justice program. Even after Ramos was imprisoned, the party continued to support the government policy to strengthen unity in view of imminent Japanese invasion. The party's decision seems to have been sincere; however, Ramos and the Ganapistas' efforts were not recognized by the government or the people in general. Instead, they were looked upon with suspicion and imprisoned by Quezon. These incidents were cause enough for Ramos and his followers to harbor personal resentment toward Quezon. If Ramos had not been imprisoned in the first place or had been released by Quezon, he could have acted as a go-between for Quezon and the Japanese military. However, it was the Japanese Army who had freed them from prison and, therefore, Ramos felt obliged to cooperate. Besides, while he was in Japan, he had been treated with respect by the ultranationalists, who considered him a struggling Asian nationalist. There was no denying that he had his political ambitions and tried to seize this opportunity for his own and his followers' benefit and to achieve the Ganapistas' final goal of independence for the country. They believed they could do so under the Japanese just as the BP had wished. Ramos's decision to cooperate with the Japanese Army was similar to that of Subhas Chandra Bose, who created the Indian National Army to fight against the British for India's freedom or Sukarno of Indonesia's struggle to expel the Dutch influence or the Burmese nationalists who had allowed themselves to be trained by the Japanese military to fight against the British. They were all aware of the brutal side of the Japanese military, but for now they wanted to "cooperate" with them. As Ramos once said, he would take independence even if it were offered by the devil.[40]

The Ganap Party immediately issued new identification cards showing the carrier's affiliation to the party.[41] Upon receiving Ramos's order to cooperate with the Japanese military, the Ganapistas worked for the Japanese forces all the more willingly. Their activities included information gathering, especially regarding anti-Japanese activities, and accompanying the Japanese military's anti-guerrilla campaigns.[42] In these instances, they were allowed to carry weapons to defend themselves from guerrilla attacks. However, some of them began using these weapons for personal purposes, such as settling prewar scores and grudges, which included the humiliation and harassment they had suffered for being Ganapistas. What made the situation worse was that after the Japanese takeover, the Ganap Party's rank and file suddenly swelled with opportunists, scoundrels, and criminals who engaged in extortion and blackmail activities. Both the prewar and new Ganapistas took advantage of their recently gained positions, which came with special responsibilities and privileges bestowed by the new power. Their actions antagonized the general citizenry and stained the party's name. [43]

Meanwhile, the guerrillas retaliated against the Ganapistas by kidnapping and killing them and their families, and the number of victims reached more than a thousand at one point. Clashes between the two camps became fierce, and this vicious cycle went on until the Japanese decided to curtail the Ganapistas' power by confiscating the weapons they had given them.[44]

In December 1942, at the end of the first year of the Japanese Occupation, all political parties were dissolved in order to mobilize the Filipinos to support Japan's war effort. Instead, the Kapisanan sa Paglilingkod sa Bagong Pilipinas, KALIBAPI (Association for Service of the New Philippines), was formed. Modeled after the organization at home, its alleged purpose was to "foster closer harmony and unanimity among all Filipinos who are devoting themselves to the reconstruction of the country." However, one of the hidden agendas behind this move was to undermine the Ganap Party's power.[45]

Benigno Ramos was appointed to head the Propaganda Office of the KALIBAPI.[46] In his capacity as propaganda officer, he wrote a Kalibapi march, entitled "Dai-Atiw ng Kalibapi." Ramos explained that the word "atiw" came from the Muslims of the south and meant "war song." By affixing "Dai" it became "official," hence "Official Kalibapi March." This march praised the Japanese as patrons of Philippine progress and prosperity. Ramos also produced an eighteen-page booklet, entitled *Syllabic Wealth of the Tagalog Dialect*. In it, Ramos demonstrated how the Tagalog language had been lost and corrupted by the Spanish colonization. He advocated using words they had inherited and to creating a new vocabulary to enrich the Tagalog language, instead of incorporating Spanish or English into it. He suggested that the new words should be derived from native words of other provinces and even the terminology of the cultural minorities of Igorot, Mangyan, and Tiruray. Ramos emphasized that losing one's own language was similar to losing self-respect.[47]

Ramos was not content with merely being the propaganda officer of the KALIBAPI. He felt disappointed that he had not been accorded a more important position despite the fact he and his followers had been whole-heartedly cooperating with the Japanese, sometimes at the risk of their lives.

## *Yoin, or Civilian Workers*

After the fall of Bataan and Corregidor in May 1942, the Japanese needed to regain order and stability to carry out their occupation policy. Destroyed roads and bridges had to be repaired so that basic necessities could be shipped from the provinces. Military installations, airfields, and harbors had to be rebuilt and reconstructed to strengthen military activities. In the beginning, labor was abundant since many people were looking for employment after the collapse of the export-oriented agriculture economy and the release of close to seventy thousand USAFFE prisoners of war. However, from the end of 1943 to the beginning of 1944, the number of applicants began to dwindle, making recruitment of labor rather difficult. This phenomenon could be attributed to the growing dissatisfaction among the people under the Japanese Occupation, the poor and dangerous working conditions, and the effective guerrilla propaganda/threats to stop working for the Japanese.[48] Therefore, the Labor Recruitment Agency was set up in April 1944 and its officers had to travel around the provinces to recruit labor with the help of the local government officials. Even before the establishment of this agency, Japanese soldiers had been going around towns and villages to procure necessary labor through mayors and local leaders in order to ensure an adequate number of laborers. In places where the Ganap influence was strong, it was easy to get young, able-bodied men. But in other areas, it was not easy, and the responsibility for recruiting workers was left to the village or town heads. As a result, men were often forcibly inducted. When the local heads failed to meet the Japanese demands, the Japanese themselves picked out men, even those just walking the streets, herded them into trucks, and hauled them away.[49]

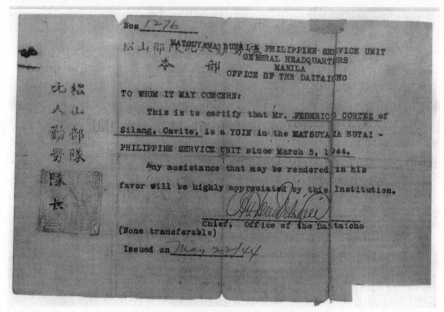

**Photo 8. Identification Card** (May 1944)
*Source: Jeremias Adia*

The bulk of Ganap members, numbering between one and three thousand, depending on the work needs, were quartered at Pier Seven in Manila Harbor. They engaged in construction or loading and unloading for the Army and Navy. They were called the Hijin Kinro Tai (Philippine Service Unit) or the Matsuyama Butai (Matsuyama Unit) after the commanding officer, a certain Col. Matsuyama, who organized it in January 1944. The head of the Philippine Service Unit was Benigno Ramos, who was called *Dai-taicho* (Supreme Commander, see photo 8). The unit not only supplied needed labor but also engaged in intelligence work for the military. Other duties included guarding storage areas and the military garrisons; transporting ammunition, rice, and medicine; procuring food through raids; digging foxholes; constructing barricades; standing guard; and serving as interpreters between the Japanese soldiers and the Filipinos.[50]

The Japanese military organized this unit for three reasons: to protect the Ganapistas from guerrilla attacks and reprisal, to provide them with a means of livelihood, and to help ease the labor shortage. When the day's work at the pier was over, the laborers were given two hours of military training.[51] These recruits were called *yoin,* meaning civilian employees in the military.

## The United Nippon Soldiers

In April 1943, the plan for recruiting local soldiers and attaching them to the Japanese military was implemented in most of the Japanese-occupied areas, such as Malaya, Sumatra, Burma, Java, Borneo, and the Philippines.[52] Training of the yoin in the Philippines seems to have begun in mid-1943, with about thirty yoins, mostly Ganap members, being trained at Fort McKinley for three months. The training included weapons handling, target practice, street fighting, and sniper tactics. In other cases, yoins were sent to places such as Bongabong, Nueva Ecija, or Sapang Buho, Bulacan, to go through intensive training for one to seven months. Some form of ideological education, such as lectures on the Nippon spirit and courses on Japanese language were given as well. Eventually, Filipinos started to call these yoins "United Nippon" soldiers, probably because the words "yoin" and "UN" had a similar ring to them, and the duties of the yoins became more like that of soldiers rather than menial laborers.[53]

Some UN soldiers in Manila were given weapons and uniforms that resembled those of the Japanese. On the pocket of the UN uniform, a small Japanese flag along with the letters "UN" and a star were sewn to differentiate them from the Japanese soldiers. They were also armed with rifles confiscated from the Americans. In the town of Atimonan, Tayabas, a stronghold of the Sakdalista movement, UN soldiers were known to local people as "Filipino soldiers belonging to the Kashima [sic] (should be Kawashima) Butai" (Unit), which was composed of about one thousand five hundred Japanese soldiers and thirty UN soldiers as of the third quarter of 1944. The majority of UN soldiers were Ganapistas, most of whom had only grade-school education. In the case of the town of Bangued, Abra, university students were recruited as yoins, probably because the Japanese wanted to train them as future UN officers.[54] In addition to the UN soldiers, there were other armed Filipino auxiliary forces found in the provinces of central Luzon, Visayas, and Mindanao.[55]

The trend of the war began to point to Japan's defeat as early as June 1942. Followed by the major defeat at the battle of Midway in August, the U.S. military landed on Guadalcanal in the Solomon Islands, causing another severe blow to the Japanese. By February 1943, the Japanese Army had conceded defeat and withdrew its surviving forces from the islands. These events encouraged anti-Japanese guerrillas to become more active, as they had secretly been listening to short wave radio broadcasts. Accordingly, the Japanese military recognized the keen need to arm the local populace in the pursuit of its war effort, particularly to put down anti-Japanese guerrilla activities. Although the training of men for the Bureau of Constabulary had started in April 1942, the number of those who escaped to join the guerrillas had gradually increased.[56] By this time, the Filipino people's unwillingness to cooperate with the Japanese military was obvious and understandable. The Japanese response to this refusal to cooperate was to form the UN military force.

Faced with diminishing support, the Japanese attempted to reverse the situation by granting the Philippines independence, provided the Filipinos collaborated more sincerely with the Japanese. Finally, in October 1943, the Philippines became the independent country of the Republic of the Philippines. The Filipino people had mixed feelings about this. Most of them knew this government would be a puppet government under Japan, but at the same time, they thought they could manipulate the Japanese by using the country's independent status. The government officials hoped they would be able to foil or nullify the Japanese demands. This way, the government officials could shield the Philippines from being totally colonized.[57] Needless to say, the Ganapistas were jubilant over the gaining of independence. Even though they saw the imperialistic and brutal aspects of the Japanese military, they also thought they could use the independent state to minimize Japanese interventions. As much as the Ganapistas were appreciative of the granting of independence, they would not have allowed the perpetual Japanese Occupation of their country, nor would they tolerate any Japanese intervention. After all, their ardent, ultimate goal was the independence of the mother country.

At the independence ceremony on 14 October 1943, two aged generals from the 1896 Revolution and the Philippine-American War, Artemio Ricarte and Emilio Aguinaldo, hoisted the Philippine flag. Ricarte's followers and the Ganapistas were satisfied that their struggle for independence had finally come to an end. But at the same time, they were greatly disappointed because neither Ricarte nor Ramos was accorded any important post in the new Republic. This meant that the followers themselves were not placed in meaningful positions in the government, central or local, despite the fact that they had worked hard for the Japanese military effort. With this feeling of dissatisfaction, the Ricartistas, mainly the organizers of the BP, planned to attempt a coup d'état at the ceremony with Ricarte's consent. However, the plan was detected by the Japanese military before it was implemented. To ease the tense situation, Ricarte was sent back to Japan for four months, from January to April 1944. With the new cabinet established and a Japanese ambassador sent to the new independent state, their frustration and anger grew deeper. A second coup d'état was planned to assassinate as many as fifty people, including Pres. Laurel and his entire cabinet, this time with the Ganapistas participating. They were also going to recruit Ilocanos (Ricarte's birthplace) and thousands of IFI adherents. This, again, remained only a plan.[58]

## The Formation of the Makapili

On 21 September, about two and a half weeks before Gen. Tomoyuki Yamashita arrived in Manila to assume command of the Fourteenth Army, Manila was raided by U.S. carrier-based planes for the first time since the occupation. Martial law was immediately declared, forcing Pres. Laurel to make the statement that the Philippines was in a *state* of (not at) war with United States and Britain. Barely ten days after Yamashita's arrival, U.S. forces began invading Leyte.[59] Thus, the general was faced with urgent problems to tackle: preparing a defense strategy for the imminent landing of the U.S. forces on Luzon, solving the problems caused by the shortage of basic commodities, and restraining the increasing incidents of guerrilla activities. To solve all these problems, he supported the idea of organizing a unified Filipino volunteer army to boost this operation. This idea, which was hatched even before the general's arrival, came from a group of Japanese military officers and some Japanese civilians drafted into the military.

Among the military officers were those who were extremely discontented with the Fourteenth Army Staff, which supported old Commonwealth politicians. One of them was Maj. Gen. Sosaku Suzuki, who was behind the establishment of the Philippine Service Unit. He had been urging the Army Staff members to install "pro-Japanese" Filipinos, such as the Ganapistas, instead of people like the prewar politicians, whom he regarded as pro-American elements. He even encouraged the staging of a coup d'état to achieve his plan. Sensing trouble, the higher officials sent him out of the Philippines before any such action could be taken. One other such person who shared Suzuki's ideas was Navy Capt. Koreshige Inuzuka, the head of the Thirty-first Garrison Unit. Earlier, Inuzuka and Ramos became acquainted with each other through the meetings of Dai Ajia Kyokai, as mentioned in Ch. 5.[60]

When Inuzuka arrived in Manila, in July 1943, he was dissatisfied with the fact that Ramos and his Ganapistas and other "pro-Japanese" Filipinos were not given important positions in the government and was therefore determined to change this policy. Thus, in mid-1944, using his own resources, he started a personal campaign by publishing pamphlets. These pamphlets alleged that Laurel and his cabinet members all belonged to the landed class and were only paying lip service to the Japanese military. Some of the Filipinos, such as Ramos, possessed the true Filipino spirit inherited from Rizal, Bonifacio, del Pilar, and other revolutionary patriots and they worked hard to return the Philippines to the bosom of the Mother Orient. Inuzuka urged the Japanese military authorities to give them the attention they deserved. At the same time, he criticized the Fourteenth Army Staff for their lack of knowledge on the Philippine situation, which resulted in utilizing the prewar old guard politicians who had dual personalities, pretending to cooperate with the military on the surface while actually sabotaging it.[61]

Another person who shared Inuzuka's perspective was Tomoji Kageyama. He was Ramos's Spanish interpreter in Japan, as we recall. Kageyama had been sent to the Philippines as a non-regular staff member of the Department of Information, formerly the Propaganda Corps. Mitsuru Toyama, an ultranationalist, had exerted some pressure for Kageyama to be appointed to that position. As soon as Kageyama arrived in the Philippines, he immediately contacted Ramos and other "pro-Japanese" Filipinos. Kageyama worked hard on their behalf for recognition by the Japanese military and protected them from guerrilla attacks. Other Japanese who supported Inuzuka included some Kenpeitai members, *Mainichi* newspaper reporters, Department of Information staff members, New Philippine Cultural Institute lecturers, and long-time Japanese residents in the Philippines. The New Philippine Cultural Institute was created by the Department of Information to nurture future leaders of the Philippines. [62] These Japanese became extremely frustrated by the inaction of the Army Staff members and bitterly criticized their failure to deal with mounting problems, including the worsening economic situation, increasing anti-Japanese guerrilla activities, and inability to prepare for an imminent American landing. They came up with the plan to create a Filipino army as one of the solutions to address these problems.

These discontented Japanese attributed the military's inability to handle the emergency to the existence of a cycle of "sabotage." Whenever proposed plans—such as tightening up on the anti-Japanese activities or increasing procurement of food—were adopted at the Army Staff meetings, most of them were never carried out due to a vicious cycle. For example, the military would submit "requests" to the Laurel government; Laurel would accept them initially but would later complain to Ambassador Murata, telling him that they could not possibly comply with such "requests." Murata would then go to the Fourteenth Army Staff to convey this message and try to persuade the commanding general to withdraw the "request." Since Murata was of the opinion that he should respect the Laurel government since the Philippines was an independent country, Murata insisted on accepting Laurel's position, and Laurel was successful most of the time. In this way, a number of the military's plans were cancelled, which was exactly what Laurel was hoping for. One way to eliminate this constant problem was to assassinate the ambassador or Pres. Laurel. Several coups d'état and assassinations were planned but nothing materialized.[63]

After several failed coup d'état and assassination attempts, these disgruntled Japanese began organizing a Filipino volunteer army in the middle of 1944. They knew that personnel of the Fourteenth Army Staff were going to be shuffled and hoped to succeed in persuading the new officers to organize a volunteer army. In July, they contacted their Filipino counterparts, and meetings were held. Those who attended included the officers of the now defunct Ganap Party, Gen. Ricarte, and other noted generals of the Philippine-American War, such as Andres Villanueva and Leon Villafuerte.[64] These old veterans reappeared to fight against the returning American forces, this time with Japanese help. Other participants in the meeting included Jose Baluyot, Pio Duran, and Aurelio Alvero. Baluyot was a businessman and publisher of the *Ang Sulo*, which advocated for Asian unity. At one time, he was Quezon's semi-official observer sent to Soviet Russia. Duran was an ultranationalist lawyer and a member of the Dai Ajia Kyokai. In 1940, he ran assembly seats in Albay under the Nacionalista Party, as mentioned earlier. Alvero was an anti-communist writer/poet and promoter of pre-Spanish Filipino culture and customs, such as using indigenous script instead of a Romanized writing system. He was also involved in politics and ran twice for Manila Municipal Board in 1937 (under the Young Philippines) and 1940 (under the Nacionalista Party), but didn't win.[65] After several meetings, they agreed to form a volunteer army. When Gen. Yamashita arrived, the "radical faction" of the military was ready to present him with a Filipino volunteer army.[66] By the time the U.S. military invaded the island of Leyte, in late October, the volunteer army was ready for its operation.

On 10 November, the above Filipinos drafted the articles and bylaws of the association, of which volunteer army was a part. The preamble stated that it was their duty to fulfill the obligation assumed by the Philippines in the Pact of Alliance with Japan, signed in October 1943, which stipulated that Filipinos were to take up arms to defend the Republic if it were attacked (Article II).[67] The preamble continued, saying that they had assembled voluntarily in order to eradicate Anglo-Saxon influence in East Asia and "in the presence of the hallowed spirits of our ancestors, to form a patriotic and nationalistic association to be known as the Kalipunang Makabayan ng mga Pilipino" (Patriotic League of Filipinos, MAKAPILI). The association had the following six departments: (1) General Affairs, (2) Enterprise, (3) Treasury, (4) Physical Culture, (5) Peace and Order, and (6) Enlightenment. The seal of the association was circular in form and contained the name of the association, designation of its office, and a design of the sampaguita, the national flower of the Philippines.[68]

General Yamashita immediately recalled one of his trusted followers, Maj. Takahide Sato from Manchuria to head the operation of the volunteer army. Thus, the Tokubetsu Kosakutai (Special Operation Unit) with around eighty members was formed and attached directly to the Fourteenth Area Army Headquarters.[69] They were mostly from the military ranks, including those who had lost their units in the fight upon landing in the Philippines; therefore, they had nowhere else to go but to the Special Operation Unit.[70] Thus, most of the soldiers had no knowledge of the Ganap Party. The unit also had some civilian draftees. Many of them came from the Interpreter Section of the Department of Information, believing that the time to fight with the pen was over since American forces were about to land.[71]

The main duties of the unit were to recruit and train Filipinos to fight alongside the Japanese against guerrillas, and in the event of U.S. invasion, to be mobilized into a flying squadron. Some members of the unit attempted in vain to contact the communist-led anti-Japanese guerrilla group Hukbalahap to form a joint front against the returning U.S. forces.[72] At the beginning of November, the headquarters of the unit was set up in Quezon City, at the Christ the King Seminary on España Extension, where about 700–800 Ganapistas and their families were accommodated.[73] Their numbers increased as the war situation worsened.

Some apprehension and resistance were expressed over the formation of the Makapili by both the Japanese and the Philippine sides. The Japanese apprehension came from Ambassador Murata and old members of the general staff, such as Naokata Utsunomiya. Ambassador Murata was not opposed to organizing such a group per se but he was afraid that these "pro-Japanese" Filipinos might resist the Laurel government. Murata was keenly aware that the military was in dire need of Filipino volunteers who would fight alongside the Japanese. The only Filipinos who answered the call were mainly the Ganap members. To Ambassador Murata's eyes, Ramos appeared to be different from those he had been dealing with, the well-to-do, Western-educated Nacionalista politicians such as Laurel, Recto, and Aquino. Murata regarded Ramos as undereducated and lacking a refined manner. He thought that the majority of Ramos's followers were "ignorant peasants and laborers." Therefore, Murata opined, Ramos was in a good position to recruit the laborers the Japanese needed but not good enough to hold an important government position.[74]

Murata and Utsunomiya had good reason to be apprehensive of the Makapili. Around the time of its formation, some of Yamashita's staff members, who were desperately preparing for the imminent landing of the U.S. forces, planned a coup d'état using the Makapili to eliminate the cabinet members. However, this action did not take place due to strong opposition, mainly from Ricarte and Murata.[75]

The opposition on the Philippine side came from the cabinet members led by Laurel, who shared a similar distrust held by Murata. They argued that since this volunteer army had been organized under the protection of the Japanese military, it would behave arrogantly and eventually threaten the sovereignty of the Republic.[76] They resisted the formation of the volunteer army; however, the acute situation of American landing did not allow them to foil this plan.

In mid-November, when Ricarte, Ramos, and Duran paid a visit to Pres. Laurel to inform him of the formation of the Makapili, Laurel suggested that they include Gen. Aguinaldo but this did not occur, partly due to Aguinaldo's reluctance. The trio likewise made a courtesy call on Ambassador Murata to explain the Makapili's administrative structure. Murata praised the organization as being the fruit of their patriotic enthusiasm and said they would have his support. However, he warned that the organization should remain as simple as possible and that it should not function as another government, inferring that they refrain from doing anything that would undermine the Laurel government.[77]

On 8 December, commemorating the successful Pearl Harbor attack three years earlier, the formal inauguration ceremony took place in front of the Legislative Building. On that very morning, the members of Laurel's cabinet were still raising some questions. Just before that date, they learned that Ramos had been given the highest position in the organization. According to their earlier understanding and the original plan, it was Ricarte who would be heading the Makapili. Somehow at the last minute, the military decided to have Ramos serve as its Supreme Head, Pres. Laurel as Honorary Supreme Advisor , and Ricarte as Highest Advisor. The cabinet members had been in a quandary since then. They asked: Was the President simply an Honorary Supreme advisor? If so, then what would happen to the President's function as Supreme Commander?

Some members of Laurel's cabinet flatly refused to attend the ceremony as a form of protest against this sudden change. Duran, then the Vice Minister of State for Home Affairs, assured them that the members of the Makapili would be working under the government.[78] Only minutes before the ceremony, they were persuaded by Murata that titles given to the trio did not signify anything and the military would be willing to change them later; the important thing was that formation of the Makapili was possible with the cooperation of Ricarte, Duran, and Ramos, who had volunteered to fight for the sake of the country and were willing to risk their own lives. Murata made somewhat threatening remarks, warning that boycotting the ceremony would not only result in a split of the cabinet, but more importantly could be interpreted as sabotage on their part against the Japanese Imperial Army.[79]

Finally, the inauguration ceremony took place and was attended by only 300–400 people, many of whom were women and children. Some Filipino soldiers were dressed in khaki-colored uniforms and caps like those worn by Japanese soldiers. At the ceremony, Gen. Ricarte unfurled the Makapili flag, which was similar to one of the Katipunan flags. The red flag had a circle in the middle, symbolizing the sun. Inside the circle was the Tagalog ancient script for "Ka" (Kalipunan, instead of Katipunan) and eight rays emanating from the circle. While the eight rays in the Katipunan flag symbolized the first eight provinces to rise up in arms against Spain, those of the Makapili flag stood for the "Eight Corners" of the world under the Emperor's guidance and benevolence. The Japanese Imperial Army tried to appeal to the Filipinos' patriotism by reminding them of the history of their struggle against foreign invaders and to entice them to join the fight against the returning Americans. The role of the Makapili was compared with that of Lapu-Lapu, who had fought the foreign invader Magellan even though his weapons were inferior to those of the Spanish conquistadors. The Makapili was also compared with the Filipino revolutionary army that had fought Spain and later the U.S.[80] After all, the Makapili had the former revolutionary generals such as Ricarte, Villafuerte, and Villanueva.

The ceremony began with a moment of silent prayer for Filipino war heroes of anti-Spanish and anti-American Wars and the Japanese and Filipino War dead from the present war. The national anthem of the Republic of the Philippines was played by the Metropolitan Constabulary Band. The Philippine and Japanese flags were raised simultaneously. Flags of other East Asian states and of Free India were also seen. Pio Duran read the Imperial Prescript declaring war on the United States of America and Great Britain. This was followed by speeches of Gen. Yamashita, Ramos, and Pres. Laurel. Both Ramos and Laurel delivered their speeches in Tagalog. Ramos described how the Makapili came to be formed: "The Makapili is a creation of the Filipinos and for the Filipinos in order to suppress disorder, to awaken the misguided elements, to ameliorate the food problems of the people, and to aid the Imperial Japanese Forces and other Asian nations in the successful prosecution of the war." He continued, saying that the Makapili was an organization formed to destroy the enemies of the nation within and without to help the people, and above all, to defend the Republic.[81] Here, Ramos was strongly insinuating that the enemies within were the anti-Japanese guerrillas and the non-cooperative Laurel cabinet members. He allegedly said that Pres. Laurel's position in the Makapili was just an honorary position and that he had no right to interfere with the activities of the organization, as written in the rules and regulations.[82]

Perhaps reacting to Ramos's speech, Pres. Laurel first emphasized the importance of unity among the Filipinos and said: "Over and above the Makapili is the government of the Republic, from which it is neither distinct nor separate and to the authority of which it must submit as all other similar organizations, for any organization that attempts to go over or obstruct the government of the Republic seeks to destroy the Republic and the work of Japan, which has facilitated its establishment."[83]

Since Murata was displeased with Ramos's speech, which insinuated the division of the nation and disregarded Pres. Laurel, he called on Laurel the following day to discuss this matter. Laurel told Murata that unlike his fellow cabinet members who did not trust Ramos, he was ready to embrace him because he knew him personally. Laurel's opinion of Ramos was that he was not a morally upright person and that the Ganap Party was merely one of the small political parties.[84] Laurel failed to tell Murata that Ramos was a socially committed poet and a fellow member of the Aklatang Bayan, or how popular the movement was in the 1930s. At one point, Laurel admired the Sakdalistas' courage in advocating for justice, and later, when the May Uprising of 1935 took place, he showed sympathy and understanding toward them.

In the meantime the Makapili members, most of whom came from the rank-and-file Ganapistas, felt that their aspirations were partly realized by seeing their leader Ramos and Gen. Ricarte sitting side by side on the platform along with the supreme commander, Gen. Yamashita. Under the leadership of these two, they were ready to fight. However, there was already a split within the organization. Two of the founders of the Makapili, Artemio Ricarte and Aurelio Alvero, were not pleased with Ramos's being appointed head of the organization. Alvero had two reasons for his concern: first, his contempt of Ramos's followers, considering the bulk of them to be "uncultured" central and southern Luzon peasants; and second, his disappointment with and distrust of Ramos. Previously, Alvero was to be appointed Head of the Department of Enlightenment of the Makapili organization. However, Ramos placed one of his own followers in that position, breaking the agreement previously entered into with Ricarte and Duran. Alvero left the Makapili and organized another armed entity, called the Bisig Bakal ng Tagala (Iron Arms of the Philippines), and made it public the second week of January 1945.[85]

Gen. Ricarte also organized an army of his own. It was called the Hukbo ng Kusang Loob sa Kapayapaan at Kaayusan ng Pilipinas (Volunteer Army for Peace and Order of the Philippines, Peace Army). Ricarte first thought of organizing a military force when the Philippines was granted independence in October 1943. He believed that an independent country should have its own military. Ricarte mentioned this idea to some Japanese high-ranking military personnel when he went back to Japan for a visit in early 1944; however, nothing came of this.

When Manila was bombed by U.S. planes in September 1944, Pres. Laurel was pressured to declare war against the U.S. After consulting with his cabinet members, Laurel skirted the issue by proclaiming that "a *state of war* against the United States and its allies existed." Ricarte, whether aware of Laurel's actual intention or not, took this opportunity to form his own military force in order to defend the country and began organizing the Peace Army around this time.[86] Ricarte believed that the Peace Army should be run by Filipinos alone and wanted to prevent the Japanese from intervening. He was apprehensive about the possibility that Ramos, as head of the Makapili, might allow the Japanese military to interfere. These were the reasons behind his forming this independent military force.

Pres. Laurel seemed to have come to trust that Ricarte would respect his authority. More importantly, Laurel was confident that the Ricarte followers were too few to present any threat to him. Therefore, Laurel formally recognized Ricarte's Peace Army at the end of November 1944, even before the inauguration of the Makapili. To show his support, Laurel was said to have donated to Ricarte's Peace Army the sum of P1 million, which at that time was called "Mickey Mouse money" because of the inflated value of the peso.[87]

Ricarte immediately began recruiting soldiers through a radio broadcast. He declared in Tagalog that it was the duty of every Filipino to rise up in defense of his mother country.[88] Over a hundred young men answered Ricarte's call, which made the total number of soldiers 400–500, the bulk being the Ricartistas. The two volunteer armies led by Alvero and Ricarte merged in the first half of January 1945—after Ricarte left for northern Luzon—along with the retreating Japanese.[89] The leadership of the Peace Army was given to Agapito Zialcita, a veteran revolutionary who had fought side by side with Ricarte some four decades earlier and had been active for the cause of independence throughout the 1910s. Despite the different names of the three volunteer organizations, the Makapili, the Bisig Bakal, and the Peace Army, the people in general perceived them as one and the same.[90]

## Rift between Ramos and Ricarte

Here let us pause to see the relationship between Ramos and Ricarte. The latter has been generally regarded as a morally upright, unyielding revolutionary of the cause of independence in Philippine history. Looking into the rift between the two may present a different perspective on Ricarte. According to him, his main justification for creating his own volunteer army was to contain Ramos's misuse of his newly acquired power. But there appears to be an underlying competitive aspect in Ricarte's motive.

Until early 1934, the relationship between Ricarte and Ramos still seemed quite amiable.[91] Ricarte admired the *Sakdal* because of its fearless criticism and exposure of the Nacionalista government. He wrote to Ramos in July 1931, saying that he still believed that liberty should be taken by force. Ricarte sent a letter of gratitude to the *Sakdal* when he received the funds raised for him.[92] The sign of the first breakup was seen in January 1935, when Ricarte was described in the *Sakdal* as one of the "enemies" of the Sakdalistas: "All those who have no honor and have been betrayers to the country are the enemies of the Sakdalistas." The "enemies" were foreigners, Filipino politicians of the "Pros" and "Antis," Communists, and Aguinaldo and Ricarte. The article alleged that in the general's house in Yokohama, one could see Quezon's picture hanging with an American flag beside it.[93] Ramos had clearly denounced Ricarte and severed relationship with him by January 1935.

Immediately after the May Uprising of 1935, *The Tribune* contacted Ricarte for his opinion, inquiring about Ramos's activities in Japan. The general, who was already indignant over the article published in the *Sakdal*, replied that Ramos was exceedingly unworthy of the cause he led.[94] Ricarte expressed the same criticism against Ramos through his wife, Agueda Esteban, when she came back to the Philippines in November 1935 to attend the inauguration of the Commonwealth government. She was persuaded by Gov. Gen. Murphy to attend the ceremony in place of the general since he still refused to pledge allegiance to the U.S. In order to obtain a passport, she had to swear allegiance to the American flag. When a public gathering was held in her honor in Bulacan town, she conveyed the message from the general to support the Commonwealth leaders. She clarified that the general had never given his consent to separate from the U.S. by force. She said that Ricarte was highly critical of the uprisings attempted by the Tanggulan Society and the Sakdalistas. Ricarte's criticism of Ramos was severe. According to Ricarte, Ramos had committed blunders in Japan and in the U.S. by using his name to raise funds to defray his transportation expenses.[95] If Ramos used Ricarte's name for fundraising, certainly many others used his name for propaganda purposes. Quezon, Roxas, and other political leaders of the time visited Ricarte in Yokohama whenever they passed through Japan on the way to or from the U.S.[96]

Ramos seemed to have always been short of funds during his stay in Japan. Initially, he and his family stayed in the detached house of a Japanese supporter. Later, Ramos moved to a simple apartment in downtown Tokyo and then to yet another simple wooden house on a Shinto shrine grounds also in Tokyo. At the end of May 1936, Ramos was treated for a serious illness and should have been hospitalized for three weeks.

However, due to a lack of funds, he refused to stay in the hospital. We also recall that Ramos could not afford to hire an interpreter when they were about to leave for Manchuria in September 1936.[97]

When the May Uprising occurred, Rash Behari Bose, an Indian freedom activist residing in Tokyo, asked Ricarte to explain the differences between himself and Ramos, as both were fighting for Philippine independence. Somehow this inquiry and Ricarte's response to Bose, alleging that Ramos had taken movement funds for his personal use, became known to Ramos. He, in turn, wrote to Bose to refute Ricarte's allegation. His letter began by first paying respect to the old general and saying that he still respected Ricarte for what he had done for the country. Ramos and the Sakdalistas had been proud of him for not pledging allegiance to the U.S. However, the general now supported the Commonwealth government and had become pro-American, and Ramos emphasized that this was the difference between the two.[98]

As early as 1931, Ricarte disapproved of radical movements and admitted supporting Quezon's independence campaign of peaceful means in his letter to his friend Jose P. Santos.[99] However, at the same time, Ricarte was saying that the idea of taking independence by force should not be discarded, as seen in his letter to the *Sakdal*.

When Quezon was trying to defeat the H-H-C Act in 1933 to get a new independence bill, he tried to rally support from anyone who was against it. To solicit more enthusiastic popular support, Quezon decided to anonymously approach Ricarte through Santos to inquire about his thoughts on the act. Ricarte wrote back saying that the act was like a pill that was sweet and tasty but at its core was a poison that would kill, strongly insisting on immediate independence.[100] Quezon used this response for propaganda purposes to rally the "Antis." Around this time, the Japanese authorities questioned Ricarte regarding his stand on the independence issue. He stated that he firmly believed in immediate independence and that when and if a conflict arose between Japan and the U.S., the Filipinos would unanimously support Japan and would declare independence from the U.S.[101]

When Quezon brought back the T-M Act and it was passed in the Philippine Assembly in May 1934, Ricarte wrote to Santos saying that it was a matter of course that the Filipino flag would be unfurled at every government building. However, the American flag also should be hoisted under the Filipino flag, stressing it would be the way to show the Filipinos' affection for the American government.[102] As early as 1934, Ricarte considered himself a "Quezonista" and supported the Commonwealth government. Meanwhile, Ramos and the Sakdalistas were strongly opposed to the T-M Act. They never stopped criticizing Quezon and his administration on the pages of the *Sakdal*. Ramos had been severely attacking Quezon as late as 1937 by calling him "the real enemy of the government in the Philippines." It is possible that it was Ramos who cut off the relationship with Ricarte after he had accepted Quezon and the Commonwealth government. Sending his own wife to the inauguration meant that Ricarte virtually accepted them. Could it be that the main reason Ricarte still refused to return to the Philippines was because he wanted to avoid Ramos's further criticism?

Ramos and Ricarte seemed to have competitive feelings in regard to the positions they might get under the Japanese-sponsored new Republic. As seen earlier, both were discontented with not having been given any important position. Ramos was said to have nurtured the possibility of becoming the president of the Republic. In fact, he announced his candidacy for the presidential race for 1941. His desire was partially fulfilled when he was designated as the head of the Makapili, which could have given him even more power than Pres. Laurel. After the Laurel government retreated to Baguio, Ramos allegedly requested that Pres. Laurel grant him a ministerial position and appoint Ricarte to be his subordinate, the vice minister.[103] If this were true, we have to ask why Ramos desired a high government position at that late stage of the war when it was obvious to everyone that Japanese defeat was imminent. Perhaps Ramos knew he was not going to survive the war, and therefore wanted to experience being in a high government position even for a short while. This could also explain why the aged anti-American war veterans, including Ricarte, had joined the Makapili to fight against the Americans. Perhaps it was a way for them to achieve their lifelong cherished dream of independence before they died.

Ricarte, too, seemed to have been expecting to be designated president of the Republic. He was indeed offered the position of the presidency by some individual Japanese military officials before being brought back to the Philippines. However, the idea of Ricarte being the president was only a suggestion and never became the official Japanese military policy. Ricarte seemed to have believed it was an official decision and boasted to his former comrade Gen. Emilio Aguinaldo that he was set up to be head of the government under the Japanese Occupation.[104]

In the early part of the Japanese Occupation in mid-1942, Ricarte penned "Balak na Pamahalaan sa Pagsasariling Pilipinas o Luviminda" (Plan for the Government of Independent Philippines, or Luviminda). He described the importance of a more authoritarian form of government (Pamahalaang Magulang) that was to be based on Filipino traditions and values. With the help of the Japanese military, the Philippines would be independent and capable of creating this kind of government, most likely with Ricarte as president.[105] However, Ricarte seemed to have forsaken this idea after the coup d'état against the Laurel government did not materialize.

### The Makapilis' Last Days

Recruitment and combat training of the Makapilis were carried on not only in Manila but also in the nearby provinces. The membership in each chapter was between ten and fifty, and some of those enlisted were female soldiers. In some towns in Bulacan and Nueva Ecija, the membership of a chapter rose as high as two to three hundred. Private houses, usually those of well-to-do Ganapistas, and public school buildings were used as barracks.[106]

Makapili songs were composed to foster unity and boost morale. One such song went like this: "Patriotic League of the Philippines/We are soldiers, you and I are soldiers/(We are of) the Asian race/A new spirit/The Makapilis are the protectors of the nation's children/Hardship will vanish/Followed by prosperity and progress."[107]

In Gapan, Nueva Ecija, sometime in mid-January 1945, the Makapili chapter was visited by members of the Hukbalahap, who offered to form a united front with them against the returning U.S. forces. This time it was the Makapili who turned down the offer. There were other attempts to establish a united front between the communists and the Ganapistas; however, nothing materialized.[108] The attempts on the part of the communists were due to the Japanese military's maneuvering. When the Japanese occupied Manila, they arrested and imprisoned communist and socialist leaders, including Crisanto Evangelista, Guillermo Capadocia, and Pedro Abad Santos. A Japanese officer by the name of Col. Kodama approached them and offered their release on the condition they would cooperate with

Japan's efforts to establish the Republic of the Philippines under Japanese aid. While some, like Evangelista, rejected the offer, Abad Santos and Capadocia agreed. Capodicia was sent out to tell the comrades to cooperate with the Japanese for the time being.[109] This explains why some of the Hukbalahap members paid a visit to the Makapilis to offer cooperation in fighting against the returning American forces.

The Makapili was an independent volunteer army in name and appearance only. In most cases, they were completely under the command of the Japanese military. The total membership of the Makapili, including those in the provinces, could have numbered between four and five thousand.[110] About a week after the Makapili inauguration, the U.S. forces landed on Mindoro Island, and their advance to Manila became only a matter of time. The Luzon Defense Operation Plan was put into effect in mid-December. The Lamon Bay area and Bicol Peninsula, in particular, were on alert as possible landing points for the American forces. In all these areas, the war was to be fought by the Japanese soldiers assisted by the Makapilis. In January 1945, a Makapili suicide squad, equipped only with bayonets, reportedly attacked the Americans who had landed in Lingayen. When the American forces entered Manila in early February 1945, the Makapilis fought a one-sided battle. Finally on 11 February, around a hundred and forty Makapili soldiers were ordered to flee from the city along with the Japanese soldiers.[111]

Ninety percent of the Makapili troops had come from the United Nippon soldiers, most of whom were rank-and-file Ganapistas. They had worked hard for the independence of the country in the prewar era and now believed that the Makapili was the only organization that could protect the Philippine independence they had just obtained. With this belief, they willingly joined, and in some cases, both father and son from the same family volunteered.[112] The non-Ganap members, comprising the remaining 10 percent, were economically desperate and thus attracted to the daily ration of rice and other basic commodities dispensed instead of daily wages.

Many of the old-timer Ganapistas did not join the Makapili after having witnessed the brutality of some Japanese soldiers, especially the Kenpeitai, toward their fellow Filipino citizens.[113] Nor did they become hooded informers, pointing out anti-Japanese elements to the military. The majority of these hooded collaborators seemed to have been those who had joined the Ganap organization after the Japanese Occupation, for personal gain or to receive material rewards, mostly food. Some were said to have killed an anti-Japanese guerrilla for a sack of rice.[114] The fact that after the war, those old-timer Ganap peasant members known to the villagers were accepted into the communist-led peasant organization, Pambansang Kaisahan ng mga Magbubukid (National Confederation of Peasants, PKM, successor to the prewar KPMP), proves they were not the hooded informers.[115]

By the early months of 1945, Ramos realized the imminent defeat of Japan. He accepted the reality that the Japanese Occupation had brought nothing but misery to his fellow countrymen. In order to save the lives of his followers, Ramos advised them not to join the Makapili, and he warned those who had already joined to lie low.[116] Around this time, the Ganapistas and their families in the nearby provinces came to Manila to avoid anti-Japanese guerrilla reprisals. Numbering some three thousand, they petitioned for the protection of the Japanese military and were all accommodated at the Makapili Headquarters (Christ the King Seminary) on España Extension.[117]

As the Makipili Headquarters soon became crowded, about seven to eight hundred of the Ganapistas were transferred to Barrio San Juan, in Caloocan. They grew their own vegetables under the direction of Salud Algabre, the Sakdalista leader of the Cabuyao uprising of 1935.[118] From January to February 1945, the Makapili/Ganap members and their families in Manila, ranging in age from newborn to elderly, all followed the retreating Japanese Army into the mountains in Rizal, Laguna, and Bulacan provinces, serving as coolies for the Japanese.[119]

The fugitive life in the mountains was miserable and gruesome for the Makapili/Ganap members and their families. A Japanese doctor who was attached to the military chanced upon some of them in the mountains of Laguna in the early part of April 1945, and reported that a few hundred Makapilis had sought refuge in the mountains of Pililla and Tanay. In Pililla, they lived in a church and were led by a Japanese officer in civilian clothes. The bulk of the Makapili soldiers and their families stayed in Tanay under the leadership of Vicente Pamatmat, whose son-in-law was Mariano Untivero, one-time representative to the Assembly on the Sakdalista Party ticket. They were nothing but skin and bones, and most of them eventually died of starvation. A young teenage girl, Mary Pamatmat, Vicente's daughter, witnessed the deaths by starvation of her parents, her sister, and all her other relatives. Later, she learned that another sister and a brother who had remained in the town had both been killed by the guerrillas, thus making her the sole survivor of her whole family.[120]

Around March 1945, a Japanese soldier who was wandering around the Igorot villages in the mountainous region of northern Luzon chanced upon a group of Makapili soldiers about whom he later wrote: "They were all equipped with Japanese arms and wore headbands with rising sun insignias...They tried to talk to me in Japanese mixed with English and Tagalog: 'We have been fighting with you ever since you landed on Luzon in order to defeat our enemy, America, and protect our independence. We believed that as long as we cooperated with you, we could obtain the independence of our mother country. We are ready to die if necessary. It might be your government's order, but you have retracted what you promised us and are now going to surrender to the Americans. What is to become of us? If arrested by the Americans or the Filipinos, we will be accused of treason and sentenced to death.'"[121] These words seemed to echo the feelings of most of the Filipino volunteer soldiers who accompanied the retreating Japanese at the end of the Occupation.

Ramos, with his second wife and a newborn baby, retreated to Baguio, as there were no other options left for them. They were reported to have all died in that area, just like Gen. Artemio Ricarte. Immediately after the war, one of Ramos's sisters learned of his death when someone who claimed to have witnessed Ramos's last moments brought his suitcases and other personal belongings to her. According to this man, Ramos and his family were going to be taken to Japan. As the plane was taking off, it was bombed by the Americans, and they were all killed. However, the exact circumstances of their deaths remain a mystery to this day. It is also possible that the retreating Japanese had executed Ramos and his family. Airplanes were scarce at that time and Ramos was not as important to the Japanese military as Laurel and Aquino. One former Kenpeitai, who admitted having executed one foreign interpreter who worked for the Japanese military, told me that toward the end of the occupation, the execution of Filipinos or other nationalities who had worked closely with the Japanese was not uncommon. These executions were carried out to prevent any inside information from being divulged to the enemy. For example, in January 1945, when a Japanese civilian was retreating to the north of Manila along with the soldiers, one of the soldiers confided to her that he had just executed some prisoners of war as well as some Ganap members. Another example can be seen in the massacre of Artemio Ricarte's kin. According to Ricarte's granddaughter Minviluz, some members of the Ricarte clan were killed by the Japanese during the battle of Manila in February 1945.[122]

Out of desperation, Gen. Yamashita and his staff organized the Makapili solely for their own operational purposes. However, not all the officers involved in its establishment had intentions of simply using them. The ultranationalist Japanese, such as Sosaku Suzuki, Koreshige Inuzuka, Tomoji Kageyama, and Shigenobu Mochizuki (the founder of New Philippine Cultural Institute), had their own vision of the future Philippines. What they wanted to see was the Philippines' eventual independence after placing the Philippines under Japanese supervision and guidance for a period of time.[123] They wanted to upgrade the lives of the poor, the peasants, and the city laborers, whom they saw as the victims of feudalism, Western colonialism, and the Nacionalista-dominated government that represented only the Filipino landed class. On the part of Ramos and the Ganapistas, initial cooperation could have been convenient and expedient; however, as they came to know these Japanese, they saw the similarities between the Ganapistas' goals and the ideals of these ultranationalist Japanese military personnel, although they were a dissenting minority in the Japanese Army. Their attempted coups d'état never left the planning stage, as we saw.

When independence was finally achieved under Japanese tutelage in October 1943, these Filipinos—including the aged revolutionary veterans of the 1896 Revolution and the Philippine-American War—felt their cherished dreams had finally been fulfilled, albeit limited and circumscribed for the time being. Therefore, they felt that independence should be protected with their lives. They were ready to die for independence as proud citizens of the new Republic. That was why they fought alongside the Japanese against the returning Americans, risking their own lives and those of their sons. Like other Asian freedom fighters, such as Indian National Army soldiers and Burmese and Indonesian nationalists, they saw an opportunity to take up arms against the returning Americans in order to protect their independence. What they experienced was yet another disaster and failure, as in the past.[124]

## CHAPTER 9

# THE TRIALS OF THE "COLLABORATORS" AND THE AFTERMATH

T HE MAKAPILI SOLDIERS were abandoned by the Japanese, and those who managed to survive suffered hostile and harsh conditions after the war. As they had feared, arrest, trial, and imprisonment awaited them.

As early as July 1944, the U.S. government was already considering how to try the Filipino collaborators. They were considered to be traitors to the Commonwealth government and to the United States of America because they had worked for the enemy; therefore, they had to be removed from authority and influence in the political and economic life of the Philippine society. Following this guideline, the Counter Intelligent Corps (CIC) of the United States Army began arresting Filipino collaborators as soon as the Americans landed on Leyte Island. After the dust from the battle of Manila had cleared, the CIC commenced its investigation of those who had been arrested; later, they were tried in the People's Court. The number of collaborators tried was around six thousand.[1]

In theory, the right of the collaborators to a trial in the People's Court rested with the Commonwealth government. But strong U.S. pressure could be seen in the creation of the People's Court and in the way the collaborators were treated. The U.S. advised the Philippine government that it would lose American economic assistance if the collaborators were not purged from the current administration.[2] The U.S. government was concerned about those Filipino politicians who had occupied important positions in the Japanese-controlled administration. At the end of September 1945, the Philippine Congress finally passed a law creating the People's Court, and eventually, fifteen judges in five divisions were appointed. Some five thousand five hundred were accused of being political, economic, or military collaborators. Roughly one-third of the military collaborators were Ganap members. In some cases, one person was accused of more than one incident of collaboration.[3]

Both former Pres. Laurel and Speaker of the National Assembly Benigno Aquino Sr., who had been flown to Japan by the Japanese military, were now imprisoned in Tokyo. Thus, the trials of the accused began with figures such as former Minister of Foreign Affairs Claro M. Recto and Finance Minister Antonio de las Alas. Since these two were considered political collaborators, they were released after posting bail.[4] This privilege was denied to the Makapilis and others who were considered military collaborators. By this time, Ricarte and Ramos were already dead in the mountains of Northern Luzon. One of the remaining prominent collaborators was Aurelio Alvero, who had left Makapili and organized his own volunteer army. He was sentenced to life imprisonment and fined P10,000 in July 1946. He was thirty-two years old at that time. Pio Duran, one of the Makapili founders, was tried as a military collaborator as well as a political collaborator and was eventually granted bail. He paid P50,000 and was released on 5 September 1946. The trials took place in Manila, the Visayas, and Mindanao. One division held trials in Pasig, exclusively for the Makapilis.[5] After four months of proceedings, only seven cases had been prosecuted: three of the accused were sentenced to death; two to life imprisonment; one to twelve years; and one minor was sent to a reformatory. Those meted death penalties were all Makapilis.[6] This was a slow process.

In January 1948, Pres. Manuel Roxas finally granted amnesty to everyone accused of political and economic collaboration, and the People's Court tried the remaining cases of the military collaborators until its abolishment in June of the same year.[7] Afterwards, the cases went to the Courts of First Instance, and those who were financially able appealed to higher courts. Some of these cases reached the Supreme Court. The majority of Ganapistas and Makapilis had no such means and had to accept the decisions handed down to them. Eventually, after serving some years in prison, most of those who had been initially sentenced to death or life imprisonment were released through amnesty or commutation of their sentences.[8]

Although the collaborators became physically free, everyone in their local neighborhoods knew the fact of their collaboration. People who had lost loved ones or had endured severe hardship at the hands of the Japanese military vented their ire and vengeance upon the former Ganapistas and Makapilis who had worked with the Japanese military. Some were lynched, others ostracized in their home villages and towns. Doors to employment were tightly closed not only to them but also to their families. Since most of them were of the economically disadvantaged class, unemployment meant a life of extreme poverty. They kept a low profile in the hope that their past would be forgotten. The Japanese Occupation of the Philippines had not only brought human and material destruction but also forced a group of simple and patriotic Filipinos into the roles of unwitting traitors to their country.[9]

## Survival after the War

After the Japanese Occupation, some former Sakdalistas and Ganapistas turned to Communist- and Socialist-led peasant and labor movements in an effort to overcome their setback. They brought Sakdalism with them, that is, their aspirations for the betterment of their people and their country's true independence, to whatever movement they were involved in.[10]

Yet, another group of Ganap members regrouped, leaving behind them a traceable past. They felt the need to be in close touch with each other, to nurse deep wounds and crushed spirits, and to pursue the unfulfilled dream of creating a society of brotherhood. They needed to reestablish an organization like the original Sakdalista Party. By this time they had learned to keep their political goals discreet, and so they set up groups in the form of religious organizations.

One such organization, established in Tondo, Manila, in 1947, was the Iglesia Sagrada ng Lahi (Church of Sacred Race).[11] A former Aglipayan priest founded this church along with three hundred members, of whom 85 percent were former Ganapistas. A few years later, in 1950, a branch was established in Atimonan, Quezon, with approximately five hundred members. The Iglesia was duly registered as a religious organization

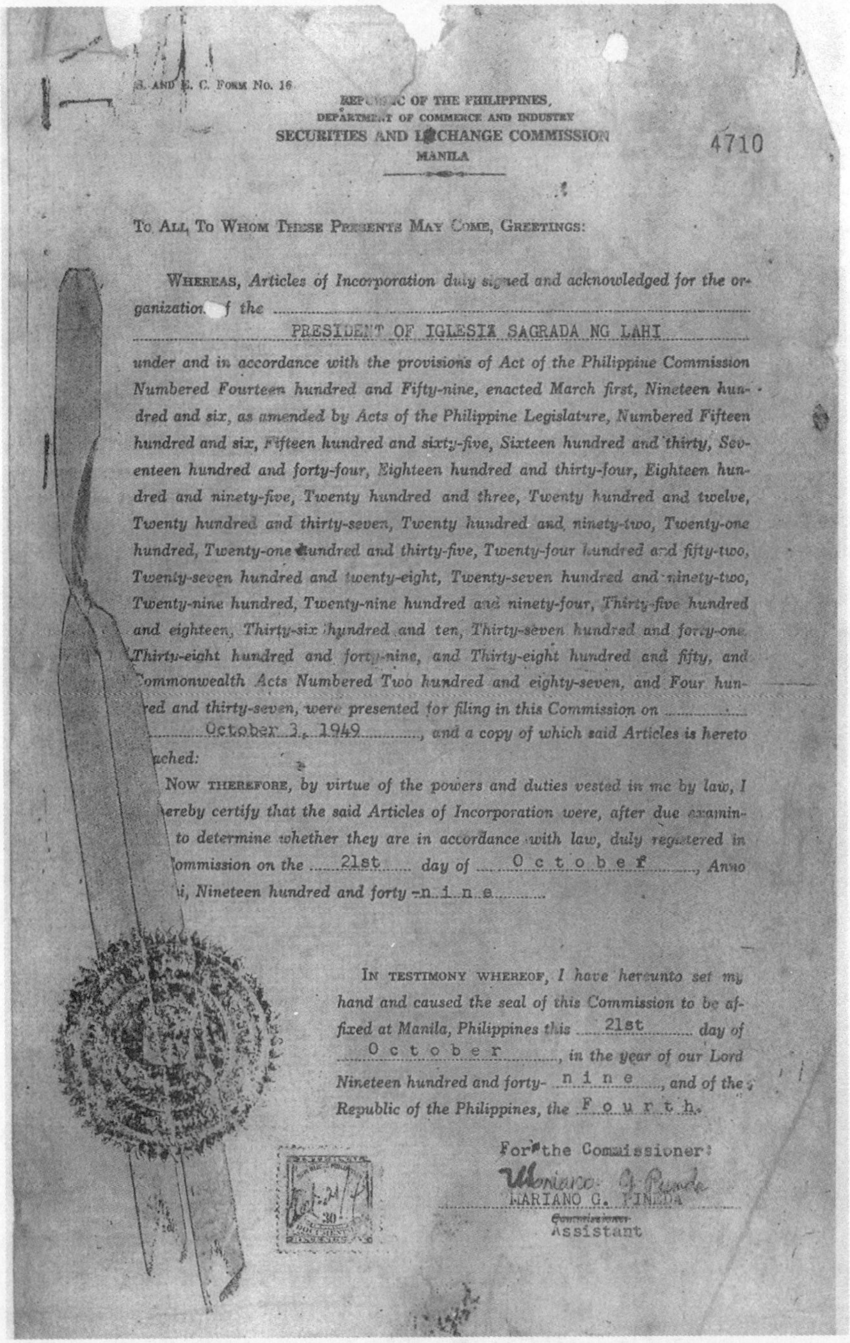

REPUBLIC OF THE PHILIPPINES,
DEPARTMENT OF COMMERCE AND INDUSTRY
**SECURITIES AND EXCHANGE COMMISSION**
MANILA

4710

TO ALL TO WHOM THESE PRESENTS MAY COME, GREETINGS:

WHEREAS, Articles of Incorporation duly signed and acknowledged for the organization of the ........................

PRESIDENT OF IGLESIA SAGRADA NG LAHI

under and in accordance with the provisions of Act of the Philippine Commission Numbered Fourteen hundred and Fifty-nine, enacted March first, Nineteen hundred and six, as amended by Acts of the Philippine Legislature, Numbered Fifteen hundred and six, Fifteen hundred and sixty-five, Sixteen hundred and thirty, Seventeen hundred and forty-four, Eighteen hundred and thirty-four, Eighteen hundred and ninety-five, Twenty hundred and three, Twenty hundred and twelve, Twenty hundred and thirty-seven, Twenty hundred and ninety-two, Twenty-one hundred, Twenty-one hundred and thirty-five, Twenty-four hundred and fifty-two, Twenty-seven hundred and twenty-eight, Twenty-seven hundred and ninety-two, Twenty-nine hundred, Twenty-nine hundred and ninety-four, Thirty-five hundred and eighteen, Thirty-six hundred and ten, Thirty-seven hundred and forty-one, Thirty-eight hundred and forty-nine, and Thirty-eight hundred and fifty, and Commonwealth Acts Numbered Two hundred and eighty-seven, and Four hundred and thirty-seven, were presented for filing in this Commission on ..................... October 3, 1949 ........................, and a copy of which said Articles is hereto attached:

Now THEREFORE, by virtue of the powers and duties vested in me by law, I hereby certify that the said Articles of Incorporation were, after due examination to determine whether they are in accordance with law, duly registered in Commission on the ....21st.... day of ....October...., Anno Domini, Nineteen hundred and forty -n.i.n.e...........

IN TESTIMONY WHEREOF, I have hereunto set my hand and caused the seal of this Commission to be affixed at Manila, Philippines this ....21st.... day of ....October...., in the year of our Lord Nineteen hundred and forty- .n.i.n.e., and of the Republic of the Philippines, the .F.o.u.r.t.h.

For the Commissioner:

MARIANO G. PINEDA
Commissioner
Assistant

**Photo 9. Iglesia Sagrada's Registration Certificate** (October 1949)
*Source: Security and Exchange Commission, Department of Commerce and Industry*

in 1959 at the Securities and Exchange Commission, Department of Commerce and Industry (see photo 9). By the 1970s, according to the president, Jeremias Adia, membership was said to have grown to around fifty thousand throughout the Philippines. Other branches were quickly established in the provinces, including Camarines Sur, Bataan, Tarlac, Leyte, and Agusan del Norte in Mindanao. In the early 1960s, the head-quarters moved to Lecheria, Calamba, in Laguna and in 1983, it moved to its present site in Silang, Cavite.[12]

Jeremias Adia's background is typical of those Ganapistas who took a spiritual path after the war. He was born in 1917 in Manila and graduated from the Philippine School of Arts and Trade in 1932. In his youth, he followed his father, Constantino Adia, into the Sakdalista movement. Constantino owned a leather shop in Santa Mesa, Manila and was a member of the Ricartista group. In the mid-1910s, Constantino was jailed for six months in connection with an armed robbery in which he attempted to steal ammunition from the U.S. Army. Constantino's arrest might have been connected to the so-called "Christmas Eve Fiasco."[13] After his release, Constantino joined the Katipunan ng Bayan and later the Tanggulan Society, both led by Patricio Dionisio. When the Tanggulan Society disintegrated, he became a follower of the newly formed Sakdalista movement. By this time, the family had moved to Cabuyao, Laguna. Constantino was devastated by the death of so many comrades at the May Uprising of 1935 and left Cabuyao for Mount Banahaw, where he helped establish the Samahan ng Tatlong Persona. He died there the following year.[14] Shortly after Ramos returned from Japan in 1938, Jeremias had a chance to meet him. He was impressed with Ramos's oratorical skills and his dedication to the cause of independence. This was when Jeremias became more actively involved in the movement. Eventually, he was appointed Sec. of the Ganap Party in early 1940, and became the Sec. Gen. during the Japanese Occupation. When the Makapili was organized, Ramos discouraged him from joining. Heeding his advice, Jeremias did not become a member of the Makapili but did join the Japanese forces retreating to the mountains to avoid guerrilla attacks. Adia was later arrested, tried by the People's Court, and spent some years in the national penitentiary in Muntinlupa.[15]

Adia's quest for reforming Filipino society brought him in touch with Communist Party members. In the early 1950s, Luis Taruc, who was then a leading figure of the Hukbong Magpapalaya ng Bayan, or HMB (National Liberation Army), contacted Jeremias to see if they could work together.

This was during the time the Communist Party was implementing an aggressive program of expansion and recruitment.[16] Luis Taruc had been active in a peasant movement in the prewar time, and before his involvement in the Socialist Party of Pedro Abad Santos, he had been active in the Sakdalista movement, attending meetings in Bulacan and helping to distribute the *Sakdal*. This was not the first time that an alliance of Communists and Sakdalistas was attempted, as we saw earlier. Taruc guaranteed the safety of Jeremias and other former Ganapistas, and many meetings were held. One of the meetings was raided, and Adia was arrested along with the Communists. He was imprisoned for three years in Muntinlupa for his involvement in the HMB.[17]

Let us now turn our attention back to the Iglesia. The church services and ceremonies remind us of the credos expressed in the *Pamahayag* of the Sakdalista Party and the *Mga Patak*, which were penned by Ramos. For instance, in his sermon, the priest strongly encourages his congregation to follow in the footsteps of a *Kaluluwang Wagas* (Pure Soul), which characterized the martyrs and heroes of the 1896 Revolution.[18] The members are reminded that since they belong to the brown race, they are the rightful inheritors of the 1896 revolution and are encouraged to emulate Rizal and Bonifacio. In addition to these two, Artemio Ricarte and Benigno Ramos are always singled out. Special ceremonies are performed on the Iglesia's Foundation Day and on the birth and death anniversaries of Rizal and Bonifacio. Church members are asked to take care of one another (*magtitinginan*) and to help each other (*magtutulungan*). The church also emphasizes that members are the rightful masters of the country and that the organization is a mutual aid society. The design of the church flag and the song sung at each flag-raising ceremony provide even more evidence of their connection to the Sakdalista movement. At the ceremony, two flags are raised, the flag of the Republic of the Philippines and the flag of the church, which is similar to the Sakdalista flag. During the ceremony, church members sing their anthem. Its lyrics are identical to the anthem the Sakdalistas used to sing in the 1930s (refer to Ch. 3).

No images of Jesus Christ can be found inside the churches. Instead, the statue of the Virgin Mary is displayed, dressed in the tricolors of the Philippine flag, to symbolize the Inang Bayan (Mother Country). Other figures venerated include Rizal and the 1896 revolutionaries. In the Silang church, a painting on the wall above the altar has a sun with multiple rays rising behind three mountains representing Luzon, Visayas, and

Mindanao. It is identical to the masthead of one of the Sakdalista publications, *The Filipino Freedom*.[19] Considering that a large number of Sakdalista members came from the IFI church, it is not surprising that the interior of the Iglesia is similar to that of the IFI, in which Rizal and the 1896 revolutionary martyrs were revered.[20]

Furthermore, when closely examining the Iglesia's creed and *Pitong Utos* (Seven Commandments), one is struck by the similarity to the prayer recited by the priests and priestesses of the Colorums at the turn at the twentieth century. The Seven Commandments are: 1) *Matang Maamo* (Gentle Eyes); 2) *Taingang Lampasan* (Forgiving Ears); 3) *Bibig na Sinusian* (Sealed Lips); 4) *Pusong Kordero* (Heart of a Lamb); 5) *Manood* (Be Observant); 6) *Mag-antay* (Have Patience); 7) *Ang Filipinas, sa mga Katutubo o sa mga Inaanak Lamang ng Filipinas* (The Philippines, only for the Natives or True Children of the Philippines).[21] This shows that the Iglesia was connected not only to the Sakdalista movement but also to the Colorum organization. A common thread running from the Colorum societies to the Sakdalista movement shows that the Colorum societies have survived to the present through the Iglesia and movements, such as the Sakdalista.[22]

Salud Algabre and Valentin de los Santos were among the first to join the Iglesia. Algabre was a Sakdalista and an Aglipayan layperson. She saw herself and her family standing in a long tradition of resistance to colonialism. According to her, someone in the family was always getting involved in uprisings to fight against oppression. For these activities, they were banished to Ilocos, Nueva Ecija, Pampanga, and other places. She stated, "In my visits to those places, I found out they were all Sakdalistas."[23] Here, she may have been intending the term "Sakdalista" to symbolize those Filipinos fighting against foreign domination. When the May Uprising occurred, most politicians and journalists trivialized the event by saying that Ramos's utopian promise fell on "the fertile ground" of ignorant followers. "The fertile ground" was this tradition of protest—to protest against whatever soiled their self-respect and dignity. Even after the experience of the Japanese Occupation, Algabre carried on the tradition in the newly established Iglesia.

Valentin de los Santos left the Iglesia in the late 1950s and organized his own religious organization called the Lapiang Malaya (Freedom Party or simply, Lapian). It was also known as Bukal na Pananampalataya (The Fountain of Faith or Bukal). Lapian was considered the political arm of the Bukal. De los Santos preached that members must adhere to the indigenous Philippine religion and rid themselves of any Western influence in their daily lives. He insisted on using the Tagalog language not only for prayers but also in everyday conversation. This was at the height of Americanism since the Americans had returned to the Philippines in 1945 as "liberators" to the Filipino people, who had nobody but the Americans to turn to. American culture, including the use of English, all the more dominated the social and cultural scenes. By the early 1960s, membership in the Lapian grew to about forty-two thousand, attracting rural folks mainly from southern Luzon. Eventually, the headquarters was established in Pasay, in the heart of Metro Manila.

De los Santos claimed that he had been in regular communication with the Deity, the spirits of Jose Rizal and the fallen heroes of the 1896 Revolution. As the name of the organization suggests, de los Santos declared the Philippines to be a U.S. colony; therefore, the Filipinos were still living in economic hardship in an unjust society. He assured his followers that if he were the president of the Philippines, he would create a prosperous society in which they would find contentment and peace. He ran for the highest seat of government during every presidential election. De los Santos had also organized numerous demonstrations at Malacañang Palace in order to appeal to the President to alleviate their poverty.[24] Other demonstrations included one in October 1966 against the summit of the seven nations allied with the U.S. in the Vietnam War. De los Santos's running for the presidency had been dismissed as a joke but the people paid serious attention when the Lapian members were massacred in May 1967.[25]

Five hundred Lapian members planned to march to Malacañang on 21 May 1967 to demand that Pres. Marcos step down. Although the demonstration was called off at the last moment, the Philippine Constabulary and the police were stationed in front of de los Santos's house in Pasay. There were conflicting stories on how it happened but whatever the cause might have been, automatic weapons were fired on Lapian members. In seconds, thirty-three were dead and fourty-seven wounded. Later, four hundred Lapian members, including de los Santos, were arrested and charged with rebellion. Eventually, de los Santos was confined at the National Mental Hospital, where he was lynched.[26]

When Valentin de los Santos was murdered in the hospital, he was around eighty-six years old (he was not sure of his birth date). He was born in Sorsogon, Bicol and studied at the Naga Seminary to become a priest but left the seminary to come to Manila. After taking up odd jobs, he landed a steady job with the American quartermaster. He also worked as a part-time mechanic and a boxer. When the Sakdalista movement began in 1930, de los Santos immediately joined the movement. After the May Uprising, he became inactive; but as soon as Ramos returned from Japan in 1938, he joined the newly-formed Ganap Party. During the Japanese Occupation, he became a *yoin* (civilian workers in the military) and worked as a mechanic. At the end of the occupation, he joined the Makapili and was arrested when the American forces landed. He was tried by the People's Court and released after serving a prison term of several years.[27]

### The Sakdalista Movement as a Rizalista Cult

As we have seen, many members, if not a majority, of the Iglesia and Lapian came from the Sakdalista movement, which declared that it was simply carrying on the teachings of Rizal. The published Sakdalista Party platform dedicated one whole page to a portrait of Rizal. Relying on Marcelino Foronda's definition of "a cult" as a movement that honors "a thing or person, including worship and veneration," we can safely say that the Sakdalista movement was a cult honoring Rizal.[28]

Some scholars who study politico-religious societies, including the Rizalista cults, point out that members of such organizations consider the heroes of the 1896 Revolution to have paid the ultimate utang na loob (debt of gratitude) to Inang Bayan (Mother Country) and that their sacrifices demand reciprocity from later generations. In this way, members' religious acts could be perceived as political and their political acts as religious, as seen in their devotion to *Dios* (God), *Kapwa* (fellow countrymen), and *Bayan* (country). Some scholars refer to Rizalista cult members as descendants of the 1896 Katipunan members. [29]

According to Prospero Covar, the Rizalistas created the cult's central doctrine from a combination of *anitism* (indigenous *anito*, or idolatory religion), Roman Catholicism (mainly Pasyon), and American Protestantism, tempered by Filipino parables, proverbs, ancient wisdom, and morality.[30] In other words, Christian teachings—Catholicism brought by Spain and Protestantism brought by America—were selectively appropriated and cognized in accordance with the traditional Filipino system of beliefs, values, and social relationships.[31] These scholars all agree that the formation of the Rizalista cults and other politico-religious societies is a manifestation of the creative strength of the Filipino masses, who have kept their moral, spiritual, and cultural values alive for generations, even under foreign regimes. These definitions and descriptions fit the nature of the Sakdalista movement, as we observe its principles and moral teachings. The Iglesia and the Lapian created after the war by some Ganap members clearly belong to Rizalista cults.

Studies by Reynaldo C. Ileto and Floro C. Quibuyen confirm the significance of Rizal's life for the anticolonial movements and uprisings that unfolded during the American colonial period. These authors point to such movements carried out by the Rizalista groups in Mounts Banahaw and San Cristobal, the Pulahanes of Samar, the Colorums of Surigao, and other similar groups in Central Visayas. John N. Schumacher, S.J, has commented that these examples belong to the fringe of society.[32] Indeed, they do. Yet the Sakdalista movement was not a fringe movement but one of the most popularly supported movements in central and southern Luzon in the 1930s. In this sense the American colonial regime was not able to marginalize the movements that sprang from the masses, contrary to Quibuyen's claims.[33]

Rizal was revered not only by the peasant masses and IFI members but also by some in the educated class, all of whom were greatly inspired by Rizal's sacrifice and martyrdom, as the 1896 and 1899 revolutionaries had been.[34] For this reason, the Sakdalista movement attracted some in the highly educated and well-to-do classes as well. When the movement was taking shape in the early 1930s, it was able to bring the "fanatical" Rizalistas up from the "dark underside" of Philippine society, to borrow Ileto's words, to the surface of a national popular protest movement and eventually into mainstream Philippine politics.[35]

# EPILOGUE

T HE SAKDALISTA MOVEMENT showed the Filipino people an alternative, independent, future society rooted in Philippine tradition and morality. The movement derived its strength from past revolutionary experiences.

Past studies on the Sakdalista uprising and movement have contributed to understanding the motives and nature of the movement. However, these studies have failed to recognize one important aspect, the connecting thread that ran through the Makapili organization, Ganap Party, Sakdalista movement, Ricartistas' military and civic organizations, peasant organizations, and IFI and politico-religious societies. All these organizations sought the country's independence throughout the American colonial period by keeping alive the legacy of the 1896 Revolution and the Philippine-American War. How did they hold on to their aspirations under rigorous Americanization process?

When the American colonial administration was set up in the early 1900s, the colonial officials tried to undermine Filipino resistance against the American forces; first, by crushing their guerrilla resistance, and second, by prosecuting thousands of Filipinos considered to be anti-American. Then the colonial regime shifted to covert operations with systematic surveillance of and infiltration into radical organizations to demoralize and eventually destroy their operations.[1] While American officials acknowledged the Filipinos'struggle and aspirations for independence, they believed that the Filipinos lacked experience for democratic self-rule. They declared that only after the Filipinos had mastered the art of politics under guidance would independence be granted. When "peace and order" had been reestablished, American tutorship began in the political, educational, and social arenas. Mass media and civic ceremonies were amply utilized. The American system of education reached an ever-wider population, and mastering English became directly connected to raising one's status in the colonial society. Filipino culture and the people's worldview came under strong American influence.

Despite this social environment, some Filipinos, believing in their ability to govern themselves, refused to accept the American notion that the Filipinos were not ready for independence. In those Filipinos' hearts, the legacy of the 1896 Revolution and the Philippine-American War was deeply held. The late historian Teodoro Agoncillo, for instance, looking back to his high school days, believed that the student strike in 1930 reached such heights, involving five to ten thousand participants, because they were inspired by the heroism and sacrifice of the 1896 revolutionaries.[2]

While the Sakdalistas severely criticized American colonial policy as oppressive and imperialistic, they recognized and appreciated the tools with which the American colonial government had provided them.[3] In fact, the Sakdalista movement thrived in the system that the U.S. colonial government had established: the right to freedom of speech, the right to hold public meetings, and the right to publish. For the Sakdalistas, the guarantee of these rights became effective means to reach the masses and to organize their movement into a political party. They were able to enter the national political arena, which had been monopolized by the elite.

Most Sakdalista leaders, including Ramos, had received an American style education. Although Ramos's educational achievements were not as high as his adversaries, they were high enough to command respect from his followers. He was able to speak and write in colonial languages and to communicate effectively with his political enemies. Within the Sakdalista leaders were holders of law degrees and graduates of overseas and U.S. universities. However, they sought to establish an independent nation modeled after their own traditions and indigenous values, not after those of the American.

It is true that the American colonial period produced a Filipino identity and that Rizal and the 1896 heroes were revered in the classrooms and their writings were published.[4] However, this was done within the framework of American tutorship so as not to endanger the establishment of the U.S.-led colonial structure. It is also true that by the time of the Japanese invasion, for most Filipinos, the memory of the Philippine-American War had faded into the distant past due to accelerated Americanization,[5] and people like the Sakdalistas became a minority. Those minority groups that held the "subversive" ideology of Philippine independence conducted their own education at home or through religious organizations, including politico-religious societies, civic organizations, or peasant and labor movements, reminding the new generations of the legacy of the past revolutions. This is how the aspiration of independence had survived under the Americanization process.

Even today, those whose backgrounds can be traced to the Sakdalista movement still believe that true independence has not yet been achieved. For instance, in December 1985, on the day of Rizal's execution, a conference was held to regain the precolonial period of self-rule. This was a national conference of all the *kapatiran* (brotherhood) groups and was held at the Puerta Real Gardens in Manila. The conference was organized by the Kapatiran Pilipinas (The Philippine Brotherhood) and attended by around three thousand people, including the members of the Iglesia and the now-defunct Lapiang Malaya. The purpose was to achieve "Unity, Peace, and Progress for the Mother Country the Philippines" while promoting "the renewal of Inner Self (*Loob*) and Unification of the Filipino citizens." The organization declared that it intended to work toward these goals by disseminating knowledge regarding the practice of precolonial spiritual traditions and by preserving their distinctive ethnic identities so that people could lead honorable and dignified lives in the atmosphere of brotherhood.[6]

If the Sakdalistas had not risen in May of 1935, would they have been able to maintain a strong opposition party and contributed to social change? Perhaps. If they had not collaborated outright with the Japanese military during the occupation period, would they have been persecuted so harshly after the war? Perhaps not. However, little can be gained by indulging in this kind of speculation. Our task is to understand how the Sakdalista movement culminated in the organization of a small Filipino paramilitary group called the Makapili. My hope is that the Filipino people in general will come to understand the true motives and intentions of the Sakdalista and Ganap Parties and the Makapilis, and that this will lead to dialogue and, eventually, reconciliation.

# APPENDIX 1

## *Tumututol Kami* (We Object)[1]
(Summary translation)

1.  We object to the unending deceit being committed by fickle politicians (*pulitikong kabilanin*) because rather than fight for immediate independence (*kagyat na kasarinlan*), what they do is to borrow immediately (from the U.S.A.). (*kagyat na pag-utang*). They want only comfort for themselves at the cost of the people.

2.  They (the government officials) destroyed the people's trust by creating a group of lucky individuals who are obedient to them and who receive help from them. These obedient individuals, in turn, live by squeezing the poor.

3.  We object to their (the government officials') clear and unending intention of making the Philippines a little America because American lifestyle fits only the Americans and will never fit us because we have our own.

4.  We object to the delay in the granting of our independence because we, who have bold hearts for independence, including those of us who are old and who have fought in the war, may grow weak, while the ones who are young are growing up and have their own thinking and beliefs (and don't understand our cause).

5.  We object to the treacherous deeds of politicians who let themselves be used by the enemies of our Freedom. It should be made known to them that the reason these acts go on without protest is because the ones perpetrating these misdeeds are our own politicians, and if it were foreigners who were committing these acts, the whole population (*buong sambayanan*) would react instantly. Another reason (they are not protesting) is that the people are trying to avoid doing anything that will harm our independence. That is the reason people are enduring the politicians' misdeeds.

6.  We object to the persecution of those who cannot pay taxes and the confiscation, in revenge, of the properties of those who do not agree with the greedy

politicians and of the little people (*mga maliliit*), who do not want to be tied to them.

7.    We object to the prosecution of the little people with hardly any evidence (*walang gaanong pinagbabatayan*), and to making it hard for them to earn a living, until they reach the point of not wanting to work anymore but to be idle.

8.    We object to the incumbent administration, which is all lopsided and wrong, with crooked reasoning and injustice, and gives our youth a wrong understanding of reason and justice.

9.    We object to the present situation in which the Country produces nothing except criminals and people who are idle and sycophantic.

# *Mga Layunin* (Objectives)[1]
(Summary translation)

1.  We demand complete and total independence from the Americans at all costs, which the Democrat Americans have written in their platform and promised in the preamble of the Jones Law. If this independence is not achieved at the end of 1935, all Sakdalistas in the government shall resign and give their posts to others.

2.  We oppose the establishment of a government that is capitalist, communist, Soviet, or Bolshevik. We also oppose the system of the Nazis of Germany and the fascists of Italy. This government would embody Filipino behavior, thoughts, feelings, intelligence, history and all such noble characteristics. We believe that only a truly Filipino government will satisfy the Filipinos.

3.  Independence of a country cannot be achieved without sacrifice (*pagpapakasakit*). The elected Sakdalistas in the government will sacrifice and shall receive only limited amount for their expenses. (List of the amount according to the government position is shown.) Sakdalistas will not collect contributions for their campaigns. Money saved will be used to pay for debts incurred to America and other initial expenses by the new government that will be established. Government employees shall earn a minimum salary of P1.20 per day since the public servants are to serve the people.

4.  Recall and impeachment law for all officials of the government should be established. (How these laws shall be applied is described.)

5.  Land taken from the poor or unjustly taken will be returned to prevent trouble (*ligalig*).

6.  Students will be sent abroad to study the making of arms for the country's benefit. Money to be used for this will come from salaries saved.

7.  Any government official shall be totally banned from joining any religious activities to prevent support of any religious group.

8. The welfare of police, constables, firemen, teachers, and government employees according to seniority, age, number of children, and work efficiency should be supported.

9. Jobs should be given for the unemployed poor to prevent criminality and to help the country's economy.

10. All Filipinos shall be given the right to train in the use of arms under the supervision of the constabulary.

11. Any abuse of authority will automatically mean dismissal from office of any government personnel.

12. Removal of pensions received by families of legislators or politicians; and the transfer of secret agents and experts to other jobs.

13. The arrest of *jueteng* (a form of gambling) collectors should be totally banned. Only their leaders (operators or *pamumuan ng jueteng*) should be arrested.

14. Any government official or member of his family linked to jueteng or similar activities shall be dismissed from office and tried.

15. Gambling shall be banned except on Sundays. The government shall not collect money connected to gambling. Everyone will be given jobs; the idle will be punished.

16. The kind of politics that should be put in force (*paiiralin*) is the one which prioritizes life over wealth; honor over duty; cleanliness (*kalinisan*) over money; freedom for all over dealings (*pagsasamahan*) (with the U.S.A.). If the government is just (*matuwid*), then wrongdoing will diminish and peace and happiness will illuminate (spread or *tatanglaw*) the household.

17. Welfare should be rendered to every household, as in Japan and America. Poor nursing mothers will be cared for.

18. Every poor man has the right to send his children to school. Fees shall be collected in the high school and at university levels. Examinations in law, medicine, etc. will be encouraged for a fee.

19. Cabinet secretaries should be removed and in their places a Council of Elders should be established to advise the governor general and the Legislature.

20. The native language (*sariling wika*) in all the Courts of Peace and Courts of First Instance should be used. All Laws will be translated in the popular (*lalong kilala*) language.

21. Change election procedures and pattern it after the American model which is simpler. Reelection will not be allowed.

22. Students shall be encouraged to finish their careers. The educational system shall be improved to make them understand the importance of freedom, their country and unity among Filipinos.

23. Remove the resident commissioner to America from office because it has not achieved anything. Likewise the commercial representative (*agente commercial*) should be removed.

24. The franchises held by the phone, gas, tranvia, autobus, Meralco, and (other) electric companies should be studied.

25. Freedom of the citizenry to hold meetings should be protected.

26. Punishment by the courts should be meted out to all government employees who enrich themselves while in office.

27. Landowners and landlords shall be prohibited from unreasonably increasing rents. Hacienda owners are obliged to provide a good environment for their tenants, build good roads, and install lights on the streets.

28. The cedula should be removed; and taxes on land and crops should be studied in order to levy appropriates taxes.

29. Interest rates on loans should be not more than 10 centavos for P1 for one year.

30. Land shall be provided to all those interested in farming.

31. The workers in the factories will have representatives who will analyze the books of the capitalists so that they will know if the factory is really profiting or not so that the workers' salary can be adjusted accordingly. Vacation and retirement benefits will be assured.

32. The situation of Filipino workers in the U.S. and Hawaii should be investigated:

so many are underemployed and who are responsible for nonpayment to those who were brought there by the Hawaiian Sugar Planters Association.

33. Houses that cost below P1,000 need no building licenses.

34. Those who suffered in the past revolution will be given the care that they deserve. The government should give them benefits. It is important to see what the veterans have done for the country.

35. The Sakdalistas stand for the following principles for farmer organizations in the places where farm disputes have been reported.
    a)  The landowner (*propietario*) is the one who pays the land tax.
    b)  Irrigation systems should be for all and the government should not charge for their use.
    c)  Loans will be recorded in the farmers' books as well as the landowners'. All loan payments will be duly noted in both books.
    d)  Interest on loans should not exceed 10 percent per annum.
    e)  Before the share of the landowner is computed, the farmer will first put aside 2 cavans (a cavan is equal to 75 liters) per hundred which he shall sell and keep the proceeds in the government's Caja de Ahorros (Savings Bank) in preparations for his old age or for his family should he die. The landowner and the tenant shall then set aside the cost of seedling and milling and whatever is left over shall be divided equally between them. If the farmer has a loan, this will not be arbitrarily taken, but will be paid according to the governing rules.
    f)  The landowner will spend for the cost of planting.
    g)  The farmer will spend for the cost of harvesting by purchasing *gapas* (an instrument for cutting rice stalks).
    h)  The delivery of the landlord's granary will be according to what has been agreed upon.

The relationship between the landowner and tenant should be like that between parent and child (*magmamagulang*); thus harmony should reign. Politics should never enter this good relationship because the poison of politics is the one that usually destroys the good characteristics of the country. These rules will be enforced for the benefit of the oppressed as well as for the landowners who are being harassed by their political enemies.

# Direct and Partial Quote of Aims and Purpose of the Ganap Party[1]

1.  "To prepare the Filipino people into a more compact and solid fraternity so that the new conditions that will inevitably arise from the actual conflict in the Far East and will effect international adjustments and the life of our country may be utilized intelligently by both the Americans and Filipino people so that a new entanglement that may lead to our subjugation by other powers be avoided."

2.  "It is our sincere desire and the aim of the Filipinos to attain the complete emancipation of the Philippines, and this is the reason why, now more than ever, we need a united front...and to place above selfish interests the welfare and security of our country."

3.  "It is our firm conviction that under the present regime, the forgotten men can secure their prosperity and advancement and that the presence of the American sovereignty is not in any manner a hindrance to their social and economic improvement. Having in the government the officials who have in their hearts the best interest and welfare of the poor, we can expect the realization of the good governmental program for the economic redemption of our masses. Although we become independent the people will remain in poverty if the present conditions will continue: the confiscation of the lands, houses, plants and beasts of burden which are contrary to the humanitarian purposes of the United States and to the altruistic utterances of President Quezon..."

4.  "The people shall become indolent, victims of vices and ignorance if our government would allow and suffer them to such, but the people shall become industrious, thrifty, and decent if the government desires them to be so, for the governing officials are the fathers of their countrymen and are always obeyed in whatever they wish and for this reason, the actions of the government reflected upon the masses. In brief, if we want to see the virtue or the evil of the officials' deeds, we have but to see the living conditions and the situation of our countrymen in the barrios, towns, fields, and riversides.

And their conditions will prove whether the good promises are carried out or simply a disregard of the miseries of our people."

5.   "We believe that our people and race must not be allowed to disintegrate as may be expected from the confiscation of real and personal properties and the destruction of their industries. We endorse the wisdom of the Social Justice program of Pres. Quezon."

6.   "We are against any measure tending to divide our people into classes of rich and poor, *responsibles* and *irresponsibles*. There can be no independence for a divided people and there can be no country for a people without union."

7.   "We advocate that our leading medical doctors be at the government's disposal and be required to render aids and services to everyone without compensation. The whole Philippine Archipelago should be divided into sanitary districts under the supervision of these doctors, especially in the filling gutters or of all dirty pools which serve as breeding places of mosquitoes, flies, and all disease-carriers. ...These medical doctors shall distribute drugs even in the form of injections or otherwise without charge."

8.   "We urge the training of all the Filipinos in the management of anti-gas implements, and establishment of safe places of refuge in case of gas attack and invasion; the increase of our army enlistment and strengthening of our air corps by encouraging civil and military aviation; and creation of a Philippine navy to defend our coasts, and the manufacture of arms and all war implements to avoid purchasing them from abroad."

9.   "We urge the recognition of the right to live to be placed above the right of properties, the interest of the people above personal grudges and political ambitions, and that municipal councils consider it as their duty to defend the life, liberty, and property of their respective jurisdictions against any action that may imperil the security and safety of their people so that the Insular government may have easy task in carrying out the administrative program for the good of all."

10.   "We demand the strict enforcement in all schools (public or private) of the teaching of good manners and right conduct."

11.   "It will be our constant endeavor to have an ever-increasing confidence and cooperation between the government and the people of the Philippines, to

instill in the minds of our communities a strong conviction that welfare and prosperity of the people are also the welfare of the government."

12. "Revival of the Senate to avoid any tendency to dictatorship on the part of the chief executive."

13. "The sending of Filipino laborers, merchants, and traders abroad to purchase lands and establish Philippine foreign trades and the marketing of our products subsidized and protected by the government."

14. "The American promise of granting our independence in 1946 will be thrown to naught if the people will become landless, propertyless [*sic*], and homeless because of their delinquency to pay the government taxes...it is the duty of the citizens to fulfill their duty toward their government, but the loss of their lands, properties, and homes is a serious matter...and we rely upon the wisdom and patriotism of our government officials to encourage the industries and to enhance the sources of livelihood of the people to avoid delinquency in the payment of taxes. We suggest the following for the consideration of our officials:

    a) That no taxes shall be imposed upon properties of less than P5,000 in value.
    b) That the government should handle and control the development of all the natural resources (as mines, petroleum, coal, manganese, etc.) and that none of the Filipino interests shall be utilized against the Filipino people; to purchase and sell the products and industries of our people in order that the inhabitants may be encouraged to work.
    c) That the prosperity of the people is the government's prosperity...and for this reason we urge the colonization of Mindanao and Sulu and all our virgin lands."

# CHRONOLOGICAL TABLE

## 1930

| | |
|---|---|
| 28 June | The first issue of the *Sakdal* is published. |
| August | Boycott of foreign-made goods begins. |
| 7 November | Communist Party of the Philippines (CPP) is formally proclaimed. |

## 1931

| | |
|---|---|
| Mid-January | Tayug Uprising occurs. |
| July | Sen. Harry B. Hawes visits Manila. |
| August | Donation campaign for Gen. Ricarte begins. |
| September | Both the CPP and Katipunan ng mga Anak-pawis (KAP) are outlawed.<br>Sec. of War Patrick J. Hurley visits Manila. |
| October | Malayang Bayan movement begins. |
| 22 November | "Meeting of Confrontation" is held in cooperation with the Union Civica Filipinas. |
| November | "Peaceful Disobedience" movement begins. |
| 4 December | Torch parade against the Eighth Independent Mission is held. |
| 9 December | Mass arrest of the Tanggulan members takes place. |

## 1932

| | |
|---|---|
| Early February | A postal ban on the *Sakdal* is ordered (remains until June). |
| May | Donation campaign to purchase a printing press begins. |
| October | An appeal to the U.S. Congress to grant the Philippines immediate independence is sent in the name of the Malayang Bayan. |
| 26 October | The Supreme Court declares the CPP illegal. |
| November | Donation campaign to send Sakdalistas' own Independent Mission begins. |
| 11 December | "Meeting ng Malayang Bayan is held at the Olympic Stadium to boost the campaign for the Sakdalistas' Mission. |

## 1933

| | |
|---|---|
| January | The Hare-Hawes-Cutting (H-H-C) Act passes in the U.S. Congress. |
| First week of March | Celerino Tiongco becomes acting editor of the *Sakdal*. |
| End of March | The Sakdalistas' own Independence Mission leaves for the U.S. |
| 22 March | Ramos pays a visit to Gen. Ricarte in Yokohama. |
| 10 April | Welcome party for Ramos is held in Honolulu. |
| End of April to June | Ramos stays in California. |
| July | *Manila Sakdal's Supplement* is published in Stockton, California. |
| | Ramos's Mission arrives in Washington, D.C. |
| 17 October | The Philippine legislature declines to accept the H-H-C Act. |
| 29 October | The Sakdalista Party is established. |
| November | *Pamahayag at Patakaran ng Lapiang Sakdalista* is published. |
| December | Quezon leaves for the U.S. to seek another independence bill. |

## 1934

| | |
|---|---|
| 1 May | The Philippine legislature accepts the Tydings-McDuffie (T-M) Act. |
| 6 June | General elections are held and the Sakdalista Party sends three representatives to the Assembly. |
| 30 July | The Constitutional Convention begins. |
| September | Two Sakdalista representatives are removed from chairmanship positions in the Assembly. |
| 24 November | Ramos ostensibly leaves for the U.S. |
| 6 December | Ramos arrives in Japan and announces his plans to stay there indefinitely. |
| Early December | Sen. Millard Tydings visits the Philippines. |
| End of December | Sakdalista members send a *Memorial* addressed to U.S. Pres. Roosevelt through Sen. Tydings. |
| 31 December | Santa Rosa Sakdalistas are harassed by the provincial governor. |

# 1935

| | |
|---|---|
| Early January | The Sakdalista Party prints one thousand copies of the *Memorial*.<br>The Sakdalista Party starts anti-T-M Act campaign.<br>Harassment of the Sakdalistas becomes more rampant. |
| Early February | Ramos's wife, two children, and his mother-in-law join him in Tokyo. Tiongco and Santos also visit Ramos. |
| March | Sakdalista Councilors in Santa Rosa are suspended by the Provincial Board. |
| April | Seven Sakdalistas in Tayabas are accused of sedition.<br>The first issue of *The Filipino Freedom* is published. |
| End of April | Copies of *Free Filipinos* are circulating in Manila and nearby provinces as well as in Tokyo. |
| 30 April | Tayabas Sakdalista leaders send a letter addressed to acting Gov. Gen. Hayden complaining about the harassment of their members by the local authorities. |
| 2 and 3 May | The Sakdalista uprising takes place. |
| 5 May | The Investigative Committee on the uprising is formed. |
| 13 May | Ramos sends a cablegram to Pres. Roosevelt, demanding the withdrawal of the U.S. government from the Philippines. |
| 14 May | The plebiscite takes place. |
| 17 May | Hayden and his party visit the affected areas by the uprising. |
| 2 June | A Sakdalista meeting is held at the party's headquarters to reflect on the uprising. |
| End of July | The Sakdalista Party's national assembly is held. |
| 18 September | The first general elections under the Commonwealth are held. |
| Early October | Ramos meets with thirty Japanese supporters in Tokyo. |
| Early November | Ramos produces a pamphlet, *The American Government Does not Like Peace in the Philippines*, addressed to the U.S. President and Congress. |
| November | The Sakdalistas prepare a *Memorial* to U.S. Sec. of War George Dean. |
| 15 November | The Commonwealth of the Philippines is established. |
| 10 December | Ramos's wife, Liboria, returns from Japan. |
| Mid-December | Salud Algabre is arrested and charged with sedition. |

**(1935, continued.)**

| | |
|---|---|
| Late December | Ramos travels to Taiwan to pay a visit to the chief of staff of the Japanese Army. |
| 29 December | Some 30 Sakdalista leaders, including Celerino Tiongco and Elpidio Santos, are arrested on charges of sedition. |

# 1936

| | |
|---|---|
| 18 August | President Quezon pardons thirty-one Sakdalistas who have been in jail. |
| Mid-September | Ramos is lodged in the Kobe police station for one night on the way to Manchuria. |
| 3 October | A series of bombings occur in Manila in another attempt of Sakdalista uprising. |
| 24 October | Five hundred Sakdalistas attempt to bomb the municipal building in Bayambang, Pangasinan, as part of the uprising. |
| 2 November | Open letter criticizing Quezon is published in the *Manila Daily Bulletin*. |

# 1937

| | |
|---|---|
| February | A united opposition against Quezon is formed. |
| March | Ramos sends a telegram to Quezon advising him to obtain absolute independence. |
| | Ramos sends telegram to Sen. Lewis Hamilton, urging the U.S. to grant the Philippines absolute independence. |
| Early April | Eugenio Salazar (B. Ramos) sends a letter to Gen. Senjuro Hayashi. |
| 23 May | Ramos's wife Liboria passes away. |
| June | Ramos publishes a pamphlet, *Quezon is the Real Enemy of the Government in the Philippines*.<br>Ramos sends an open letter to the Philippine Commonwealth government: "Suggestions to the Commonwealth Government." |

**(1937, continued.)**

| | |
|---|---|
| September | Ramos sends a telegram to High Commissioner McNutt, urging him to look into tax abuses in Atimonan, Tayabas. The Sakdalista Party prepares a *Memorial for the Joint Preparatory Committee*. Sakdalista representatives attend the Joint Preparatory Committee Hearing. |
| October | Ricardo Enrile, Ramos's valet, returns to Manila for a short visit. |
| End of November | Japanese Diet member Koike Shiro visits Manila. |
| 14 December | Provincial and municipal elections are held. The Sakdalista Party runs on the Popular Front ticket. |

## 1938

| | |
|---|---|
| February | Gaudencio Bautista, former official of the Sakdalista Party, comes to Tokyo and tries to see Ramos. |
| April | The Sakdalista Party merges with the peasant group Dumating Na. The Sakdalista women organize the Patriotic League for women. |
| June | Quezon visits Japan and meets with Ramos. |
| 28 August | Ramos returns to the Philippines and is immediately arrested, but is released after filing a bond. |
| 12 September | The Sakdalista Party changes its name to Ganap Party. |
| 7 October | The first issue of the *Ganap* comes out. |
| 8 November | Elections for the National Assembly are held. The Ganap Party is defeated. |

## 1939

| | |
|---|---|
| 3 January | The Court of First Instance of Manila rules the Sakdalista Party an illegal association. |
| January | The party members are issued ladaw (membership cards). |

**(1939, continued.)**

| | |
|---|---|
| February | The Ganap Party publishes *Panawagan sa Lahat ng Lapian at Kababayan ukol sa Paghahanda ng Pansagot sa Kasarinlan kung Umalis na ang Estados Unidos* (Call to All the Party (Members) and Fellow Countrymen about the Guarantee for Independence When the U.S. Leaves). |
| 12 May | Ramos is arrested on swindling charges. He pleads not guilty before the Manila Municipal Court and is later released on bail. |
| June | The Patriotic League for Women publishes its organ, *Hirang*. |
| Early July | Ramos announces his candidacy for the presidential election for 1941. Ramos publishes *Mga Patak ng Luha ng Bayang Api*. |
| Mid-November | Ramos is arrested again. |
| 7 December | Ramos is sentenced at the Laguna Court of First Instance to four to five years. |
| Early December | Ramos is given an accumulated maximum jail sentence of sixteen years in the courts of Manila, Laguna, and Bulacan. Later, his sentence is reduced to twelve years on charges of rebellion, illegal association, and estafa (swindling). |

## 1940

| | |
|---|---|
| Early January | Ramos is sent to Bilibid Prison. |
| Mid-May | The Ganap Party sends a *Memorial* to the U.S. Pres. and Congress, reiterating its firm stand on immediate independence. |
| October | The Ganap Party puts up candidates for local as well as national elections. |
| 10 December | General elections are held, but the Ganap Party candidates face dismal failure. |
| End of December | The Court of Appeals rules that the Sakdalista Party is illegal. |

## 1941

| | |
|---|---|
| 27 June | The case of illegal association of the Sakdalista Party is elevated by the Court of Appeals to the Supreme Court. |
| 11 November | Presidential and general elections are held. |

**(1941, continued.)**

| Mid-December | Many Ganap members are arrested on fifth-column charges. |
| 19 December | Gen. Ricarte is flown to Aparri in northern Luzon. |

## 1942

| 2 January | The Japanese military occupies the Philippines. |
| Mid-January | The Bagong Pagkakaisa is formed. |
| 3 April | Ramos, Tiongco, and other Ganap members are released from prison. |
| 4 December | All political parties, including the Ganap Party, are dissolved. |
| 30 December | The Kalibapi is formally launched and the Ganap Party is absorbed into it. |

## 1943

| June | Filipinos (mainly the Ganapistas) start military training at Fort McKinley and elsewhere. |
| 14 October | Independence of the Philippines is granted. |

## 1944

| September | Gen. Tomoyuki Yamashita arrives. |
| Mid-October | U.S. forces invade Leyte. |
| 10 November | The articles and by-laws of the Makapili are drafted. |
| 8 December | Formal inauguration of the Makapili is held. |

## 1945

| End of January | Makapili suicide squad fights a one-sided battle in Manila and elsewhere. |
| January | Ganapistas/Makapilis and their families retreat to the mountains with the Japanese military. Ramos retreats to Baguio and reportedly dies there. |
| September | People's Court trial begins. |

# NOTES

## Prologue

1. For such cases, see trial court documents of the United States of America Commonwealth of the Philippines People's Court, University of the Philippines. For portrayal of Filipino soldiers, see Josephine de Jesus Quimbo, "Survivors' Schematic Reconstruction of the Japanese Occupation of Los Baños," *Philippine Studies* 56, no. 2 (2008): 206. The only article that I came across in which the Makapilis were treated as victims of the Japanese Occupation is by Angelito L. Santos, "Gleanings from a Cruel War," in Under Japanese Rule, ed. Renato Constantino (Quezon City: Foundation for Nationalist Studies, Inc., 1994), 5–63.

2. For instance, Prime Min. Yasuhiro Nakasone expressed deep regret to Pres. Ferdinand Marcos on his visit to Manila in 1983. See Satoshi Nakano, "The Politics of Mourning," in *Philippines-Japan Relations*, ed. Setsuho Ikehata and Lydia N. Yu Jose (Quezon City: Ateneo de Manila University Press, 2003): 340–41. More recently, in 2006, Japanese Ambassador to the Philippines Ryuichiro Yamazaki expressed a heartfelt apology for the massacre of Filipinos at the hands of the desperate Japanese soldiers. See "Remarks by Ambassador Ryuichiro" (2006), http://ph.emb-japan.go.jp/pressandspeech/2006%20speeches/liberationof manila.htm.

3. Reconciliation efforts can be seen among the groups of former Japanese soldiers, but their primary motive for coming to the Philippines was to memorialize the death of their comrades. For more details on the Bridge for Peace project, see http://bridgeforpeace.jp. The other project is the Battle of Manila, organized by social scientists. Their task is to gather historical materials from the U.S., the Philippines, and Japan on the battle of Manila that took place in February 1945. Based on these facts, they hope to commence discussion among these three countries, leading to reconciliation between the Philippines and Japan. This ongoing Battle of Manila Project was organized by Dr. Satoshi Nakano of Hitotsubashi University in Tokyo.

4. The conference was filmed and televised by NHK on 15 August 2005. It was entitled "60 nenme no taiwa—firipin sabakareta tainichi kyouryokusha—" (Dialogue after 60 years—Judgment on the Japanese Collaborators in the Philippines—). It was produced by Sabara Production Company and directed by Mariko Kanamoto.

## Chapter 1

1. For details on the uprisings in Bulacan, Laguna, and Cavite, see "Appendix II: Action by Constabulary prepared by Lieut. Colonel F. W. Manley," and "Appendix no. 3 (should be III), dated May 25, 1935: Sakdal Uprising Report: Action of Municipal Authorities" of Report of the Committee Appointed by Acting Governor General J. R. Hayden to Investigate the Uprisings of May 2 and 3, 1935 (Report of the Committee) in Papers 1934–35, concerning the Sakdals, folder 25-26; "Public Order-Sakdals, Dunham Committee" (Public Order) Hayden Papers (HP), Michigan Historical Collections, Bentley Historical Library, University of Michigan.

2. For details of the Navotas incident, see "Appendix N: The Christmas Eve Fiasco and a Brief Outline of the Ricarte and Other Similar Movements from the Time of the Breaking up of the Insurrection of 1899–1901" in Artemio Ricarte, *Memoirs of General Artemio Ricarte* (Manila: National Heroes Commission, 1963), 159–69. See also *Consolidacion Nacional*, 3 January 1915.

3. For information on the proclamation, see "Christmas Eve Fiasco," 158–59, 169. See also *Consolidacion Nacional*, 3 January 1915.

4. Most of the details in this paragraph come from "Face to Face with the Generala (*sic*)," *The Sunday Tribune*, 12 May 1935; and the Cabuyao section of "Appendix II," in Report of the Committee, 1–6; and "Appendix no. 3," 3–5, folder 25-26, in Public Order, HP. The information about the Cabuyao Sakdalistas wearing red bands across their shoulders and *anting-anting* comes from an interview with Jeremias Adia, whose father was one of the participants, on 27 November 1985, at

his residence in Cabuyao, Laguna. See also appendix D, "An Interview with Salud Algabre," in David Sturtevant, *Popular Uprisings in the Philippines, 1840–1940* (Ithaca: Cornell University Press, 1976), 286–99.

5. See "Appendix II," 3, ibid. Another source indicates 700 Sakdalistas were reportedly involved in the attack on Cabuyao. See "When Laguna Sakdalistas Fell," *Philippines Free Press*, 11 May 1935, 33. See also Amadis Ma Guerrero, "Sakdalista Uprising: Requiem to a Mass Movement," *Philippine Graphic*, 13 May 1970, 7.

6. "Face to Face with the Generala [*sic*]," 3.

7. *The Tribune*, 3 May 1935. See also Sturtevant, "An Interview with Salud Algabre," *Popular Uprisings*, 295.

8. Later investigation revealed that most of the revolutionaries had been shot in the back, showing that they had been running away. The constabulary was accused of using deadly "dum-dum" bullets in suppressing the uprisings. These bullets had already been outlawed in World War I as "inhumane." See "Witnesses Remember Santa Rosa," *The Sunday Tribune Magazine*, 1 May 1949, 8.

9. *The Philippines Herald*, 4 and 11 May 1935.

10. *The Tribune*, 5 May 1935; *The Philippines Herald*, 4 May 1935.

11. See "Report of the Committee," 7–8, folder 25-26, "Public Order," HP Information on the initial development of the uprisings. See 3, 4, 5 May issues of major Manila-based dailies, such as *The Tribune*, the *Manila Daily Bulletin*, and *The Philippines Herald*.

12. See Sakdalista Box, Series 7, Subject File, 1934–1936, Manuel L. Quezon Papers (QP). The number of casualties in the QP is the same as in "Appendix II," in "Report of the Committee." However, the latter does not include Tanza. The *Philippine Graphic* and dailies, such as *The Philippines Herald* and *The Tribune*, give slightly different figures. See "Sakdalista Uprising Crushed," *Philippine Graphic*, 9 May 1935, 6, and the latter two dailies, 4 May 1935.

13. See "Radio sent, no. 209," folder 25-24 (no title), HP. Hayden had earlier estimated the Sakdalistas to number between 60,000 and 300,000. See "Radiogram sent, no. 204 on May 7, 1935 to Sec. of War Cox," ibid., HP. Other sources gave a different estimation. For instance, the governor of Nueva Ecija estimated that there were 6,000 Sakdalistas in Nueva Ecija; of these, 2,000 were in Gapan. He estimated that half this number accounted for fully pledged Sakdalistas and the other half were sympathizers. See appendix no. 3, 11, "Report of the Committee," folder 25-26, "Public Order," HP.

14. For those who dismissed the uprising as foolish, see "Ignorance," *Far Eastern Freemason* (May 1935): 107. See also *The Philippines Herald*, 4 and 15 May 1935; *The Tribune*, 3 and 5 May 1935. Manuel Quezon used the incident to bargain

with the U.S. Congress, blaming the Philippines' economic depression on U.S. legislation limiting the amount of Philippine products that could be exported to the U.S. See *The Tribune*, 5 May 1935; *New York Times*, 5 May 1935; and other major American dailies, which commented that one of the causes of the Filipino uprisings was the shortsighted U.S. trade policy, such as the one incorporated in the Tydings-McDuffie Act. For more on economic problems, see "Report of the Secretary of the Interior on the Sakdalista Uprising, 5 June 1935," QP; "Report of the Secretary of Labor Ramon Torres to Acting Governor General, May 7, 1935," folder no. 25-26, "Public Order," HP. "Sakdalism in Bulacan," an article focusing on the economic aspect of uprising, appeared in three installments in *The Tribune* issues for 21, 22, and 23 May 1935. For other sources, see the *Manila Daily Bulletin*, 18 May 1935; *The Sunday Tribune*, 19 May 1935; and *The Philippines Herald*, 11 May 1935.

15. The negligence of government officials was cited by Jose P. Laurel. See *The Sunday Tribune*, 19 May 1935. Also see *The Philippines Herald*, 11 May 1935; Conrado Benitez, "Sakdalista," *Philippine Magazine*, May 1935, 240 and 252; *Manila Daily Bulletin*, 21, 23, and 27 May 1935. For the journalists' opinions, see A .V. H. Hartendorp, "The Sakdalista Protest," *Philippine Magazine*, May 1935, 233. See also the *Manila Daily Bulletin*, 23 May 1925. See also W(alter) R(obb), "Sakdals," *American Chamber of Commerce Journal* (May 1935): 10–11. This article compared the Sakdalista uprising to the '96 Revolution.

16. "Report of the Committee," 4, folder 25-26, "Public Order," HP. The *Manila Daily Bulletin*, 8 May 1935 issue also noted the same.

17. See Joseph Ralston Hayden, *The Philippines: A Study in National Development* (New York: The Macmillan Company, 1942), 376–400.

18. See Milagros C. Guerrero, "Peasant Discontent and the Sakdalista Uprising," *Praxis* (August–September 1968): 40–56. Roy Manning Stubbs's work has two chapters on the Sakdalista movement. Other movements included were: (1) the Kapisanang Makabola Makasinag (Association of the Worthy Kabola [*sic*]); (2) the Tayug Colorums; and (3) the Tangulan (Tanggulan). See "Philippine Radicalism: The Central Luzon Uprisings, 1925–1935" (PhD diss., University of California, 1951). The word "Colorum" is said to have derived from the ending prayer phrase of the group, "per omnia saecula saeculorum." For more details, see Milagros Guerrero, "The Colorum Uprisings: 1924–1931," *Asian Studies* 5, no. 1 (April 1967): 65.

19. David R. Sturtevant, *Popular Uprisings in the Philippines*, 215–55 and 264–65. Other studies on the Sakdalista movement include Teresita Z. Hachero-Pascual, "The Sakdalista Movement: A Historical Assessment" (PhD diss., University of

Santo Tomas, 1984). Hachero-Pascual interviewed surviving Sakdalista members and introduced Sakdalista documents not previously used. However, no new major insights are gained and her conclusions are similar to those of the previous studies. Carmen Tiongco-Enriquez has a short article, "Revolt in the Grassroots," in *Filipino Heritage: The Making of a Nation,* vol. 9 (Manila: Lahing Pilipino Publishing Inc., 1978), 2517–20. She also wrote "Lapiang Sakdalista: Hibik ng Bayang Api" (The Sakdalista Party: Supplication of the Oppressed People) (a typewritten manuscript of about fifty pages that has no bibliography and is missing a couple of pages), which was given to me by the author. It mentions Benigno Ramos's efforts to advance moral purification, which, unfortunately, were not fully elaborated on and the narration centers on the May 1935 uprising. It has valuable interviews with the Sakdalistas from Santa Rosa, which confirm the Aglipayan membership in the movement and the members' profound belief in God and Christ. Also worthy of note is Grant K. Goodman's "Japan and Philippine Radicalism: The Case of Benigno Ramos," in *Four Aspects of Philippine-Japan Relations, 1930–40* (New Haven: Yale University Southeast Asia Program, 1967), 133–94. This study's main focus is on Ramos's activities in Japan between 1934 and 1938, and Manuel Quezon's scheme to bring him back home.

20. At the time of the uprising, two journalists saw the connection. One was Walter Robb, as mentioned in fn15; the other was Leon Ma. Guerrero. Guerrero said that if Katipunan founder Andres Bonifacio were alive, he would certainly have led one of the Sakdalista uprisings, referring to the1936 uprising. See Leon Ma. Guerrero, "Was Bonifacio a Sakdalista?" *Philippines Free Press,* 28 November 1936, 4, 30, and 36.

21. Milagros C. Guerrero, "Luzon at War: Contradictions in Philippine Society, 1898–1902" (PhD diss., University of Michigan, 1977), 167–69, 194–96, 210–11, 216. Guerrero further hints that the Sakdalista movement may have been built explicitly on earlier organizations, such as the Colorum movement. See Milagros C. Guerrero, "The Colorum Uprisings: 1924–1931," 78.

22. Reynaldo C. Ileto, *Pasyon and Revolution: Popular Movements in the Philippines, 1840–1910* (Quezon City: Ateneo de Manila University Press, 1979).

23. Ibid., 1–3 and 253–54.

24. For instance, the participants of the Christmas Eve Fiasco in Navotas uprising, in 1914, told the governor of Rizal "that (politicians' behavior) is all politics, deceit." See appendix N: "The Christmas Eve Fiasco," 163, in *Memoirs of Artemio Ricarte.*

25. "Christmas Eve Fiasco," 159, 173.

26. *The Philippines Herald,* 15 June 1924. The initiation rites of Legionarios

del Trabajo, organized in 1917, were similar to those of the '96 Katipunan society. One of the organization's founders, Crisanto Evangelista, eventually left the society because he disagreed with its initiation practices and later established the Communist Party of the Philippines. See Philippine Commonwealth, Department of Labor, *Report of the Fact-Finding Survey of Rural Problems in the Philippines to the Secretary of Labor and to the President of the Philippines* (*Survey Report*) (Manila: 1937), 98.

27. For more on Ang Labi ng Katipunan, see *Survey Report*, 99. See also Serafin E. Macaraig, *Social Problems* (Manila: The Educational Supply Co., 1929), 408 and 410–11. The Katipunan had elaborate initiation rituals, promoted nationalism, and wore native attire as their uniform.For more information on Katipunan Mipanampun, see above-mentioned *Survey Report*, 100-102. For information on Dimas Alang activities and its role as a smoke screen for the Revolutionary Army, see "Confidential Report," 23 and 29 November 1910; 17 May, 26 June, and 7 and15 September 1912, Philippine Constabulary Report (PCR), in Harry Hill Bandholtz Papers (HBP), Michigan Historical Collection, Bentley Historical Library, University of Michigan. See also *Survey Report*, 95; Ileto, "Orators and the Crowd," in *Reappraising the Empire*, ed. Peter W. Stanley (Cambridge and London: Committee on American-East Asian Relations of the Department of History, in collaboration with the Council on East Asian Studies, Harvard University, 1984), 105 and 107. In Malabon, the uniform of the Dimas Alang was similar to the Katipunan's. See "Confidential Report," 14 December 1911, PCR.

28. See "Confidential Report," 27 December 1912, PCR.

29. A former '96 revolutionary also made a similar statement. See "Confidential Report," 18 February 1912, PCR.

## Chapter 2

1. The Filipinos held jobs mainly in the agricultural fields, canneries, hotels, and restaurants. For the number of Filipinos, see C. M. Goethe, "Filipino Immigration Viewed as a Peril," in *Letters in Exile: An Introductory Reader on the History of Filipinos in America*, ed. UCLA Asian American Studies Center (Los Angeles: UCLA Asian American Studies Center, 1976), 72–73. The official count was 45,208 on the U.S. mainland, 30,467 of them in California. See U.S. Bureau of the Census, *Sixteenth Census of the United States: 1940* (Washington D. C.: Bureau of Printing, 1940), 2.

2. To address this injustice, a mass meeting of 300 Filipinos was held. See Emory S. Bogardus, "Anti-Filipino Race Riots," in *Letters in Exile*, 51–62.

See also Michael P. Showalter, "The Watsonville Anti-Filipino Riot of 1930: A Reconsideration of Fermin Tobera's Murder," *Historical Society of Southern California* (Winter 1989): 345.

3. *San Francisco Chronicle*, 23 January 1930.

4. Before the Watsonville incident, numerous anti-Filipino riots had occurred on the West Coast. For details, see Bogardus, "Anti-Filipino Race Riots," 51–62, *Manila Daily Bulletin*, 31 January 1930. For more details on the arrested youth, see Howard A. De Witt, *Violence in the Fields: California Filipino Farm Labor Unionization during the Great Depression* (Saratoga, California: Century Twenty-One Publishing, 1980), 30–48.

5. The Philippine Chamber of Commerce sent a formal protest to Washington as well as to local officials. Gov. Gen. Dwight Davis also cabled the Bureau of Insular Affairs to request adequate protection for the Filipinos. See the *Manila Daily Bulletin*, 27 January 1930.

6. The Manila municipal meeting was attended by a diverse range of people, including educators such as Dean Jorge Bocobo and Conrado Benitez, both of the University of the Philippines (UP); members of the legislature, such as Reps. Tomas Confessor and Francisco Varona; labor leaders; and newspaper editors, such as Joaquin Balmori. See the *Manila Daily Bulletin* and *The Manila Times*, 28 January 1930.

7. *Manila Daily Bulletin* and *The Manila Times*, 31 January 1930.

8. An American correspondent estimated the crowd to be one thousand five hundred while the *La Defensa Catolico* estimated fifty thousand. See "'Humiliation Day' Observed At Luneta Mass Meeting," *Philippines Free Press*, 8 February 1930, 37. Both *The Tribune* and the *Manila Daily Bulletin* reported 15,000 in their 4 February 1930 editions.

9. For more on Varona's speech, see *The Tribune*, 4 February 1930, and the *Manila Daily Bulletin*, 3 February 1930. Other speakers included Dean Jorge Bocobo of UP.

10. On the anniversary of the deaths of Fathers Gomez, Burgos, and Zamora, which falls on 17 February, the Ilocano Civic League included a commemoration of the death of Tobera, an Ilocano. In Calamba, Laguna, 64-year-old Feliciano Rizal, father of a municipal policeman, shot himself as a protest against the "brutal attack by white residents of California on the Filipino laborers." See *The Tribune* issues 24–31 January and 4, 12, and 16 February 1930. See also the *New York Herald*, 17 March 1930. For more on the protest march in California, see De Witt, *Violence in the Fields*, 44.

11. Letter addressed to General Francis Parker, Chief of Bureau of Insular

Affairs, dated 23 January 1930, E 21, Personal Name Information, Group Record (GR) 350, Bureau of Insular Affairs (BIA), United States National Archives and Records Administration (NARA).

12. Teodoro A. Agoncillo, "Student Activism of the 1930s," *Solidarity*, July–August 1976, 22–28.

13. *Manila Daily Bulletin*, 19 and 20 February 1930.

14. Later, the students' parents organized a parents committee and participated in the mass rallies in support of their children. A delegation of the committee called on Gov. Gen. Davis and Sen. Manuel Quezon, pleading with them to accept the students' demands. *Manila Daily Bulletin*, 7 March 1930. See also Agoncillo, "Student Activism," 22–28.

15. *Manila Daily Bulletin*, 11 March 1930. See also Agoncillo, "Student Activism," 23; *Philippines Free Press*, 15 March 1930, 40; 26 April 1930, 37; and *The Tribune*, 14 October 1930. The four schools were the Manila North High School, West High School, East High School, and the Philippine School of Commerce. For more details on the student strike, see Taihei Okada, "School Strikes in the Philippines under U.S. Colonialism: With a Particular Focus on the 1930 High School Strike," *Tonan Ajia: Rekishi to Bunka*, no. 40 (2011): 27–55.

16. Agoncillo, "Student Activism," 24. According to Agoncillo, shortly before the Manila High School incident, a similar incident occurred at UP, where an American professor uttered racially discriminatory words to the students.

17. *Manila Daily Bulletin*, 17 March 1930; *New York Herald*, 17 March 1930; *New York Times*, 17 March 1930. Two similar incidents took place in Iloilo at around the same time. See *New York Herald*, 15 March 1930.

18. Before Tobera's remains reached the Philippines, he was honored with memorial services in several cities, including Los Angeles, Honolulu, Shanghai, and Hong Kong, *The Tribune*, 12 and 14 March 1930. See also the *Manila Daily Bulletin*, 13 March 1930.

19. Letter addressed to Gen. Francis Parker, Chief of Bureau of Insular Affairs, dated 23 January 1930, and letter addressed to Patrick Hurley, Sec. of War, dated 28 March 1930, Box 149, 57/27/15, GR 350, BIA, NARA.

20. See *The Philippines Herald*, 8 March 1930. See also "Huwag Tayong Padala sa Katsang ng mga Dambuhala," *Sakdal*, 30 August 1930, 2; Yasotaro Moori, "Hito Daitoryo no Nihon Homon wa Nani o Imisuruka" (What Does the Philippine President's Visit to Japan Signify?), *Kokusai Panfurtto Tsushin*, 11 August 1938, 3.

21. Interview with Francisco Ramos (Benigno's younger brother) in Teresia Z. Hachero-Pascual, "The Sakdalista Movement: A Historical Assessment" (PhD

diss., University of Santo Tomas, 1984), 315. See also *The Tribune* (3d edition), 5 May 1935.

22.  Ramos's salary as division director was P1,560 a year, which was said to be about four times that of the average Manila office worker. See "Benigno Ramos," *Personal Record*, BIA, NA, quoted in Stubbs, "Philippine Radicalism," 131. See also *The Tribune* (3d edition), 5 May 1935.

23.  Ramos requested more time but his plea was ignored and he was forced to resign, *The Sunday Tribune*, 5 May 1935; "Hindi Pinaalis Kundi Kusang Umalis," *Sakdal*, 8 February 1936, 3; "Ang Buhay ni Gng. Liboria de Castro ni Ramos; ang Pangbibira sa Kasaysayan ng Babaing Pilipina," *Sakdal*, 5 June 1937, 1.

24.  Varona was a former president of the Congreso Obrero de Filipinas, a federation of labors unions and one of Ramos's *compadres* (godfathers to Ramos's children). See Roy Stubbs, "Philippine Radicalism," 134. Stubbs erroneously claims that the initial issue of the *Sakdal* came out on 13 October 1930. This date has been quoted by other researchers such as Sturtevant and Goodman. Stubbs's error seems to have come from a report, "The Sakdal Party," written by Col. Guillermo Francisco to the chief of Constabulary, which in turn was given to Hayden. See "Radiogram no. 209, dated 9 May 1935," folder no. 25-24 (no title) in HP. The *Sakdal* itself confirms it was first published on 28 June 1930. See, "Sariling Diwa: Ang Ikalawang Taon Namin," 25 June 1932, 2; and "Sariling Diwa: Ikawalong Taon ng Paglilingkod," 26 June 1937, 2, both in *Sakdal*. On Masangkay and Varona, see *The Sunday Tribune*, 5 May 1935. On Masangkay being a Ricarte supporter, see "Confidential Report," 28 March 1912, PCR.

25.  Other supporters included Gregorio Aglipay, Toribio Teodoro, and Alfonso E. Mendoza, who were all critical of Quezon and his administration, *Survey Report*, 112.

26.  See "Patakaran ng 'Sakdal,'" in Editorial box, *Sakdal*, 28 November 1931, 2.

27.  As of April 1931, Benigno Ramos was registered as the owner, publisher, editor, and business manager. The paper's office was located at 2326 Juan Luna Street in Manila, and the subscription rate was P2.50 a year. For subscribers abroad, the price doubled. For the publication numbers, see "Ang Sinumpaan ng Aming Patnugot," 4 April 1931, 3; and 3 October 1931, 4, both in *Sakdal*.

28.  The list of publications registered in the Bureau of Posts, as of December 1929, reveals that the most popular daily newspapers were the *Taliba* (Tagalog), followed by the *Pagkakaisa* (Tagalog) with 17,355. The third-ranked paper was the English-language *The Tribune*. The weekly magazines had larger circulations. The *Liwayway* (Tagalog) had 69,785, and the *Philippines Free Press* (English) had

28,000. See Jesus Z. Valenzuela, *History of Journalism in the Philippine Islands* (Manila: Privately published, 1933), 196–200.

29. Interview with Leticia Ramos-Uyboco, Ramos's daughter, on 14 April 1983, at Alabang, Muntinlupa, Metro Manila.

30. Jeremias Adia, former Ganap Party member, claimed that there was at least one copy of the *Sakdal* in every barrio in the provinces surrounding Manila. Interview with Adia on 20 April 1985, at his residence in Cabuyao, Laguna. See also Walter Robb, "Sakdals," *American Chamber of Commerce Journal* 15 (May 1935): 10–11. Robb estimated the readership to be about three hundred thousand. For information on the weekly *Sakdal* being for the masses, see Conrado Benitez, "Sakdal," *Philippine Magazine*, May 1935, 252.

31. "Ang Kailangan ng Bayan," 26 September 1931, 3; and "Takot ang Lahat ng Periodiko," 26 September 1931, 1, both in *Sakdal*.

32. "Nangaral ang Kostable sa Pasig," 26 December 1931, 3. The Sakdalistas compared the constabulary's harassment to Rizal's experience. See "Nakabilanggo na naman si Dr. Rizal," 31 January 1931, 3; and "Bawal ang 'Sakdal' sa Senado," 1 November 1930, 4, all in *Sakdal*.

33. "Ikinagalak ni Hen. Ricarte ang Kampanya Nitong 'Sakdal,'" 1 November 1930, 3; and "Isang Liham ni Hen. Ricarte," 28 March 1931, 3, both in *Sakdal*.

34. "Philippine Constabulary Report, 1932," BIA, NARA, quoted in Stubbs, "Philippine Radicalism," 141.

35. See Santo Domingo section of "History and Cultural Life of Luisiana," 2, Historical Data of Laguna 45, *Historical Data Papers* (HDP), typescript, ca. 1950–1951. For Malayang Bayan, see "Kung Ano ang Malayang Bayan," *Sakdal*, 24 December 1932, 2.

36. Quoting from Zola, see Yasotaro Moori, "Hito Daitoryo no Nihon Homon wa Nani o Imisuruka," 3. For the original Sanskrit, see "Opo, ang Sagot Namin," *Sakdal*, 25 April 1936, 4.

37. Underscoring and translation are mine. A torn page from the Tagalog version of the Bible, "Ang Sulat ni Santiago," p. 369, was given to me by a former Sakdalista member but no publication facts were given. The modern version of the Bible reads "upang kayo'y maging ganap at walang pagkukulang." There is no word "sakdal." See *Mabuting Balita para sa Ating Panahon: Tagalog Popular Version New Testament* (Manila: Philippine Bible Society1973), 655. The English Bible reads: "And let steadfastness have its full effect, that you may be perfect and complete, lacking in nothing." See "The Letter of James," in *The New Oxford Annotated Bible*, ed. Herbert G. May and B. Metzer (New York: Oxford University Press, 1962), 1469. Former Sakdalistas informed me of this interpretation during one of their

reunions in Alabang, Muntinlupa, Metro Manila, on 14 April 1983. Leticia Ramos-Uyboco, Ramos's daughter, also told me about this interpretation.

38. Regarding Illustrisimo's definition, see Vicente Marasigan, *A Banahaw Guru* (Quezon City: Ateneo de Manila University Press, 1985), 72.

39. "Kolorum ang mga Beterano sa Atimonan?" *Sakdal*, 7 February 1931, 4.

40. "Ang mga Miting ng 'Sakdal,'" *Sakdal*, 18 October 1930, 4.

41. "Ang Ating Tunay na Kalaban," 13 September 1930, 3; "Ang Miting ng 'Sakdal' sa Gagalangin," 20 September 1930, 2; "Panawagan," 13 December 1930, 4; and "Ano ang Dapat Gawain?" 16 May 1931, 1, all in *Sakdal*. Manuel Roxas, who headed the Philippine Independence Mission in 1929, became convinced through observing the political atmosphere in Washington that independence was imminent and that tariff preferences for Philippine goods would come to an end. Therefore, upon his return, he established a nonpartisan patriotic society called Ang Bagong Katipunan (The New Katipunan), or National Association for Independence, on 30 November 1930, Bonifacio's birthday. The call for self-sufficiency received enthusiastic support from the people; however, Quezon and the economic interests behind him were lukewarm toward this and Roxas's movement soon dissolved. See Hayden, *The Philippines*, 349, 707, and 911. See also *The Philippines Herald*, 18 September, and 15 and 23 November 1930.

42. "Ang Suliranin ng Di Pagboto," 18 October 1930, 4; "Bayang Dukha," 6 September 1930, 2, both in *Sakdal*.

43. Details on the Tayug uprising appeared in *The Tribune*, 13–17 and 21–23 January 1931; *The Philippines Herald*, 17 January 1931; *Independent*, 17 and 24 January 1931; *New York Times*, 16 and 18 January 1931; and the *Washington Daily News*, 12 January 1931. See also A. V. H. Hartendorp, "The Tayug 'Colorums,'" no. 27 (February 1931): 563–67; and "Kings for a Day," 17 January 1931, 4, 40, and 44, both in the *Philippine Magazine*; Walter Robb, "What Ho, The Guard," *American Chamber of Commerce Journal* 11, no. 2 (February 1931): 3, 18, 25, and 26; Blas Villamor, *Tayug Colorums: Reseña Historica de la Conspiracion en Tayug en 1834 y de la Sedicion en Tayug en 1931* (Bangued, Abra: n.p., 1931); "Annual Report of the Sec. of the Interior," *Annual Report of the Governor General of the Philippines Islands, 1931* (Washington, D.C.: U.S. Government Printing Office, 1932), 89; and Sturtevant, *Popular Uprisings*, 175–92. For in-depth analysis, see Cynthia B. Urgena, "The Colorum Uprising of Pangasinan" (MA thesis, University of the Philippines, 1960); Milagros C. Guerrero, "The Colorum Uprisings: 1924–1931," *Journal of Asian Studies* 5 (April 1967): 65–78.

44. The organization Kapisanan Makabola Makasinag (Association of Brilliant Kabola Supporters) had 12,000 members, the majority of whom had

suffered at the hands of landlords, usurers, or land-grabbers. Kabola promised to create a society of equality, justice, and prosperity. For more details on Kabola's uprising, see Stubbs, "Philippine Radicalism," 24–53. He translated it as "Association of the Worthy Kabola." Also see Sturtevant, *Popular Uprisings*, 178–80, and the *Manila Daily Bulletin*, 6 March 1925. An American newspaper described the group as quasi-religious, quasi-political, and closely resembling the Communists of Bolshevist Russia. See *The Washington Post*, 5 March 1925.

45. Calosa was Aglipayan and Protestant at the same time. See Sturtevant, *Popular Uprisings*, 273 and 275. Tolosa/Calosa also associated with well-known Communists in Nueva Ecija. See Urgena, "The Colorum Uprising of Pangasinan," 18.

46. "Mga Sukat Masabi," 17 January 1931, 1; "Kung Ako'y Kostable," 7 February 1931, 4; and "Iba't Ibang Balita," 7 March 1931, 2, all in *Sakdal*.

47. Ramos was briefly arrested in March 1931, perhaps due to his never-ceasing public criticism of the government. For more on his arrest, see "Dinakip ng Secreto ang Editor Namin," *Sakdal*, 28 March 1931, 3.

48. "Ang Kailangan ng Bayan," *Sakdal*, 26 September 1931, 3.

49. Bernardita Reyes Churchill, *The Philippine Independence Missions to the United States 1919–1934* (Manila: National Historical Institute, 1983), 253–54.

50. "Maraming Salamat sa Inyong Lahat! Ani Hen. Ricarte," 19 September 1931, 1; "Kay Heneral Ricarte," 1 August 1931, 3; "Si Ricarte Lamang ang Tanging Di Magbabago sa Kampanyang Sumpa sa Republica," 15 August 1931, 1; and "Artemio Ricarte," 26 September 1931, 3, all in *Sakdal*. This was not the first time Ramos appealed for donations to help Ricarte. When the Kanto Earthquake hit Japan in 1923, Ramos wrote to the *El Debate* asking readers to send donations to Ricarte. See Kaneshiro Ohta, *Kikoku* (Haunting Cries of the Ghost) (Tokyo: Hiripin Kyokai, 1972), 84.

51. This was seen in Mayumo, Bulacan. See "Hindi Papapasukin sa Pilipinas ang Bangkay ni Hen. Ricarte," *Sakdal*, 1 August 1931, 1.

52. Others included groups such as the workers of the Malabon Sugar Company; members of Palihan ng Bayan; employees of the Manila Railroad Company; the Department of Veterano de la Revolucion of Malabon, Rizal; La Revolucion of Cebu; and groups of *Sakdal* supporters in the provinces. See "Sampung Libong Piso ang Hanggahan ng Abuluyan para kay Hen. A. Ricarte," 1 August 1931, 1; "Mahigit Nang P400 ang Naipadala kay Hen. Artemio Ricarte," 15 August 1931, 1; "Lalong Sumisigla ang Ambagan kay Hen. A. Ricarte," 5 September 1931, 4; 12 September 1931, 3; and "P1712 na ang Naipadala kay Hen. Ricarte," 19 September 1931, 1, all in *Sakdal*.

53. Ricarte's letter was dated 23 November 1931. Original text: "LA LIBERTAD NO SE PIDE SINO SE TOMA POR MEDIO DEL MAS PRECIOSO TESORO QUE POSEE EL HOMBRE. Cual es, la sangre y la propia vida." The capitalized part of the text must have been done by the *Sakdal.* See "Carta de Ricarte a Lapus," *Sakdal,* 12 December 1931, 1. A total of P2,051.44 was sent to Ricarte through Yokohama Specie Bank on 2 October 1931. See "Ang Ulat ni G. Lapus ukol sa Ambagan kay Heneral Ricarte," *Sakdal,* 24 October 1931, 4. For details on the arrest in Gapan, see "Hindi Kaya ni Gov. Santos ang Pamamahala sa N.E.?" in *Sakdal,* 5 September 1931, 2.

54. For information on Union Civica's aims and membership, see "Dadalo Sina Gabaldon"; "Mga Iba Pang Nagsilagda sa Pamahayag ng Kasarinlan"; and "Ang Lupong Sanggunian ng 'Union Civica Filipinas,'" 21 November 1931, 1. "Ang Nagsisibuo ng Ktt. Sangguniang Pambansa ng Union Civica Filipina," 2; and "Ang Pagkasapi Namin sa 'Union,'" 28 November 1931, 1, both in *Sakdal.* See also "Sasapi si Quezon sa Union," *Sakdal,* 17 March 1932, 1. Other principles of the Union Civica included: "We ought to know that our redemption lies in our own hands"; "We should be conscious of the fact that money that goes out of our country never returns"; and "We ought to inculcate in the minds of our sons that the money of the Filipinos is for the Filipinos." For the original Spanish, see "Decalogo de la 'Union,'" *Sakdal,* 12 December 1931, 1. The English translation is adapted from *The Tribune,* 9 December 1931.

55. Vice Gov. Gen. George C. Butte believed the Union was an attempt to revive the Democrata Party, and he predicted that it might act as an opposition movement. See *The Philippines Herald,* 11 May 1935. See also Stubbs, "Philippine Radicalism," 138. The participants included such personalities as Teodoro Sandiko, Isauro Gabaldon, Gregorio Aglipay, Isabelo de los Reyes, and Vicente Sotto. The *Sakdal* subsequently published several articles written by Vicente Sotto. See p. 1 of the *Sakdal* issues of 1 August and 7 November 1931. Palihan ng Bayan, organized by Eusebio A. Godoy, grew rapidly in the provinces of Laguna, Tayabas, and Batangas; and it had a membership of about forty thousand as of 1934. See *Survey Report,* 106–8; see also *The Tribune,* 21 September 1934.

56. "Miting ng Pagtutuus sa Opera House," and "Ang Pamahayag ng 'Union Civica Filipina,'" both in *Sakdal,* 21 November 1931, 1.

57. "Ang Pamahayag ng 'Union Civica Filipina,'" and "Puera Mision!" both in *Sakdal,* 21 November 1931, 1. 58. For the resolution, see "Walang Kaparis na Tagumpay ang 'Miting ng Pagtutuus,'" 28 November 1931, 3; see also "Los Sakdalistas contra La Mision," 5 December 1931, 1, both in *Sakdal.* The top leaders of the Union Civica signed this resolution. See "Comentarios Semanales," *Sakdal,*

5 December 1931, 1. For related articles on this meeting, see *Sakdal*, 21 and 28 November 1931; and 5, 12, and 26 December 1931.

59. "Walang Kaparis na Tagumpay ang 'Miting ng Pagtutuus'"; and "Los Sakdalistas contra La Mision" *Sakdal*.

60. For information on the resolutions and Ramos's speech, see the *Manila Daily Bulletin*, 23 November 1931. Other speakers included Eusebio Godoy and Isauro Gabaldon. By September 1934, the Sakdalista organization and the Palihan ng Bayan were not on good terms and no longer cooperated with each other after the president of the Palihan declared that the Palihan "had stood for the government and fought against the Sakdalistas and communists." See *The Tribune*, 14 November 1934. See also "Shocking Questions to Quezon's Henchmen," *Sakdal*, 15 September 1934, 1.

61. "Maulit Kaya ang Nangyari kina Andres Bonifacio?" *Sakdal*, 28 November 1931, 4. A group of veterans of the anti-Spanish and Philippine-American Wars sent a congratulatory note to the *Sakdal* and renewed their support for the complete independence the Malayang Bayan (*Sakdal*) movement was seeking.

62. "Ang Manifesto ng Bayang Malaya sa Ating mga Pinuno," 24 October 1931, 1; "Maikling Balita," 7 November 1931, 1; "Ilan sa mga Gabay na Pagtitibayin sa Miting ng Malayang Bayan," ibid., 3; "Samahan 'Malayang Bayan' sa Nabotas, Rizal," 5 December 1931, 4; "Vet. ng Rebolusyon," 26 December 1931, 4; and "Lupon ng Malayang Bayan," 12 December 1931, 3, all in *Sakdal*.

63. *Manila Daily Bulletin*, 4 December 1931; and *The Tribune* and *Manila Daily Bulletin*, 5 December 1931.

64. "Nakahanda na Ba Kayo," 5 December 1931, 3; and "Sariling Diwa," 5 December 1931, 2, both in *Sakdal*. 65. "Ang Kapasyahan (*sic*) ng Bayang Pagtitibayin sa Miting," *Sakdal*, 31 October 1931, 1.

66. The annual report was for the year 1933–1934. See fn9 in Hayden, *The Philippines*, 916. Eligio S. Cayetano's father was a Sakdalista in Bulacan, Bulacan. He joined this campaign and did not send Eligio to public school; therefore, Eligio did not know how to speak in English. Interview with Cayetano on 27 December 1986, at Matungao, Bulacan, Bulacan Province.

67. "Huag Ninyong Labuin ang Salitaan," *Sakdal*, 9 July 1932, 1.

68. Other issues included reforming Banco Nacional Filipino, investigating the suspicious wealth of the heads (of the government offices), and promoting the use of Tagalog as the national language. See "Ang Ukol sa Sedula at sa Asyenda," *Sakdal*, 22 January 1932, 2.

69. Some of those arrested turned out to be Communist Party members. See *The Tribune*, 11 December 1931; *The Sunday Tribune*, 13 December 1931; *La*

*Opinion*, 11 December 1931; and *The Philippines Herald*, 10 December 1931. See also Stubbs, "Philippine Radicalism," 113. For information on Dionisio's effort, see Sturtevant, *Popular Uprisings*, 210.

70. Five Sakdalistas in Atimonan, whom I interviewed, for example, revealed that they had been Tanggulan members before they joined the Sakdalista movement. Interview with former Sakdalistas (names withheld) on 24 April 1986, in Atimonan, Quezon. For former Tanggulan members becoming Sakdalistas in Bulacan, see Brian Fegan, "Dionisio Macapagal: Rebel Matures," in *Lives at the Margin: Biography of Filipinos, Obscure, Ordinary, and Heroic*, ed. Alfred W. McCoy (Quezon City: Ateneo de Manila University Press, 2000), 354–55.

71. Butte pointed out that these problems should have been tackled by past governor generals and said that it was hard for an acting governor general, such as himself, to settle them. See Cablegram, "To Sec. of War from Acting Governor General Butte," 14 December 1931, 4865, RG 350, BIA, NARA.

72. Seven years earlier in 1920, Dionisio had organized a similar secret society, called Hijos del Pueblo (Sons of the Country), or HIDELPO, whose membership grew to about sixty thousand. Only laborers and low-salaried employees of the government were admitted to this organization. In the meantime, Dionisio was arrested for leading an uprising against the government under another secret society. When Katipunan ng Bayan was organized, it absorbed some members of HIDELPO. See *Survey Report*, 100.

73. *Survey Report*, 110.

74. The other organization that fused with the Tanggulan Society was the Alitaptap Gubat (Firefly in the Wild). See *Survey Report*, 108–12. This section of the *Survey Report* was written by Dionisio himself. Acting Gov. Gen. Butte estimated Tanggulan membership to be between 12,000 and 15,000 just before the crackdown. See Cablegram, "To Sec.of War from Acting Gov. Gen. Butte," 14 December 1931, NARA. The initiation rites of both organizations, the Tanggulan Society and the Kapatirang Magsasaka, were similar to those of Bonifacio's Katipunan. See Brian Fegan, "Dionisio Macapagal: Rebel Matures," 350–53. See also Fegan, "The Social History of a Central Luzon Barrio," in *Philippine Social History: Global Trade and Local Transformations*, ed. Alfred W. McCoy and Ed. C. de Jesus (Quezon City: Ateneo de Manila University Press; Sydney: George Allen and Unwin Australia Publishing, Ltd., 1984), 108.

75. For Dionisio's affiliation with KAP, see Guillermo Capadocia, "The Philippine Labor Movement," 37; "Notes which may be used in the milestone in the history of the CCPI," 2, both in Military Intelligence Service, Personal File: Guillermo Capadocia, ca. 1950, Capadocia Papers (CP), typescript. This document

was made available to me by Dr. Brian Fegan. See also Jim Richardson, "The Genesis of the Philippine Communist Party" (PhD Diss., University of London, 1984), 281 and *Komunista* (Quezon City: Ateneo de Manila University Press, 2011), 188–95.

76. Benedict J. Kerkvliet, *The Huk Rebellion: A Study of Peasant Revolt in the Philippines* (Quezon City: New Day Publishers, 1979), 28. There were no dues or fees in the Tanggulan Society; instead, their activities were funded by voluntary contributions.

77. For more on Tanggulan Society and ordering of uniforms, see Brian Fegan, "Dionisio Macapagal," 353. For the Ilocano counterparts to the Tanggulan Society, see Brian Fegan, "Central Luzon Barrio," 110. See also the cablegram "To Sec. of War from Acting Gov. Gen. Butte," 14 December 1931, NARA. In an attempt to show close ties with Gen. Artemio Ricarte, the Tanggulan Society tried to raise money for his cause. An array of alleged correspondence appeared to support the claim of ties with Ricarte. On the alleged letters from Ricarte, see *The Philippines Herald*, 10 December 1931; and *The Sunday Tribune*, 13 December 1931.

78. For Dionisio's articles in the *Sakdal*, see "Paliwanag ng Paguluhan ng 'Tanggulan' sa mga Kinauukulan," 28 March 1931, 1; and "Walang Kinalaman ang 'Kapisanang Tanggulan' sa Kaguluhang Nililikha rin ng mga Kostable sa mga Lalawigan," 12 December 1931, 3. For information on the close relationship between the two, see "Ang Miting ng 'Sakdal' sa Bugyon, Kalumpit," 28 March 1931, 2; and "Mga Miting ng 'Sakdal,'" 30 May 1931, 3, both in *Sakdal*. See also Roy Stubbs, "Philippine Radicalism," 107. For Dionisio serving as one of Ramos's lawyers, see "Dinakip ng Secreto ang Editor Naming si Benigno Ramos Noon Biernes Nagdaan," *Sakdal*, 28 March 1931, 3.

79. Sturtevant, *Popular Uprisings*, 205. For information on their literary backgrounds, see Virgilio S. Almario, *Balagtasismo Versus Modernismo* (Quezon City: Ateneo de Manila University Press, 1984), 53 and 86.

80. *Survey Report*, 113. See also the Dionisio interview in Sturtevant, *Popular Uprisings*, 213.

81. Cablegram sent by Butte to the Sec. of War, 14 December 1931, NARA. See also *Survey Report*, 112, and the Dionisio interview in Sturtevant, *Popular Uprisings*, 217fn3; Stubbs, "Philippine Radicalism," 107–9; "Radio Sent no. 209," folder no. 25-24 (no title), HP.

82. Before the disbanding of the Tanggulan Society, the Manila City Court of First Instance convicted Ramos in mid-November of libel on grounds that the paper had published a "defamatory" article regarding an allegedly anomalous refund of customs duties. See *The Philippines Herald*, 13 November 1931. For defiant articles, see "Ang 'Sakdal' ay Magpapatuloy sa Kanyang Tungkulin," 22

January 1932, 1; and "Sakdal Is Not an Imported Paper," 30 January 1932, 4, both in *Sakdal*. The ban must have been imposed shortly after 6 February as Ramos was explaining to the readers why the price of the newspaper had been raised, with one of the reasons being postal expense. See "Nagtaas Kami ng Halaga," *Sakdal*, 6 February 1932, 3.

83. For information on the shared printing press, see Guillermo Capadocia, "Notes which may be used in the milestone in the history of the CCPI," CP. For the new campaign, see "Mga Kusang Ambagan sa Sariling Limbagan," 24 March 1932, 2; 21 May 1932, 4; 18 June 1932, 3; and 9 July 1932, 4, all in *Sakdal*.

84. For the Communists' utilizing the *Sakdal*, see Jim Richardson, "Hard Times: The Philippine Communist Party, 1933–1935" (unpublished manuscript), 1995, 36. I thank Dr. Jim Richardson for sharing this paper with me. For Evangelista's articles in the *Sakdal*, see "Open Letter to the Philippine Capitalist Press," which appeared in two installments on 26 December 1931 and 2 January 1932. Evangelista discusses the miserable living conditions of the poor, who were victims of the landlords, the caciques, and their ally and master, the American imperialists.

85. Alfred B. Saulo, *Communism in the Philippines: An Introduction* (Quezon City: Ateneo de Manila University Press, 1990), 22–23. The party leaders were found guilty and banished to the provinces for eight years. In October 1932, the Supreme Court unanimously affirmed the lower court decision, declaring the Communist Party illegal and therefore outlawed.

86. For information on Sakdalista attitudes toward the Communists, see "Takot ang Lahat ng Periodiko," 26 September 1931, 1; "Mga Tanong na Aming Sinasagot ukol kay Hen. Aguinaldo," 15 August 1931, 3; and "Sa Dukha Nanggagaling ang Salapi ng Pamahalaan," 17 March 1932, 2, all in *Sakdal*. According to Kojiro Sada, who interviewed Ramos in Tokyo, on 14 January 1936, Ramos explicitly said that he wanted to emphasize the differences between the Sakdalistas and the Communists after the latter's mass arrest. Kojiro Sada, *Nanyo Sosho: Hiripin-hen* (The South Sea Series: The Philippines) (Tokyo: Toa Keizai Chosa Kyoku, 1939), 429.

87. "Sariling Diwa: Ang Ikalawang Taon Namin," *Sakdal*, 25 June 1932, 2.

88. Churchill, *The Philippine Independent Missions to the United States*, 275–76.

89. The supporters of the act included Rafael Palma, president; and Jorge Bocobo, dean of the Law School, at the UP. The latter gave an impassioned speech at the "National Humiliation Day" rally, inspired by Tobera's death. Information on the opposition and supporters comes from Frank Golay, *Face of Empire: United*

*States-Philippine Relations, 1898–1946* (Madison: University of Wisconsin Center for Southeast Asian Studies, 1997), 312. In one of the general meetings that took place on 12 February at the Sakdalista headquarters, Narciso Lapus and Hermenegildo Reyes were dismissed from the movement due to their support of the H-H-C Act. See "Nag-iisa Kami," 4 February 1933, 1; and "Abuluyan ng Bayang Api," 4 March 1933, 1, both in *Sakdal*.

90. In addition, Quezon and his supporters considered the immigration clause humiliating (as it excluded practically all Filipino laborers in the U.S. mainland), the powers of the new High Commissioner too indefinite, and the postindependence military and naval reservations inconsistent with true independence. See Churchill, *The Philippine Independence Missions*, 290; and Golay, *Face of Empire*, 322.

91. "Kabuwan ng Batas Hawes-Cutting," 18 February 1933, 3; and "Quo Vadis?" 4 March 1933, 3, both in *Sakdal*.

92. "An Appeal," *Sakdal*, 24 December 1932, 1.

93. "Pilipinas ng Pilipino at Di Pilipinas ng Dayuhan ang Ibig Namin," *Sakdal*, 26 November 1932, 1. This was not the Sakdalistas' first attempt to conduct such a campaign. Originally, Narciso Lapus was to be sent and a donation campaign was launched in December 1931, but nothing came of this. See "Si G. Narciso Lapus," *Sakdal*, 26 December 1931, 1. Perhaps due to this incident, Lapus later left the Sakdalista movement and supported the H-H-C Act. Even earlier, in 1930, Gen. Emilio Aguinaldo had announced that he would make a trip to demand immediate independence. However, the necessary support was not forthcoming and he had to give up the plan. See Churchill, *The Philippine Independence Missions*, 247.

94. For information on the Sakdalistas' enthusiastic support, see "Mga Balita sa Kilusan," 26 November 1932, 1; and "Sa Lahat ng Maka-Sakdal," 19 November 1932, 4, both in *Sakdal*. The Sakdalistas used "Malayang Bayan" and "Bayang Malaya" interchangeably.

95. Among the speakers were Felino Cajucom, a lawyer who later became the president of the movement, and Bishop Gregorio Aglipay. "Sa Miting ng Bayang Malaya" and "Sa Enero ang Alis ng mga Sugo ng Bayang Malaya," *Sakdal*, 17 December 1932, 1. Similar meetings took place in the provinces such as Ragay, Camarines Sur, on 31 December 1932. See "Miting ng mga Sakdalista sa Ragay, Cams. Sur," 4 February 1933, 4; and "Mga Miting na Nairaos," 4 February 1933, 1, both in *Sakdal*.

96. For more on Tiongco taking over the editorship, see "Abuluyan ng Bayang Api"; "Ang Pangsamantalang Patnugot Namin"; "Mga Manunulat"; and "Sworn Statement," all in *Sakdal*, 4 March 1933, 1.

97. For donations, see *Sakdal*, 4 March 1933, 4; and 8 April 1933, 1. See also "Salamin ng Dangal," 8 April 1933, 3; "Sariling Diwa," 18 February 1933, 2; "Well Wishers Donate to Sakdal Independence Fund," 1 July 1933, 3, all in *Sakdal*. The leading dailies in Manila did not even mention Ramos's leaving for the States.

98. "Alang-alang sa Ipagwawagi ng Katwiran ng Ating Bayan," 4 February 1933, 2; and "'Mga Dapat Mabatid,'" 22 April 1933, 4. For Ramos's exact words, see "Hindi Maaring Masilaw si Ramos," 18 February 1933, 1, all in *Sakdal*.

99. "Ang Ikinaaalipin ng Ibang Bayan ay di Pagkaunawa sa Kalayaan," *Sakdal*, 26 May 1934, 1.

100. "Liham ng Mabunying Hral Ricarte, na Nagbabalita ng Pagkadalaw ng Aming Patnugot," *Sakdal*, 8 April 1933, 1. There is no reason to suspect that Ricarte's letter was a fake, such as those allegedly sent to the Tanggulan Society, since there was already a documented relationship between the two. However, the photo published with this latest letter showed only Ricarte's face, not a picture of a dinner with Ramos, as Satoshi Ara claims, in "Firipin no Rikarute shogun ni kansuru ichi kosatsu" (A Study on the General Ricarte of the Philippines), *Kokusai Seiji*, no. 120 (February 1999): 226fn21.

101. Picture with the caption "Magandang Gabi," *Sakdal*, 1 July 1933, 1. Note that the dates of Ramos's tour to the U.S. are at odds with Roy Stubbs's assertion (p. 156) that Ramos and his party left for the U.S. in November 1933, a date repeated by later scholars, such as Goodman and Sturtevant. In addition to the above documents, a group photo was taken in Stockton, California, that has the following inscription: "A Wellcome (*sic*) Meeting in Honor of Benigno Ramos and Ramon Crespo...Sponsored by Filipinos of Stockton, California, 18 April 1933..." This photo was given to me by Mr. Jeremias Adia.

102. "Ganappu-to ni Kansuru Kenkyu" (A Study of the Ganap Party), written by a certain Hayase, April 1944, 10 (mimeographed), in Koreshige Inuzuka, "Hito ni okeru dai 31 keibitai no sakusen (The Operation of the 31st Garrison in the Philippines), dated April 1944," 8–89, Itaku (entrusted by the Inuzuka family), 26 May 1960, National Institute of Defense Studies (NIDS), Tokyo, Japan. This wartime document describes Ramos's U.S. trip in detail. See also Nippi Irei Kai, ed., *Hito Senki* (Record of the Battle of the Philippines) (Tokyo: Nippi Irei Kai, 1958), 241, which is based on Hayase's writing.

103. *Sakdal*, 15 July 1933, 3. Publication details for the *Manila Sakdal's Supplement* were listed as follows: Editor, Benigno Ramos; Manager, Tomas D. Española; Assistant Manager, Ramon Crespo. Office address: 303 South El Dorado, Stockton, California. See "Sakdal," *Sakdal*, 29 July 1933, 3. For the papers published in the U.S., see "Sakdalistas In and Out," *Sakdal*, 29 June 1935, 4. See also "Be a

Militant Campaigner!" *Sakdal*, 15 July 1933, 3. The *Manila Sakdal's Supplement* was reprinted in the *Sakdal* starting 1 July, appearing at the rate of one page in the English issue to each of four successive Tagalog issues.

104. "Benigno Ramos's Understudy," *Philippines Free Press*, 18 April 1936, 10–11 and 50; and "Ang Sugo ng Bayang Api at si G. T. D. Española," *Sakdal*, 15 July 1933, 1. In the latter article, Ramos erroneously says Española was from Cebu.

105. "Kababayan: Read This," *Sakdal*, 1 July 1933, 3.

106. "Sariling Diwa," 15 July 1933, 2; "Reveries and Experiences of Our Editor," 29 July 1933, 1; and "Liham ng Sugo ng Bayang Api sa Kanyang Giliw na Maybahay," 29 July 1933, 1, all in *Sakdal*. See also "Benigno Ramos' Understudy," *Philippines Free Press*, 10. On Ramos's meeting with the American senators, see "Ganappu to ni Kansuru Kenkyu," 10.

107. Bernardita Churchill, *The Philippine Independence Missions*, 288.

## Chapter 3

1. "Pinatunayan ng mga Pangyayari," *Sakdal*, 12 January 1935, 1. See also "Ang Sakdalista sa Harap ng Sariling Suliranin," *The Filipino Freedom*, 4th week of July 1935, 1.

2. *Pamahayag at Patakaran ng Lapiang Sakdalista* (Manila: Fradica Press, 1933), 19. Mr. Jeremias Adia made this document available to me.

3. The preface is located on the page before "Tumututol Kami," in *Pamahayag*. Nine points of objection against the government and government officials are listed in "Tumututol Kami." See "Tumututol Kami," n.p., which is translated and summarized in appendix 1. Federalists were those who cooperated with the U.S. occupation force at the turn of twentieth century.

4. "Sa Buzon ng Sakdal," *Sakdal*, 15 September 1934, 3.

5. *Pamahayag*, inside front cover. For the star, see "Sariling Diwa," *Sakdal*, 6 April 1935, 2. Some members, such as Adia, understood the heart on the palm to be "Ang puso ng bayan ay kailangang hawakan natin. Ginagawa natin ang sariling suwerte" (A Nation's heart must be grasped. We must make our own destiny). The emblem was designed by Ramos. Interview with Adia on 26 April 1985, at his residence in Cabuyao, Laguna.

6. *Pamahayag* front cover. The quotation attributed to Bonifacio is from the *Teachings of the Katipunan*, which was said to have been written by Bonifacio but later polished by Emilio Jacinto. The English translation here is a quotation from Agoncillo's translation in Teodoro Agoncillo, *Revolt of the Masses: The Story of Bonifacio and the Katipunan* (Quezon City: University of the Philippines, 1956), 84.

7. On the page after "Diwa ng Sakdalista" (Spirit of the Sakdals), in *Pamahayag*, n.p.

8. "Diwa ng Sakdalista" and the following page, n.p.

9. These sentiments were widely shared at the time. About a year after the Sakdalista Party was formed, Joaquin Manibo published his *Pasyon ng Bayan sa Kahapo't Ngay-on* (Passion of the Country in the Past and Present) (Bauan, Batangas: Juan Press, 1934), which voiced similar criticisms of leading politicians. See Ileto, *Pasyon and Revolution*, 250–53. See also Evelyn Ansay-Miranda, "Ang Kilusang Pang-Independensya sa Pananaw ng Oligarkiya at ng Masa Noong Panahong 1930," *Historical Bulletin* 26, nos. 1–4 (January–December 1982): 123–26.

10. For more on the Sakdalista Party's critique of current social conditions, see "Pamahayag at Patakaran ng Lapiang Sakdalista," in *Pamahayag*, 1–8. See also "Tumututol Kami."

11. The thirty-five objectives are summarized in appendix 2.

12. *Pamahayag*, 23. For information on Felino Cajucom, see Stubbs, "Philippine Radicalism," 154.

13. For councilors' names, see *Pamahayag*, 23. The members represented their birthplaces even if they currently resided in Manila or other parts of Luzon. The representative for Panay was Tomas Española (a native of Antique Province), who had hosted Ramos during his visit to Stockton, California. Laguna representative Gregorio Tobias of Santa Cruz was said to have sold part of his land for the cause of the Sakdalista Party. Interview with Luis Taruc on 22 August 1986 in Quezon City. He became one of the leaders of the anti-Japanese guerrilla force during the Japanese Occupation period.

14. "Tuntuning Pang-Loob," in *Pamahayag*, 24–25. At least in the town of Cabuyao, membership dues were 10 centavos per week. However, this practice and amount may have applied only to that town. See "History and Cultural Life of the Town (of Cabuyao)," 7, Historical Data of Laguna, 46, HDP.

15. "Lupong 'Sakdalista' na Nakatatag na sa mga Bayanbayan," 3; "Ang mga Miting sa Ilocos, Bikol at Kabisayaan," 3; "Kabalitaan: Libu-libo ang Nagsikatig sa Simulain ng Lapian Sakdalista sa Tarlak, Tarlak," 3; and "Ang Laguna sa Kilusang Sakdalista," 4, all in *Sakdal*, 18 November 1933. See also "Partido Sakdalista de Filipinas," 3; and "Ang Sakdalista sa Camarines Sur," 4; 27 January 1934, in *Sakdal*.

16. "Pamanhik sa mga Sakdalista," *Sakdal*, 6 January 1934, 4. To further boost the election campaign, numerous Sakdal meetings were held. For instance, see "Mga Miting na Nairaos," *Sakdal*, 6 January 1934, 4.

17. "Masiglang Totoo ang Kilos ng mga Sakdalsita," *Sakdal*, 6 January 1934, 1.

18. "Kablegrama sa Kasarinlan," *Sakdal*, 27 January 1934, 1. Also in January 1934, the party announced plans to bring the case before the U.S. Supreme Court to prove the Treaty of Paris illegal. See "Move of Startling Nature Planned by Sakdalista Leaders," 27 January 1934, 1, and "Ang Pagtutol ni Don Felipe Agoncillo sa Tratado de Paris," 7 July 1934, 1, both in *Sakdal*.

19. "Ang Ikinaalipin ng Ibang Bayan," *Sakdal*, 26 May 1934, 1.

20. *The Sunday Tribune*, 10 June 1934. Although incomplete, Quezon garnered 71,005 votes and Timog, 19,474 votes so far as of mid-June. See *Philippines Free Press*, 16 June 1934, 35.

21. *Manila Daily Bulletin*, 9 May 1935.

22. For instance, Municipal Pres.-elect Nemesio Esmilla could barely speak any English or Spanish but had already served as the town's executive for three consecutive terms before becoming a Sakdalista Party member. He was considered the most energetic mayor the town had ever had. See *The Tribune*, 19 June 1934. Laguna towns that showed strong Sakdalista Party support were Longos, Majayjay, Nagcarlan, Pangil, and Pila. *The Sunday Tribune*, 17 June 1934. See also *The Tribune*, 7, 8, 9, 11, 17, and 19 June 1934; 4 and 9 May 1935.

23. "History and Cultural Life of San Fernando," n.p. Historical Data of Pampanga 77, HDP.

24. "Murphy to Sec. of War Dern," cablegram, 12 June 1934, BIA, NARA, quoted in Stubbs, "Philippine Radicalism," 166fn69.

25. *The Tribune*, 7 June 1934. Sakdalista platform mentions that mines should be used for the benefit of the Filipinos. See "Sa Pagkakaroon Natin ng Kasarinlan," in *Pamahayag*, 37. During the election campaign, the Sakdalista candidates announced that the Philippines' natural resources should be used to support the country, and they wanted to abolish a number of taxes, including the cedula tax. See Isidro L. Retizos, "Why Sakdalistas Won In Laguna and Other Places," *The Herald Mid-Week Magazine*, 27 June 1934, 6–9. Retizos called the Sakdalista Party "a new Socialist party."

26. *The Tribune*, 8 June 1934.

27. *The Tribune*, 7 June 1934; and *The Sunday Tribune*, 10 June 1934. The Sakdalista Party's victory was attributed to the fact that the party's opponents had underestimated its strength and failed to counter its propaganda. See *The Tribune*, 14 and 21 June 1934.

28. For Almazan and Untivero, see *The Tribune*, 15 June 1934. On election day, a prominent pro-administration citizen of Tayabas went to Atimonan to offer the Sakdalistas all the municipal positions if they would vote for Quezon. The Sakdalistas replied that they would gladly sacrifice all elective positions in

the municipality but would fight for the national legislative positions of senator and representative because these were the ones who made the people suffer by shouldering the cost of the big salaries they received from the government. See *The Tribune*, 7 June 1934, and *The Sunday Tribune*, 10 June 1934.

29. The following are Sakdalista Party candidates who ran in the 1934 elections: Candidates for senators, Esteban Coruña (3rd district); Celerino Tiongco (4th district); Dr. Jose T. Timog (5th district). Candidates for representatives, Sixto Sablay (Bulacan, 1st district); Paulo V. Capa (Bulacan, 2dd district); Luis Javier (Cavite); Aurelio C. Almazan (Laguna, 1st district); Mariano S. Untivero (Laguna, 2nd district); Antonio Velisasrio (Manila, 2nd district); Frisco Villanueva (Manila, 2d district); Quintin Santos de Dios (Rizal, 1st district); Elpidio Santos (Rizal, 2nd district); Dionisio C. Mayor (Tayabas, 1st district); and Antonio Z. Argosino (Tayabas, 2nd district). (Narciso Lapus ran in Pampanga under no party.) Candidates for governors, Pio Centeno (Bulacan); Leon Pelaez (Marinduque); Gregorio Tobias (Laguna); Jose Jabson (Rizal); Jose Ner Abueg (Cavite); Felino Cajucom (Nueva Ecija); Ciriaco V. Campomanes (Tayabas); Evaristo Magbag (Tarlac); Teodoro de Leon (Pampanga); Isabelo Magno (Camarines Norte). See the *Philippines Free Press*, 16 June 1934, 34–35, 42. See also the United States of America, Commonwealth of the Philippines, *Court of Appeals: The People of the Philippines versus Fruto R. Santos et al. – Criminal Case No. 51558* (Manila), 24–25.

30. Between 1932 and 1935, a quarter of the adult citizens in Laguna were unable to pay their cedula tax. For the economic condition in Laguna and Tayabas, see Daniel F. Doeppers, "The Philippines in the Great Depression: A Geography of Pain," in *Weathering the Storm: The Economies of Southeast Asia in the 1930s Depression*, ed. Peter Boomgaard and Ian Brown (Singapore: Institute of Southeast Asia Studies, 2000), 69–70.

31. Some of the strike leaders, such as Teodoro Asedillo, escaped to the mountains in Laguna after a big clash between the authorities and the strikers. Doeppers, "Metropolitan Manila in the Great Depression: Crisis for Whom?" *The Journal of Asian Studies* 50, no. 3 (August 1991): 531–32.

32. *Philippines Free Press*, 16 June 1934, 35.

33. *The Sunday Tribune*, 10 June 1934.

34. *The Tribune*, 7 June 1934.

35. "Ang Pilosopya Sakdalista," *Sakdal*, 21 July 1934, 3.

36. For details on these rallies, see Series 7, Subject File 1934–36, Sakdalista Box, Ex. 36–38, 40–41, QP.

37. "To Provincial Commander, Tayabas: Subject: Sakdalista Meeting, Lucena, July 11, 1934," Ex. 38, File 1934–1936, QP.

38. "Ang Dalawang Landas," *Sakdal*, 30 March 1935, 2. It is obvious that the author of the article is referring to the statement in Jesus' Sermon on the Mount. See Matthew 7:13–14, in *The New Oxford Annotated Bible*, 1179.

39. "Ang Dalawang Landas," ibid.

40. "To Provincial Commander, Tayabas: Subject: Sakdalista Meeting, Atimonan," Ex. 37, Subject File 1934–1936, QP.

41. In July, an election was held to further solidify the party. The following candidates were elected: President, Benigno Ramos; Acting President, Celerino Tiongco; Vice President, Venancio R. Aznar; Secretary, Simeon de Sena; Vice Secretary, Paulino J. Cifra; Treasurer, Jose E. League; and Auditor, Marcelino Tenorio. Regional representatives were also elected. See "Patnugutang Pangbansa ng Lapiang Sakdalista," *Sakdal*, 30 March 1935, 2.

42. "Patnugutang Pangbansa ng Lapiang Sakdalista," 2.

43. To reduce importation, the Sakdalista Party also advocated growing medicinal plants to produce herbal medicines. Other proposals included making public defenders available to the poor without charge; investigating all franchises the legislature had granted to foreign corporations; filing legal complaints against all independence missions that had been sent by the Legislature on the grounds that they violated the Constitution of the Philippines; constructing commercial vessels to transport Philippine products to foreign countries; changing the salaries of representatives and senators (presumably from a fixed monthly basis) to a per-session basis; transferring the power of appointments from the politicians to an independent board; changing the government from a presidential form to a parliamentary one so the cabinet would be responsible to the people rather than to the governor general; and changing the title of high officials from "Honorable" to just plain "Mister." See *The Sunday Tribune*, 24 June 1934.

44. *The Tribune*, 6 and 12 September 1934. Some of the Sakdalista proposals, such as the total abolition of the cedula tax, paralleled those of other legislators, such as Representatives Diokno and Karag. However, the proposal did not pass. It failed by just one vote. See *The Tribune*, 27 October 1934. In November 1937, Pres. Quezon proposed to abolish the cedula tax and later the National Assembly passed the resolution to abolish it. See *Court of Appeals: The People of the Philippines versus Fruto R. Santos et al. – Criminal Case No. 51558*, 58.

45. "Mga Lupong Sakdalistang Nakatatag na sa mga Bayan-bayan," 3 March 1934, 3; "Mga Lupong Sakdalista sa Bayan-Bayan," 26 May 1934, 3, both in *Sakdal*.

46. "Kumikilos ang Atimonan," *Sakdal*, 14 July 1934, 2.

47. "Ang Sampong (*sic*) Tuntunin," *Sakdal*, 15 September 1934, 4. For "Ang Tuntunin ng Umiibig sa Simulain ng 'Sakdal.'"

48. "Resolution," *Sakdal*, 14 July 1934, 2.

49. "Sa Kilusang Sakdalista," *Sakdal*, 14 July 1934, 3.

50. For Ramos's announcement of the departure, see "Namatay ang Anak ng Patnugot," *Sakdal*, 3 November 1934, 4. For information on Crespo becoming Ramos's secretary, see *Pamahayag at Patakaran*, 23. Also see Ramon Paz Crespo file, no. 79-4, Peoples Court Papers (PCP), Main Library Archives, University of the Philippines, Special Collections, Filipiniana Section (UPFS), Quezon City. During his stay in Japan, Crespo married a Japanese woman, Migiko Saso, in June 1936. See "Ang Katangian ng Isang Haponesa," *Sakdal*, 1 July 1936, 1.

51. For their arrival date, see "Liham ng Kasamang Naglalakbay," *Sakdal*, 5 January 1935, 1. For Ramos's change of heart, see "Ang Limang Tuta ni Paredes," *Sakdal*, 4 May 1935, 1. Japanese police surveillance records show that Ramos's wife and two children went to Japan at the same time as Ramos and his two attendants. However, this detail was added to the records incorrectly because the Japanese police had not yet begun tracking Ramos in Japan. Ramos's daughter remembers that she, her mother, grandmother, and brother accompanied some Sakdalistas to Japan a month after her father had gone there. Her memory agrees with a Japanese journalist's account, which was based on an interview with Ramos. For the Japanese police surveillance report, see Naimusho Keihokyoku (Home Ministry, Police Bureau) *Gaiji keisatsu gaikyo* (Police General Situation on Foreign Affairs) (*Japanese Police Report*) (Tokyo: Ryukei Shosha, 1980) vol. 1 (1935): 168. This document was made available to me by Dr. Lydia N. Yu Jose of Ateneo de Manila University. For the Japanese journalist's account, see Yasotaro Moori, "Hito daitoryo no nihon homon wa nani wo imi suruka" (What does Philippine President's Visit to Japan Signify?) *Kokusai Panfuretto Tsushin*, 11 August 1938, 22. Information also comes from an interview with Leticia Ramos-Uyboco.

52. *Japanese Police Report* 1 (1935): 168. Leticia Ramos-Uyboco remembers the exact address of their host, Maruyama, which matches the police record. Ramos must have made prior arrangements to meet with these Japanese. It is possible that Artemio Ricarte introduced Ramos to them. It is also possible that some local Japanese of ultranationalist leanings in the Philippines could have arranged it. For instance, Eikichi Imamura, who was engaged in the lumber business and was a prominent member of the Japanese community in Manila, was a member of the Genyosha, headed by Mitsuru Toyama. See Seitaro Kanegae, *Aruitekita michi* (The Path I Took) (Tokyo: Kokusei-sha, 1968), 365. At least one local Japanese, Toshihide Ishita, was openly sympathetic to the Sakdalista cause. He was a Philippine-born Japanese residing in Calamba, Laguna, and his articles appeared in the Sakdalista Party publications. For his articles, see "Thoughts Uncensored,"

*Sakdal*, 19 June 1937, 1; and "In My Opinion," *The Filipino Freedom*, 6 April 1937, 5. Information on Ishita also comes from the interview with Adia on 25 April 1985, in Cabuyao, Laguna. It is possible that people like Imamura and Ishita facilitated making contacts for Ramos in Japan.

53. On Kageyama's background, see Koreshige Inuzuka, "Hito ni okeru dai 31 keibitai no sakusen," Itaku, 26 May 1960, 80–88, NIDS. Information on Ramos's meeting with Gen. Matsui came from Uzuhiko Ashizu, "Ramosu himei ni taoreru: Hito dokuritsu kakumei senshi shoden" (Ramos Succumbs with an Unfulfilled Wish: Short Biography of a Filipino Independent Revolutionary Fighter), *Shin Seiryoku*, no. 142, April 1971, 9. For Matsumoto's background, see Grant K. Goodman, "Japan and Philippine Radicalism: The Case of Benigno Ramos," 144. According to Ramos-Uyboco, Ricarte introduced Ramos to Mitsuru Toyama, who in turn got in touch with Kunpei Matsumoto and other ultranationalists such as Maruyama and members of Dai Nippon Seisan party. For information on the party, see Lydia N. Yu Jose, *Filipinos in Japan and Okinawa: 1880s to 1972* (Tokyo: Research Institute for the Language and Cultures of Asia and Africa, Tokyo University of Foreign Studies, 2002), 36.

54. Goodman, "Japan and Philippine Radicalism," 143–44. See also Crespo file, no. 79-4, PCP, UPFS. Leticia Ramos-Uyboco, who was in her mid-teens at the time, saw Gen. Artemio Ricarte visiting their residence occasionally. Once she heard her father trying to convince the general to return to the Philippines. To this, Ricarte answered that he would rather die in Japan than see "tyrants" in the Philippines. Then Ramos said that he was just testing Ricarte's patriotism, and they all laughed. As for Ramos's Japanese name, Goodman states that it was Sakurada Shigenosuke. See "Japan and Philippine Radicalism,"143.

55. Ashizu, "Ramosu himei ni taoreru," 11–13.

56. For information about the development of the political parties, see Dapen (Ta-peng) Liang, *The Development of Philippine Political Parties* (Hong Kong: South China Morning Post [printed but not published], 1939), 236–39. See also Hayden, *The Philippines*, 364–75. For the Sakdalistas' criticism, see "The Coalition of the Major Parties," *Sakdal*, 2 February 1935, 1.

57. Golay, *Face of Empire*, 335.

58. "Ang Ikalawang Pulong ng mga Delegadong Sakdalista," *Sakdal*, 5 January 1935, 1.

59. "Ang Ginagawang Pagsulat ng Ibang Pahayagan sa mga Balitang Natatamo," *Sakdal*, 5 January 1935, 2. See also "Lapiang Sakdalista sa Filipinas," *Sakdal*, 12 January 1935, 1.

60. "The Speech of Tydings Should Not Be Left Unchallenged," *Sakdal*, 5

January 1935, 1. For details on Tydings' address, see *The Tribune* and *The Philippines Herald*, 22 December 1934. See also Golay, *Face of Empire*, 336.

61. "Lapiang Sakdalista sa Pilipinas; Lupong Panlalawigan Maynila, S.P.," *Sakdal*, 26 January 1935, 4.

62. "Nabunyag sa San Pablo, Laguna ang Kasinungalingan ng mga Maka-Commonwealth," *Sakdal*, 26 January 1935, 1.

63. "Buong Siglang Naidaos ang Miting ng Sakdal sa Intramuros; Dinaluhan ng Mahigit na 6,000 Tao," *Sakdal*, 16 February 1935, 2. However, this meeting was not reported by other major dailies.

64. Three regional campaign committees were set up. One covered the provinces of Nueva Ecija, Pampanga, and Tarlac; the second covered Manila, Rizal, Bataan, and Cavite; and the third covered Tayabas, Laguna, and Marinduque. "Magsisimula sa 23 ang Pangatawanang Kampanya," *Sakdal*, 16 March 1935, 4.

65. "Hanggang sa Leyte ay Namamayani ang Sakdalismo," 13 April 1935, 3. For the campaign in Tayabas and Bataan, see "Mahalaga Para sa Tayabas," 30 March 1935, 4. "Tagumpay ang Miting ng mga Sakdalista sa Orani, Bataan," 13 April 1935, 3, all in *Sakdal*.

66. "Sa 27 ng Abril ang 'Debate' U.P.-Sakdalista," 13 April 1935, 1; (no title), 27 April 1935, 2; and "Malaking Pagtatalo sa Harap ng Bayan," 2, all in *Sakdal*. See also *The Philippines Herald*, 27 April 1935. Unfortunately, I have not yet been able to locate the contents of this debate.

67. "Maka-Sakdal: Ang Sigaw nang Api,'" *Sakdal*, 25 August 1934, 2. This poem should not be confused with Ramos's poem of the same title, "Sigaw nang Api."

68. "Paniniwala sa Katarungan ng Dios at Pananalig sa Simulain ng Lapian ay Katubusan ng Lahi/ Magtutuloy Tayong Lahat," *Sakdal*, 2 March 1935, 1.

69. In the case of Pila, Laguna, the Sakdalistas' stronghold, the Rizal Day celebration of the Sakdalistas was launched by none other than the municipal mayor. For details, see "Kabalitaan ng Naglalakbay: Ang Pila, Laguna sa Pamunuan ng mga Sakdalista," *Sakdal*, 12 January 1935, 2.

70. "Bayang Magiting," *Sakdal*, 7 July 1934, 4.

71. "Mga 'Sakdalistang Lihim na Naglilibot," 26 January 1935, 2; "Tugon ni Asunar kay Perfectio," 2 February 1935, 1, 4; "Mga Kilusang Lihim sa Lalawigan Tayabas," 9 February 1935, 1; "Ang Kilusan sa Lucena," 16 March 1935, 3, all in *Sakdal*. See also "Magtapat Tayo sa Bayan," *Sakdal*, 2 March 1935, 1. Another such group was the Santiago de Galicia movement operating in the Barrio of Colonia, San Ildefonso, Bulacan. This movement was headed by four women who were allegedly taking orders from a "warrior" named Santiago de Galicia. Some people

said that this group belonged to the Colorum. Consequently, Sakdalistas in this area were warned not to join this kind of organization. See "Lilipad sa Alapaap," *Sakdal*, 3 November 1934, 1.

72. "Pamamahayag ng Patnugutan," *Sakdal*, 21 July 1934, 1, 4.

73. "Narito Na si Gen. Ricarte at Nagpapagalaw ng mga Galamay," *Sakdal*, 13 April l935, 1.

74. For March 1935, see "Sworn Statement," *Sakdal*, 30 March 1935, 1.

75. "Ang Utang na Loob nina Quezon at Ramos," *Sakdal*, 14 July 1934, 1. See also Sakdalista Box, Ex. 36, 37, 1934–36, QP.

76. "Ang Sagot sa 'Mabuhay,'" *Sakdal*, 21 July 1934, 1.

77. Ramos invited Quezon to participate in a public debate. For Ramos's defense, see "Ang Utang na Loob nina Quezon at Ramos," and the Ilocano version, "Awis ni Apu B. Ramos, Pangulo ti Sakdalista," both in *Sakdal*, 14 July 1934, 1, 3, respectively.

78. Sakdalista Box, Ex. 36, 37, 1934–36, QP.

79. "The Why of Sakdalism," *Philippines Free Press*, 21 July 1934, 8–10, 28. Even Quezon's opponents, such as Sen.-elect Juan Sumulong and Dean Conrado Benitez, shared the same opinion. See *The Tribune*, 14 and 15 June 1934. For more on Benitez's opinion, see *Philippines Free Press*, July 1934, 9. See also "Unfounded Attacks against the Representatives of Laguna," and "Scandalous Mistakes," both in *Sakdal*, 28 July 1934, 1.

80. "Sariling Diwa: At Humanda Na Kayo," 15 September 1934, 2 and Ayaw Nang Pagsasalita Sina Kint. Untivero at Almazan, 3 November 1934, 1. both in *Sakdal*.

81. "Kahinahinalang Pangyayari," *Sakdal*, 5 January 1935, 4.

82. *The Tribune*, 4 and 9 May 1935. See also the *Manila Daily Bulletin*, 5 May 1935.

83. Even before the 1934 elections (in July 1933), a Sakdalista meeting in Agdagan, Tayabas, was disallowed because the group was unable to obtain a permit from the municipal mayor, who claimed he was acting on orders from the Sec. of the Interior, Leon Guinto. See "Ang P. Puno ng Sakdal," *Sakdal*, 1 July 1933, 4. After the June 1934 election, however, it was alleged that Quezon had been pressuring Gen. Basilio Valdez of the Philippine constabulary to suppress Sakdal activities on grounds that the Sakdal movement was subversive. See "Sariling Diwa," *Sakdal*, 28 July 1934, 2. For the withholding of permits, see "Naliligalig ang mga Pulitiko," 5 January 1935, 1; and "Patalastas sa Lahat ng Kapanalig,"12 January 1935 3, both in *Sakdal*.

84. "Pulis na Amerikanong Lumusob sa Pulong ng mga Sakdalista," *Sakdal*, 2 March 1935, 3.

85. "May mga Paring Pilipino na Kasangkapan Din sa Pangaalipin," *Sakdal*, 12 January 1935, 2.

86. Those who did attend were ready to be arrested; however, no arrests were made. See "Ang Sakdalista sa Harap ng mga Kanyon Pang Rapido sa Nueva Ecija," 16 March 1935, 4; and "Sariling Diwa: Sa Harap ng mga Alagad ng Batas," 16 March 1935, 2, both in *Sakdal*.

87. The four Sakdalistas were Jose Ner Abueg, Ignacio Martinez, Narciso Galvez, and Filomeno Prodon. All four continued their speaking activities in Sakdalista campaigns, and two of them were soon appointed to the regional committees coordinating Sakdalista efforts against the T-M Act. See "Tulungan sina Abueg at mga Kasama," *Sakdal*, 2 March 1935, 1.

88. "Sariling Diwa: Iligtas Natin ang Bayan sa Rebolucion," *Sakdal*, 15 September 1934, 2.

89. The real author of the letter is said to be Hiroshi Tamura, a major in the Japanese army in Taiwan. See "Telegram Received from Governor General Hayden to Grew," 8 May, and "To Governor General from Grew," 9 May 1935, File 811b.00, Box 5291, RG 59, General Record, Department of State, NARA. See also "Ayaw Paraanin ng Sakdal sa Correo," Sakdal, 27 April 1935.

90. The following issues of *The Filipino Freedom* were made available to me: 4th week of July 1935; 19 January; 16 and 23 March; 6 April; 4 May; 1, 8, 15, and 22 June, all in 1937. *The Filipino Freedom* occasionally included a section in the Visayan language. The editor was listed as Antonio Velisario and the office address was in Sampaloc, Manila. According to Walter Robb, the party had no fewer than six or seven publications. However, I have not been able to locate all of the publications he mentions. One of them was *Sulô* (Torch), published by the Torch Publishing Company. The paper's main theme was the oppression of the peasants and the poverty of the people, and its editors wished to resume the revolution of 1896 and carry it out to the end. For more on these publications, see W(alter) R(obb), "Sakdals," *American Chamber of Commerce Journal* 15 (May 1935): 10.

91. The quotation from the Bible is from Roman 3:4. The original Tagalog text is "Sabihin ang katotohanan, kasakdalang masumpungang ang lahat ng tao'y sinungaling, Dios lamang ang totoo." I have not been able to find this exact wording in any recent Tagalog version of the Bible. Del Pilar's Tagalog original text that appeared in the masthead of *The Filipino Freedom* is "Ibigin ninyo ang Bayang iyan na siyang kabuuan ng lahat ng ating katangian at kadakilaan. Ang pagpapabaya sa kanya ay pagpayag na maalipin tayo at maalipin pati ating mga anak."

92. For the protest in Gapan, see "Nasaan ang Kagyat na Pagsasarili ang Sigaw ng mga Sakdalista sa Gapan nang Nagdaan Doon Sina Kal. Guinto at Paredes," 16 March 1935, 1; and "Isinigaw ni Dr. Lotuaco ang Damdamin ni Kal. Guinto,

Pinalaya ni Espiker Paredes," 16 March 1935, 2, both in *Sakdal*. For the Visayas, see *The Tribune*, 30 March 1935. For government speeches, see *The Tribune*, 5, 8, 12, 13, 27, and 30 March 1935. See also "Speaker Paredes Talks to the People," *Philippines Free Press*, 16 March 1935, 8, 33.

93. *The Philippines Herald*, 15 April 1935.

94. At this time, government officials also discussed potential solutions to the conflicts between landlords and tenants. They were particularly concerned about the distribution of sugar benefit payments, which had resulted in serious disputes between landlords and tenants. See *The Tribune*, 2 April 1935.

95. *The Philippines Herald*, 2 April 1935.

96. "Memorandum to His Excellency Acting Governor General J. R. Hayden from Sec. of Department of Agriculture and Commerce, Eulogio Rodriguez, dated 2 April 1935," in "Departmental Order dated April 12," folder no. 25-26 Part 2, "Public Order," H.P.

97. "General Circular No. 11," folder 25-24 (no title), HP. This circular was quoted in another memorandum, dated 15 April 1935, that Rodriguez sent to Hayden.

98. "The Reason for Sakdalism," *Philippines Free Press*, 13 April 1935, n.p. (inside the cover page).

99. "Mga Taong Pamahalaan," *Sakdal*, 13 April 1935, 2. See also *The Philippines Herald* and *The Tribune*, 26 April 1935. The government also sought to drive a wedge between the labor movement and the Sakdalistas. See *The Tribune*, 2 May 1935.

100. On Barros, see Teodoro A. Agoncillo, *Maikling Kuwentong Tagalog: 1886–1948* (Tagalog Short Stories: 1886–1948) (Quezon City: Wika Publishing, 1949), 22. On Jose P. Laurel, see *Political-Social Problems* (Manila: National Teachers' College, 1936), 31. The Sakdalistas were also seen as people to be feared. When sending unwilling children to bed, some mothers and nursemaids used to threaten them by saying, "Ayan na ang mga Sakdalista!" (The Sakdalistas are coming!). But this image could only have been formed after the May Uprising. See E. V. Ventura and M. Mendez, *From Journalism to Diplomacy* (Quezon City: University of the Philippines Press, 1978), 66–67.

101. "Sakdalistas in Verse," *Philippines Free Press*, 8 June 1935, 46–47.

102. "Pinipilit sa Kaalipinan ang Bayan,"13 April 1935, 1; "Sakdalista,"13 April 1935, 2; and "May Balitang Hahalayin si Gg. B. Ramos," 1 September 1934, 1, all in *Sakdal*.

103. "Magpalaganap at Magpakatibay," 9 February 1935, 2; "Sa Araw ng Plebisito," 27 April 1935, 2, both in *Sakdal*. 104. "Inuusig sa Matuwid," *Sakdal*, 3 November 1934, 1.

105. "Hindi Lalahok sa Plebesito," *Sakdal*, 27 April 1935, 1.

106. For the affidavits, see "Evidence against Tomas Rueda," "Evidence against Juan Peñaranda," and "Evidence against Ciriaco Campomanes," in Sakdalista Box, Series 7, Subject File, 1934–36, QP.

107. *The Tribune*, 20, 21, and 26 April 1935. Campomanes was presumed to be a Ricartista, having been a member of the Ricarte-inspired Tanggulan Society. He ordered the uniforms for the uprising and joined Ricarte's group during the Japanese Occupation.

108. The signatories of the letter, dated 29 April, included Jose Timog, Pedro Torres, and Dionisio Mayor. See the *Manila Daily Bulletin*, 1 May 1935.

109. *The Tribune*, 9 May 1935. For Hayden's letter to Dionisio Mayor, see *Court of Appeals: The People of the Philippines versus Fruto R. Santos et al. – Criminal Case No. 51558*, 62–66.

110. "Report of the Sec. of the Interior on the Sakdalista Uprising," June 1935, Series 7, Subject File 1934–35, Sakdalista Box, QP.

111. "General Basilio Valdez Report," 31 May 1935, Series 7, QP.

112. "Confidential Memorandum for the Superintendent by Basilio J. Valdez 2 May 1935," folder 25-23 "Untitled," HP.

113. *Manila Daily Bulletin*, 9 May 1935.


# Chapter 4

1. *Manila Daily Bulletin*, 7 May 1935. On 14 May, Ramos sent a telegram to Pres. Roosevelt demanding immediate U.S. withdrawal from the Philippines. He said that the revolution (the May Uprising) was caused by nonfulfillment of an American promise. This defiant attitude further proves his leadership of the uprising. For his telegrams, see James Biedzynski, "American Perception of the Sakdals," *Bulletin of the American Historical Collection* 18, no. 3 (July–September 1990): 90.

2. Guillermo Capadocia, "Notes which may be used in the milestone in the history of the CCPI,'" CP, 2. See also Dionisio interview in Sturtevant, *Popular Uprisings*, 227fn1.

3. A copy of this periodical can be located among the Hayden Papers. See folder no. 25-24 (no title), HP.

4. The article was signed "Benigno R. Ramos, President and envoy [*shisetsu*] of the Sakdalista Party." See *Free Filipinos* (Japanese section), 1. While Ramos was in Japan, the *Sakdal* weekly began printing his address in Japan: "Nichido Bldg., Room 26, 1, Nishigochome, Ginza, Kyobashi-ku, Tokyo, Japan." See *Sakdal*, 16 July 1938, 2.

5. Joseph Grew, American Ambassador to Japan, to Joseph Hayden, Acting Governor General, 13 May 1935. BIA quoted by Grant K. Goodman, "Japan and Philippine Radicalism," 145.

6. Ramon Paz Crespo file, no. 79-4, PCP. UPFS. Crespo says this paper was named *The Filipino Freedom*. He must have been confused, because *The Filipino Freedom* was written mostly in Tagalog and aimed primarily at local audiences. It also carried accounts of recent events in the Philippines, which meant it had to have been written locally and for local consumption. *Free Filipinos*, on the other hand, was multilingual, aimed at foreign audiences, and carried no time-sensitive information.

7. It seems that the police informer misremembered the name "Malayang Tao" (Free People) as "Tagalog Malaya," and it is most likely that this report actually refers to *Free Filipinos*. See *Japanese Police Report* 2 (1936): 375.

8. Leon Ma. Guerrero, "How Japan Looks at Ramos," *Philippines Free Press*, 1 June 1935, 4–5.

9. The other names, R. Paz, Marcelo Alaras, and Juan de Mesa, are not known to me. I have not come across these names in any of the *Sakdal* issues I have read so far. R. Paz could be the first and middle names of his secretary.

10. Other articles denounced Gov. Gen. Frank Murphy, Laguna Gov. Juan Cailles, and Quintin Paredes for suppressing the people's right to protest against the constitution and the T-M Act.

11. *The Philippines Herald*, 4 May 1935. At the time of the "Christmas Eve Fiasco," certain agents of the U.S. Military Information Division allegedly convinced the Ricartistas that the Scouts and constabulary would mutiny in order for them to start the revolution. See McCoy, *Policing America's Empire*, 195. It seems that this fabrication was remembered as a piece of information and accepted as a possibility by Ramos and his followers.

12. *Sakdal*, 4 May 1935, 1.

13. After Ramos returned from Japan in 1938, he was eventually arrested and a trial was held. Gaudencio Bautista, former secretary general of the Sakdalista Party, who had turned into one of Quezon's informers, became a government witness. He testified that Ramos had been informed of the planned uprising but tried in vain to delay it. The telegrams were court evidence submitted by Bautista. See the *Manila Daily Bulletin*, 11 August 1939. See also *The Tribune*, 8 December 1939.

14. *The Philippines Herald* and the *Manila Daily Bulletin*, 4 May 1935. Ramos's letter was never verified.

15. Other leaders to whom Ramos disclosed his real plan included Juan de la Cruz, Apolonio Villacorte, Paulo Capa, Gaudecio Bautista, and Arseno Batitis.

See *The Tribune*, 8 December 1939. The absences of Santos and Tiongco from the Philippines was noted in "Sariling Diwa: Dapat na Pasyahan ng Nakararami," *Sakdal*, 2 March 1935, 2. Tiongco's passport indicated that he had obtained his visa to Japan on 28 January 1935 and returned to the Philippines on 26 March 1935. His passport was shown to me by Mrs. Carmen Tiongco-Enriquez, granddaughter of C. Tiongco. See also "Bomei no Sakudaru Toshu Ramusra Kikoku" (The Head of Sakdalista Party Ramos and Others Who Were Exiled in Japan Are Returning Home) *Hiripin Joho*, no. 18 (August 1938): 13. For information on the reunion of the Ramos family, see *Japanese Police Report* 1(1935): 168. See also Yasotaro Moori, "Hito Daitoryo," 3; and an interview with Leticia Ramos-Uyboco.

16. Algabre interview in Sturtevant, *Popular Uprisings*, 293. See also Crisostomo interview in Hachero-Pascual, "The Sakdalista Movement," 205.

17. "Hindi Lalahok sa Plebisito ang mga Sakdalista," *Sakdal*, 22 April 1935, 1.

18. See *The Philippines Herald*, 13 May 1935; and *The Tribune*, 14 May 1935.

19. *The Philippines Herald*, 11 May 1935.

20. See *The Philippines Herald*, 3 May 1935. In the aftermath of the uprising, many Sakdalistas from Laguna and Rizal fled to the mountains of Montalban, Antipolo, San Mateo, Marikina, and Cainta in Rizal Province. See *The Tribune*, 7, 10, and 11 May 1935; *Manila Daily Bulletin*, 10 May 1935; and *The Philippines Herald*, 6 and 11 May 1935.

21. This kind of rumor circulated in the towns of Rizal, Bulacan, and Tayabas. See *The Tribune*, 7 and 9 May, and 9 July 1935. *Manila Daily Bulletin*, 9 May 1935. For more rumors, see "Memorandum for Superintendent by Captain Jose P. Guido, Assistant Superintendent of Intelligence Division dated 9 May 1935," folder 25-26, "Untitled," HP. See also "Memorandum for the Adjutant General of the Philippine Constabulary from the Provincial Commander of Pampanga, 18 July 1935," Sakdalista Box, QP.

22. *The Tribune*, 5 May 1935; *Manila Daily Bulletin*, 8 May 1935; and *The Philippines Herald*, 11 and 16 May 1935.

23. The number of people arrested, released after investigation, and prosecuted in connection with the May Uprising are as follows:

| PROVINCE | ARRESTED | RELEASED | PROSECUTED |
|---|---|---|---|
| Laguna | 384 | 164 | 220 |
| Bulacan | 365 | 256 | 99 |
| Rizal | 344 | 333 | 11 |
| Cavite | 47 | 45 | 2 |
| TOTAL | 1,140 | 798 | 332 |

*Source*: Series 7, Subject File, 1934–1936, Sakdalista Box, QP. In Cavite, the Provincial Fiscal accused 53 more Sakdalistas on 21 May 1935, but they had not yet been included in this list.

24. "Memorandum for His Excellency the Acting Governor General of the Philippines dated 8 May 1935 by Eulogio Rodriguez," folder 25-23, "Papers on Sakdalistas," HP. A band of the Asedillo-Encallado was hiding in the same area and most likely assisted the fugitive Sakdalistas. Teodoro Asedillo, one of the strike leaders mentioned in fn31 of chapter 3, escaped to the mountains. Nicolas Encallado, a veteran of the revolution, continued resistance against U.S. occupation. See the *Manila Daily Bulletin*, 29 July 1935.

25. *Manila Daily Bulletin*, 9 May 1935. See also "Affidavit in the case of Gapan, Nueva Ecija," folder 25-26, "Untitled," HP.

26. *The Tribune*, 8, 11, and 14 May 1935; the *Manila Daily Bulletin*, 10 May 1935; and *The Philippines Herald*, 11 May 1935.

27. *The Tribune*, 14 May 1935. Some of the areas affected by the uprising had a low ratio of "no" votes because many Sakdalistas did not vote. See "Partial Result of the Plebiscite on the Constitution Held on 14 May 1935, According to Official Reports Received up to 3:30 P.M., May 15, 1935," folder 25-23, "Untitled," HP. 28. See *The Philippines Herald*, 7 and 19 October 1935; *Manila Daily Bulletin*, 3 October 1935. Among those charged and convicted were the two Sakdalista representatives from Laguna, Almazan and Untivero. See *The Philippines Herald*, 4 May 1935; *Official Gazette*, Commonwealth of the Philippines 37, no. 100 (1937). These two appealed to the Supreme Court and were eventually acquitted in February 1939. "Sakdals Acquitted," *Philippines Free Press*, 18 February 1939, 30.

29. An interview with Conrado Generalla, Algabre's son, on 16 December 1988, in Quezon City. See also *The Philippines Herald*, 26 July 1935; the *Manila Daily Bulletin*, 29 July 1935. See also Sturtevant, *Popular Uprisings in the Philippines*, 286–99. Conrado reveals that Algabre's arrest brought hardship to her family. At one point, her baby got so hungry that she crawled over to a nursing dog to feed herself. For more on Algabre, see Pretancio Dealino "Salud A. Generalla: Disciple of Sakdalism," *Chronicle Magazine*, 7 June 1969, 7–9.

30. In the case of Pasig, Rizal, and San Pablo, Laguna, see "Sakdals Are on Warpath Again," *The Whip*, 19 August 1935, 11. Interview with Carlos Tech, a long-time resident of Pasig, on 3 July 1988, at his residence in Pasig. See also *The Tribune*, 15 May 1935. The landlords in Pampanga and Nueva Ecija, who had already created private armies, must have been alerted. See Benedict Kerkvliet, *The Huk Rebellion: A Study of Peasant Revolt in the Philippines* (Quezon City: New Day Publishers, 1977), 56.

31. *The Tribune*, 17 and 23 May 1935.

32. *The Tribune*, 31 May 1935; and the *Manila Daily Bulletin*, 1 June 1935.

33. Earlier, a meeting had been held between the Sakdalista officials and Vice Gov. Gen. Hayden. The Sakdalistas complained to Hayden about the oppressive treatment by the government officials, such as suppressing their meetings and suspending their mailing privileges. See "Sa Pakikipanayam," *Sakdal*, 22 June 1935, 1. For further details on the meeting, see the *Manila Daily Bulletin*, 3 June 1935. For information on the *Sakdal* mail ban, see "Sa Buzon ng Sakdal," *Sakdal*, 29 June 1935, 1.

34. For details about the meeting, see *The Philippines Herald*, 9 May 1935; and the *Manila Daily Bulletin*, 10 May 1935. According to Timog, most of the radicals in Tayabas were found in the towns of Sariaya, Lukban, and Pagbilao.

35. The KLK was established around 1935 by Angel Lorenzo in the lowlands near Mount Banahaw. See Michael Gonzalez, "The Edge of Structures: A Study of Religious Ideology and Filipino Culture" (MA thesis, Sydney University, 1985), 122. For information on the Sakdalistas' perspective on KLK, see "Patuloy ang Kilos ng Litaw na Katalinuhan," 11 January 1936, 4; "Ukol sa 'Litaw na Katalinuhan,'" 25 January 1936, 1, both in *Sakdal*.

36. "Pangungusap ng Patnugot," 6 July 1935; 1, 22 June 1935, 2; "Ang Dios at Kasaysayan ang Hahatol Sa Atin," 1 February 1936, 2; and "Ang Kahulugan ng Pagpapakasakit," 30 May 1936, 3, among others. See also "Panawagan at Pagpapagunita," 22 June 1935, 1; "Ang Kaalipinan ng Pag-iisip," 22 June 1935, 1, all in *Sakdal*.

37. "Truth About Sakdalism," *Sakdal*, 13 July 1935, 1.

38. "Lipos ng Hinagpis ang Hukom Rovina nang Ilagda ang Hatol sa Sapat na Alagad ng Sakdalismo," *Sakdal*, 27 July 1935, 1.

39. "Hindi Magtataas ng Kamay," and "Hindi Dapat Lumahok sa Halalan," 13 July 1935, 2, both in *Sakdal*.

40. "Ang Lupon sa 'Kapuluan ng Malayang Tao' ay Bumabati," *Sakdal*, 27 July 1935, 1. Ramos sent his letter in the name of the "Committee in the Archipelago of Free People," trying to give the impression that such a committee existed and its representatives were in Tokyo.

41. *Manila Daily Bulletin*, 29 July 1935. See also *Whip*, 29 July and 9 September 1935; and "Lapian Sakdalista: Lukban, Tayabas," QP. Celerino Tiongco was of the opinion that if the Sakdalistas had their own party candidates, they should vote; but if they had none, then they should not vote. See "Ang Sakdalista sa Harap ng Sariling Suliranin: Dapat o Hindi Dapat Humalal ang Lapian ng Bayang Api," and "A Dangerous Game," *The Filipino Freedom*, 4th week of July 1935, 1.

42. "Sa Hapay ng Talahip," 13 July, 1; "Hindi Dapat Maniniwala," 14

September 1935, 4; "Mga Miting na Naidaos," 13 July 1935, 3; and "Kabalitaan," 16 June 1935, 3, all in *Sakdal*. See also *Taliba,* 11 September 1935.

43. Hayden, *The Philippines*, 413.

44. The Visayan Sakdalistas, including Iloilo and Cebu, supported Aguinaldo. The Cebu Sakdalistas even passed a resolution endorsing the candidacy of General Aguinaldo. The Aglipayan Sakdalistas must have supported Aglipay, although some leading members of the Aglipayan Church were reported to have cast lots with Aguinaldo. *Whip*, 29 July; and 12 August 1935.

45. Hayden, *The Philippines*, 426.

46. *"A Frank, Unequivocal But Respectful Enunciation of the Filipinos' Demand for Real Independence Based on the Promises of the American People from the Incipiency of the American Regime to the Passage of the Jones Law; Presented by the Sakdalista Delegation to the Hon. Secretary of War and the Congressional Delegation of the United States of America on November 13th, 1935"* (Manila: n.p. 1935), 4–6. Emilio Aguinaldo and his supporters planned to stage a separate demonstration protesting against alleged frauds committed in the last elections. See *The Philippines Herald*, 21 October 1935.

47. For information about another revolt, see *The Tribune*, 22 and 23 October 1935. The signers of the *Memorial* included the two delegates to the National Assembly, Untivero and Almazan, and the directorate of the Sakdalista Party, among whom were Celerino Tiongco (Sakdalista National Assembly president), Elpidio M. Santos (vice president), Simeon de Sena (secretary), Felicisimo Lauson (acting general president of the party), Gaudencio V. Bautista (acting secretary general of the party), and Salud Algabre (Sakdalista National Assembly delegate). For more details, see *Court of Appeals: The People of the Philippines versus Fruto R. Santos et al. – Criminal Case No. 51558*, 27-29. The Court of Appeals had acquitted them in March 1940; however, the case was later brought to the Supreme Court. See "Nasa Ktt. Hukuman Ang 'Illegal Association,'" *Hirang,* 9 July 1941, 1. For the Sakdalista orators' arrest, see "Sa Hapay ng Talahib," 13 July 1935, 1; "Sakdalistas Are Persecuted," 11 January 1936, 1, both in *Sakdal*.

48. For details on the parade, see *The Tribune*, 16 November 1935, and other local newspapers. One hundred thousand marched in the military and civic parades. See the *Manila Daily Bulletin*, 16 November 1935. For more on Quezon's pardon, see the *Manila Daily Bulletin*, 17 November 1935.

49. O. S. Villasin, "Inauguration Day in a Sakdal Town," *Philippine Magazine*, December 1935, 608.

50. Another rumor alleged that the combined forces of Sakdalistas, Communists, KLK, Katipunan ng mga Anak-pawis sa Pilipinas, and some agrarian organizations in Rizal, Laguna, Nueva Ecija, Cavite, Tayabas, and Bulacan were

going to stage an uprising on 24 December (Christmas Eve) or 30 December (Rizal Day). For more on the rumors, see the *Manila Daily Bulletin*, 24, 28, and 30 December 1935; *Monday Mail*, 30 December 1935. For information on Liboria Ramos's arrival, see "Ginagawang Lahat ang Paraan," 11 January 1936, 1; "Natuklasan ni Martinez," 30 May 1936, 1, both in *Sakdal*. See also *Monday Mail*, 30 December 1935.

51. For more information on Algabre, see the *Manila Daily Bulletin*, 19 December 1935. Others arrested included Jose Tinawin, Simeon de Sena, Dr. Ciriaco Campomanes, Dr. Quintin Santos de Dios, Santiago Salvador (shoe factory owner), Antonio Velisario (editor of *The Filipino Freedom*), Fruto R. Santos (Ricartista and Malabon leader, who was 85 years old), and Candida Gomez. Fourteen of them were sent to either Bilibid Prison or the women's correctional institution. Tiongco and two others were out on bail. See the *Manila Daily Bulletin*, 29 and 30 December 1935; and 3 January 1936. See also *The Tribune*, 3 January 1936.

52. *Manila Daily Bulletin*, 30 April and 12 May 1936.

53. For information on rumors of another uprising, see the *Manila Daily Bulletin*, 12 May 1936. For details on the conditional pardon, see *The Tribune*, 19 and 20 August 1936; *Manila Daily Bulletin*, 19, 20, and 29 August 1936. Later in March 1937, 21 Sakdalistas from Cavite were released. See "Pinalaya Na ang mga Sakdalistas sa Kabite," *Sakdal*, 27 March 1937, 1. The municipal president and other prominent residents of the town acted as guarantors for the released Sakdalistas.

54. *Manila Daily Bulletin*, 24 December 1935.

55. *Manila Daily Bulletin*, 29 and 30 April 1936.

56. *The Tribune*, 29 December 1935; 4 January 1936. For information on the Sakdalista Party's denial, see "Ang 'Tagumpay'ay Walang Kinalaman sa Sakdalista," 2 May 1936, 2; "Mga Balitang Pinasisinungalingan," 2 May 1936, 3, both in *Sakdal*.

57. "Walang Kinalaman ang Lapiang Sakdalista sa Binabalak na Aklasan ng mga Manggagawa," *Sakdal*, 6 June 1936, 1; and the *Manila Daily Bulletin*, 9 June 1936. For more on Lauson's presidency, see "Sa Lahat ng Lupon Sakdalista," 7 December 1935, 4, *Sakdal*.

58. Another book recommended was *Ala-ala sa mga Anak ng Himagsikan ng Filipinas* (Recollection of the Children of the Philippine Revolution). The list of books can be found in "Agitador Pulitiko," *Sakdal*, 7 December 1935, 4. For the response, see "A Thought for the New Year," *Sakdal*, 11 January 1936, 1.

59. "Mga Tuntuning Sakdalism," 11 January 1936, 1; and "Hindi Lamang Kalaban ang Nais Magwasak ng Ating Lapian," 11 July 1936, 2, both in *Sakdal*.

60. *The Tribune*, 4 January 1936. The group in San Ildefonso is presumed to have joined the Kalipunang Pangbansa ng mga Magbubukid sa Pilipinas (KPMP), as many Sakdalistas were found in the KPMP. See Kerkvliet, *The Huk Rebellion*, 48. See also Brian Fegan, "The Social History of a Central Luzon Barrio," in *Philippine Social History*, 108; and "Pagunita sa Ilang Sakdalista," *Sakdal*, 11 January 1936, 2. At the same time, it is interesting to note that some joined the party after the uprising because they were deeply moved by the sacrifice made by the participants. Interview with Inocencio Bernardo on 9 August 1990, at Ugong, Pasig, Metro Manila.

61. *The Tribune*, 29 May 1936.

62. "Pinagtibay ang Kable ni Ben Ramos," 11 July 1936, 1; and "Naging Masigla ang Pagtitipon ng Maka-kalayaan," 25 July 1936, 3, both in *Sakdal*.

63. *The Tribune*, 25 September and 2 October 1936.

64. *Manila Daily Bulletin*, 28 January 1938.

65. D. L. Francisco, "From the Mouths of the Sakdals," *Philippines Free Press*, 14 November 1936, 30. For Penullar's involvement in the Tayug Uprising, see *New York Times*, 4 March 1931.

66. This plan was discussed at Adia's residence although he was not directly involved in it. Interview with Adia on 17 August 1985, in Cabuyao, Laguna. See also *The Sunday Tribune*, 4 October 1936; and the *Manila Daily Bulletin*, 5 October 1936.

67. *The Sunday Tribune*, 4 October 1936. See also the *Manila Daily Bulletin*, 5 October 1936; and *The Tribune*, 6 and 7 October 1936. Information also comes from an interview with Adia, 17 August 1985.

68. For more details on this incident, see *Court of Appeals: The People of the Philippines versus Fruto R. Santos, et al.*

69. Yojiro Ishizaka, *Mayon no Kemuri* (The Smoke of Mt. Mayon) (Tokyo: Shueisha, 1977), 169.

70. These rebels were to assassinate all government officials, including the archbishop and the American high commissioner, should they resist, although the assassination plot was later proven to be a fabrication. Acting Gov. Gen. Weldon Jones denied these plots as fictitious in his communication to the War Department. See Lewis E. Gleeck Jr., *The American Half-Century (1898–1946)* (Manila: Historical Conservation Society, 1984), 335.

71. For information on the plot, see Radiogram to Sec. of War from Jones dated 22 October 1936, 4865 in RG 350 NARA; the *Manila Daily Bulletin*, 8, 10, 16, 19, 21, and 29 October 1936; *The Tribune*, 28 and 30 October 1936; "Arrested Sakdals Reveal Terrorist Scheme," *Philippine Graphic*, 22 October 1936, 7; *New York Times*, 19 October 1936. As a result, 11 of the 14 Sakdalistas linked to the October

uprising were sentenced by the Court of First Instance to prison terms ranging from four months to five years in addition to a fine of Pl,000 each. See the *Manila Daily Bulletin*, 27 April 1937.

72. *The Tribune*, 9 and 20 October 1936; the *Manila Daily Bulletin*, 8 and 9 October 1936. "Ano't sa Tuwing Magkakaroon ng Kaguluhan ay mga Sakdalista ang Binabagsakan?" 1; and "Mga Halaw na Balita," 3, both in *Sakdal*, 24 October 1936.

73. *Manila Daily Bulletin*, 5 October 1936; and *The Tribune*, 6 October 1936. The towns especially targeted included Muntinlupa, Pasig, Marikina, Taytay, Cainta, Mandaluyong, San Juan, Caloocan, Pasay, Malabon, and Makati.

74. *Manila Daily Bulletin*, 27 April 1937.

75. For the conventional interpretation of the cause of the October uprising, see Walter Robb in *Chicago Daily News*, 23 October 1936. Filemon Tutay, "Shadows in Nueva Ecija," *Philippines Free Press*, 14 November 1936, 10–11, 46. The participants of the uprising in Pangasinan were branded as "gullible, innocent" people with "blind, misguided patriotism." They were portrayed as being on the verge of starvation and having been promised "booty" if they would join the attack on the town. See D. L. Francisco, "From the Mouths of the Sakdals," 30. For Leon Ma. Guerrero's article, see "Was Bonifacio a Sakdal?" *Philippines Free Press*, 28 November 1936, 4.

76. *Pamahayag at Patakaran ng Lapiang Sakdalista*, 23. See also *Court of Appeals: The People of the Philippines versus Fruto R. Santos et al. – Criminal Case No. 51558*, 25.

77. D. L. Francisco, "Sakdal Head Confesses," *Philippines Free Press*, 7 November 1936, 4, 30, and 36.

78. Francisco was impressed with Villanueva, saying "This man has guts! ...within him something of the stuff of which heroes and martyrs are made." See "Sakdal Head Confesses," *Philippines Free Press*, 7 November 1936, 30 and 36.

79. *Taliba*, 7 July 1938, reprinted in *Sakdal*, under the headline "Bilanggong Tumanggi sa Patawad ng Pang. Quezon," 16 July 1938, 1.

80. D. L. Francisco, "From the Mouths of the Sakdals," 30–32.

81. *Manila Daily Bulletin*, 3 and 16 December 1936. The rumors were perhaps based on Ramos's letters to C. Tiongco, which were intercepted. They simply said "Buhayin ang Sakdal sa Politica" (Revive the Sakdalista Party in Politics), and "Ihanap ng comercio sa Pasig" (Look for Business in Pasig). Perhaps this meant to seek advice from Santos in Pasig. See the *Manila Daily Bulletin*, 19 October 1936.

82. "Patalastas," *Sakdal*, 5 December 1936, 4. For Lauson's plea, see the *Manila Daily Bulletin*, 19 December 1936.

83. "Mga Lupong Tutol Pa Rin," 12 June 1937, 3; "Miting Sakdalista," 19

June 1937, 4; "Ang Bagong Pamunuan ng Lupon Bayan sa Tondo," 19 June 1937, 2; and "Mga Miting Sakdalista sa Lalawigang Kabite," 19 June 1937, 2, all in *Sakdal*. For details of the criticism against Lauson, see "Sundot, Himas at Paalala sa mga Naging Dating Kasama," 12 June 1937, 4; and "Mga Lupong Tutol Pa Rin," 26 June 1937, 2, both in *Sakdal*.

## Chapter 5

1. Luis Taruc represented Pedro Abad Santos of the Socialist Party. Interview with Taruc on 22 August 1986, in Quezon City. A lengthy letter of condolence addressed to Ramos was sent by Tomas Española in California. See "Sipi ng Liham ni G. Tomas Española," *Sakdal*, 18 September 1937, 2.

2. "Mga Balita sa Libing ng Ginang," 5 June 1937, 4; "Yumaong Parang Martir"; "Salitang Pangkasalukuyan: Ang Libing," "Sa Sariling 'Observatorio'"; and "Higit sa 80,000 Nakipaghatid sa Libing," all in 12 June 1937, 3, *Sakdal*. See also the *Manila Daily Bulletin*, 25 May 1937. One participant reported that he had never seen such a huge crowd in any funeral procession in Manila. Interview with Adia on 18 May 1985, in Cabuyao, Laguna.

3. "Tunay na Martir," *The Filipino Freedom*, 8 June 1937, 1. Ramos's passage came from "Nakikiramay ang Lapiang Sakdalista," *The Filipino Freedom*, 1 June 1937, 8. Ramos's daughter, Leticia Ramos-Uyboco, recited exactly the same passage during our interview.

4. For difficulties imposed, see "Tunay na Martir." For instance, when the Cavite Sakdalistas wanted to hire a truck in order to attend the funeral, they were refused simply because they were Sakdalistas. On the strength of the party, see "100,000 Sakdalistas on Parade," *Sakdal*, 12 June 1937, 1.

5. *Manila Daily Bulletin*, 15 and 17 October, and 31 December 1937; *The Tribune*, 5 November 1937.

6. *Japanese Police Reports* 3: 196.

7. For instance "Balagtasan sa Kuento nina Trotzky at Mussolini," 1 June 1937, 1; and "Ang mga Pulitiko sa Herusalem," 22 June 1937, 1, *The Filipino Freedom*. Around April 1937, the party came up with a new official organ called the *Sakdalista* in order to get around the postal ban on the *Sakdal*. Celerino Tiongco, *Sakdal* publisher, requested that the new paper be accepted as second-class mail material but his request was rejected. Due to its "seditious" and "subversive" content, Usec. of Justice Jose P. Melencio upheld the right as the director of Posts to refuse to allow the newspaper to be classified as second-class mail material. See *The Tribune*, 12 May 1937. So far, I have not located the *Sakdalista*.

8. "Kataka-taka, blg. 16," 9 January 1937, 1. On the Republic Ramos tried to establish, see "Bagong Uri ng Pamahalaan," 13 February 1937, 3, both in *Sakdal*.

9. *The Tribune*, 12 and 15 October; and 11 November 1937; *Manila Daily Bulletin*, 12, 13, and 15 October; and 8, 10, and 31 December 1937.

10. The municipalities in Laguna included San Pedro and Calamba. The towns in Rizal Province were Muntinlupa, San Juan del Monte, and Mandaluyong. *Manila Daily Bulletin*, 21 and 26 January 1938.

11. *The Tribune*, 29 April 1938.

12. D. L. Francisco, "Will 'Sakdals' Rise Again?" *Philippines Free Press*, 21 December 1935, 12–13. The towns affected by peasant unrest were San Jose, San Ildefonso, Meycauayan, Marilao, and Malolos in Bulacan; Gapan, Peñaranda, Santa Rosa, Cabiao, San Jose, Zaragoza, and Cabanatuan in Nueva Ecija. See "Let's End Agrarianism" (editorial), *Agricultural Life* (January–February 1936): 41. For the tenants who faced eviction in various haciendas, including the Tunasan Estate in San Pedro, Laguna, and Hacienda Esperanza in Nueva Ecija, see "Mga Magsasakang Humawak ng Sandata," *Sakdal*, 31 July 1937, 1. See also Michael J. Connelly, S.J., *Church Lands and Peasant Unrest in the Philippines: Agrarian Conflict in 20th Century Luzon* (Quezon City: Ateneo de Manila University Press, 1992), 130–54. Thirty-eight incidents of unrest occurred in Central Luzon in 1936. The number gradually increased and jumped to 137 in 1939. These numbers were culled from the articles that appeared in the *The Tribune*; and in Kerkvliet, *The Huk Rebellions*, 40 table 7.

13. *Manila Daily Bulletin*, 3 May 1938; *The Tribune*, 24 and 27 April 1938.

14. The area where the survey was conducted included Nueva Ecija, Tarlac, Bulacan, Pampanga, Rizal, and Laguna. See *Survey Report*, 409–38.

15. Quezon issued the proclamation that the Philippine Rice Share Tenancy Act would be in full force and effect in all the municipalities of Bulacan, Nueva Ecija, Pampanga, Pangasinan, and Tarlac. For details, see Percy A. Hill, "Agrarian Unrest: The New Tenancy Law," *Philippine Magazine*, March 1937, 116–17, 142–44. See also the *Manila Daily Bulletin*, 13 and 24 May 1937; *The Tribune*, 17 August 1937.

16. For details, see *The Tribune*, 20 August 1937.

17. For details, see Golay, *Face of Empire*, 380–81.

18. Connolly, S.J., *Church Lands and Peasant Unrest in the Philippines*, 192.

19. Signatories included Gregorio Aglipay (Republican Party), Celerino Tiongco (acting president of the Sakdalista Party), Vicente Sotto (Union Civica de Filipinas), Miguel Cornejo (Fascist Party), Manuel Joven (Anak-pawis, or KAP), and Alfonso Vedua (National Socialist Party), among others. See the *Manila Daily Bulletin*, 2 November 1936.

20. The speakers represented the Socialist Party, Nacionalista Consolidado Pro, Sakdalista Party, Union Civica de Filipinas, Communist Party, and Nacionalista Consolidado Anti. See "Isang Mahalagang Pagpupulong," *Sakdal*, 13 February 1937, 1. For more on the opposition groups, see James S. Allen, *The Radical Left on the Eve of War* (Quezon City: Foundation for Nationalist Studies, Inc., 1985), 13. In addition, the following parties and organizations were involved: Manila Democrata (those who refused to go along when the "Pros" and "Antis" merged, Young Philippines, Radical Party (of Representative Mendoza), National Labor Party, Bloque Popular (of dissenting Nacionalista Party), Nuclio Totalitario Filipino (a fascist group), Toilers League, and the New Philippines Party (organized by dissidents from the Young Philippines). See Hayden, *The Philippines*, 445.

21. It was prompted by the Nazi rise to power as well as by a growing realization that extreme sectarianism and dogmatism were not beneficial. For more details, see J. Richardson, *Komunista*, 217.

22. G. Capadocia, "Notes which may be used in the milestone in the history of the CCPI,'" 2, CP. It seems a nationalist like Ramos could not escape from regionalism, as evidenced by his emphasis on being a Bulaqueño.

23. According to Kojiro Sada, Ramos explicitly said that he had wanted to emphasize the differences between the Sakdalistas and the Communists after the mass arrests. See *Nanyo Sosho: Hiripin-hen*, 429.

24. Jim Richardson, "Hard Times: The Philippine Communist Party, 1933–35," 37. This was incorporated in Chapter 8 of *Komunista*, 208–47.See also Theodore Friend, *Between Two Empires* (Manila: Solidaridad Publishing House, 1969) 120–21.

25. Richardson, "Hard Times," 36–37.

26. Ibid., 38. See also Severo Dava, *Mga Katutuhanan ukol sa Sakdal at Lapiang Sakdalista sa Kalupi ni Benigno Ramos* (The Truths about the *Sakdal* and the Sakdalista Party that are in Benigno Ramos's Billfold) (Manila: n.p., n.d.). This pamphlet was made available to me by Dr. Jim Richardson.

27. "Lumibot ang Masamang Sakit ni Severo Dava," *Sakdal*, 2 February 1935, 2.

28. "Pilipinas ng Pilipino," 26 November 1932, 1; and "Sariling Diwa," 19 November 1932, 2, both in *Sakdal*.

29. For criticism against the Communists, see the following *Sakdal* issues: "Mamatay ang Sakdal—Ang Malakas na Sigaw ng mga Ahente ng Russia," 2 July 1932, 2; "Mahal Si Lenin Kay sa Ating Rizal," 29 October 1932, 2; "Diyata't Naghahamon?" 18 February 1933, 1; "Matang-Lawin," 26 May 1934, 3; "Welga, Tangkilikin," 1 September 1934, 4; "Patuloy ang mga Komunista sa Pagsasabog ng Lason Laban sa Ating Kalayaan," 21 July 1934, 2; "Puera Komunista, Puera

Pulitiko," 25 August 1934, 1; "Sariling Diwa: Ang Salitang Komunista," 22 August 1934, 2; "The Sakdalistas are against the Communists," 25 August 1934, 4; "Ang Ibig ng mga Komunista," 3 November 1934, 3; "Sakdalismo Laban sa Komunismo," 2 March 1935, 1; and "Hindi Tinanggap ang Komunismo," 6 February 1935, 1.

30. For the Communists' discussions, see G. Capadocia, "Notes which may be used in the milestone in the history of the CCPI,'" 11, CP. For self-criticism, see Jim. Richardson, "The Genesis of the Philippine Communist Party" (PhD diss., School of Oriental and African Studies, University of London, 1984), 279.

31. Richardson states that the efforts of the Communist Party regarding the Sakdalistas have been analyzed as a classic case of "winning over" the rank-and-file while exposing the leadership as opportunists and betrayers. See Richardson, "Hard Times," 39. As a later event would show, some Communist members in the peasant organization, namely the KPMP, worked closely with the Sakdalista Party.

32. For example, see G. Capadocia's article, "Ang Pamahalaan at ang mga Komunista," *Sakdal*, 25 September 1937, 2.

33. "Ipakikilala ng Sakdalista ang Tunay na Bayan," *Sakdal*, 19 June 1937, 1.

34. The Sakdalista followers were so determined that some sold their carabaos (water buffalos) and mortgaged their lands to raise money to cover their expenses in coming to Manila. See "Ipakikilala ng Sakdalista ang Tunay na Bayan." Sakdalistas from Naga in the Bicol Region announced that they were coming to Manila whether the authorities granted them a permit to assemble or not. See the *Manila Daily Bulletin,* 29 July, and 13 August 1937; and *The Tribune*, 15 August 1937. For the educational campaign, the authorities explained the futility of uprising in Cavite, where 36,000 Sakdalistas resided. See *The Tribune*, 28 July, and 13 and 15 August 1937.

35. For more on the harassment of the Sakdalistas, see "Isang Pangkat ng mga Sakdalista ang Nakipagkita sa Alto Kom. McNutt," *Sakdal*, 19 June 1937, 4. Around mid-August, the letters from Ramos in Tokyo addressed to Ricardo Enrile, who was visiting Manila, were opened. See the *Manila Daily Bulletin*, 13 August 1937. See also *The Tribune*, 13 and 14 August,; and 16 September 1937.

36. *Manila Daily Bulletin*, 14 and 17 August, and 13 September 1937; and *The Tribune*, 17 August 1937.

37. *To the Honorable Chairman and Members of the Joint Preparatory Committee on Philippine Affairs, This Memorandum is Respectfully Submitted* (Manila: n.p., 1937), 1–15. Two hundred copies of the *Memorial* were printed. See "Ilang Pangyayaring Katangitangi," *Sakdal*, 25 September 1937, 1.

38. In addition to Santos, the remaining three Sakdalistas were all from Cavite. It is assumed that they were allowed to appear before the committee

since Fernando Manuzon, president of the Cavite Sakdalista branch, declared they were opposed to any means other than diplomacy to obtain independence. He emphatically rejected any help from other nations, including Japan. See *The Tribune*, 3 June 1937. The fifth Sakdalista, Celerino Tiongco, represented the Sakdalista Party to the Popular Front at this time.

39. The memorial that Manuzon read had been created by the Cavite chapter but the contents are the same as the one submitted by the Sakdalista Party. *A Memorial: Lapiang Sakdalista sa Filipinas Derectorio Provincial Cavite*, Cavite (Manila[?]: n.p., 1937), 1–14.

40. For the content of their speeches, see *Joint Preparatory Committee on Philippine Affairs: Report of May 20, 1938* 2: 611–26. See also *To the Honorable Chairman and Members of the Joint Preparatory Committee on Philippine Affairs, This Memorandum is respectfully Submitted.*

41. Quezon must have realized this and therefore demanded early independence, although he withdrew his demand immediately. Copra producers, who had predicted this predicament, supported Quezon's bid for early independence. See Steve MacIsaac, "The Struggle for Economic Development in the Philippine Commonwealth, 1935–1940," *Philippine Studies* 50, no. 2 (2002): 160–64.

42. Tiongco, at that time, was the chairman of the National Executive Council of the Popular Front. See "Pagkakaisa ng Bayan (Popular Front) Briefs on Economic Problems of the Philippines by Hon. Juan Sumulong et al. September 10, 1937," in *Joint Preparatory Committee on Philippine Affairs* 3:651–61. For the Communist Party, see "Brief Submitted by the Central Executive Committee of the Communist Party of the Philippines," in *Joint Preparatory Committee*, 887–900. The Communist Party was not exactly legalized but the imprisoned leaders were released in December 1936 and the party was allowed some limited activities. Absolute pardon was granted in December 1938.

43. "Ilang Pangyayaring Katangitangi sa Pagharap ng mga Sakdalista sa Lupon," *Sakdal*, 25 September 1937, 1.

44. Other Popular Front candidates for governor included Pedro Abad Santos for Pampanga, Luis Ferrer Jr. for Cavite, Jose Robles Jr. for Nueva Ecija, Sofronio Española for Palawan, Mariano Serrano for Bulacan, and Vicente Sotto for Cebu. See *The Philippines Herald*, 6, 7, and 11 December 1937. For the Popular Front's membership, see Hayden, *The Philippines*, 444–45.

45. In Lucban, three other opposition parties ran against the Nacionalista Party: the Democrata-Nacionalista Consolidado Coalition Party, the Kaliitliitang Nacionalista Consolidato Anti, and the Popular Front. See *The Philippines Herald*, 9 December 1937.

46. *The Philippines Herald*, 15 December 1937.

47. The Supreme Court decision of 8 December 1937 declared the Nacionalista Party (Partido Nacionalista), which was called Partido Nacionalista Pro Independencia in 1934, to be the majority "fusion" party of the "Antis" and the "Pros" and the Popular Front to be the leading opposition party. See *The Philippines Herald*, 8 December 1937. Close fights between the majority and the opposition parties were seen in Nueva Ecija and Cavite. Although Iloilo lost governorship, the majority provincial council posts went to the Popular Front. In Manila, two out of ten seats went to the oppositional candidates Carmen Planas and Manuel de la Fuente. See *The Philippines Herald*, 15 and 16 December 1937. The victory of Planas was a clear indication of the power of women voters.

48. The representatives came from the following towns: San Miguel, Bulacan; Pasig, Marikina, Mandaluyong, Malabon, and Pasay, Rizal; Gen. Trias, Cavite; Muñoz, Aliaga, Gapan, San Antonio, and Nueva Ecija. "Ang Lupong Kababaihan Sakdalista sa San Isidro, Cavite," 9 April 1938, 1; see a photo, 4 June 1938, 1, in *Sakdal*.

49. *Pamahayag at Patakaran ng Samahang Makabayan ng mga Babaing Pilipina* (Proclamation and Principles of the Patriotic League of Filipino Women) (Manila: Samahang Makabayan ng mga Babaing Filipina, 1937). Under the American colonial government, the organization of women's societies had been encouraged, although these organizations, such as the Philippine Association of University Women, the Red Cross, the Anti-Tuberculosis Society, the Asociacion de Damas Filipinas, and the National Federation of Women's Club, were for the elite and influential women of society. For more details, see Encarnacion Alzona, *The Filipino Woman: Her Social, Economic, and Political Status, 1565–1933* (Manila: University of the Philippines Press, 1934).

50. *Pamahayag at Patakaran*, 2.

51. This was why they were against the campaign of the Catholic Women's League, which was urging women to vote for the plebiscite in 1935. They criticized the League because it was against the Pope, who said not to use the Church for politics. See "Ang Dalaga't Binata," 23 July 1932, 3; "Kasiraan ng Ating Dangal ang Pagboboto ng mga Babae," 27 April 1935, 1; and "Sariling Diwa," 27 April 1935, 2, all in *Sakdal*.

52. "Gumising Ka, Bayan," *The Filipino Freedom*, 4th week of July 1935, 3.

53. Interview with Capt. Junsuke Hitomi, one of the officers of the Propaganda Corps, on 7 May 1990 in Kyoto City, Japan. Also see Ishizaka, *Mayon no Kemuri*, 79 and 150–51.

54. Quezon signed the information service bill that included exercising censorship of radio broadcasts. Commonwealth Act 2 of 7-11-1936 and *First*

*Report of the High Commissioner, 1935–36*, quoted in Golay, *Face of Empire*, 356–57. For the content of the new law, see the *Manila Daily Bulletin*, 2 November 1936. Another law signed by Quezon required publishers of newspapers, magazines, and other periodicals to file with the director of Posts before printing anything. See the *Manila Daily Bulletin*, 28 and 30 October 1936.

55. For instance, Patricio Dionisio of the Tanggulan Society, Jacinto Manahan of KPMP, Hermenegildo Cruz, Lope K. Santos, and Amado Castro, who were once radical antiadministration labor leaders, were all given government positions or became pro-Quezon. See also Alfred McCoy, "Quezon's Commonwealth: The Emergence of Philippine Authoritarianism," in *Philippine Colonial Democracy*, ed. R. Paredes (New Haven: Yale University Southeast Asia Studies, Yale Center for International and Area Studies, 1988), 135; Melinda Tria Kerkvliet, *Manila Workers' Unions, 1900–1950* (Quezon City: New Day Publishers 1992), 32. For Quezon's move to unify labor organizations, see Guillermo Capadocia, "The Philippine Labor Movement," 41, CP.

56. William J. Pomeroy, *The Philippines: Colonialism, Collaboration, and Resistance* (New York: International Publisher, 1992), 93. 57. The magazine was the 13 February 1937 issue of the *Philippines Free Press* mentioned in "Kataka-taka, blg. 27," *Sakdal*, 27 March 1937, 1. So far I have not located Celerino Tiongco'se *Sakdalista*. It is possible the *Philippine Free Press* was mistaken.

58. "Ang Kampanya ng mga Sip-sip," 31 July 1937, 3; "Partido Sakdalista de Filipinas," 18 September 1937, 4; and "Nasa Pilipinas ang Paghahari-harian," 26 June 1937, 2, all in *Sakdal*.

59. Benigno Ramos, *Quezon is the Real Enemy of the Government in the Philippines* (Manila: n.p., n.d.). It is assumed the booklet was published in June of 1937.

60. *The Tribune* and the *Manila Daily Bulletin*, both 15 September 1937.

61. Ibid.

62. Theodore Friend, *Between Two Empires*, 180.

63. For instance, on 23 April 1935, Ramos spoke before the representatives of the Asian countries that were European colonies. In June 1936, he spoke in Shizuoka at the general meeting of the Ajia Seinen Kyodan, or Congress of Young Asia. On the platform was a banner: "Young Asia, Unite!" For the contents of Ramos's speech, see "Speech of Mr. Benigno R. Ramos," and its Tagalog version "Kailangan Lumaya Kami upang Makatulong sa Daigdig," *Sakdal*, 1 August 1936, 1. A photo of his lecture in June appeared in the *Sakdal*, 5 August 1936, 1.

64. B. R. Ramos, "Firipin to Nippon" (The Philippines and Japan), *Kaizo* (May 1936): 42–51.

65. For the Nacionalista candidates of 1907, see Michael Cullinane, *Ilustrado Politics: Filipino Elite Responses to American Rule, 1898–1908* (Quezon City: Ateneo de Manila University Press, 2003), 305. Information on Quezon and Tiongco's mestizo appearance came from an interview with Adia on 17 August 1985, in Cabuyao, Laguna.

66. "Our Party" probably referred to the Dai Nippon Seisan Party. Ashizu, "Ramosu himei ni taoreru" (Ramos Dies by Violence), *Shin Seiryoku* (The New Power), no. 142 (April 1971): 31–32. The Dai Nippon Seisan Party, at a board meeting, also passed a resolution not to allow the authorities to take Ramos away. The party resolution came from the *Japanese Police Reports* 2 (1936): 374.

67. Uzuhiko Ashizu, "Ramosu himei ni taoreru," 31–32.

68. The Japanese title "Sakudaristasu o shokai suru" (Introducing Sakdalistas) originally appeared in the *Kokusai Pamphlet*. The reprinted form is in Uzuhiko Ashizu, "Zoku B. R. Ramosu Kenkyu" (Continuation, Study on B. R. Ramos), *Shin Seiryoku*, no. 145 (July 1971): 10–13. According to Ashizu, these publications were all funded by the Dai Nippon Seisan Party. For the English translation of "Sakdudaristasu o shokai suru," see Grant K. Goodman, "An Interview with Benigno Ramos: Translated from the Japanese," *Philippine Studies* 37 (1989): 217–20.

69. Edwin L. Nerville, Charge d'Affaires ad interim of the American Embassy, sent a copy of the petition to the Sec. of State. When the Division of Far Eastern Affairs of the State Department received the copy translated into English, it concluded "no action required" and lambasted the party as "the bigoted impertinence of an organization which can present such a resolution in the midst of Japanese swashbuckling in China." See 811B.01/272, RG 59, NARA. See also Lydia N. Yu-Jose, *Filipinos in Japan and Okinawa*, 36.

70. Leon Ma. Guerrero Jr., "How Japan Looks at Ramos," *Philippines Free Press*, 1 June 1935, 4–5.

71. Koike was the founder of the Aikoku Seiji Domei (League for Patriotic Politics), a member of the Ishin Konwakai (Restoration Friendly Discussion Society) and of the Taiwan Konwakai (Taiwan Friendly Discussion Society). See Goodman, "Japan and Philippine Radicalism," 153–56.

72. *Dai Ajia Shugi* (August 1936): 56–58, and (November 1936): 35. On the Dai Ajia Kyokai, see Lydia N. Yu-Jose, "Japanese Organizations and the Philippines, 1930s–1941," *The Journal of International Studies* 33 (April 1994): 83–110. Its Philippine branch was organized in mid-1934. See Grant K. Goodman, "Japanese Pan-Asianism in the Philippines: The Hiripin Dai Ajia Kyokai," in *Studies on Asia*, ed. Robert Sakai (Lincoln, Nebraska: University of Nebraska Press, 1966),

133–43. Pio Duran, a lawyer and advocate for the unity of Asia with Japan as its head, was one of the active members and visited Japan in 1935 and 1939. There were two articles on the Dai Ajia Kyokai, or Malaking Samahang Asiatika, written by Takeyo Nakatani, that appeared in the *Sakdal* issues of 11 July and 1 August issue of 1936.

73. *Japanese Police Reports* 2: 374.

74. *Sakdal* (extra), 21 September 1936, 1.

75. "Ibinilanggo si B. R.," "Sariling Diwa," and "Ramos and Staff Jailed in Kobe, Japan," *Sakdal* (extra), 21 September 1936, 1.

76. *Japanese Police Reports* 3 (1937): 196.

77. Ashizu, "Ramosu himei ni taoreru," 14–15.

78. For the telegram, see "Ang Kable ng Patnugot sa Presidente Roosevelt," *Sakdal*, 29 June 1935, 1. The pamphlet is found in 811B.01/273, RG 59, NARA. The pamphlet was stamped: "American Consulate, Kobe Japan, Received November 4, 1935." It is not clear whether the document was sent to the American Consulate in Kobe to be forwarded to the addressee or the Consulate came into possession of the document by chance.

79. Benigno R. Ramos, *The American Government Does Not Like Peace in the Philippines* (Tokyo Japan [?]: n.p., November 1935). This was reprinted in the *Sakdal*, 5 December 1936, 1.

80. Radiogram Message, dated March 10 and 15, 1937, Series 5: General Correspondence File, Box 105, QP. Ramos also sent the letter to Quezon dated 13 March 1938, with the same content. The radiogram and the letter were brought to my attention by Dr. Florentino Rodao of the Universidad Complutense de Madrid. Ramos also sent a cablegram to High Commissioner McNutt. See "Ang Goviernong Kaaway ng Dukha," 28 August 1937, 1. "Ang Kable ni G. Ramos sa Mataas na Komisionado," 25 September 1937, 1 both in *Sakdal*.

81. "Pamanhik ng Patnugot," *Sakdal*, 28 August 1937, 1.

82. For cultivating goodwill between the two countries, see Motoe Terami-Wada, "Cultivating Goodwill between Japan and the Philippines in the 1930s," in *Philippines-Japan Relations*, ed. Setsuho Ikehata, and Lydia N. Yu Jose (Quezon City: Ateneo de Manila University Press, 2003), 155–84. For the meeting with Arita and Quezon, see Manuel L. Quezon, *The Good Fight* (Manila: Cacho Hermanos, Inc., 1985), 175–80.

## Chapter 6

1. For Ramos's utterance, see *Japanese Police Reports* 3 (1937): 195.

2. Ibid., 196. The Philippine Society of Japan was established in August

1935 to promote goodwill between the two countries. For details, see Grant K. Goodman, "The Philippine Society of Japan," *Monumenta Nipponica* 22, nos. 1–2 (1967): 131–46; Lydia N. Yu-Jose, "Japanese Organizations and the Philippines, 1930s–1941," *Journal of International Studies* 33 (April 1994): 83–110; Shinzo Hayase, *Hukkokuban: Firipin Joho: Kaisetsu: Somokuroku: Sakuin* (Reprint: Firipin Joho: Commentary: List of Content: Indices) (Tokyo: Ryukei Shosha, 2003), 3–23.

3. *Manila Daily Bulletin*, 2 April 1937.

4. Other suggestions were: the government should be more vigilant on how foreigners take photos of Filipinos, especially the Ifugaos, Aetas, and Moros, because their appearance could bring shame to all Filipinos. At the same time, the government should treat them with respect and make them wear shoes. See "Mungkahi sa Pamahalaan ng Commonwealth," *Sakdal*, 5 June 1937, 1. A reprint appeared in the following two issues of the *Sakdal*: 12 and 19 June 1937.

5. For Ramos's letter addressed to the Secretary of State dated October 20, 1937, see 811B.00/92, Box 5291, RG 59, NARA. "Ramosu no Kankokusho" (A Written Advice of Ramos), *Hiripin Joho*, no.10 (December1937): 21, quoting the *Manila Daily Bulletin*, dated 27 November 1937. In April 1938, Ramos sent a telegram to Sec. of State Cordell Hull in protest against the opening of an air route between Java and the Philippines, saying it would be dangerous to the defense of the Islands because it would make it easier for a foreign enemy, insinuating Japan, to attack the Philippines. See Goodman, "Japan and Philippine Radicalism," 163.

6. *Japanese Police Reports* 4 (1938): 209–10.

7. *Manila Daily Bulletin*, 11 August 1939.

8. The bombed American gunboat was the USS *Panay*, which was carrying evacuees from Nanjing. See *The Philippines Herald*, 13 December 1937. See also Golay, *Face of Empire*, 392. By this time, Quezon had strong doubts about the self-sustenance of the defense plan and openly expressed his feelings of uncertainty. See Ricardo Trota Jose, *The Philippine Army, 1935–1942* (Quezon City: Ateneo de Manila University Press, 1992), 112–13.

9. Quezon had already been assured the previous year by Foreign Minister Arita that Japan had no intention of invading the Philippines. Satoshi Nakano, *Firipin Dokuritsu Mondai-shi* (History of Philippine Independence Issues) (Tokyo: Ryukei Shosha, 1997), 225.

10. *The Philippines Herald*, 29 June 1938.

11. For how Quezon staged the meeting and what took place between Quezon and Ramos, see Grant K. Goodman, "Japan and Philippine Radicalism: The Case of Benigno Ramos," 164–70. See also *The Sunday Tribune*, 11 September 1938; Ken' ichi Goto, "M. Hatta Oyobi M. Keson no Hojitu ni Kansuru Shiteki Kosatu"

(Historical Inquiry into M. Hatta's and M. Quezon's Visits to Japan), ed. Waseda Daigaku Shaken, *Ajia no Dento to Kindaika* (Tradition and Modernization in Asia) (Tokyo: Waseda Daigaku Shaken, 1990), 419–20.

12.  Mitsuo Matsumura, "Nihon Bomei San-nen no Seikatsu o Hito Dokuritsu undo no Shishi Ramosu ni Kiku" (Interview with Ramos, the fighter for Philippine Independence who was in Japan for a Three-Year Exile) *Hanashi* (October 1938): 144–47.

13.  "Bomei no Sakudarutoshu Ramosura Kikoku" (Ramos, the Exiled Head of the Sakdalista Party, and Others Returned Home) *Hiripin Joho*, no. 18 (August 1938): 13–14.

14.  Shortly before Ramos's departure from Japan, the party chairman of the Dai Nippon Seisan Party and Ramos exchanged a written oath saying that the party would support the Sakdalista aim of complete independence. For the translation of this oath, see Lydia Yu-Jose, *Filipinos in Japan*, 39. Ramos also donated ¥20 to the Japanese Army Ministry. See *Japanese Police Reports* 4 (1938): 209–10.

15.  *Manila Daily Bulletin*, 29 August 1938; and *The Tribune*, 30 August 1938. The latter reported that the number of those who came to welcome Ramos was 8,000. In Santa Cruz, Laguna, the Sakdalistas held a celebration, thinking that independence would come within a year after Ramos's return. See *The Tribune*, 28 August 1938.

16.  Ramos was brought to prison accompanied by Manila's Police Chief Antonio Torres, former Rep. Francisco Varona, and Tomas Morato. See the *Manila Daily Bulletin*, 29 August 1938. Morato had been re-elected as mayor of Calauag, Tayabas, with the Sakdalistas' support and was one of those who had accompanied Quezon on his last trip to Japan. For Morato, see Goodman, "Japan and Philippine Radicalism,"165.

17.  From prison, Ramos proceeded to the La Loma Cemetery to visit the graves of his youngest child and his wife, whose funeral he had not been able to attend. *The Tribune*, 29 August 1938, and "Return of Ramos" *Philippines Free Press*, 3 September 1938, 5. For bail, see *The Tribune*, 3 September 1938. For Ramos' announcement, see *The Tribune* and the *Manila Daily Bulletin*, both 29 August 1938.

18.  *The Tribune*, 30 August 1938.

19.  The recipients of the telegrams included Iwane Matsui, commander in chief of the Japanese forces, and Sadao Araki, Minister of Education and the members of the Privy Council. See the *Manila Daily Bulletin*, 30 August 1938.

20.  *Manila Daily Bulletin*, 30 August 1938.

21.  Initially, the party was named the General Party. "Ang Palatuntunan ng Asemblea Nacional Sakdalista sa Ika-Limang Pagpupulong," *Sakdal*, 10 September

1938, 2. The new organ of the Ganap Party, *Ganap*, came out on 7 October and was registered with the post office a week later. See *Ganap*, 15 October 1938, 1.

22. "Panunumpa ng mga Makabayan" in *Mga Patak ng Luha ng Bayang Api* (Manila: n.p., 1939), 37. "Ganap member," or "Ganapista," was used to designate Ganap Party members as well as those who support the party. The old Sakdalista Party members and its supporters were not included. The words "Sakdalista movement" used in this book refers to the whole movement from its establishment to the end, including the Ganap Party era.

23. *Partido "Ganap" de Filipinas: Manifesto to the People* (Manila: n.p., 1938), 1–3. In order to emphasize that the Ganap Party was the continuation of the old Sakdalista Party and that the basic demand of independence had not changed, the *Partido "Ganap" de Filipinas* included *Memorials* sent to the Congressional Mission headed by Tydings in December 1934, to the U.S. Pres., and to the U.S. Congress in November 1935 and May 1937. For Quezon's accumulation of power during the Commonwealth period, see McCoy "Quezon's Commonwealth," 114–60.

24. *The Tribune* and the *Manila Daily Bulletin*, 29 August 1938.

25. *Paritido "Ganap" de Filipinas*, 2–3.

26. For a summary of Ganap Party platform, see appendix 3. The party leadership was composed of President, Gregorio Tobias (proprietor); First Vice Presdent, Ruperto Santiago (industrialist); Second Vice President, Dr. Quintin de Dios (agriculturist, i.e., landlord); Secretary, Paulo Capa (agricultural proprietor); Treasurer, Marcelino Tenorio (proprietor); and Counsel, Antonio de los Reyes (attorney). Ramos himself became chairman and was in charge of the press and propaganda. See *Partido "Ganap" de Filipinas*, 3–5.

27. The telegram was sent on 24 October 1938. See "Sakdal Party in the Philippine Islands," 28875, RG 350, BIA, NARA.

28. An example of this supportive attitude can be seen in a cartoon in which Quezon and the Ganap Party are both showing a cool reception to High Commissioner Francis Sayre. This cartoon appeared in the *Philippines Free Press* in October 1939, and was reprinted in McCoy, "Quezon's Commonwealth," 146.

29. *The Tribune*, 30 August; 7 October; 5 and 8 November 1938. Those who criticized Ramos included Gaudencio Bautista, Felicisimo Lauson, Filomeno Prodon, and Narciso Lapus, See *The Tribune*, 5 November 1938. By May 1939, Ramon Crespo, Ramos's secretary, eventually joined the anti-Ramos Sakdalista Party. See *The Philippines Herald*, 6 May 1939. Lapus must have rejoined the party as well.

30. "Hinahamon si Gg. Ramos sa Isang Balagtasan," *Ganap*, 15 October 1938, 3. As of October 1938, the Ganap Party founder was Benigno Ramos and the manager was Marcelino Tenorio. Celerino Tiongco was thought to be opposed

to Ramos when he initially returned from Japan. Judging from the fact that he became the owner/manager of the *Ganap* around August of the following year, we assume that he had reconciled with Ramos. See *Ganap*, 26 August 1939, 2; see also *The Tribune*, 7 September 1938.

31. *The Philippines Herald*, 24 October 1938; also see Hayden, *The Philippines*, 446.

32. *The Tribune*, 4 October 1938. Narciso Lapus, who spearheaded the donation campaign for the ailing Gen. Artemio Ricarte in 1931, assisted the general when he returned to the Philippines in December 1941, as we shall see later.

33. The Ganap Party candidates and Ganap-supported candidates in the provinces and Manila were: Nueva Ecija, Vicente M. Sison (Ganap G) and Felipe Buencamino Jr. (Nacionalista N); Tayabas, Dionisio Mayor (G) and Jose Timog (G); Cavite, Fernando Manuzon (G); Laguna, Aurelio Almazan (G); Pampanga, Lorenso Galang (G) and Antipas Soriano (G); Bataan, Agripino Bautista (Popular Front); Albay, Venancio Mangampo (G) and Ignacio Concepcion (G); Sorsogon, Zergio Grafit (G) and Celestino M. Sito (G); Tarlac, Antonio C. Manalatoc (G); and Manila, Gregorio Perfecto (N) and Antonio Velisario (G). In Manila, 13 candidates ran for the National Assembly: Nacionalista, 3; Alianza Democratica-Frente Popular-Young Philippines-Bloque Popular, 5; Communist Party, 2; Ganap Party, 1; Independent, 2. See *The Tribune*, 8 November 1938; and "Don Gregorio Perfecto Es el Candidado del 'Ganap' para el Norte de Manila," *Ganap*, 15 October 1938, 1.

34. *The Tribune*, 7 September 1938.

35. *Manila Daily Bulletin*, 7 and 14 September 1938.

36. Ramos gave this speech in Cabanatuan, Nueva Ecija, on 7 October, and was reported in the *Manila Daily Bulletin*, 8 October 1938, which in turn was reported in *Hiripin Joho*, no. 20 (October 1938): 19. For Japanese criticism, see Kojiro Sada, *Nanyo Sosho: Hiripi-hen* (The South Sea Series: The Philippines) (Tokyo: Toa Keizai Chosa Kyoku, 1939), 439.

37. The other speakers represented the parties of the Democrata, Republican, Socialist, Young Philippines, and Young Mindanao, in addition to Sakdalistas. See *The Tribune*, 7 October 1938; see also Hayden, *The Philippines*, 447. Five hundred Sakdalistas gathered and chose Anselmo Rivera and Aurelio Tanquico for the candidates from Nueva Ecija. See *The Tribune*, 21 September 1938.

38. *The Philippines Herald*, 29 October 1938.

39. Ibid. The Socialist and the Communist Parties merged at the end of October 1938, a week or so before the elections.

40. Sison garnered more votes than the Popular Front candidate Ignacio Nabong. See *The Philippines Herald*, 9 November 1938.

41. For Fernando Manuzon's (Cavite) campaign speech supporting Quezon, see *The Tribune*, 21 September 1938.

42. "Sa Buzon ng Ganap," *Ganap*, 26 November 1938, 2.

43. *The Tribune*, 4 January 1939.

44. *The Philippines Herald*, 5 May 1939.

45. *Mga Patak ng Luha ng Bayang Api* (Manila: n.p., 1939).

46. Ileto, *Pasyon and Revolution*, 121.

47. "Pauna," *Mga Patak ng Luha ng Bayang Api*, 2–22.

48. "Ramos will Seek to Unify His Countrymen," and "Walang Kalayaang Dumating sa mga Taong Walang Bayan, at Walang Bayang Nabuo sa mga Taong Di Nagkakasundo," both in *Sakdal*, 10 September 1938, 1.

49. "Pagunita sa Tunay na Damdamin ng Bayan" (Reminder of the Real Feelings of the People), 28–37; and "Tuntuning Pangloob" (Rule for the Insiders [officials]), 40, both in *Patak*.

50. The secret group members were Elpidio Santos, Ciriaco Campomanes, Simeon de Sena, and Paulo Capa. Ramos was called *tandis*, which is a pre-Spanish Tagalog word for principal chieftain and the official title of Sikatuna, Lakandula, and other Philippine warriors. See *The Philippines Herald*, 6 May 1939.

51. *The Philippines Herald*, 5 May 1939.

52. "Ang Hapon ay Bantay ng mga Bayan sa Silangan," *Sakdal*, 10 September 1938, 1.

53. Tagalog original: "Salamat kung hindi umalis, nguni't kung umalis, paano naman ang magiging lagay natin?"

54. *Panawagan sa Lahat ng Lapian at Kababayan ukol sa Paghahanda ng Pansagot sa Kasarinlan Kung Umalis na ang Estados Unidos* (Call to All the Party [Members] and Fellow Countrymen about the Guarantee for Independence When the U.S. Leaves) (Manila: n.p., 1939), 3 and 12. On the contribution, see *Ganap*, 2 March 1940, 1; see also *The Philippines Herald*, 5 and 13 May 1939; and *Photo News*, 1 November 1939, 45.

55. For ladaw, see *The Philippines Herald*, 6 May 1939.

56. *The Sunday Tribune*, 5 February 1939.

57. Those accused with him were Gregorio Tobias and Ricardo Enrile. *Philippines Herald*, 13 and 16 May 1939. "Proceed with Ramos Trials," *Philippine Graphic*, 1 June 1939, 28. Later, Tobias and Enrile were dismissed.

58. Ramos paid a call on Sec. of the Interior Rafael Alunan and clarified his stand. See *The Philippines Herald*, 16 May 1939; *The Tribune*, 4 July 1939; and the *Manila Daily Bulletin*, 8 August 1939; see also "They Want to be 'Emperors,'" *Philippines Free Press*, 4 November 1939, 2.

59. These speeches were heard in Polo, Bulacan, and in Navotas, Rizal. See "March of Ramos," *Philippines Free Press*, 25 November 1939, 35.

60. The charges against Ramos were: three estafas and one illegal association at the Manila Municipal Court; two illegal collections of contributions at Bulacan Court; one rebellion and three estafas at Laguna Court; sedition charges at Rizal and Cavite Courts. See the *Manila Daily Bulletin*, 8 August, and 8, 9 and 10 December 1939; *The Tribune*, 9, 21, 23, and 24 December 1939; *The Philippines Herald*, 8, 13, and 21 December 1939, 31 May 1940; "Courts: 'Stop Ramos!'" *Philippines Free Press*, 4 November 1939, 37; and "Hahatulan si Ramos," *Ganap*, 2 March 1940, 3. At the end of December 1940, the Court of Appeals handed down the decision that the Sakdalista Party was illegal, giving Ramos an indeterminate sentence ranging from six months to two years for illegal association, having agitated the "laboring class" into breaking the laws of the land and leading them into bloody riots. This sentence was added on top of what he had accumulated. See "Lapiang Sakdal Outlawed," *Philippines Free Press*, 4 January 1941, 51. The case of illegal association of the Sakdalista Party was elevated by the Court of Appeals to the Supreme Court in June 1941. See "Nasa Ktt. Hukuman ang 'Illegal Association,'" *Hirang*, 9 July 1941, 1.

61. Ramos withdrew his appeal to the Appellate Court of First Instance, as the Supreme Court had denied his appeal from a decision of the Court of First Instance of Laguna. *The Philippines Herald*, 31 May 1940.

62. "Our Calvary has Come," *Ganap*, 16 December 1939, 1.

63. The *Hirang*'s temporary office address was the same as that of the Ganap headquarters.

64. "Hindi Muna Kami Lalabas," *Hirang*, 9 July 1941, 3.

65. *Memorial Sent to the President and Congress of the United States by the Ganap Party of the Philippines* (Manila: n.p., 1940), 2–6.

66. "They Want to be 'Emperors,'" 2.

67. *The Philippines Herald*, 18 November 1940. For Tiongco and Agplipay, see *The Tribune*, 10 October 1940; "Mrs. Aglipay for President" (should be Vice President), *Philippines Free Press*, 4 January 1941, 48. One hundred seventy-six candidates ran for governorship in forty-eight provinces. The Ganap candidates were as follows: Bulacan, Esteban Coruna; Camarines Sur, Ricardo Valdivia; Cavite, Engracio Salazar y Bedan; Laguna, Mariano Untivero; Marinduque, Teodulo Frayre; Nueva Ecija, Vicente Sison; Rizal, Ramon Paz Crespo; and Tayabas, Genaro D. Saez. *The Philippines Herald*, 18 November 1940.

68. *The Philippines Herald*, 19 and 20 November 1940.

69. *The Philippines Herald*, 25 November 1940.

70. *The Philippine Herald*, 5 and 7 December 1940. For instance, Carmen Planas, who won the Manila councilor's seat in 1937 under the Young Philippines, campaigned under the Democrata Nacional-Popular Front this time.

71. "(No title)," 20 November 1940, 4; "Hindi Naguurong ang mga Kandidato ng Ganap sa Binyang, Laguna," 20 November 1940, 2; and "Gamitin Natin ng Buong Laya ang Ating Halal sa Pagpili," 4 December 1940, 1, all in *Hirang*. On the eve of the election, Juan Sumulong appealed to the voters to vote for them if they were against a dictatorial government and in favor of a democratic, honest government. *The Philippines Herald*, 9 December 1940.

72. *The Tribune*, 10 October 1940; and "Malaki ang Pag-asa sa Maynila," *Hirang*, 4 December 1940. 1.

73. The opposition candidates who won the seats in the Municipal Board included Carmen Planas, Pascual Santos, and Segundo Agustin. *The Philippines Herald*, 11 December 1940; *The Tribune*, 15 December 1940. For the two governors, see *The Philippines Herald*, 11 December 1940.

74. Hayden, *The Philippines*, 451–52.

75. *The Philippines Herald*, 9 December 1940. See also Hayden, *The Philippines*, 456.

76. *The Philippines Herald*, 29 October 1941.

77. *The Philippines Herald*, 8 October 1941. Three major presidential candidates ran in this election: Manuel Quezon for the Nacionalista Party, Juan Sumulong for the Democrata Nacional-Popular Front, and Hilarrio Moncado for the Modernist Party, in addition to Celerino Tiongco. The Communists and Socialists, such as Juan Feleo, Guillermo Capadocia, and Luis Taruc, ran under the Popular Front Pedro Abad Santos faction. See ibid., 20 September, 29 October, and 1 November 1941.

78. *The Philippines Herald*, 8 October 1941.

79. Ibid., 5 and 8 November 1941.

80. The left wing of the Popular Front was also supported by the KPMP. See *The Philippines Herald*, 24 October 1941. For the provinces and candidates considered to be a serious threat to the majority party, see Eugenio Santos, "Your Candidates' Chances," *The Herald Mid-Week Magazine*, 5 November 1941, 9–10; *The Philippines Herald*, 30 October 1941.

81. *The Philippines Herald*, 10 November 1941.

82. Hayden, *The Philippines*, 450.

83. *The Philippines Herald*, 15 November 1941.

84. Ibid., 8 and 19 November 1941.

85. *The Philippines Herald*, 13 and 14 November 1941. In two Quezon City precincts, Quezon lost to Celerino Tiongco and also lost another precinct to Sumulong. See *The Philippines Herald*, 12 November 1941.

86. *Philippines Free Press*, 28 June 1941, 4; *The Tribune*, 8 and 11 July 1941. In mid-November, President Quezon proclaimed Civilian Defense Week to be observed from 11–16 November. This was in concert with what had been proclaimed in the U.S. See *The Philippines Herald*, 6 November 1941.

87. Teodoro Agoncillo, *The Fateful Years: Japan's Adventure in the Philippines, 1941–1945*, vol. 1 (Quezon City: R. P. Garcia Publishing Co., 1965), 72–74.

88. Other Filipinos suspected of being fifth-columnists were the Colorum members. Foreign fifth-columnists included Italians, Germans, and pro-Wang Chiwei Chinese. The Communist Party declared full support to the Philippine government and the armed forces of the U.S. See *The Tribune*, 14, 16, 17, and 19 December 1941; see also "Fifth Columnists at Work," *Philippines Free Press*, 20 December 1941, 18–19. Arrested Ganap leaders included Celerino Tiongco, Gregorio Tobias, Paulo Capa, Quintin Santos de Dios, and Jeremias Adia. See Adia interview on 28 March 1989. On torture, see also Adia interview.

89. *The Tribune*, 14 December 1941.

90. Civilian Emergency Administration was created in April 1941 to handle the various phases of civilian defense work. For details, see Teodoro Agoncillo, *The Fateful Years* 2, 51–52; see also *The Tribune*, 19 December 1941.

91. "The 'Fifth Column' Fever," *Hirang*, 1st issue of July 1940, 1.

# Chapter 7

1. Others opposed to the administration included the employees of the Department of Agriculture, the Cavite navy yard, newspaper companies, such as the *Manila Daily Bulletin*, the Panay autobus company, and some wealthy residents. Even policemen were found among them. See *The Tribune*, 8, 9, and 11 May 1935; *The Philippines Herald*, 9 May 1935; and the *Manila Daily Bulletin*, 23 May 1935; see also "The Copy of the Philippine Constabulary Report to Governor General dated 8 May 1935," folder no. 25-23, "Untitled," HP. Many issues of the *Sakdal* included several poems and essays composed either by the subscribers or by well-known Tagalog poets and writers, including Carlos Ronquillo, Sixto Salibay, and Serafin C. Guinigundo, who were all presumed to be Sakdalista supporters, if not members. For Carlos Ronquillo's essay, see "Ang Panganib ng Ating mga Lupa," 17 October 1931, 4; on Sixto Salibay, see "Ipinagbawal ang Miting ng 'Sakdal' sa Pasay, Rizal," 18 April 1931, 3; for Guinigundo's poem, see "Inuusig sa Matuwid," 3 November 1934, 1, all in *Sakdal*.

2. For Aznar, see Virgilio Almario, "Book Burning at Plaza Moriones," in Milagros Guerrero, *Under Stars and Stripes, Kasaysayan: The Story of the Filipino People* 6 (Manila: Asia Publishing Company Ltd., 1998), 218. For Tiongco, see *The Tribune*, 2 June 1934. Some local-level leaders, such as Vicente Pamatmat of Santa Cruz, Laguna, possessed the means to buy a piano and a refrigerator by the early 1940s, as reported by a Japanese soldier who had stayed with Pamatmat's family. Information on Pamatmat came from an interview with Takuya Maeda, on 6 August 1991, in Himeji City, Japan.

3. Please refer to Ch. 6, fn 26.

4. "The Christmas Eve Fiasco," 136 and 187.

5. Diokno was, at the time, a member of a revolutionary committee based in Tokyo. See "Confidential Report," 14 and 20 October 1909; and 15 December 1910, in PCR. Because of the establishment of the Philippine Revolutionary Council, it is no wonder that the Balintawak celebration of 1911 generated a heated atmosphere and was attended by 20,000, which is a conservative estimate. Participants were all wearing native shirts and blouses. Many men even put on red trousers, part of the Katipunan uniform, shouting "Panahon na" (It is now time). See "Confidential Report," 4 September 1911; see also *El Renacimiento Filipino*, 14 September 1911, quoted in Soledad Borromeo-Buehler, *The Cry of Balintawak: A Contrived Controversy* (Quezon City: Ateneo de Manila University Press, 1998), xv; and Reynaldo C. Ileto, "Orators and the Crowd," 96.

6. Letter dated 13 February 1911 in "Confidential Report" PCR. See also letter dated 26 February 1912 addressed to Policarpo Pimentel in Ilocos Sur, 10 May 1910, and 18 April 1911 in "Confidential Report." Kropotkin is a Russian anarchist theoretician.

7. The military organizations included Viper Battalion, Sandatajanes (Armed People), Bolo Battalions (Machete Battalions), Mapagsumikap (Endeavor), Pagkakaisa (Unity), Dugo Ko (My Blood), Infinito Club (Infinite Club), and Anak ng Bayan (Child of the Nation). See "Christmas Eve Fiasco," 212–13; see also "Confidential Report," 18 April, and 10 and 11 May 1910, PCR.

8. "Confidential Report," 20 October 1909; 7 December 1909; 6 and 14 January 1910; and 5 December 1911, PCR.

9. "Christmas Eve Fiasco," 207–8; see also "Confidential Report," 26 June 1912, PCP.

10. On the Constitution, see "Christmas Eve Fiasco," 137–56, 213. The forces from towns near Manila were to go to a town in Bulacan where they would connect with Ricarte, who was supposedly leading a Japanese army. From there, they were to go to Meycauayan to receive arms and uniforms. For this so-called Balintawak Affair, see "Christmas Eve Fiasco," 215.

11. "Christmas Eve Fiasco," 216. In mid-1915, the police authorities received information that a certain Carriaga, a Ricarte follower, was said to be planning to capture Fort McKinley and to establish independence. The authorities also received a report that Dimas Alang was seething with activity and that another revolt was expected to develop. For details, see *The Washington Post*, 24 July 1915. For techniques of surveillance, intelligence, and penetration into radical nationalist groups, see Alfred W. McCoy, *Policing America's Empire* (Madison: The University of Wisconsin Press, 2009), 59–125.

12. Ohta, *Kikoku*, 80–81. See the communication from the Governor General to the War Department's Chief of the Bureau of Insular Affairs, quoted in Grant K. Goodman, "General Artemio Ricarte and Japan," 53.

13. *New York Tribune*, 30 December 1915.

14. For del Pilar, see "Confidential Report," 18 October 1909, PCR. After returning from Guam, del Pilar had been aiding the authorities in keeping public peace. Therefore, his organizing the Magtanggol invites suspicion. It could have been done as a way to spy on the group. For Ricarte's misgivings on del Pilar, see *Memoir*, 125. For Villafuerte, see *Survey Report*, 101. For more on Magtanggol, see "Swindling 'Patriots,'" *Philippines Free Press*, 13 April 1929, 4–5. See also the *New York Tribune*, 8 April 1929.

15. "Swindling 'Patriots,'" 4–5; see also *New York Tribune*, 8 April 1929.

16. "Magpatuloy Kayo," 15 September 1934, 3; and "Buzon ng Sakdal," 3 March 1934, 1, in *Sakdal*. For the Sakdalistas' view on Aguinaldo, see "Asociacion de veteranos de la revolucion"; and "Tumitiwalag ang Det. No. 1," both 9 February 1935, 1. "Tumiwalag na ang Veteranos sa Imus, Kabite," 21 May 1932, 4; and "Ang Ukol kina Bonifacio at Aguinaldo," 29 October 1932, 2, all in *Sakdal*.

17. The other peasant organizations included Oras Na, in Bulacan; Pahahon Na, in Tunasan; Laguna, Dumating Na; and Handa Na, both in the Buenavista Estate in Bulacan. For other organizations, such as Araw Na and Nagkaisa Na, see G. Capadocia, "The Philippine Labor Movement," 59, CP. See also B. Fegan, "The Social History of a Central Luzon Barrio," in *Philippine Social History*, 111.

18. For more details on the church-owned estates, see Michael J. Connolly, S.J., *Church Lands and Peasant Unrest in the Philippines*. Ramos's defending the peasants' plight, see ibid., 102. See also *The Sunday Times* (Manila), 29 September 1929; and *The Philippines Herald*, 29 September 1929, and 15 April 1930.

19. For example, the way Salud Algabre was exploited by a landlord was narrated during her interview. See "An Interview with Salud Algabre," in Sturtevant, *Popular Uprisings in the Philippines*, 290–91; on peasants being exploited, see B.

Kerkvliet, *The Huk Rebellion*, 19–25; Marshall S. McLennan, "Changing Human Ecology on the Central Luzon Plain: Nueva Ecija, 1705–1939," in *Philippine Social History*, 70–77; and B. Fegan, "The Social History of a Central Luzon Barrio," in *Philippine Social History*, 10; and Milagros C. Guerrero, "Provincial and Municipal Elites of Luzon during the Revolution," in *Philippine Social History*, 155–56. See also, J. Richardson, *Komunista*, 45–50.

20. After 1916, as stipulated in the Jones Bill, the franchise was expanded but it was still limited to males over 21 years of age who could read and write in the vernacular language.

21. For more details on the formation of peasant associations such as KPMP and KP, see J. Richardson, *Komunista*, 50–59.

22. Melinda Tria Kerkvliet, *Manila Workers' Unions, 1900–1950*, 64. Arsenio Batitis of Santa Rosa, Laguna, was one of the first to join the Sakdalista movement. He was a construction worker in Manila when he first read the *Sakdal*. He was deeply moved, and when he lost his job, he decided to go back to his province to establish the movement there. For his active involvement in the movement, see "Sa Buzon ng Sakdal," *Sakdal*, 6 December 1930, 4. Interview with Arsenio Batitis on 6 December 1986 in Santa Rosa, Laguna. Celerino Tiongco was recruited by Batitis. Interview with Carmen Tiongco-Enriquez on 16 December 1988, in Pasay City, Metro Manila.

23. Daniel F. Doeppers, *Manila 1900–1941: Social Change in Late Colonial Metropolis* (Quezon City: Ateneo de Manila University Press, 1984), 117, 516–17; "Metropolitan Manila in the Great Depression: Crisis for Whom?": 514–19; and *Annual Report of the Governor General of the Philippine Islands 1931* (Washington: United States Government Printing Office, 1932), 89.

24. One organization consisted of Filipino servants of American officers stationed at Fort McKinley. Others included workers in Intramuros and in Plaza Santa Cruz, where American soldiers patronized cabarets and bars. Yet another group, in the blue-collar Tondo neighborhood, was organized solely to boycott foreign businesses. For more details, see Serafin E. Macaraig, *Social Problems* (Manila: The Educational Supply Co., 1929), 414–15.

25. Manila laborers had been historically well organized into labor unions since the end of the nineteenth century. In the 1920s and 1930s, especially, many were members of the Congreso Obrera. For more details, see Jim Richardson, *Komunista*, 94–96, 107–140.

26. For the formation of IFI, see Pedro S. de Achutegui and Miguel A. Bernad, *Religious Revolution in the Philippines* 1–3 (Manila: Ateneo de Manila University Press, 1960, 1966, 1969). See also, Lewis Bliss Whittemore, *Struggle for Freedom:*

*History of the Philippine Independent Church* (Greenwich, Conn.: Seabury Press, 1961); Mary Dorita Clifford, "Iglesia Filipina Independiente: The Revolutionary Church," in *Studies in Philippine Church History*, ed. Gerald H. Anderson (Ithaca and London: Cornell University Press, 1969), 223–55; Ellsworth Chandlee, "The Liturgy of the Philippine Independent Church," in *Studies in Philippine Church History*, 256–76; see also William Henry Scott, "The Union Obrera Democratica, First Filipino Labor Union," *Social Science and Humanities Review* 47, nos. 1–4 (January–December 1983): 137–42.

27. Whittemore, *Struggle for Freedom*, 128; see also Hayden, *The Philippines*, 571.

28. Other reasons for the IFI decline included manipulation by the constabulary. See Alfred W. McCoy, *Policing America's Empire*, 109. For the IFI in the provinces, see Daniel F. Doeppers, "Changing Patterns of Aglipayan Adherence in the Philippines, 1918–1970," *Philippine Studies* 25 (1977): 265–77. See also John A. Larkin, *Colonial Society in a Philippine Province: The Pampangans* (Berkley: University of California Press, 1972), 180–81; and Hayden, *The Philippines*, 572.

29. For Aglipay as founder of the Katipunan chapter, see William Henry Scott, *Ilocano Responses to American Aggression, 1900–1901* (Quezon City: New Day Publishers, 1986), 126. When Ricarte secretly returned to the Philippines in 1903, Aglipay supported his effort. See "Christmas Eve Fiasco," 181. On the Aglipayan priests' activities, see "Confidential Report," 19 November 1909, 22 January 1911, and 9 July and 6 October 1910, PCR.

30. "An Interview with Salud Algabre," in Sturtevant, *Popular Uprisings*, 292; see also "Ang Kinatawang Arsenio Bonifacio ang Nag-utos na Pigilin ang Miting ng Sakdal," 3 October 1931, 1; "Nang Umalis si Obispo Aglipay," 4 April 1931, 4; and "Isang Malaking Parangal ang Gagawin ng Malolos Bul. kay Obispo Aglipay," 1 August 1931, 3, all in *Sakdal*.

31. Francis A. Gealogo, "Time, Identity, and Nation in the Aglipayan *Novenario ng Balintawak* and *Calendariong Manghang*," *Philippine Studies* 58, nos. 1–2 (June 2010): 150–66.

32. Michael M. Gonzales, "The Edge of Structure," 7 and 229. The groups themselves sometimes acted in ways that contributed to this impression. For instance, in 1902, a Colorum group in a barrio of Catmon, Santa Maria, Bulacan, applied to register as a religious organization but was denied. The group's founder changed the name to Aglipayan Church and it was given recognition. See "San Vicente, Santa Maria," Historical Data of Bulacan, HDP, 19, 53.

33. *Sakdal* allotted plenty of space for articles on Rizal, particularly around

the time of the anniversary of his birthday in June and his execution in December. Rizal not only became a model to emulate but, for some admirers, a source of *Kapangyarihan* (potency, or power). See Reynaldo Ileto, "Rizal and the Underside of Philippine History," in *Moral Order and the Question of Change: Essays on Southeast Asian Thought*, ed. David K. Wyatt and Alexander Woodside, Monograph Series no. 24 (New Haven, Connecticut: Yale University Southeast Asia Studies, 1982), 322. See also Sturtevant, *Popular Uprisings*, 141–94. However, as far as the Sakdalistas were concerned—at least as evidenced by the articles appearing in the available *Sakdal* issues—Rizal was to be revered and emulated only for his exemplary sacrifice, not as a source of personal power.

34. Vicente Marasigan, *A Banana Guru*, 4, 71–72, 139. To avoid harassment for being Sakdalistas and to seek a more spiritual path, the Samahan ng Tatlong Persona was established after the May 1935 Uprising. Ramos's residence was located in 2326 Juan Luna, Gagalangin, Tondo. Close to this address, at 2296, was the residence of Tomas Martinez, who was a Sakdalista, and Agapito Illustrisimo used to stay at this residence whenever he came to Manila. Interview with Adia on 5 October 1985, in Cabuyao, Laguna. Most likely, Illustrisimo and Ramos met whenever the former visited Manila.

35. Another such organization closely associated with the Sakdalista movement was Bathalismo (Godism). See Venacio P. Wagan, *Bathalismo, Inc. (Inang Mahiwaga)* (Manila ?: n.p., n.d.), 9, 43, and 45–46. The fluidity of the membership in the various religious societies can be seen. For instance, in Barrio San Vicente of Santa Maria, Bulacan, some Aglipayan members supported the Sabadistas (those who congregated on Saturdays). In the late 1930s, some Sakdalistas joined a new religious organization known as "Iglesia ng Dios kay Cristo Jesus, Haligi at Bahay ng Katotohanan" (Church of God for Jesus Christ, The Pillar and the House of Truth). See "San Vicente, Santa Maria," *Historical Data of Bulacan* 19, 63.

36. "Ang Lahat ng Iglesias Evangelicas Dito sa Pilipinas," *Sakdal*, 25 April 1931, 3. A pastor of the Church of Christ was mentioned in the same article. It may be Iglesia ni Kristo. For the historical background of IEMELIF, see Richard L. Deats, "Nicolas Zamora: Religious Nationalist," in *Studies in Philippine Church History*, 325–36; see also T. Valentino Sitoy Jr., *Comity and Unity: Ardent Aspirations of Six Decades of Protestantism in the Philippines (1901–1961)* (Quezon City: National Council of Churches in the Philippines, 1989), 57.

37. Teodoro M. Kalaw, *Five Precepts from Our Ancient Morality*, trans. Maria Kalaw Katigbak (Manila: privately published, 1951). *Komedya*, which recites *awit* and *corido*, can be included here.

38. Ramos was the second of seven children—three boys and four girls—born to Catalino Ramos, a former Katipunero, and Benigna Pantaleon, a volunteer nurse on the battlefront. See Hayase, "Ganap to ni Kansuru Kenkyu" (Study on the Ganap Party),12, NIDS. For his birth date, see Benigno Ramos, *Gumising Ka, Aking Bayan: Mga Piling Tula*, comp. Delfin L. Tolentino (Quezon City: Ateneo de Manila University Press, 1998), xi. Information on Ramos's early life, unless otherwise indicated, come from interviews with Leticia Ramos-Uyboco, Amada Ramos, widow of Ramos's brother Francisco, and Luwalhati Samonte, daughter of Ramos's sister Enriqueta, on 23 August 1985, at Taliptip, Bulacan.

39. Isaac Cruz, "Benigno Ramos: Founder of the Sakdalista," *Philippines Free Press*, 4 February 1961, 16.

40. Other members of Aklatang Bayan included Hermenegildo Cruz, Rosauro Almario, Carlos Ronquillo, Iñigo Ed. Regalado, Lope K. Santos, Faustino Aguilar, Patricio Mariano, Julian Cruz Balmaseda, Pedro Gatmaitan, Severino Reyes, and Amado V. Hernandez. See Virgilio S. Almario, *Balagtasismo Versus Modernismo* (Quezon City: Ateneo de Manila University Press, 1984), 53 and 86. For Ramos's career as a poet, see Julian Cruz Balmaseda, comp., "Mga Diwang Naghihimagsik," n.p.

41. For Ramos's being invited to literary gatherings, see "Parangal sa Hari ng mga Manunulat," *Renacimiento Filipino* (Seccion Tagala), 7 April 1911, 23. The critics were Rosauro Almario, Martin Martires, and Julian Cruz Balmaseda. For the comments of his literary colleagues, see the following: Rosauro Almario, "Tampal sa Tampal," quoted in Almario, *Balagtasismo versus Modernismo*, 87; M. Martires, "Benigno 'Ruben' Ramos, alias Ben Ruben, Ang 'Sakdalero,'" *Alitaptap*, 20 November 1930; and Julian Cruz Balmaseda, comp., "Mga Diwang Naghihimagsik." Both Martires and Balmaseda's comments are found in the Balmaseda Collection.

42. Ramos hid behind names such as "Ben Ruben," "Gat Lotus," "Batikuling," "Ramon Galvez Pantaleon," "Wistano Biroy," "Taliptip," "B...," "Robespierre," and "Nilad." *The Tribune* (3d edition), 5 May 1935. As a journalist, Ramos had his own column, "Sukat Masabi," in *Pagkakaisa*. See Martires, "Benigno 'Ruben' Ramos." The name of the column was later transferred to the *Sakdal*. The information on Ramos using "R" as his middle name came from interview with Adia, on 20 April 1985, in Cabuyao.

43. Balmaseda, comp., "Mga Diwang Naghihimagsik," which includes one hundred twenty-four poems written by Ramos. Teodoro Agoncillo lists a total of one hundred thirty-five poems. For more details, see Teodoro Agoncillo, *Tagalog Periodical Literature* (Manila: Institute of National Language, 1953).

44. "!Bulkan!" originally appeared in *Renacimiento Filipino*, 21 February 1911. It was reprinted in Ramos, *Gumising Ka*, 1–4. Balmaseda states that it was originally

published in *Pagkakaisa*, but does not give the date of publication. "Asyenda" originally appeared in *Pagkakaisa*. According to Tolentino, it was published around 1929–1930. See Ramos, *Gumising Ka*, 172. Benigno Ramos, *Pancho Villa: Maikling Kasaysayan ng Bantog at Kilabot na Taong Ito sa Mehiko* (Pancho Villa, Short History of a Famous and Fearful Person in Mexico) (Manila: Imprenta y Liberia de P. Sayo Vda. de Soriano, 1916).

45. Tagalog original: "Kung kahapon ako'y inapi ng Dasal/ngayon ay lalo pang kaapiapihan; namatay ang aking magiting na Rizal/at patuloy pa rin ang kanyang kaaway . . ." See "Mga Diwang Naghihimagsik." "Pilipinas" was originally published in *Pagkakaisa*, but the compilation gives no dates.

46. "Balagtasan ng Kalayaan," in "Mga Diwang Naghihimagsik."

47. "Alaala" originally appeared in *Renacimiento Filipino*, 7 September 1911. This issue is in the "Mga Diwang Naghihimagsik." It was reprinted in Ramos, *Gumising Ka*, 52–54.

48. "!Bayani!" was originally published in *Renacimiento Filipino*, 28 December 1911, available in the Balmaseda Collection; reprinted in Ramos, *Gumising Ka*, 71–74.

49. "Bagong Hudyo" originally appeared in *Sampagita*, 6 April 1926. Balmaseda says that "Ang Diyos Ko" originally appeared in *Pagkakaisa*. This poem was reprinted in *Sakdal* under one of Ramos's pen names, Eugenio Salazar. See "Ang Diyos Ko," *Sakdal*, 27 December 1930, 2.

50. "Talsik" was serialized irregularly in *Renacimiento Filipino* from 14 February to 21 May 1911; the Filipiniana Section of UP's main library in Diliman has a copy in typescript. For women, see Ben Ruben, "Ang Kalinisan ng Ating mga Babae," *Sakdal*, 18 October 1930, 3. This was declared to be a reprint of what Ramos had written in 1924.

51. "Ang Laruang Bigay sa Atin ng Amerika," *Sakdal*, 18 October 1930, 3. This was declared to be a reprint of what Ramos had written in 1922.

52. G. K. Goodman, "Japan and Philippine Radicalism," 136.

53. "Panulat," *Sakdal*, 30 August 1930, 1.

54. "Si Bernardo Carpio: Ang Hari sa Alamat ng mga Tagalog," *Sakdal*, 21 May 1932, 3. For the legend of Bernardo Carpio and its influence on Bonifacio and the people in the nineteenth century, see Reynaldo Ileto, "Bernardo Carpio: *Awit* and Revolution," in *Perceptions of the Past in Southeast Asia*, ed. A. J. S. Reid and D. G. Marr (Singapore: Heinemann Educational Publishers, 1979), 379–400. Bonifacio's 1895 visit to the cave of Pamintinan in Montalban was considered to be a conscious effort to connect his activities with the popular folk hero Carpio. See Ileto, *Pasyon and Revolution*, 127.

55. "Ako Ang Diwa ng Kalayaan," *Sakdal*, 12 September 1931, 3.

56. The word "Pahayag" is commonly translated as "Manifesto," but on the basis of the work's content, I have followed the lead of Setsuho Ikehata, who translated it as "Revelation." See Ikehata, *Firipin Kakumei to Katorishizumu* (Philippine Revolution and Catholicism) (Tokyo: Keiso shobo, 1987), 116.

57. Excerpts of Jacinto's "Pahayag" are taken from Ileto, *Pasyon and Revolution*, 109–12. For reprint of "Pahayag," see *Pasyon and Revolution*, 109fn23.

58. The masthead of *Sakdal* issue of 23 August 1930.

59. "Sariling Diwa," *Sakdal*, 1 July 1933, 2.

60. "Sariling Diwa," "Ngayon Dapat Lumitaw ang mga Rizal," 13 December 1930, 2; "Mga Sukat Masabi," 7 March 1931, 4; "Sang-ayon kay Wistano Biroy," 6 February 1932, 3; and "Mga Sukat Masabi," 1 October 1932, 1, all in *Sakdal*.

61. "Huwag Isipin ang Pagkatakot Kundi ang Pagpapakasakit," 6 December 1930, 3; "Sariling Diwa: Kaululan at Katinuan," 26 January 1935, 2; "Buzon ng Sakdal," 28 February 1931, 3; "May Balitang Hahalayin si G. B. Ramos Upang Manglamig ang mga Sakdalista," 1 September 1934, 1; and "Venga Esa Tirania que es Senal de Vuestra Caida," 26 December 1931, 1, all in *Sakdal*. Many other articles compared Ramos's hardships to those of Rizal's. For instance, see "Mga Pangyayaring Dapat Ihayag," 22 January 3; "Walang Progreso o Pagsulong," 22 January 1932, 1; and "Sariling Diwa: Kaululan at Katinuan," 26 January 1935, 2, all in *Sakdal*.

62. "Sa Tama ng Ilaw: Ang Aming Tagapamahala Sang-ayon kay G. Zosimo O. Maderal," *Sakdal*, 6 December 1930, 3. Perhaps "white bird" was used as an allusion to the dove that descended on Jesus at his Baptism or the dove that Noah sent out to see if the flood was ending.

63. "Sa Tama ng Ilaw."

64. Ibid. For similar sentiment expressed, see "Nobela ni F. V. Reyes na Kadiwa ng Sakdal," 8 October 1932, 2; and "Ang Aming Paglalakbay sa Tayabas ay Napuspos ng Tagumpay ng Simulaing Pang Bayan," 18 April 1931, 3, both in *Sakdal*. For Ramos being compared to Bonifacio, see "Huwag Isipin ang Pagkatakot Kundi ang Pagpapakasakit," *Sakdal*, 6 December 1930, 3.

65. The Sakdalistas compared Ramos with Lope K. Santos and Hermenegildo Cruz. Santos was a former governor of Rizal and Nueva Vizcaya, and later became a senator. Cruz, formerly a pro-labor activist and orator, became a senator and was later appointed to the Bureau of Labor. Both became editors of pro-Nacionalista periodicals, and they wrote and delivered Tagalog speeches for Quezon and Osmeña. The Sakdalistas called Cruz "bata ni Quezon" (Quezon's henchman).. Others included in the criticism were Faustino Aguilar, a well-known Tagalog

writer, later the director of the Bureau of Labor and a senator, and the list goes on. See "Lahat ng May Panitik Ay Ikinabit, Lahat ng May Bunganga, May Mantika," *Sakdal*, 17 March 1932, 1; see also Melinda Tria Kerkvliet, *Manila Workers' Unions*, 32; and "May Pagunita ang Malaki," *Sakdal*, 25 August 1934, 1. If Ramos had not been dismissed from his position as an employee of the Senate, perhaps he would have remained a reformist trying to change the social situation from within, like those the Sakdalistas criticized.

66. By contrast, Quezon was a mestizo and could not speak fluent Tagalog. Unlike Quezon, to whom provincial officials kowtowed with pompous ceremonies and entertainment, Ramos affected a native style of interaction. Interview with Aida on 29 November 1986 in Cabuyao, Laguna. See also "Sa Miting, Kostable; Sa Pahayagan, Paglait; Iyan ang Ginamit sa Amin ng mga Makatiyan,"14 January 1933, 1; "Bagong Lider ng Bayan," 15 September 1934, 3, both in *Sakdal*. On Quezon, see "Sariling Diwa: Anong Kaalipinan Iyan/What Slavery Is This?" *Sakdal*, 26 December 1931, 2.

67. For instance, Jorge Bocobo and Manuel Quezon looked up to Japan as a model to emulate. See Grant K. Goodman, "Nitobe's Bushido: The Samurai Ethic in a Philippine Setting," in *Festschrift: in Honor of Dr. Marcelino Foronda, Jr.*, ed. Emerita S. Quito (Manila: De La Salle University Press, 1987), 56–71. For others who tried to forge strong ties with Japan in the early 1930s, see Motoe Terami-Wada, "Cultivating Goodwill between Japan and the Philippines in the 1930s," in *Philippines-Japan Relations*, ed. Setsuho Ikehata, and Lydia N. Yu Jose (Quezon City: Ateneo de Manila University Press, 2003), 155–84.

68. For expectations of help from Russia, see Jim Richardson, "The Genesis of the Philippine Communist Party," 113. See also *Komunista*, 83.

69. For instance, see (no title) 12 December 1931, 4; "Bago Kayo Bumoto, Basahin Ninyo ang Bilang na Ito ng 'Sakdal,'" 30 May 1931, 1; (no title), 4 February 1933, 3; and 11 June 1932, 2; "Nanguupat sa pagaakalang masisira ang pananalig ng mga Sakdal," 27 July 1935, 3; and "Iglesia Filipina Independiente Paroquia ng Maria Clara," 27 February 1936, 3, all in *Sakdal*.

70. "Nang Tubusin ni Moises," *Sakdal*, 18 February 1933, 1; "Ang 'Ebionismo' ni Jesucristo," 25 June 1932, 3; "Ang mga Hudyo at si Kristo," 26 December 1931, 3; "Ang Maralitang Hesus," 24 March 1932, 3; "An Agitation and Agitators," 16 July 1932, 1, all in *Sakdal*. In addition to Christ, the writer included parallels to Mohammed, the Buddha, Luther, Washington, Bolivar, Lincoln, Rizal, Bonifacio, and del Pilar. See "Lumagay Tayo sa Katuwiran at Saka Humatol Pagkatapos," *Sakdal*, 16 July 1932, 1; see also *Sakdal* issues for 16 February 1935, 2; 30 March 1935, 1; and 14 September 1935, 2.

71. "Ang Sakdalista," *Sakdal*, 7 December 1935, 2. For information on

Patenia being an active Sakdalista, see interview with Adia on 10 January 1987, in Cabuyao, Laguna. In Patenia's other articles, he quoted from New Testament books, such as Matthew, James, Luke, Romans, Hebrews, and Revelation, and from Old Testament books, such as Genesis, Zephaniah I and II, Chronicles, Psalms, Micah, Isaiah, and Jeremiah. Patenia was the president of the International Bible Studies Association and a leading member of the Jehovah's Witnesses. For other articles by Patenia, for example, see "Bakit Inuusig ang mga Saksi ni Jehoba at mga Sakdalista?" *Sakdal*, 11 January 1936, 1.

72. The Samahang ng Tatlong Persona members thought Amang Illustrisimo had ordered Ramos to go to the U.S. and Japan. Therefore, Ramos's trips abroad were also considered divine orders. See Marasigan, *A Banahaw Guru*, 79–80.

73. "Teokrasya ang Makalulunas sa Pagdaralita ng Sangkatauhan," 11 January 1936, 2, and "Walang Kapanatagan sa Di Makasisiyang mga Pamahalaan sa Daigdig," 1 February 1936, 1, in *Sakdal*.

74. For Baltazar's poems in *Sakdal*, see "Lubayan na ang mga Kuwentong Iyan," 4 June 1932, 4. For Baltazar being praised as a patriotic poet, see "Ang Kalayaan sa Pagsasalita at Pagsulat," 9 March 1932, 2; and "Ang Laging Hinahamak Na 'Pilosopo,'" 8 October 1932, 3, in *Sakdal*.

75. "Nagkasagutan ang Pangulo ng Pulo at ang Aming Direktor ukol kay J. Manahan," *Sakdal*, 5 December 1931, 4.

76. "Mga Pagtatapat ng Bayang Api," 15 July 1933, 1; and 29 July 1933, 1, both in *Sakdal*. For Rizal's sacrifice, see "Sariling Diwa: Ngayon Dapat Lumitaw ang mga Rizal,"13 December 1930, 2. Other articles stressed the sacrifices made by the Heroes; for instance, see (no title), 17 October, 3, 28 November 1931, 1; "Ang Bayani ng Gutom," 1 August 1931, 1; and "Mga Luha't Hinagpis," 4 February 1933, 2. For similar articles, see "Think of That," 1 July 1933, 3; "Ang Kalabaw na Gatasan," 1 July 1933, 4; and "Quo Vadis," 5 January 1935, 2, all in *Sakdal*.

77. "Iyo't Iyon din...!" 22 April 1933, 2; "Salaping Niwaldas ng mga Nasionalista," 30 May 1931, 1; and "Sariling Diwa," 15 August 1931, 2, all in *Sakdal*.

78. In 1897, on the anniversary of Rizal's death, the Katipunan appealed to the people to follow his example by being willing to die for the sake of the country. See Reynaldo C. Ileto, "Rizal and the Underside of Philippine History," 274–337. The following articles echo the same sentiment as in 1897: "Si Rizal ang Bayaning Walang Kapantay sa Buong Daigdig," 20 December 1930, 3; and "Ang Kalbaryo ng mga Sakdalista," 4 May 1935, 1, both in *Sakdal*.

79. Ambeth R. Ocampo, *Rizal Without the Overcoat* (Manila: Anvil Publishing, Inc., 1990), 23 and 86. The English translation of the two novels was undertaken

by Charles E. Derbyshire under the titles *The Social Cancer* (for *Noli me tangere*) and *The Reign of Greed* (for *El Filibusterismo*).

80. "Basahin at Isipin," 8 October 1932, 1; and "Umabot ng Diplomang Nandakip," 22 April 1933, 4, both in *Sakdal*.

81. "Mga Talsik ng Apoy," 21 February 1931, 2; and "Mga Sukat Masabi," 14 November 1931, 3, both in *Sakdal*.

82. "Umabot ng Diplomang Nandakip," *Sakdal*, 22 April 1933, 4.

83. Jose Rizal, *Noli me tangere*, trans. Ma. Soledad Lacson-Locsin (Manila: Bookmark, 1996), 404.

84. Jose Rizal, *El Filibusterismo*, trans. Ma. Soledad Lacson-Locsin (Manila: Bookmark, 1997), 410.

85. According to some Sakdalista contributors, Rizal had first thought of leading the revolution when he was in Berlin trying to complete his second novel, *El Fili*, in 1887. (Actually, Rizal started to write *El Fili* in 1888 after he returned from the Philippines.) See "Mali ang Palagay ni Jacinto Manahan na si Dr. Rizal ay Kalaban ng Himagsikan," 12 September 1931, 3; "Si Dr. Jose Rizal ay Kalaban ng Panghihimagsik ni A. Bonifacio," 19 September 1931, 4; and "Tinangka ni Dr. Rizal," 15 October 1932, 3, all in *Sakdal*. There was a dispute in the early 1930s between the two historians Gregorio Zaide and Arsenio Manuel, the former asserting that Rizal supported the 1896 Revolution and the latter denying it. Manuel's argument seems to have been accepted since then. For details, see Floro C. Quibuyen, *A Nation Aborted: Rizal, American Hegemony, and Philippine Nationalism* (Quezon City: Ateneo de Manila University Press, 2008), 44–48.

86. *El Fili*, 69.

87. "Pagunita sa mga Magulang," 6 February 1932, 4; "Tinangka ni Dr. Rizal na Siya ang Maging Patnugot ng Paghihimagsik sa Sangkapuluan," 15 October 1932, 3; and "Si Rizal ang Bayaning Higit sa Lahat," 21 May 1932, 3, all in *Sakdal*.

88. "Mga Pangyayaring Magkatutugon sa Pagbabangon ng Katuwiran; Mga Tanda ng Magkakawangis na mga Pangyayari," 1 February 1936, 2; "Sariling Diwa: Kailangan ang Init upang Mahinog ang Bunga," 8 February 1936, 2; and "Si Rizal ang Nagsimula, si Ramos ang Tatapos," 5 September 1936, 2, all in *Sakdal*.

89. "Buhay Pa ang Ating Rizal, Narito at Nangungusap," *Sakdal*, 2 January 1932, 1. Though expressing the voice of Rizal, the style of this passage is reminiscent of Emilio Jacinto's *Pahayag* and Ramos's "Ako ang Diwa ng Kalayaan" as we saw earlier.

90. *El Filibusterismo*, 407–11; *Noli*, 436.

91. "Gunitain Ninyo Kami: Ang Tuntunin ng Umiibig sa Simulain ng 'Sakdal,'"

*Sakdal*, 28 November 1931, 2. The form of decalogues created by Bonifacio, Jacinto, and Mabini to inspire people at the end of the nineteenth century had been popular. For instance, the codes of laborers such as their duties and obligations, were listed and circulated among labor union members in the 1910s and 1920s. For more details, see Richardson, *Komunista*, 31.

92. For "Decalogue," see Teodoro A. Agoncillo, *The Revolt of the Masses*, 94. Apolinario Mabini also wrote *True Decalogue* and stressed that people must radically change their attitudes, ways of thinking, and behavior toward each other, because that is what had made their colonization possible. For details of Mabini's philosophy, see Cesar Adib Majul, *Apolinario Mabini: Revolutionary* (Manila: National Heroes Commission, 1970) 52–56, 218.

93. "Ang Limang Utos Ni Bathala," *Sakdal*, 21 May 1932, 4.

94. For proverbs, see (no title), *Sakdal*, 14 November 1931, 4; "Lumalakas na ang Katotohanan," 16 March 1935, 1; "Mga Kawikaan," 14 November 1931, 4; and "Ang Patakaran at Aral ng KKK ng mga Anak ng Bayan," 28 November 1931, 3, all in *Sakdal*. For the original "Teachings of the Katipunan," see Teodoro A. Agoncillo, *The Revolt of the Masses*, 83–84.

95. John N. Schumacher, S.J., "Propagandists' Philippine Past," in *The Making of a Nation: Essays on Nineteenth-century Filipino Nationalism* (Quezon City: Ateneo de Manila University Press, 1991), 116; and "The Civic and Religious Ethic of Emilio Jacinto," in *Morality, Religion and the Filipino*, ed. Rene B. Javellana, S.J. (Quezon City: Ateneo de Manila University Press, 1994), 95fn24.

96. It is not a coincidence that the stronghold of the Sakdalista movement, namely, Laguna, Cavite, Bulacan, Bataan, Batangas, Pampanga, Nueva Ecija, not to mention Manila, were the Katipunan's strongholds.

97. Ramon Rubio, "Ano ang Sakdalismo?" *Sakdal Supplement* (n.d.), April 1935, 2. The issue was dated April but there is strong evidence that the supplement came after the May Uprising because one article discussed the plebiscite. See "Ang Pangulo ng E.U. ay Wawalang Bisa ang Halalan ng Plebisito" (The President of the U.S. will Have No Effect on the Plebiscite Election). The article questioned why the elections had not been postponed if a disturbance had actually occurred. It also mentioned the fact that some Sakdalista leaders sent a petition, dated 9 May, asking for postponement of the plebiscite.

98. "Ano ang Sakdalismo?" 14, 32.

99. Ibid., 18.

100. *Pamahayag*, 45.

101. Even today, one finds among lowland Filipinos a widespread sentiment that the poor are more moral, less greedy, and more compassionate than the rich.

For the Bicol case, see Fenella Cannell, *Power and Intimacy* (London: Cambridge University Press, 1999), 101.

102. Gaudencio Tobias, "Patria Amore," *Sakdal*, 2 March 1935, 2.

103. The interviewee's words were: "We have shown that we have rights. We know that we have rights and are willing to die for them. We have shown America that the Filipinos want their independence. I don't care if we go to Bilibid (the national penitentiary) for a long time. I do not care if we are killed." See Hayden, *The Philippines*, 397.

## Chapter 8

1. Benedict Anderson, *Under Three Flags: Anarchism and the Anti-Colonial Imagination* (London, New York: Verso, 2005), 124–25.

2. John N. Schumacher, S.J., *The Propaganda Movement: 1880–1895, The Creator of a Filipino Consciousness, the Makers of Revolution* (Quezon City: Ateneo de Manila University Press, 1997), 290. See also Setsuho Ikehata,"Firipin Kakumei to Nihon no Kan'yo," (The Philippine Revolution and the Japanese Involvement) in *Seiki Tenkanki ni Okeru Nihon-Firipin Kankei* (The Japan-Philippine Relations at the Turn of the Century) (Tokyo: Institute for the Study of Languages and Cultures of Asia and Africa, University of Tokyo of Foreign Languages and Culture, 1989), 1–36.

3. "Zakken: Manira Hanto Dosei no Ken" (Miscellaneous: Movement of Manila Rebels), in *Nihon Gaiko Monjo* (Japanese Diplomatic Documents) (Tokyo: Ministry of Foreign Affairs, 1971), 969–72. See also Josefa Saniel, *Japan and the Philippines, 1868–1898* (Quezon City: University of the Philippines, 1969), 171–75.

4. Agoncillo, *The Revolt of the Masses*, 80. See also appendix A, "The Memories of Dr. Pio Valenzuela," in National Historical Institute, ed., *Minutes of the Katipunan* (Manila: National Historical Institute, 1978), 105.

5. Agoncillo, *The Revolt of the Masses*, 132.

6. Takuya Ozaki, *Chomin Sakamoto Shiro* (Tokyo: Chominkai, 1932), 208.

7. For the social nature of the visit, see Josefa Saniel, *Japan and the Philippines, 1868–1898*, 192–94. See also Setsuho Ikehata, "Firipin Kakumei no Ridashippu ni Kansuru Kenkyu" (A Study on the Leadership on the Philippine Revolution), *Toyo Bunka Kkenkyusyo Kiyo*, no. 80 (1980): 114.

8. Ikehata, "Firipin Kakumei to Nihon no Kan'yo," 8.

9. *Minutes of the Katipunan*, 143, 164, 191, and 212–13.

10. For details on some Filipino efforts to obtain arms in Japan and secure Japanese assistance, see Mariano Ponce, *Cartas Sobre la Revolucion, 1897–1900*

(Manila: Bureau of Printing, 1932); Josefa Saniel, *Japan and the Philippines, 1868–1898*; Grant K. Goodman, "Japan and the Philippine Revolution: Image and Legend," *Journal of Oriental Studies* (January 1970): 100–12; and Ikehata, "Firipin Kakumei to nihon no kan'yo," 1–36.

11. Most of these Japanese volunteers were actually military personnel. They left the military and came to the Philippines as civilians. No doubt, the Japanese military was behind this move. See Motoe Terami-Wada, "Japanese Residents and the Philippine Revolution," in *The Japanese in the Philippines: 1880s to 1980s* (Manila: National Historical Commission of the Philippines, 2010), 15–16. On the arrest of civilian Japanese, see John R. M. Taylor, *The Philippine Insurrection against the United States: A Compilation and Introduction by John R. M. Taylor* (Pasay: Eugenio Lopez Foundation, 1971) 5: 486.

12. "A Letter to Aguinaldo from Sandiko, dated August 9, 1898," in "Communications Showing Relations of Japanese and Filipinos in the Philippine Islands," in *Harry Hill Bandholtz Papers* (HBP), Michigan Historical Collection, Bentley Historical Library, University of Michigan.

13. "A Letter to Aguinaldo from T. Sandiko, dated October 31, 1898"; "Translation of a Rough Draft of a Letter from Mariano Trias to Captain S. Narahara, Captured among the Former's Papers by Captain Cole, 4th Cavalry, December 1900"; "A Letter to Aguinaldo from Agent, August 26, 1899," all found in HBP. Another Filipino revolutionary general, Mariano Trias, wrote to Capt. Narahara in 1900 and said that Filipinos and Japanese "should view each other as sisters and not as two peoples—I would desire to see the people in close bonds of fraternity with the Japanese people." See "Translation of a Rough Draft."

14. "Confidential Report," dated 2 August, 24 September, 14 October, and 18 December 1909; 5 February, 3 March, and 8 August 1910, PCR. See also McCoy, *Policing America's Empire*, 181, and 183–85. Many rumors of war between the two countries are reported in the constabulary reports between 1906 and 1913. For rumors, see also Ileto, *Pasyon and Revolution*, 255 and 298–99.

15. For instance, see "Confidential Report," dated 11 January and 6 August 1908; 24 September, 8 December 1909, and 8 August 1910, PCR. The Japanese Ministry of Foreign Affairs report shows that indeed Ramos (Ishikawa) and Vicente Lucban arrived in Japan in August 1909 to try to obtain Japanese assurance for Philippine independence. See Shinzo Hayase, "Nanpo `Imin; to `Nanshin,'" ("Emmigration" to the South and "Advance to the South") in *Firipin Kin-Gendaishi no naka no Nihonjin* (The Japanese in Modern and Contemporary Philippine History), (Tokyo:Iwanami Shoten, 2012), 81.

16. The fact was that Salvador had never left the Philippines. See, Ileto, *Pasyon and Revolution*, 298–99.

17. Both Teodoro M. Kalaw (1930) and Carlos Quirino (1964), who wrote the preface to the publications of the *Minutes of the Katipunan*, cast strong doubts as to the authenticity of some of the events recorded in the minutes. *Minutes of the Katipunan*, V and IX. When the *Minutes* were published in 1930, some former Katipunan members publicly declared that the *Minutes* "are false, fabricated, and manipulated by one who did not have any knowledge of the functions, practice, and procedures of the K.K.K...." See Borromeo-Buehler, *The Cry of Balintawak*, 95–97.

18. *Minutes of the Katipunan*, 19.

19. The daughter of Jose Dizon, one of the alleged delegates sent to Japan to purchase arms, said her father had never been to Japan. See Teodoro Agoncillo, *The Revolt of the Masses*, 338fn3.

20. *Minutes of the Katipunan*, 19, 48, 54, 59, and 69–70.

21. Appendix A, "The Memoirs of Dr. Pio Valenzuela," *Minutes of the Katipunan*, 92.

22. Grant K. Goodman, "The Problem of Philippine Independence and Japan: The First Three Decades of American Colonial Rule," *Southeast Asia, An International Quarterly* 1, no. 3 (Summer 1971): 166. See also McCoy, *Policing America's Empire*, 184–85.

23. Rumors of Gen. Ricarte returning from Japan with Japanese assistance, see Ileto, "Orators and the Crowd," 105.

24. *Manila Daily Bulletin*, 8 and 9 December 1939.

25. The following works were helpful in analyzing the function of rumor: John Demos, *Entertaining Satan, Witchcraft and the Culture of Early New England* (NY: Oxford University Press, 1982); Gordon Allport and Leo Postman, *The Psychology of Rumor* (NY: Russell and Russell, 1947); Tamotsu Shibutani, *Improvised News: A Sociological Study of Rumor* (Indianapolis: Bobbs-Merrill, 1966); Pamela Stewart and Andrew Strathern, *Witchcraft, Sorcery, Rumors and Gossip* (Cambridge, UK: Cambridge University Press, 2004); Georges Lefebvre, *The Great Fear of 1789: Rural Panic in Revolutionary France* (New York: Schocken Books, 1973); and Ranajit Guha, *Elementary Aspects of Peasant Insurgency in Colonial India* (Delhi: Oxford University Press, 1992), especially chap. six, "Transmission."

26. Some Filipinos might have known Ricarte's return to the Philippines before his actual landing as he announced it a few weeks before he left Japan through NHK International radio broadcast. Ohta, *Kikoku*, 119–20.

27. *The Tribune*, 4 January 1942.

28. Interview with Bibiana Tuazon-Ishita on 15 April 1989, in Osaka City, Japan. See also Shizuo Hosokawa, *Manira e no Michi* (The Road to Manila) (Tokyo: Tokyo Shiryu Sha, 1961), 203–4.

29. Interview with Minviluz Dominguez (Maria Luisa Fleetwood) on 7 July 1995, in Fremont, California. Interview with Capt. Junsuke Hitomi on 27 February 1991, in Kyoto City, Japan. See also Motoe Terami-Wada, "The Japanese Propaganda Corps in the Philippines: Laying the Foundation," in *Japanese Cultural Policies in Southeast Asia during World War II*, ed. Grant K. Goodman (New York: St. Martin's Press, 1991), 23. For details on Ricarte's visits in the towns of Luzon, see Ohta, *Kikoku*, 270–86; also see Ishizaka, *Mayon no Kemuri*, 73.

30. Marasigan, *A Banahaw Guru*, 107–8, 121, and 126–28. Some say Illustrisimo was executed by President Quezon's Own Guerilla Group (PQOG). See "Dolores, Historical Data of Quezon," 84, 17.

31. It seems the organization was named so simply because it was a "new unity" of the anti-Quezon groups. However, a Ricartista organization called "Pagkakaisa" existed along with an organ called *Pagkakaisa*, published in the 1930s, which often published Gen. Ricarte's statements. The name of the group could have derived from either of these groups. See Antonio Abad, *General Macario L. Sakay: Was He a Bandit or a Patriot?* (Manila: J. B. Feliciano & Son, 1955), 33.

32. Other political parties represented in the BP were the Nacionalista, Popular Front, Democrata, Young Philippines, and other minor parties and organizations; socialists and communists were not included. Individual members included Jose Turiano Santiago (Katipunan official and Ricartista), Fruto Santos (who joined the Propaganda Corps), Ciriaco Campomanes (the old Sakdalista Party leader in Tayabas), Felicisimo Lauson (the old Sakdalista Party leader), Narciso Lapus (the old Sakdalista Party member who collected the donations for Ricarte), Pascual de Leon (writer), and Francisco Torrontegui (a former Manila city councilor). See C. Bernardo file, no. 48-2, B. Eslete file, no. 110-11; L. F. Santos file, no. 247-22, People's Court Papers (PCP), University of the Philippines Filipiniana Section (UPFS)

33. V. Correa file, no. 78-11; and Eslete file, PCP, UPFS.

34. Bernardo file, PCP, UPFS. A similar allegation had been made during Quezon's presidency. For details, see McCoy, "Quezon's Commonwealth," 137.

35. Bernardo file.

36. The guideline is contained in "Nanpo Senryochi Gyosei Jisshi Yoryo," (Guidelines Governing the Administration of the Southern Occupied Area) *Shiryoshu: Nanpo no Gunsei*, (Compilation of Historical Documents: Military Administration in the Southern Areas) ed. Boeicho Boei Kenkyujo Senshibu (Defense Agency, National Institute for Defense Studies [NIDS], Office of Military History) (Tokyo: Asagumo Shimbunsha, 1985), 91–92. See also "Taibei Senso ni Tomonau Hito Shori Hosakuan," (Proposed Measures Managing the Philippines with the Commencement

of War against the U.S.A.) Nansei Gunsei, no. 62, NIDS. On Ricarte's role, see Setsuho Ikehata, "Firipin ni okeru Nihongusei no Ichi Kosatsu: Rikarute Shogun no Yakuwari o Megutte" (A Study on the Japanese Military Administration in the Philippines: Focus on Gen. Artemio Ricarte's Role), *Ajia Kenkyu* 22, no. 2 (July 1975): 48–49.

37. N. Lapus file, no. 173-5; C. Campomanes file, no. 61-5, PCP, UPFS. See also Frank Reel, *The Case of General Yamashita* (Chicago: The University of Chicago Press, 1949), 126–27.

38. Tiongco, who was already of advanced age, died in the following month, perhaps due to harsh prison conditions. See Carmen Tiongco-Enriquez, "Revolt in the Grassroots," 2520. For Ramos's release, see *Firipin Joho*, no. 59 (March 1942): 87; see also, Hayase, "Ganappu-to ni Kansuru Kenkyu." According to Adia the other Ganapistas including himself, who were arrested earlier in December were released on or around 30 December just before the Japanese entry to Manila; see Adia interview on 28 March 1989.

39. "Ramos's Loyalty," *Philippines Free Press*, 20 December 1941, 32. See also *The Tribune*, 17 December 1941. Earlier, Quezon seemed to have considered releasing Ramos on bail and ordered Sec. of Justice Abad Santos to release him under bail bond. However, Solicitor Gen. Roman Ozaeta refused on the ground that Ramos's bail bond had been cancelled. See Roman Ozaeta, "Manuel L. Quezon, a Personal Appraisal," *Philippine Journal of Education*, quoted in Teresita Hachero-Pascual, "The Sakdalista Movement: A Historical Assessment," 229.

40. R. Crespo file, no. 79-4, PCP, UPFS.

41. The identification cards were printed in both Tagalog and Japanese and signed by the "Patnugutang Pambansa ng Sakdal-Ganap" (National Director of Sakdal-Ganap) with the signature of Benigno Ramos as Tandis (governor) and Antonio Velisario as Pangulo (president.) The sample of ladaw is found in J. Juco file, PCP, UPFS.

42. In some towns, Ganap Party members assisted municipal officials in organizing meetings in which Japanese military officials and Ramos spoke about the purpose of the Japanese Occupation and the need for Filipinos' cooperation. A. V. H. Hartendorp, *Japanese Occupation of the Philippine* 2 (Manila: Bookmark, 1967), 1:301.

43. For instance, the residents of Gagalangin, Tondo, and Sampaloc, in Manila, complained to the authorities that the Ganapistas organized themselves into volunteer fire brigades and solicited contributions for protection. Eventually, some sixty alleged Ganapistas were rounded up for questioning. *The Tribune*, 8 August 1942. Pres. Laurel observed that numerous opportunists began joining the Ganap Party after the Japanese Occupation. See Shozo Murata, *Murara Shozo Iko*,

*Hito Nikki* (Murata Shozo's Posthumous Manuscript: Philippine Diary or Murara Diary), ed. Shintaro Fukushima (Tokyo: Hara Shobo, 1969), 307.

44. *Hiripin Joho*, no. 59 (March 1942): 87. For the numbers of Ganapista victims, see Hayase, "Ganappu-to ni Kansuru Kenkyu." See also interview with Takashi Hayashi, the *kenpeitai* in charge of the Ganapistas, on 11 August 1991, in Tokyo, Japan. One of the victims was Agapito Illustrisimo, as we have seen.

45. Setsuho Ikehata, "Filipin ni Okeru Nihon Gunsei no Ichi Kosatsu," 54. For the Kalibapi's goals, see Teodoro A. Agoncillo, *The Fateful Years: Japan's Adventure in the Philippines*, 364–65. See also Ricardo T. Jose, "The Association for Service to the New Philippines (KALIBAPI) during the Japanese Occupation: Attempting to Transport a Japanese Wartime Concept to the Philippines," *The Journal of Sophia Asian Studies*, no. 19 (2001): 149–85.

46. *The Tribune*, 29 and 30 January 1943.

47. When the march was introduced to the public, the lyricist's name was not announced, so it became a topic of debate, especially among the Tagalog poets. Their opinions were divided; one group said it must have been Ramos since he was the propaganda officer. The other group argued that the lyrics were so bad that such a recognized poet like Ramos could not have penned it. See Agoncillo, *The Fateful Years*, 625. On "Dai Atiw," see Benigno Ramoz, *Syllabic Wealth of the Tagalog Dialect* (Manila: n.p., Kalibapi? 1943), 8–10. This could have been written both in English and Filipino but my research found only the English version. Many Kalibapi publications had several versions: English, Tagalog, Ilocano, Cebuano, etc. By this time, Ramos was spelling his last name "Ramoz."

48. *The Tribune*, 29 October 1942; 27 January and 6 February 1943; 13 and 22 April, 1 and 10 June, 18 and 19 July, and 15 November 1944. See also Setsuho Ikehata, "Mining Industry Development and Local Anti-Japanese Resistance," in *The Philippines under Japan*, ed. Setsuho Ikehata, and Ricardo T. Jose (Quezon City: Ateneo de Manila University Press, 1999), 152.

49. J. Pedro file, no. 220-225, and about a hundred other files, PCP, UPFS.

50. A. Adriano file, no. 3-12, and other dozens of files, PCP, UPFS.

51. According to Ambassador Murata, there were about 1,000 men, including their families, in that unit. There were another 1,000 laborers sent from Taiwan. See Murata, *Murata Diary*, 105. See also J. Juco file, no. 165-20, PCP, UPFS; and "Dai 14 Gun Kankei Joho Shiryo Tsuzuri: (A Pad of Information Material Related to the 14th Army) Joho Gyomu Renraku Jiko," February 1944, Hito Boei, no. 3, NIDS.

52. The plan was based on the "Heiho Kitei Shiko Saisoku" (Details in Implementing Military Auxiliary Regulations), Hito Zenpan, 78, NIDS.

53. A. Adriano file, no. 3-12, and other dozens of files, PCP, UPFS. During

the course of my interviews with the former *yoins*, or UN soldiers, I had a hard time differentiating the two words as they used them interchangeably.

54. C. Amador file, PCP, UPFS, which stated: "I applied as private of the Kashima (*sic*) Butai in Oct. 1944." For recruitment of university students, see Supreme Commander for Allied Powers, Box 1940, RG 331, NARA..

55. Other auxiliary forces included the Pambansang Pagkakaisa ng mga Anak ni Rizal (National Unity of the Children of Rizal or Pampar) in Laguna and Rizal Provinces; Shin'nichi Tai (the Pro-Japanese Unit) in Nueva Ecija; the Kaigun Jiyutai (Navy Free Unit) in Zamboanga; and Standing Army in Negros Occidental. See J. Yakan file, no. 284-6, M. Dizon file, no. 98-7; C. Pillas file, no. 266-7, PCP, UPFS. Some of the Kaigun Jiyutai members were sent to Manila for further training. Interview with a former member (name withheld), in Zamboanga City, on 23 November 1998.

56. *The Tribune*, 1 November and 21 December 1944, and 28 January 1945. By the end of 1944, the number of escapees had significantly increased. See A. V. H. Hartendorp, *Japanese Occupation of the Philippines* 2 (Manila: Bookmark, 1967), 2:379fn; Ricardo T. Jose, *Captive Arms: The Constabulary under the Japanese, 1942–1944*, Professorial Chair Paper Series no. 97-5, College of Social Sciences and Philosophy (Quezon City: College of Social Sciences and Philosophy, University of the Philippines, Diliman, 1997), 95–97. In November 1944, the authorities attempted to organize armed units based in each barrio (village) to do the police work, with the intention of suppressing anti-Japanese activities. These units were called the Home Guards, but not much actual activity was seen.

57. For instance, on Pres. Laurel's efforts, see Ricardo T. Jose, "Test of Wills: Diplomacy between Japan and the Laurel Government," in *Philippine-Japan Relations*, ed. Setsuho Ikehata, and Lydia N. Yu Jose (Quezon City: Ateneo de Manila University Press, 2003), 185–222. For the Filipino writers and artists' efforts to utilize the situation, see Motoe Terami-Wada, "Cultural Front in the Philippines, 1942–1945: Japanese Propaganda and Filipino Resistance in Mass Media" (MA thesis, University of the Philippines, 1984).

58. On Ricarte's return to the Philippines, see *The Tribune*, 4 April 1944. For more details on coup d'états and assassination plans, see Ikehata, "Firipin ni Okeru," 55–60. Also see Ohta, "Kikoku," 150.

59. *The Tribune*, 23 and 24 September, and 22 October 1944.

60. Major Gen. Suzuki had been advocating the use of Ganapistas and Muslims in the Japanese war effort. See Koreshige Inuzuka, "Hito ni Okeru Dai 31 Keibitai no Sakusen," 80–88, NIDS.

61. Inuzuka, "Hito no Jihei to Sono Taisaku," (Problems of the Philippines

and Its Counter Measure) July 1944, attached to Inuzuka, "Hito ni okeru." Inuzuka once approached Pres. Laurel about having Ramos appointed as Sec. of the Interior. Laurel had Teofilo Sison in mind for that post and Ramos was to be a member of the Commission on Social Policy Research. See Murata, *Murata Diary*, 94 and 103.

62. For details on the New Philippine Cultural Institute, see Motoe Terami-Wada, "Lt. Shigenobu Mochizuki and the New Philippine Cultural Institute," *Journal of Southeast Asian Studies* 27, no. 1 (March, 1996): 104–23. The supporters' names can be culled from Tokubetsu Kosakutai Meibo, (List of the members attached to the Special Operation Unit) in Takashi Iwamura, *Makapiri Aika* (A Makapili Elegy) (Kobe: privately published, n.d.) 27–28. A part of this book can be found at http://www.h3.dion.ne.jp/~ya.ike/makapili-1-3.htm. This information was brought to my attention by Dr. Satoshi Ara of Fukushima University.

63. The assassination on Laurel's life was planned around March 1944. In July, an attempt was made on Ambassador Murata's life. See Motoe Terami-Wada, "The Filipino Volunteer Armies," 74–78. Claro M. Recto heard a rumor that if Ramos weren't appointed to an important position in the government, some Japanese Army and Navy officers would carry out a coup d'état. See *Murata Diary*, 33. See also the letter written by Takashi Hayashi, a Kenpeitai member, to Iwamura, dated 20 February 1990, in Takashi Iwamura, *Ruson no Sen'yu wa Ima Izuko?* (Where are the Fellow Soldiers Who Fought in Luzon?) (Kobe: privately published, n.d.), n.p. See also interview with Hayashi. L. E. L. Sluimers in his paper, "Samurai, Pemuda und Sakdalista: Die Japaner Und Der Radikalismus in Indonesien und den Philippinen 1941–1945" (Samurai, Pemuda, and Sakdalista: Japan and Radicalism in Indonesia and in the Philippines, 1941–1945) (unpublished paper, 1972), discusses the split within the military on whether to support the "pro-Japanese" Filipinos or prewar Nacionalista politicians along the lines recommended by the *Kodoha* (Imperial Way Faction), an ultranationalist faction that wanted to bring about a revolution and its opponent, *Toseiha* (Control Faction). However, in the Japanese Army in the Philippines, this matter was not so simplistic and could not be separated along these lines.

64. A. V. H. Hartendorp, *The Japanese Occupation of the Philippines* 2, 2:610fn4. Andres Villanueva was a former Cavite Katipunero. See "Christmas Eve Fiasco,"174. See also Ileto, *Pasyon and Revolution*, 213. Leon Villafuerte fought with Sakay and later organized the military group called Magtanggol, mentioned in chap. 7. See also Ileto, *Pasyon and Revolution*, 240fn9.

65. For more details on Alvero, see Grant K. Goodman, "Aurelio Alvero: Traitor or Patriot?" *Journal of Southeast Asian Studies* 27 (March 1996): 95–103. See also Motoe Terami-Wada, "Filipino Volunteer Armies," 86–94. For Alvero's

running for the Municipal Board, see *The Philippines Herald*, 11 December 1937, and 5 December 1940.

66. Hayashi's letter, dated 20 February 1990. Takahide Sato letter, dated 12 December 1979, in Iwamura, "Ruson no Sen'yu," 23; Teodoro Agoncillo, *The Fateful Years*, 831–33. For the names of those Filipinos who attended the meeting, see Hartendorp, *The Japanese Occupation of the Philippines*, 2:610. For information on Baluyot, see Jose Baluyot file, no. 35, PCP, UPFS. It is not known how deeply Captain Inuzuka was involved in the formation of the Makapili. Since his name does not appear in the list of the Tokubetsu Kosakutai (the Special Operation Unit), it is assumed he had left the Philippines by then.

67. For more details on the Pact, see Ricardo T. Jose, "Test of Wills," 210–11. President Laurel proclaimed in September 1944 that the Republic had but one course to pursue, to render every aid and assistance to the Japanese government, "short of conscription of Filipino manhood for active military service."

68. "Articles of Association of the Kalipunang Makabayan ng mga Pilipino" and "By-laws of the Kalipunang Makabayan ng mga Pilipino" are found in Felix Lopez file, no. 179-15, PCP, UPFS.

69. The members included twelve officers, nineteen noncommissioned officers, seventeen soldiers, and thirty-three civilian draftees. See Tokubetsu Kosakutai Meibo, (List of Special Operation Unit) in Takashi Iwamura, *Makapiri*, 27–28.

70. Interviews with Hiroshi Arita, on 9 February 1991, in Sanda City, Hyogo, and Takuya Maeda on 6 August 1991, in Himeji City, Hyogo. Maeda shed light on the military members of the unit.

71. Letter from Junsuke Hitomi, the former officer of the Department of Information, to Motoe Terami-Wada, dated 20 December 1990.

72. The unit's duties also included such activities as distributing food, clothing, and cosmetics in an attempt to win the Filipinos over since these items had become extremely scarce. See Hayashi's letter; see also Felix Lopez file, no. 179-15, PCP, UPFS. For contact with the Huks, see Takahide Sato's letter in Iwamura, *Ruson no Sen'yu*, 26.

73. Hayashi's letter to Iwamura. Koji Nakamura, the *Mainichi* newspaper correspondent sent to the Philippines, states the number of trainers to be several thousands. See "Hiripin Seifu no Yokogao," (Profile of the Philippine Government) in *Hiroku Daitoa shi: Hito Hen*, (Secret Record of the Great East Asian History: The Philippines) ed. Yoshio Tamura (Tokyo: Fuji Shoen, 1953), 87.

74. In Murata's opinion, Ricarte was too simplistic in his thinking and was not particularly intelligent but had courage. He thought Duran had brains but no

courage. As for Ramos, he had neither and was too "shabby" to be appointed to a government post. See *Murata Diary*, 243–44, 278, and 280.

75. Kaneshiro Ohta, *Hito Dokuritsu no Shishi, Rikarute Shogun Shouden* (A Short Biography of Gen. Ricarte, Zealous Fighter for the Philippine Independence) (Tokyo: Firipin Tomono-kai, 1953), 30. However, Theodore Friends says that Ramos was the one who proposed a coup d'état against the Laurel government, replacing all the cabinet members except Laurel. Yamashita's Chief of Staff, Muto, liked this idea. See Theodore Friend, *Between Two Empires*, 244. I place more credibility on Ohta's account because he was present when the possible coup d'état using the Makapilis was discussed. See also Ikehata, "Firipin ni Okeru," 59.

76. *Murata Diary*, 278–313. Laurel was not against the formation of such a volunteer army. He later donated some money to Ricarte's volunteer army. For details, see Motoe Terami-Wada, "Filipino Volunteer Armies," 79–86.

77. Meeting with Murata, see *Murata Diary*, 266 and 280. On 23 November, Gen. Yamashita met with the three. See *The Tribune*, 7 December 1944.

78. Duran must have been placed in the Laurel cabinet under pressure of the Japanese military after Laurel refused to place either Ramos or Ricarte in his cabinet. See Jose P. Laurel, *War Memoirs of Dr. Jose P. Laurel* (Manila: Jose Laurel Memorial Foundation, 1980), 25. Ricarte felt it was important to place in the government Filipinos who would wholeheartedly collaborate with Japan, instead of the uncooperative members of the Laurel administration. See "Rikarute Shogun wo Kakomu Zadankai (A Round-Table Talk with Gen. Ricarte), "Taihi Senden Joho," (Information on Propaganda for the Philippines) Senden Sanko Shiro Sono 3, (Propaganda Material No. 3) 2 December 1944, in Shobu Shudan Hodobu, (Shobu Group, Department of Information) 8 December 1944, Hito Zenpan 141, NIDS; "Aikoku Doshikai ni Kansuru Kakugi Naiyo," (The Content of the Cabinet Meeting on the Patriotic League) Senden Joho Sokuho dai 41 Go, (Newsflash on Propaganda Information No. 41) 9 December 1944, in Shobu Shudan Hodobu, and 9 December 1944, Hito Zenpan 141, NIDS.

79. *Murata Diary*, 301. See also *War Memoirs of Dr. Jose P. Laurel*, 25.

80. *The Tribune*, 9 and 10 December 1944. According to Laurel, fewer than one hundred attended. See *War Memoirs*, 25. The design of the Makapili flag was taken from the Magdalo faction's flag, which was hoisted in Imus, Cavite, in 1897 before the Naic convention.

81. *The Tribune*, 9 December 1944.

82. Furthermore, Ramos allegedly said that the families and friends of those who had been arrested by the Kenpeitai could contact him for some compensation. He allegedly gave the phone number where he could be reached, and said that he

and the members would do their best to work for the release of those who had been arrested. See *Murata Diary*, 306–7.

83. For Laurel's speech, see *The Tribune*, 9 December 1944. President Laurel's warning to Ramos so impressed some people present that it became a topic of conversation among them after the ceremony. For the impression of the people, see Jose Baluyot, file no. 35-23. PCP, UPFA. See also Claro M. Recto, *Three Years of Enemy Occupation* (Manila: People's Publishers, 1946), 58–59.

84. *Murata Diary*, 306–7.

85. "People vs. Alvero," *Philippine Report: Reports of Cases Decided by the Supreme Court of the Philippines from April 1 to June 30, 1950*, vol. 86 (*Philippine Report*) (Manila: Bureau of Printing, 1958), 76–77. The word "Tagala" comes from Katagalugan but is used to designate the whole Philippines. For the name, see Aurelio Alvero, *A Matter of Nomenclature* (Muntinglupa: [New] Bilibid Prison, 1945), 1–16. For more details on the Bisig Bakal ng Tagala, see Motoe Terami-Wada, "The Filipino Volunteer Armies," 86–89.

86. Ohta, *Kikoku*, 144 and 268. For Laurel's proclamation, see *The Tribune*, 24 September 1944.

87. For Laurel's donation, see C. Lazaro file, no. 175-7, PCP, UPFA. Civilian donors included F. C. de la Rama, who became a millionaire through shady dealings with the Japanese military. He donated P12,000,000. See Ohta, *Kikoku*, 160.

88. For Ricarte's broadcast, see *The Tribune*, 26 November 1944. During the Japanese Occupation, Ricarte wrote a booklet to encourage the youth to selflessly dedicate themselves to the cause of independence. See *Sa mga Kabataan Filipino* (n.p., n.d.).

89. N. Lapuz file, no. 178-5; B. Honor file, no. 150-11, PCP, UPFA. For more details on the Peace Army, see Motoe Terami-Wada, "The Filipino Volunteer Armies," 89–90.

90. In 1912, Zialcita unsuccessfully ran for the Assembly from the north district of Manila. See "Confidential Report," dated 10 January 1910, 23 October 1910, and 28 May 1912, PCR. In some of the prosecution papers of the People's Court Trial, the following description can be read: "The Peace Army, also called 'Makapili'...."

91. Ricarte sent Christmas and New Year's greetings to Sakdalista members in late 1933. See "Ang Bati ng Ating General," *Sakdal*, 6 June 1934, 1.

92. For Ricarte's letters, see 28 March, 3; 1 August, 4; 19 September, 3; 5 December, 1; and 12 December 1931, 1, all in *Sakdal*.

93. "Lahat ng Walang Dangal at Taksil sa Bayan ay Kalaban ng mga Sakdalista," *Sakdal*, 26 January 1935, 1.

94. *The Tribune*, 21 May 1935.

95. *The Tribune,* 14 December 1935. Ricarte also accused Ramos of spending the contribution on his family, who had joined him in Tokyo in January 1935. His wife joined him in Japan mainly to receive treatment for her illness. She came from a family of some means, and her family contributed to some of the expenses when the Sakdalista Party purchased the printing machine. It seems that Ramos's wife's family could well afford the travel as well as the medical expenses. Ramos-Uyboco interview. See also *Japanese Police Reports* 2 (1936): 374. Ricarte's accusation of Ramos reminds us of the one he made against Makario Sakay, calling him a common bandit and cattle thief. For details, see "Christmas Eve Fiasco," in *Memoirs of General Ricarte*, 185.

96. Goodman, "General Artemio Ricarte," 55–56 and 59.

97. About Ramos's living in a small apartment, see *Japanese Police Reports* 2 (1936): 374. Information on Ramos's living on a Shinto shrine grounds came from Prof. Shizuo Suzuki. On Ramos's sickness, see "May Karamdaman si Ramos," *Sakdal*, 6 June 1936, 1. Salud Algabre pleaded with the members to remember Ramos and support his efforts. See "Nangungusap si Gng. S. Algabre," *Sakdal*, 25 July 1936, 4.

98. "Sagot ng 'Ama ng Sakdal' sa mga Tuligsa ni Artemio Ricarte," *Sakdal*, 29 June 1935, 1. This article was originally written in English and appeared in *The Filipino Freedom*, in the June 24 issue, which was translated into Tagalog for the *Sakdal*.

99. Jose P. Santos, ed., *Mga Liham ni Heneral Artemio Ricarte kay Jose P. Santos, 1935*, in Satoshi Ara, "Firipin no Rikarute Shogun ni Kansuru Ichi Kosatsu" (A Study of Gen. Ricarte of the Philippines), *Kokusai Seiji*, no. 120 (February 1999): 215.

100. Theodore Friend, *Between Two Empires*, 119–20.

101. Satoshi Ara, "Firipin no Rikarute Shogun," 217.

102. Ara, "Filipino no Rikarute Shogun," 215–16. By 1935, Ricarte acknowledged the improvements the U.S. had introduced in the Philippines and was thankful for the American promise of independence. See Ma. Luisa D. Fleetwood, *General Artemio Ricarte* (Vibora) (Manila: National Historical Institute, 1997), 11.

103. *Murata Diary*, 370.

104. Friend, *Between Two Empires*, 214–15. For more on the Japanese military's plan for Ricarte, see Ohta, *Kikoku*, 118. See also Setsuho Ikehata "Filipin ni Okeru," 45. For Ricarte's words to Aguinaldo, see Armando J. Malay, "Introduction," in Artemio Ricarte, *Memoirs of General Artemio Ricarte*, xxiii.

105. Ara, "Firipin no Rikarute Shogun," 219.

106. For Makapili activities and numbers, see Takuya Maeda, letter dated 15 April 1990, in Iwamura, *Ruson*, 68–69, and my interview with Maeda. See also Shinsaku Hoshina, *Rakurui Sensen: Hito no Omoide* (Heartbreaking Operation: Memories of the Philippines) (Tokyo: privately published, n.d), 35–43; Kota Wada, *Jagaimo Jinsei* (Potato Life) (Tokyo: privately published, 1986), 54–67. See also P. de la Cruz file, no. 83-12, PCP, UPFS.

107. Tagalog original: Katipunang Makabayan ng mga Pilipino/Kawal kami, kawal tayo/Mga Lahing Asiatiko/Ang diwang bago/Makapili ang tanggulan ng mga anak ng bayan/Ang hirap ay maparam/Kasunod ay kasaganaan at kaunlaran. Interview with Cayetano Zurbano on 12 August 1985 in Santa Rosa, Laguna. There seem to be different Makapili songs in different areas.

108. Atsuo Yajima, "Gapan no Omoide, (Recollections of Gapan)" in *Hi to Tsuchi to*, (Sun and Earth) ed. Hi to Tsuchi to Editorial Board (Tokyo: privately published, 1974), 196–236. Interview with Atsuo Yajima, on 23 July 1984, at his residence in Nishinomiya City, Japan. See also Takahide Sato's letter in Iwamura, *Ruson no Sen'yu*, 26.

109. Capadocia, "Note which may be used," 16.

110. Nakamura estimates several thousands. See Koji Nakamura, "Hiripin Seifu no Yokogao," 87. Also see interview with Nakamura on 5 July 1982, in Tokyo, Japan. Hartendorp estimates not more than five thousand. See A. V. H. Hartendorp, *The Japanese Occupation of the Philippines*, 2:610. In Tayabas alone, three thousand Ganapistas, some of whom were the Makapili, and their families were evacuated to the mountains by the Japanese. Iwamura, *Makapiri Aika*, 36.

111. For the Luzon Defense Operation Plan, see *Senshi Sosho: Rikugun Sogo Sakusen 2, Russon Kessen* (War History Series, "Sho" [Victory] Army Operation 2: The Decisive Battle of Luzon) (Tokyo: Asagumo Shuppansha, 1972), 1–31. For the Makapili's fights, see *The Tribune*, 7, 30, and 31 January 1945. See also Yoshiro Akinaga, *Hito Kobo-sen* (Defense War in the Philippines) (Tokyo: Masu Shobo, 1956), 159; Yuzuru Kojima, *Manira Kaigun Rikusen tai* (Manila Navy Landing Party) (Tokyo: Shincho-sha, 1970), 94–95.

112. N. Estrada file, no. 112-6 and C. Campomanes file, no. 61-5; F. Ordoño file, no. 206-3, PCP.

113. For instance, Dionisio Macapagal of Barrio Buga in San Miguel, Bulacan, had been a staunch Sakdalista-turned-Ganapista. Most Ganapistas in his town did not collaborate with the Japanese military. Fegan, *Dionisio Makapagal*, 356–57.

114. Hernando J. Abaya, *Betrayal in the Philippines* (Quezon City: Malaya Books Inc. 1970), 57.

115. Fegan, "The Social History," 112 and 116. The Ganapistas who joined the party in the prewar time all testified during the interviews that they never became hooded informers although they had acted as informers of known anti-Japanese guerrillas.

116. Ramos's exact words to Adia were, "Mayroon na kayong sariling ladaw. Hayaan ninyo ang iba ang sumama" (You already have your own identification card. Let others join instead.) Interview with Adia on 28 March 1989, in Cabuyao, Laguna. When Ramos and his family retreated to the mountain area in northern Luzon, he was heard to have said, "The Japanese military has used me and now it has forsaken me. Gen. Honma said that the Philippines was for the Filipinos..." By this time he was disgusted with the Japanese. See Ohta, *Kikoku*, 168–69.

117. The number of Makapili and their families increased fourfold in a few months. Interview with Takashi Hayashi who claims it was called "Quezon University" instead of "Christ the King Seminary."

118. Algabre in turn received orders from Antonio Velisario, a former Sakdalista Party president. A ration of rice was given to them by the Japanese military. See Salud Generalla Algabre File, no. 133, PCP. Algabre said there were only sixty of them. Hayashi, who assigned the Ganapistas to Barrio San Jose, claimed there were seven to eight hundred in the beginning. See Hayashi interview. See also Iwamura, *Ruson no Sen'yu*, 71.

119. The mountains in which they took refuge were Taytay, Antipolo, Santa Inez, and Ipo. Iwamura interview on 6 August 1991, in Kobe City, Japan, and some memoirs by the Japanese soldiers, which are too numerous to cite here.

120. For the Japanese doctor's narrative, see Tadashi Moriya, *Hiripin Sensen no Ningen Gunzo* (A Group of People at the Battlefront in the Philippines) (Tokyo: Keiso Shobo, 1977), 76–91. On the Pamatmat family, see interview with Mary Pamatmat, on 9 September 1997, in Quezon City, Metro Manila. Some wandering Japanese soldiers near Mount Banahaw were cared for by the Ganapistas. See Tadahiko Obo, *Ah, Kusamakura: Hito sensen no shito* (Ah, Bivouac: Fight to the Death at the War Front in the Philippines) (Tokyo: Geibundo 1995), 236–38.

121. Isao Ishida, *Ruson no Kiri* (Fog of Luzon) (Tokyo: Asahi Shinbunsha, 1971), 183–84. See also Shin'ichi Ose's, letter to me, dated 11 November 1992. Ose gave military training to the Makapili and retreated to the mountains with them. He also described the Makapili's disappointment.

122. On Ramos's death, see my interview with Ramos-Uyboco. Ramos's possible execution is my supposition, based on a war memoir, an interview with Mikio Matsunobe, former Kenpeitai, and testimony from Minviluz Dominguez. Interview with Mikio Matsunobu on 3 July 1982 in Kawasaki City, Japan. For the

massacre of the Ricarte clan, see also Ohta, *Kikoku*, 245. For execution of the Ganap members, see Sachiko Ohmori, *Death Valley* (Ohita: privately published, 1996), 38. Around the mid-1980s, a man who claimed to be Benigno Ramos showed up at one of Ramos's sisters' residences in Bulacan. By this time, all of Ramos's sisters and brothers had passed away, and their children, Ramos's nieces and nephews, had never met their uncle. Although Ramos's death was still not certain, as the family had not seen the remains, they gave the benefit of the doubt to this man. Every time he paid a visit, the family gave him some money. Even Ramos's daughter, Leticia, was not sure if he was her father. In July 1987, the late Prof. Shizuo Suzuki, the late Mr. Jeremias Adia, the former Ganap Party official, and I paid a visit to this man who lived on Bosoboso Mountain in Rizal province. Ramos's nephew was our guide. This man looked much younger than ninety years old (the age Ramos would have been at that time). Since what he told us did not match historical facts, we concluded that he was an imposter.

123. One of the graduates of the New Philippine Cultural Institute in Tagaytay told me that he was impressed by Lt. Mochizuki because he had said that after the Philippines obtained independence, they should fight even against Japan if she decided to invade. See interview in Terami-Wada, "Lt. Shigenobu Mochizuki and the New Philippine Cultural Institute," 121.

124. For the reasons they fought to the end, see F. Española file, no. 110-10; A. Adriano file, no. 3-12; N. Estrada file, no. 112-6; C. Campomanes file, no. 61-5; and F. Ordoño file, no. 206-3, all in PCP, UPFA. See also Motoe Terami-Wada, "The Filipino Volunteer Armies," 85–86.

# Chapter 9

1. David Joel Steinberg, *Philippine Collaboration in World War II* (Ann Arbor: The University of Michigan Press, 1967), 108–9 and 200fn23.

2. U.S. pressure was seen in the directive sent by Harold Ickis, Sec. of the Interior, in September. See *The Manila Times*, 14 September 1945. For the full text of his directive, see Hernando J. Abaya, *Betrayal in the Philippines* (Quezon City: Malaya Books Inc., 1970), 116–17. For different policies toward the collaboration issue within the U.S. government, including Gen. MacArthur, see Satoshi Nakano, "Firipin no Tainichi Kyoroku Mondai to Amerika Gasshukok" (The Japanese Collaboration Issue in the Philippines and the U.S.A. *Rekishigaku Kenkyu*, no. 600 (November 1989): 57–67.

3. The fifteen judges were not appointed immediately. Some divisions, such as the first and the fifth divisions, had only two judges for quite some time and

they were reshuffled constantly among the five divisions. See Ma. Felisa Sijuco Tan, "Settling the Score: The Court Trials of the Filipino Informers and Paramilitary Collaborators (1945–1952)" (PhD diss., University of the Philippines, 2009), 266–79. The estimation that one-third of the accused were the Ganap members is based on my research reviewing approximately 2,400cases out of around 4,000 available records of the People's Court housed in the University of the Philippines.

4. Recto and de las Alas paid P30,000 and P20,000, respectively. On the trial, see Steinberg, *Philippine Collaboration in World War II*, 147–63; Nakano, "Firipin no Tainichi Kyoroku," 57–67. At the start, news of the People's Court trial cases appeared almost every day in the dailies in Manila. For instance, see *The Manila Times*, September 1945 to January 1948.

5. On Alvero, see A. Alvero file, no. 16-4, PCP, UPFS. He was charged on twenty-two counts, including economic, political, and military collaborations. See *Report of Cases Decided by the Supreme Court of the Philippines from April 1 to June 30, 1950*, vol. 86 (Manila: Bureau of Printing, 1953), 59–103. On Duran, see Tan, "Settling the Score," 219. For the special trial for the Makapili, see "Settling the Score," 266–79. The Borong-Borong Makapilis were tried in the Pasig court. It seems that they were criminal elements who had joined the Makapili to take advantage of the situation.

6. *Free Philippines*, 15 and 22 September 1945, 2 and 6 February, and 20 July 1946.

7. Steinberg, *Philippine Collaboration in World War II*, 147–63; Nakano, "Firipin no Tainichi Kyoryoku Mondai," 57–67. The army also tried the military collaborators as war criminals. The collaborators included Makapilis, Ganapistas, members of Kaigun Jiutai, Pampar, Shin'nich-tai, and Bisig Bakal ng Tagala. For more details, see Tan, "Settling the Score," 48.

8. Those who appealed to higher courts included Aurelio Alvero and Minviluz Dominguez, Ricarte's granddaughter. Alvero served only a little over four years of his life sentence. Interview with Lucila A. Salazar (Mrs. Aurelio Alvero), on 9 December 1992, in Quezon City, Metro Manila. For more trial results, see the *Official Gazettes* of the Commonwealth of the Philippines as well as of the Republic of the Philippines.

9. The soldiers from India, Burma, and Indonesia, who fought with the Japanese against their colonial powers, such as the British and Dutch, had totally different treatment by their fellow countrymen.

10. According to Luis Taruc, the former commander of the National Liberation Army (Hukbong Magpapalaya ng Bayan), it was easy to recruit former

Ganapistas to his organization after the war. Interview with Taruc on 22 August 1986, in Quezon City, Metro Manila.

11. The names of some of those who founded the Iglesia often appeared in the pages of the *Sakdal* and *Ganap* newspapers published in the1930s and 1940s, such as Bonifacio Villareal and Miguel Adan.

12. The background of Iglesia is based on the following material made available to me by an Iglesia member. Bonifacio P. Villareal, "Ang Kasaysayan ng Pagkatatag ng Sagrada ng Lahi sa Quezon" (History of Establishing the Church of Sacred Race in Quezon) (typescript, n.d.), in *Salaysay ni G. Olimpia Parafina (95 ang edad)* (An Account of Mrs. Olimpia Parafina [95 years old]). Still today, when the members attend services at this church, they carry a sacred book, entitled *Narito Na Ako* (I Am Here) which traces the history of the Malay people to 400,000 B.C., just like the Old Testament on the history of the Hebrews. *Narito Na Ako* was made available to me by Mr. Adia. Placedo Bronto, ed. Anastacio Naval, *Narito Na Ako: Mga Bagay na Dapat Nating Malaman* (I am Here: What We Should Know) (Manila [?]: Juan P. Omega, n.d.).

13. According to Adia, his maternal uncle, Ladislao Luna, who fought in both the 1896 Revolution and the Philippine-American War, was imprisoned with Gen. Ricarte by the Americans and died in prison. Interview with Adia on 20 April 1985 in Cabuyao, Laguna.

14. For Constantino Adia as one of the founders, see Marasigan, *Banahaw Guru*, 78.

15. J. Adia file, no. 3-6. PCP, UPFS.

16. William J. Pomeroy, *The Philippines: Colonialism, Collaboration, and Resistance!* (New York: International Publishers, 1992), 197.

17. Others arrested included Mariano P. Balgos of the Communist Party. See the *Manila Daily Mirror*, 28 March 1951, and interview with Adia on 27 November 1985, in Cabuyao, Laguna. If there had been no military intrusion, a united front of the sort between the former Ganapistas and the Communists could have been possible. Balgos's father was a Ricartista, and Balgos himself used to be a member of IFI and the Tanggulan Society. Information on Balgos and Luis Taruc's involvement with the Sakdalista movement came from an interview with Taruc on 22 August 1986, in Quezon City, Metro Manila. See also his autobiography, *Born of the People* (New York: International Publishers, 1953), 29. Many overlapping affiliations existed between the Ganapistas and the Communists, hence similar sentiments. In view of this, it was not hard for the Communists to work with former Ganapistas.

18. The following observation is based on my visits to the Iglesia Sagrada ng Lahi churches in Silang, Cavite, and Atimonan, Quezon, during the period 1985–1987.

19. Another statue of Mary in Silang has two knives penetrating her heart. These knives symbolize the two foreign colonial powers that dominated the Philippines. In the church in Atimonan, the altar has no statues of the Tatlong Persona, or of the Holy Family. Instead, there is a bust of Jose Rizal wrapped in a white cloth and placed on a hollowed-out piece of wood. At the bottom are seven framed pictures of the '96 revolutionary heroes and the image of Inang Bayan. The description of the churches and their activities are based on my observations in Silang as well as in Atimonan.

20. On the IFI interior, see James Allen, *The Radical Left*, 20. On Rizalista cults, see Marcelino A. Foronda, "The Canonization of Rizal," *The Journal of History*, VIII 2 (1960): 95–137; and Foronda, *The Cults Honoring Rizal* (Manila: R. P. Garcia, 1961); see also Michael M. Gonzales, "The Edge of Structures."

21. For the recitation of the Colorums, see Artemio Ricarte, *Memoirs of General Artemio Ricarte*, 83. On the Colorums, see Santiago Alvarez, *The Katipunan and the Revolution: Memoirs of a General* (Quezon City: Ateneo de Manila University Press, 1992), 207–10. See also Reynaldo C. Ileto, *Pasyon and Revolution*, 205–6; and Setsuho Ikehata, *Firipin Kakumei to Katorishizumu* (The Philippine Revolution and Catholicism) (Tokyo: Keiso Shobo, 1987), 241–43. Dennis Shoesmith, who studied the Rizalista cults in Bukidnon, Mindanao, states that they share much of the organizational character, beliefs, and religious practices with the Colorums. For details, see Dennis Shoesmith, "The Glorious Religion of Jose Rizal: Radical Consciousness in a Contemporary Folk Religious Movement in the Southern Philippines," in *Peasant and Politics: Grassroots Reaction to Change in Asia*, ed. D. B. Miller (Melbourne: Edward Arnold pty. ltd., 1978), 149–79.

22. For more on the Iglesia, see Motoe Terami-Wada, "Iglesia Sagrada ng Lahi: Upholding the Unfinished Revolution," in *The Philippine Revolution and Beyond* 2, ed. Elmer A. Ordoñez (Manila: Philippine Centennial Commission; National Commission For Culture and the Arts, 1998), 641–51.

23. "An Interview with Salud Algabre," in Sturtevant, *Popular Uprisings*, 298–99.

24. Information on the other name of Lapiang Malaya came from David Sturtevant, "Rizalistas—Contemporary Revitalization Movements in the Philippines," in *Agrarian Unrest in the Philippines*, ed. David Sturtevant (Athens, Ohio: Ohio University Center for International Studies, 1969), 18. On the Lapiang Malaya, see Elizabeth A. Pastores, "Religious Leadership in the Lapiang Malaya:

A Historical Note," in *Filipino Religious Psychology*, ed. Leonardo N. Mercado (Tacloban City: Divine Word University, 1977), 149–58.

25. For the demonstration of 1966, see Sturtevant, *Popular Uprisings in the Philippines*, 258. The massacre incident gave an impact to writers like Ricardo Lee who wrote a short story based on this incident, depicting the discrepancy between the rich and the poor in Philippine society. See "Si Tatang, si Freddie, si Tandang Senyong, at iba pang mga Tauhan ng Aking Kuwento" (Tatang, Freddie, Old man Senyo, and Other Characters of My Story), in *Asia Leader Magazine*, 8 October 1971.

26. After the incident, constabulary reports flowed in stating that in the provinces of Quezon, Laguna, Cavite, Batangas, Camarines Sur and Norte, Albay, and Sorsogon, Lapian members had been regrouping for an alleged vendetta. They had been preparing to go to Manila to free their fellow members from the constabulary. The authorities also uncovered the existence of a women's auxiliary corps of the Lapian army in a barrio in Pampanga. See "The Fanatic," 3 June 1967, 7–8; "Tatang and the Lapiang Malaya," 8 June 1967, 1, 8, and 91, both in the *Philippines Free Press*. See also *The Philippines Herald*, 27, 28, 29, and 30 May 1967; the *Manila Daily Bulletin*, 26 May 1967.

27. V. (de los) Santos file, no. 247-34, PCP, UPFS. At one time, he was with Matsuyama Butai. Interview with Adia on 24 April 1987, in Cabuayo, Laguna.

28. For the definition, see Marcelino A. Foronda, "Cults Honoring Rizal," 47. Foronda quotes the *Catholic Concise Dictionary*.

29. Gonzales, "The Edge of Structures," 147, 246–59, and 279; Floro Quibuyen, *And Woman Will Prevail Over Man: Symbolic Sexual Inversion and Counter-Hegemonic Discourse in Mt. Banahaw*, *The Case of the Ciudad Mistica de Dios*, Philippine Studies Occasional Paper No. 10 (Honolulu: Center for Philippine Studies, 1991), 9; and Consolacion R. Alaras, "Pamathalaan," in *The Filipino Spiritual Culture Series 1*, ed. Teresita B. Obusan and Angelina Enriquez (Manila: Mamamathala, Inc., 1994), 69–70.

30. Prospero R. Covar, "General Characterization of Contemporary Religious Movements in the Philippines," *Asian Studies* 13, no. 2 (August 1975): 79–92. We can also add *korido*, *awit*, and *komedya*, which often contain moral lessons and ethical teachings. See also Covar, "Potensiya, Bisa, at Anting-anting," *Asian Studies* 18 (April, August, and December 1980): 71–78.

31. Leonardo Mercado states that Christian teachings, or folk Catholicism, of the Philippines is "the pre-Spanish Philippines (spiritual practices) continuing in the guise of Christianity," Leonardo N. Mercado, SVD, *Christ in the Philippines* (Tacloban City: Divine Word University Publications, 1982), 7. Quite a few other studies support his contention, including F. Landa Jocano, *Folk Christianity*

(Quezon City: Trinity Research Institute, 1981); and Jose M. de Mesa, "Holy Week and Popular Devotion," in *Morality, Religion and the Filipino*, 221, to name a few. O. W. Wolters uses the term "localization" for the phenomenon. See O. W. Wolters, *History, Culture, and Religion in Southeast Asian Perspectives* (Ithaca, NY: Southeast Asia Program, Cornell University, 1999), 55 and 223. The skillful Philippine "localization" was persuasively narrated in Ileto's *Pasyon and Revolution*. See also Vicente Rafael, *Contracting Colonialism* (Quezon City: Ateneo de Manila University Press, 1988). Mobilization of local belief systems to combat colonial power can be found throughout Southeast Asia where foreign colonial powers dominated. See Reynaldo C. Ileto, "Religion and Anti-Colonial Movements," in *The Cambridge History of Southeast Asia* 2, ed. Nicholas Tarling (Cambridge: Cambridge University Press, 1992), 2:197–248.

32. Ileto, "Rizal and the Underside of Philippine History," 323; Floro C. Quibuyen, *A Nation Aborted: Rizal, American Hegemony, and Philippine Nationalism* (Quezon City: Ateneo de Manila University Press, 1999), 281–84. (I quoted the 1999 version here as it was commented on by Schumacher.) For Schumacher's comment, see John N. Schumacher, S.J., "Rizal and Filipino Nationalism: A New Approach," *Philippine Studies* 48 (4th Quarter, 2000): 562.

33. Quibuyen, *A Nation Aborted* (Quezon City: Ateneo de Manila University Press, 2008), 343.

34. Schumacher, S.J., gives an example of how in 1899 the people of Bicol had been inspired to support the anti-American struggle upon hearing about Rizal's life. See Schumacher, "Rizal and Filipino Nationalism," 563. See also Quibuyen, *A Nation Aborted* (1999), 63–64.

35. For Ileto's words, see "Rizal and the Underside of Philippine History," 323. The Tatlong Persona group considered Rizal to be a human being although special veneration was given to him for his sacrifice. See Marasigan, S.J., "Banahaw Guru," 20. The IFI eventually decanonized Rizal. See Foronda, "Cults," 48.

## Epilogue

1. Alfred McCoy, *Policing America's Empire*, 126–205.

2. For Agoncillo's statement, see Ch. 2. With Americanization came the opportunity for large numbers of Filipinos to immigrate to the U.S., and yet some of them enthusiastically welcomed Ramos on his visit to the U.S. and supported the Sakdalista movement. Perhaps their aspirations for independence became even stronger when they experienced racial discrimination in their adopted country.

3. For Sakdalistas' criticism of the U.S., see "Ang Roma ng mga Caesar

Kahapon ay Siya Namang Amerika Ngayon," 27 December 1930, 1; "Sa Panahon ng Mabunying Dukha," 2 January 1932, 3; "Simulain ng Sakdal," 12 January 1935, 2; "Sariling Diwa," 22 April 1933, 2; "Hindi Bawal ang Bastos na Pelikula," 23 July 1932, 4; "Hindi Naparito ang America laban sa mga Pilipino," 16 March 1935, 1; and "Slavery under the Guise of Liberty," 1 September 1934, 1, all in *Sakdal*. Ramos had compared the U.S. to Rome in antiquity in that it was an oppressive imperialistic and capitalistic country. Brutality committed during the Watsonville racial conflict and vulgar aspects of American culture were noted. For their appreciation of the U.S., see the Sakdalista Party platform. It stated that the U.S. had good intentions in the Philippines and the Sakdalistas appreciated the American colonial government for having taught the Filipinos the elements of self-governance and that these principles should be followed for the good of the people, for without them the cause of independence would be in vain. Some may say that this was nothing but diplomatic rhetoric.

4. Resil B. Mojares, "Guillermo Tolentino's *Grupo de Filipinos Ilustre* and the Making of National Pantheon," *Philippine Studies* 58, nos. 1–2 (June 2010): 179.

5. Reynaldo Ileto, "The Wars with the United States and Japan in the Making of Post-1946 Philippine Politics," *Proceedings of the Symposium: The Philippine-Japan Relationship in an Evolving Paradigm* (Manila: Yuchengco Center, 2006), 100–101. On the effect of the education system, see Bienvenido Lumbera, "From Colonizer to Liberator: How U.S. Colonialism Succeeded in Reinventing Itself after the Pacific War," in *Vestiges of War: The Philippine-American War and the Aftermath of an Imperial Dream, 1899–1999*, ed. Angel Velasco Shaw and Luis H. Francia (New York: New York University Press, 2002), 202.

6. The image of the precolonial period as "paradise lost" was inherited from the Katipunan era, which had roots in Rizal's annotation of *Sucesos de las Islas Filipinas*. For more details, see the conference pamphlet, "Unang Pagtitipon Espirituwal ng Kapatiran Pilipinas," (The First Spiritual Forum of the Philippine Brotherhood) n.p., 30 December 1985. On the conference, see *Times Journal*, 26 January 1986.

## Appendices

1. "Tumututol Kami," Pamahayag, n.p.
2. "Mga Layunin," Pamahayag, 8–18.
3. Partido "Ganap" de Filipinas (Manila: 1938), 1–4.

# BIBLIOGRAPHY

**Manuscript Collections**

Boeicho Boei Kenkyujo Senshishitsu (Defense Agency, National Institute for Defense Studies, Office of Military History), Tokyo.
    Hito Boei (The Philippine Defense), 3.
    Hito Zenpan (The Philippines General), 78, 141.
    Itaku (Entrusted) 26 (not opened to the public).
Filipiniana Section, Special Collections, Main Library Archives, University of the Philippines, Quezon City.
    People's Court Papers.
Michigan Historical Collections, Bentley Historical Library, University of Michigan, Ann Arbor, Michigan.
    Harry Hill Bandholtz Papers (HBP).
    Joseph Ralston Hayden Papers.
Military Intelligence Service. Armed Forces of the Philippines, Manila.
    Personal File: Guillermo Capadocia.
Philippine National Archives (PNA), Manila.
    Japanese War Crime Records.
Philippine National Library, Manila.
    Manuel L. Quezon Papers.
    Historical Data Papers, ca. 1950–1953.
    Julian Cruz Balmaseda Collection.

U. S. National Archives and Records Administration in the Washington D. C. area.
    Records of the Bureau of Insular Affairs (BIA). Record Group (RG) 350.
    Genearal Records of the Department of State. RG 59
    Supreme Commander for the Allied Powers. RG 331.


**Documents of the Sakdalista Movement and the Party**

*A Frank, Unequivocal but Respectful Enunciation of the Filipinos' Demand for Real Independence
    Based on the Promises of the American People from the Incipiency of the American Regime
    to the Passage of the Jones Law; Presented by the Sakdalista Delegation to the Hon.
    Secretary of War and the Congressional Delegation of the United States of America on
    November 13th, 1935.* Manila: Sakdalista Party, 1935.
*A Memorial: Lapiang Sakdalista sa Filipinas Directorio Provincial Cavite, Cavite.* Manila: N.p.,
    1937.
*Memorial.* Manila: N.p., Sakdalista Party, 13 November 1935.
*Memorial Sent to the President and Congress of the United States by the Ganap Party of the
    Philippines.* Manila: Ganap Party, 19 May 1940.
*Pamahayag at Patakaran ng Lapiang Sakdalista.* Manila: Sakdalista Party, 29 October 1933.
*Pamahayag at Patakaran ng Samahang Makabayan ng mga Babaing Pilipina.* Manila: Samahang
    Makabayan ng mga Babaing Pilipina, 1937.
*Panawagan sa Lahat ng Lapian at Kababayan ukol sa Paghahanda ng Pansagot sa Kasarinlan
    kung Umalis na ang Estados Unidos.* Manila: Ganap Party, 1939.
*Partido "Ganap" De Filipinas: Manifesto to the People.* Manila: Ganap Party, 1938.
*Sakdalista Memorial: The People of the Philippines for Immediate, Complete, Absolute
    Independence and against the Tydings-McDuffie Law, through the Sakdalista Party.* N.
    p., 23 December 1934.
*The Sakdalista Party of the Philippine Islands to the President and Congress of the United States.*
    Manila: Sakdalista Party, 1937.
*To The Honorable Chairman and Members of the Joint Preparatory Committee on Philippine
    Affairs, This Memorandum is Respectfully Submitted.* Manila: Sakdalista Party, 1937


**Newspapers and Periodicals**

*Agricultural Life*, 1936.
*Alitaptap*, 1930.
*American Chamber of Commerce Journal*, 1935.
*Chicago Cable News*, 1936.
*Chicago Daily News*, 1936.
*Chicago Tribune*, 1936.
*Chronicle Magazine*, 1969.
*Consolidacion Nacional*, 1915.
*Dai Ajia Shugi*, 1936.
*El Ideal*, 1914–1915.
*El Renacimiento Filipino*, 1911–1912.

*Evening Star*, 1935.
*Express* (San Antonio, Texas), 1931.
*Far Eastern Freemason*, 1935.
*The Filipino Freedom*, July 1935, 1937.
*Free Filipinos*, 1 April 1935.
*Ganap*, 1938–1940.
*Hanashi*, 1938.
*Hirang*, 1940–1941.
*Hiripin Joho* (*Philippine Information*), 1937–1942.
*Independent*, 1931.
*Kokusai Panfuretto* (*International Pamphlet*), 1938.
*La Defensa Catolico*, 1930.
*La Opinion*, 1931.
*Literary Digest*, 1931.
*Liwayway*, 1923.
*Manila Daily Bulletin*, 1925, 1930, 1935–1939.
*Manila Daily Mirror*, 1951.
*Monday Mail*, 1935.
*Moto Hito Zairyu Hojin Manira Kai Kaiho* (*Bulletin for the Former Japanese Residents in Manila*), 1983.
*New York Herald*, 1930.
*New York Tribune*, 1915.
*New York World Telegram*, 1935.
*Philippine Graphic*, 1935–1936, 1939, 1970.
*Philippine Magazine*, 1931, 1935.
*Philippines Free Press*, 1929, 1934–1939, 1941, 1967.
*Photo News*, 1939.
*Sakdal*, 1930–1938.
*Sampaguita*, 1926–1927.
*San Francisco Chronicle*, 1930
*Shin Seiryoku* (*New Power*), 1971.
*Sunday Times*, 1929.
*The Herald Mid-Week Magazine*, 1934.
*The Manila Times*, 1935–1938.
*The New York Times*, 1931.
*The Philippines Herald*, 1931, 1935–1939, 1967.
*The Sunday Tribune*, 1934–1936.
*The Sunday Tribune Magazine*, 1930, 1931, 1935, 1949.
*The Tribune*, 1930, 1931, 1934–1936, 1941.
*The Washington Post*, 1915, 1925.
*Times Journal*, 1986.
*Washington Herald*, 1935.
*Whip*, 1935.

**Published and Unpublished Sources**

Abad, Antonio. *General Macario L. Sakay: Was He a Bandit or a Patriot?* Manila: J. B. Feliciano & Son, 1955.

Abaya, Hernando J. *Betrayal in the Philippines*. Quezon City: Malaya Books Inc., 1970.

Achutegui, Pedro S. de, and Miguel A. Bernad. *Religious Revolution in the Philippines*. Vols. 1–3. Manila: Ateneo de Manila University Press, 1960, 1966, 1969, respectively.

Agatsuma, Hitoshi. *Hito Senki* (Record of the Battle in the Philippines). Tokyo: Nippi Ireikai, 1958.

Agoncillo, Teodoro, ed. *Maikling Kwentong Tagalog: 1886–1948*. Quezon City: Wika Publishing, 1949.

———— *Tagalog Periodical Literature*. Manila: Institute of National Language, 1953.

————. *The Revolt of the Masses: The Story of Bonifacio and the Katipunan*. Quezon City: University of the Philippines, 1956.

————. *Malolos: Crisis of the Republic*. Quezon City: University of the Philippines, 1960.

————, comp. and trans. *The Writings and Trial of Andres Bonifacio*. Manila: The Manila Bonifacio Centennial Commission in cooperation with the University of the Philippines, 1963.

————. *The Fateful Years: Japan's Adventure in the Philippines, 1941–1945*. Vols. 1–2. Quezon City: R. P. Garcia Publishing, 1965.

————. "Student Activism of the 1930s." *Solid Varity* (July–August 1976): 22–28.

Akinaga, Yoshiro. *Hito Kobo-sen* (Defense War in the Philippines). Tokyo: Masu Shobo, 1956.

Alaras, Consolacion R. "Pamathalaan." In *The Filipino Spiritual Culture Series 1*, edited by Teresita B. Obusan and Angelina Enriquez, 69–78. Manila: Mamamathala, Inc., 1994.

Allen, James S. *The Radical Left on the Eve of the War*. Quezon City: Foundation for Nationalist Studies, Inc., 1985.

Allport, Gorden, and Leo Postman. *The Psychology of Rumor*. NY: Russell and Russell, 1947.

Almario, Virgilio S. *Balagtasismo Versus Modernismo*. Quezon City: Ateneo de Manila University Press, 1984.

————, ed. *Walong Dekada ng Makabagong Tulang Pilipino*. Manila: Philippine Education Co., 1981.

Alvarez, Santiago. *The Katipunan and the Revolution: Memoirs of a General*. Quezon City: Ateneo de Manila University Press, 1992.

Alvero, Aurelio. *A Matter of Nomenclature*. Muntinlupa: [New] Bilibid Prison, 1945.

Alzona, Encarnacion. *The Filipino Woman: Her Social, Economic, and Political Status, 1565–1933*. Manila: University of the Philippines Press, 1934.

Amistoso, Mercedes Y. "General Artemio Ricarte, 1896–1915." M.A. thesis, Ateneo de Manila University, 1974.

Anderson, Benedict. "Cacique Democracy in the Philippines: Origins and Dreams." In *The Spectre of Comparisons: Nationalism, Southeast Asia, and the World*, 192–203. London and New York: Verso, 1998.

————. *Imagined Communities: Reflections on the Origin and Spread of Nationalism*. London, New York: Verso, 1999.

————. *Under Three Flags: Anarchism and the Anti-colonial Imagination*. London, New York: Verso, 2005.

*Annual Report of the Governor-General of the Philippines Islands, 1931*. Washington, D.C.: U.S. Government Printing Office, 1932.

Ansay-Miranda, Evelyn. "Ang Kilusang Pang-Independensya sa Pananaw ng Oligarkiya at ng Masa noong Panahong 1930." *Historical Bulletin* 26, nos. 1–4 (January–December 1982): 117–27.

Apilado, Mariano C. *Revolutionary Spirituality: A Study of the Protestant Role in the American Colonial Rule of the Philippines, 1898–1928*. Quezon City: New Day Publishers, 1999.

Ara, Satoshi. "Firipin no Rikarute Shogun ni Kansuru Ichi Kosatsu" (A Study of General Ricarte of the Philippines). *Kokusai Seiji*, no. 12 (February 1999): 212–21.

Ashizu, Uzuhiko. "Ramos himei ni taoreru: Hito dokuritsu kakumei senshi shoden" (Ramos Died with an Unfulfilled Wish: A Short Biography of a Philippine Independence Fighter). *Shin Seiryoku* (New Power) (April 1971): 2–30.

———. "Zoku: B. R. Kenkyu" (Study of B. R. Ramos II). *Shin Seiryoku* (July 1971): 8–25.

———. "Kaigai Bomeisha o Mukaeta Nihonjin" (Japanese Who Welcomed Foreign Political Refugees). *Dento to Gendai* (January 1971): 110–17.

Benitez, Conrado. "Sakdal." *Philippine Magazine*, May 1935, 240, 252.

Biedzynski, James C. "American Perceptions of the Sakdals." *Bulletin of the American Historical Collection* 18, no. 3 (July–September, 1990): 85–94.

Boeicho Boei Kenkyujo Senshibu (National Institute for Defense Studies, War History Department). *Senshi Sosho, Sho-go Rikugun Sakusen 2: Ruson Kessen* (War History Series, Sho Army Operation 2: The Decisive Battle of Luzon). Tokyo: Asagumo Shinbun-sha, 1972.

Bogardus, Emory S. "Anti- Filipino Race Riot." In *Letters in Exile: An Introductory Reader on the History of Filipinos in America*, 51–62. Los Angeles: UCLA Asian American Studies Center, 1976.

Bridge for Peace. http://bridgeforpeace.jp.

Bronto, Placedo. *Narito na Ako: Mga Bagay na Dapat Nating Malaman* (I am Here: Things We Must Know). Edited by Anastacio Naval. Manila (?) Juan P. Omega, n.d.

Cannell, Fenella. *Power and Intimacy*. London: Cambridge University Press, 1999.

Chandlee, Ellsworth. "The Liturgy of the Philippine Independent Church." In *Studies in Philippine Church History*, edited by Gerald H. Anderson, 256–76. Ithaca and London: Cornell University Press, 1969.

Churchill, Bernardita R. *The Philippine Independent Missions to the United States, 1919–1934*. Manila: National Historical Institute, 1983.

Clifford, Mary Dorita. "Iglesia Filipina Independiente: The Revolutionary Church." In *Studies in Philippine Church History*, edited by Gerald H. Anderson, 223–55. Ithaca and London: Cornell University Press, 1969.

Clymer, Kenton J. *Protestant Missionaries in the Philippines, 1898–1916: An Inquiry into the American Colonial Mentality*. Chicago: University of Illinois Press, 1986.

Cohn, Norman. *The Pursuit of the Millennium: Revolutionary Millenarians and Mystical Anarchists of the Middle Ages*. London: Granada, 1978.

Connolly, Michael J., S.J. *Church Lands and Peasant Unrest in the Philippines: Agrarian Conflict in 20th-Century Luzon*. Quezon City: Ateneo de Manila University Press, 1992.

Covar, Prospero R. "General Characterization of Contemporary Religious Movements in the Philippines." *Asian Studies* 13, no. 2 (August 1975): 79–92.

———. "The Iglesia Watawat ng Lahi: An Anthropological Study of a Social Movement in the Philippines." PhD diss., University of Arizona, 1975.

———. "Potensiya, Bisa, at Anting-anting." *Asian Studies* 18 (April, August, December 1980): 71–78.

Cruz, Isaac. "Benigno Ramos: Founder of the Sakdalista." *Philippines Free Press*, 4 February 1961, 16, 56.

Cullamar, Evelyn Tan. *Babaylanism in Negros: 1896–1907*. Manila: New Day Publishers, 1986.

Cullinane, Michael. "The Politics of Collaboration in Tayabas Province: The Early Political Career of Manuel Luis Quezon, 1903–1906." In *Reappraising an Empire: New Perspectives on Philippine-American History*, edited Peter W. Stanley, 60–84. Cambridge and London: The Committee on American-East Asian Relations of the Department of History and the Council on East Asian Studies of Harvard University, 1984.

———. Playing the Game: The Rise of Sergio Osmeña, 1898–1907.In *Philippine Colonial Democracy*, edited by Ruby R. Paredes, 70–113. New Haven: Yale University Southeast Asia Studies, Yale Center for International and Area Studies, 1988.

———. *Ilustrado Politics: Filipino Elite Response to American Rule, 1898–1908*. Quezon City: Ateneo de Manila University Press, 2003.

Dava, Severo. *Mga Katutuhanan ukol sa Sakdal at Lapiang Sakdalista sa Kalupi ni Benigno Ramos* (The Truths about the Sakdal and the Sakdal Party that are in Benigno Ramos's Billfold). Manila: N.p., n.d.

De Witt, Howard. *Violence in the Fields: California Filipino Farm Labor Unionization during the Great Depression*. Saratoga, California: Century Twenty One Publishing, 1980.

Dealino, Presentacion. "Salud A. Generalla: Disciple of Sakdalism." *Chronicle Magazine*, 7 June 1969, 7–9.

Deats, Richard L. "Nicolas Zamora: Religious Nationalist." In *Studies in Philippine Church History*, edited by Gerald H. Anderson, 325–36. Ithaca and London: Cornell University Press, 1969.

Demos, John. *Entertaining Satan, Witchcraft and the Culture of Early New England*. NY: Oxford University Press, 1982.

Doeppers, Daniel F. "Changing Patterns of Aglipayan Adherents in the Philippines, 1918–1970." *Philippine Studies* 25 (1977): 265–77.

———. *Manila 1900–1941 Social Change in a Late Colonial*. Quezon City: Ateneo de Manila University Press, 1984.

———. "Metropolitan Manila in the Great Depression: Crisis for Whom?" *The Journal of Asian Studies* 50, no. 3 (August 1991): 511–35.

———. "The Philippines in the Great Depression: A Geography of Pain." In *Weathering the Storm: The Economies of Southeast Asia in the 1930s Depression*, edited by Peter Boomgaard and Ian Brown, 53–82. Singapore: Institute of Southeast Asia Studies, 2000.

Edgerton, Ronald K. "Joseph Ralston Hayden: The Education of a Colonialist." In *Compadre Colonialism: Philippine-American Relations, 1898–1946*, edited by Norman G. Owen, 81–104. Ermita, Manila: Solidaridad, 1971.

Elwood, Douglas J. "Varieties of Christianity in the Philippines." In *Studies in Philippine Church History*, edited by Gerald H. Anderson, 366–86. Ithaca and London: Cornell University Press, 1969.

Fast, Jonathan, and Jim Richardson. *Roots of Dependency*. Quezon City: Foundation of Nationalist Studies, 1979.

Fegan, Brian. "Light in the East: Continuities in Central Luzon Peasant Movements 1896-1970." Unpublished manuscript. 1978.

———. "The Social History of a Central Luzon Barrio." In *Philippine Social History: Global Trade and Local Transformations*, edited by Alfred W. McCoy and Ed. C. de Jesus, 91–130. Quezon City: Ateneo de Manila University Press; Sydney: George Allen and Unwin Australia Publishing, Ltd., 1984.

———. "Dionisio Macapagal: Rebel Matures." In *Lives at the Margin: Biography of Filipinos, Obscure, Ordinary, and Heroic*, edited by Alfred W. McCoy, 337–87. Quezon City: Ateneo de Manila University Press, 2000.

Fernando, Felipe D. "Aurelio Tolentino: Playwright, Poet, and Patriot." *Philippine Studies* 12 (January 1964): 83–92.

Fleetwood, Ma. Luisa D. *General Artemio Ricarte (Vibora)*. Manila: National Historical Institute, 1997.

Foronda, Marcelino A. "The Canonization of Rizal." *The Journal of History* 7, no. 2 (1960): 93–140.

———. *Cults Honoring Rizal*. Manila: R. P. Garcia, 1961.

Francisco, D. L. "When Laguna Sakdalistas Fell." *Philippines Free Press*, 11 May 1935, 4–5, 32–35.

———. "Will 'Sakdals' Rise Again?" *Philippines Free Press*, 21 December 1935, 12–13.

———. "Sakdal Head Confesses." *Philippines Free Press*, 7 November 1936, 4, 30, 36.

———. "From the Mouths of the Sakdals." *Philippines Free Press*, 14 November 1936, 30–32.

Friend, Theodore. *Between Two Empires: Philippine Ordeal and Development from the Great Depression through the Pacific War, 1929–1946*. Manila: Solidaridad Publishing House, 1969.

Gealogo, Francis A. "Time, Identity, and Nation in the Aglipayan Novenario ng Balintawak and Calendariong Manghang." *Philippine Studies* 58, nos. 1–2 (June 2010): 147–68.

Geothe, C. M. "Filipino Immigration Viewed as a Peril." In *Letters in Exile: An Introductory Reader on the History of Filipinos in America*, 72–73. Los Angeles: UCLA Asian American Studies Center, 1976.

Gleeck, Lewis E., Jr. *The American Half-Century (1898–1946)*. Manila: Historical Conservation Society, 1984.

Golay, Frank H. *Face of Empire: United States-Philippine Relations, 1898–1946*. Madison: University of Wisconsin Center for Southeast Asian Studies, 1997.

Gonzales, Michael Manuel. "The Edge of Structures: A Study of Religious Ideology and Filipino Culture." M.A. thesis, Sydney University, 1985.

Goodman, Grant K. "General Artemio Ricarte and Japan." *Journal of Southeast Asian History* 7 (1966): 48–60.

———. "Japanese Pan-Asianism in the Philippines: The Hiripin Dai Ajia Kyokai." In *Studies on Asia*, edited by Robert Sakai, 133-43. Lincoln, Nebraska: University of Nebraska, 1966.

———. "The Philippine Society of Japan." *Monumenta Nipponica* 22, nos. 1–2 (1967): 131–46.

———. "Japan and Philippine Radicalism: The Case of Benigno Ramos." In *Four Aspects of Philippine-Japanese Relations, 1930–40*, 123–92. New Haven: Yale University Southeast Asian Program, 1967.

———. "Japan and the Philippine Revolution: Image and Legend." *Journal of Oriental Studies* (January 1970): 100–12.

———."The Problem of Philippine Independence and Japan: The First Three Decades of American Colonial Rule," *Southeast Asia, An International Quarterly* 1, no. 3 (Summer 1971): 165–72.

———. "Nitobe's Bushido: The Samurai Ethic in a Philippine Setting." In *Festschrift: In honor of Dr. Marcelino Foronda, Jr.,* edited by Emerita S. Quito, 56–71. Manila: De La Salle University Press, 1987.

———. "An Interview with Benigno Ramos: Translated from the Japanese." *Philippine Studies* 37 (1989): 217–20.

———. "Aurelio Alvero: Traitor or Patriot?" *Journal of Southeast Asian Studies* 27 (March 1996): 95–103.

———. "Japanophobia and Japanophilia in the Philippines in the Aftermath of the Spanish-American War in 1898." In *1898: España y el Pacifico,* edited by Miguel Luque Talavan, J. Onrubia and F. Aguado, 553–56 Madrid: Asociacion Española de Esutudios del Pacifico, 1999.

Gopinath, Aruna. *Manuel L. Quezon: The Tutelary Democrat.* Quezon City: New Day Publishers, 1987.

Goto, Ken'ichi. "M. hatta oyobi M. keson no hojitu ni kansuru shiteki kosatsu" (Historical Study regarding M. Hatta and M. Quezon's Visits to Japan). In *Ajia no dento to kindaika (Tradition and Modernization in Asia),* edited by Waseda Daigalu Shaken, 401–29. Tokyo: Waseda University, 1990.

Guerrero, Amadis Ma. "Sakdal Uprising: Requiem to a Mass Movement." *Philippine Graphic,* 13 May 1970, 6–7, 43.

Guerrero, Leon Ma. "How Japan Looks at Ramos." *Philippines Free Press,* 1 June 1935, 4–5.

———. "Was Bonifacio a Sakdal?" *Philippine Free Press,* 28 November 1936, 4, 30, 36.

Guerrero, Milagros C. "The Colorum Uprisings: 1924–1931." *Asian Studies* 5 (April 1967): 65–78.

———. "Peasant Discontent and the Sakdal Uprising." *Praxis* (August–September 1968): 40–56.

———. "Luzon at War: Contradictions in Philippine Society, 1898–1902." PhD diss., University of Michigan, 1977.

———. "The Provincial and Municipal Elites of Luzon during the Revolution, 1898–1902." In *Philippine Social History: Global Trade and Local Transformation,* edited by Alfred McCoy and Ed. de Jesus, 155–90. Quezon City: Ateneo de Manila University Press; Sydney: George Allen and Unwin Australia Pty., Ltd., 1984.

———. *Under Stars and Stripes; Kasaysayan: The Story of the Filipino People.* Vol. 6. Manila: Asia Publishing Company, 1998.

Guha, Ranajit. *Elementary Aspects of Peasant Insurgency in Colonial India.* Delhi: Oxford University Press, 1992.

Hachero-Pascual, Teresita Z. "The Sakdalista Movement: A Historical Assessment." PhD diss., University of Santo Tomas, 1984.

Hartendorp, A. V. H. "The Tayug 'Colorums.'" *Philippine Magazine,* February 1931, 563–67.

———. "The Sakdal Protest." *Philippine Magazine,* June 1935, 230–34.

———. *The Japanese Occupation of the Philippines.* 2 vols. Manila: Bookmark, 1967.

Hayase, Shinzo. *Hukkokuban: Firipin Joho: Kaisetsu: Somokuroku: Sakuin* (Reprint: Firipin Joho: Commentary: List of Content: Indexes). Tokyo: Ryukei Shosha, 2003.

—. Firipin Kin-Gendaishino naka no Nihonjin.(The Japanese in the Philippine Modern and Contemporary History). Tokyo: Iwanami Shoten, 2012.

Hayden, Joseph Ralston. *The Philippines: A Study in National Development*. New York: The Macmillan Co., 1941.

Higashiguchi, Tamaki. *Hito Sakusen to Kawashima Heidan* (Operations in the Philippines and the Kawashima Army Corps). N.p.: Privately published, 1968.

Hill, Percy A. "Agrarian Unrest: The New Tenancy Law." *Philippine Magazine*, March 1937, 116–17, 142–44.

Horikawa, Shizuo. *Manira e no Michi* (The Road to Manila). Tokyo: Tokyo Shiryu Sha, 1961.

Hoshina, Shinsaku. *Rakurui Sensen: Hito no Omoide* (Heart-Breaking Operation: Memories of the Philippines). Tokyo: Privately published, n.d.

Ikehata, Setsuho. "Filipin ni Okeru Nihon Gunsei: Rikarute Shogun no Yakuwari o Megutte" (A Study on the Japanese Military Administration in the Philippines: Focus on Gen. Artemio Ricarte's Role). *Ajia Kenkyu* 22, no. 2 (July 1975): 40–73.

—. "Firipin Kakumei no Ridashippu ni Kansuru Kenkyu" (A Study on the Philippine Revolution's Leadership). *Toyo Bunka Kenkyusyo Kiyo*, no. 80 (1980): 41–194.

—. *Firipin Kakumei to Katorishizumu* (Philippine Revolution and Catholicism). Tokyo: Keiso Shobo, 1987.

—. *Popular Catholicism in the Nineteenth-Century Philippines: The Case of the Cofradia de San Jose*. Translation of Contemporary Japanese Scholarship on Southeast Asia 1. Ithaca, New York: Southeast Asia Program, Cornell University, 1990.

—. *The Japanese Military Administration in the Philippines and the Tragedy of Gen. Artemio Ricarte*. Trans. Elpidio R. Sta. Romana. Singapore: Department of Japanese Studies, National University of Singapore, 1991 (English translation of "Firipin ni okeru nihon gunsei").

—. "Firipin Kakumei to Nihon no Kanyo" (The Philippine Revolution and the Japanese Involvement). In *Seiki Tenkan-ki ni Okeru Nihon-firipin Kankei*. (The Japan-Philippine Relations at the Turn of the Century) by S. Ikehata, M. Terami, S. Hayase. *AA ken Tonan Ajia Kenkyu*, no. 1. Tokyo: Institute for the Study of Languages and Cultures of Asia and Africa, University of Tokyo of Foreign Languages and Cultures (1989): 1–36.

—. "Mining Industry Development and Local Anti-Japanese Resistance." In *The Philippines under Japan*, edited by Setsuho Ikehata and Ricardo T. Jose, 127–70. Quezon City: Ateneo de Manila University Press, 1999.

Ileto, Reynaldo C. *Pasyon and Revolution: Popular Movements in the Philippines, 1840–1910*. Quezon City: Ateneo de Manila University Press, 1979.

—. "Bernardo Carpio: *Awit* and Revolution." In *Perceptions of the Past in Southeast Asia*, edited by Anthony J. S. Reid and D. G. Marr, 379–400. Singapore: Heinemann Educational Publishers, 1979.

—. "Rizal and the Underside of Philippine History." In *Moral Order and the Question of Change: Essays in Southeast Thought*, edited by David Wyatt and Alexander Woodside, 274–337. New Haven: Yale University Southeast Asian Studies, 1982.

—. "Orators and the Crowd." In *Reappraising the Empire*, edited by Peter W. Stanley, 85–114. Cambridge and London: Committee on American-East Asian Relations of the Department of History in collaboration with the Council on East Asian Studies, Harvard University, 1984.

————. "Religion and Anti-colonial Movements." In *The Cambridge History of Southeast Asia*, edited by Nicholas Tarling, vol. 2: 197–248. Cambridge: Cambridge University Press, 1992.

————. *Filipinos and their Revolution: Event, Discourse, and Historiography*. Quezon City: Ateneo de Manila University Press, 1998.

Ishida, Isao. *Ruson no Kiri* (Fog of Luzon). Tokyo: Asahi Shinbunsya, 1971.

Ishizaka, Yojiro. *Mayon no Kemuri* (Smoke of Mt. Mayon). Tokyo: Shueisha, 1977.

Iwamura, Takashi. *Makapiri Aika* (Makapili Elegy). Kobe: Privately published, n.d.

————. *Ruson no Sen'yu wa Ima Izuko?* (Where Are the Comrades in Luzon Now?) Kobe: Privately published, n.d.

Jocano, F. Landa. *Folk Christianity*. Quezon City: Trinity Research Institute, 1981.

*Joint Preparatory Committee on Philippine Affairs: Report of May 20, 1938*. 3 vols. Washington: United States Government Printing Office, 1938.

Jose, Ricardo Trota. *The Philippine Army, 1935–1942*. Quezon City: Ateneo de Manila University Press, 1992.

————. *Captive Arms: The Constabulary under the Japanese, 19421–944*. Professorial Chair Paper Series no. 97-5, College of Social Sciences and Philosophy. Quezon City: College of Social Sciences and Philosophy, University of the Philippines, Diliman, Quezon City, 1997.

————. "The Association for Service to the New Philippines (KALIBAPI) during the Japanese Occupation: Attempting to Transport a Japanese Wartime Concept to the Philippines." *The Journal of Sophia Asian Studies*, no. 19 (2001): 149–85

————. "Test of Will: Diplomacy between Japan and the Laurel Government." In *Philippines-Japan Relations*, edited by Setsuho Ikehata, and Lydia N. Yu-Jose, 185–222. Quezon City: Ateneo de Manila University Press, 2003.

Jose, Lydia N. Yu. "Japanese Organizations and the Philippines, 1930s–1941." *Journal of International Studies* 33 (April 1994): 83–110.

————. *Filipinos in Japan and Okinawa: 1880s to 1972*. Tokyo: Research Institute for the Language and Cultures of Asia and Africa, Tokyo University of Foreign Studies, 2002.

Kalaw, Teodoro M. *Five Precepts from Our Ancient Morality*, translated by Maria Kalaw Katigbak. Manila: Privately published, 1951.

Kanegae, Seitaro. *Aruitekita Michi* (The Path I Took). Tokyo: Kokusei Sha, 1968.

Kerkvliet, Benedict J. *The Huk Rebellion: A Study of Peasant Revolt in the Philippines*. Quezon City: New Day Publishers, 1977.

Kerkvliet, Melinda Tria. *Manila Workers' Union, 1900–1950*. Quezon City: New Day Publishers, 1992.

Larkin, John A. *Colonial Society in a Philippine Province: The Pampangans*. Berkley: University of California Press, 1972.

Laurel, Jose P. *Political-Social Problems*. Manila: National Teachers' College, 1936.

————. *War Memoirs of Dr. Jose P. Laurel*. Manila: Jose Laurel Memorial Foundation, 1980.

Lefebvre, Georges. *The Great Fear of 1789: Rural Panic in Revolutionary France*. New York: Schocken Books, 1973.

Liang, Dapen (Ta-peng). *The Development of Philippine Political Parties*. Hong Kong: South China Morning Post (printed, not published), 1939.

Lumbera, Bienvenido. "From Colonizer to Liberator: How U.S. Colonialism Succeeded in Reinventing Itself After the Pacific War." In *Vestiges of War: The Philippine-American*

*War and the Aftermath of an Imperial Dream, 1899–1999*, edited by Angel Velasco Shaw and Luis H. Francia. New York: New York University Press, 2002.

Mabini, Apolinario. *The Letters of Apolinario Mabini*. National Heroes Commission, comp. and trans. Manila: National Heroes Commission, 1965.

*Mabuting Balita para sa Ating Panahon: Tagalog Popular Version New Testament*. Manila: Philippine Bible Society, 1973.

Macaraig, Serafin E. *Social Problems*. Manila: The Educational Supply Co., 1929.

MacIsaac, Steve. "The Struggle for Economic Development in the Philippine Commonwealth, 1935–1940." *Philippine Studies* 50, no. 2 (2002): 141–67.

Majul, Cesar Adib. *Apolinario Mabini: Revolutionary*. Manila: National Heroes Commission, 1970.

Manibo, Joaquin. *Pasyon ng Bayan Kahapon at Ngay-on* (Passion of the Nation in the Past and Present). Bauan, Batangas: Javier Press, 1934.

Manuel, Arsenio. *Dictionary of Philippine Biography*. Quezon City: Philippine Publications, 1970.

Marasigan, Vicente. *A Banahaw Guru*. Quezon City: Ateneo de Manila University Press, 1985.

Matusmura, Mitsuo. "Nihon Bomei San'nen no Seikatsu o Hito Dokuritsu Undo no Shishi Ramosu-shi ni Kiku" (Interview with Mr. Ramos, a Philippine Independence Movement Fighter, on His Three-Year Exile in Japan). *Hanashi*, October 1938, 144–47.

May, Herbert G., and Bruce Metzger, eds. *The New Oxford Annotated Bible*. New York: Oxford University Press, 1977.

McCoy, Alfred W. "Quezon's Commonwealth: The Emergence of Philippine Authoritarianism." In *Philippine Colonial Democracy*, edited by R. Paredes, 114–60. New Haven: Yale University Southeast Asia Studies, Yale Center for International and Area Studies, 1988.

———. *Policing America's Empire*. Madison: University of Wisconsin Press, 2009.

McLennan, Marshall S. *The Central Luzon Plain Land and Society on the Island Frontier*. Quezon City: Alemars-Phoenix Publishing House, Inc., 1980.

———. "Changing Human Ecology on the Central Luzon Plain: Nueva Ecija, 1705–1939." In *Philippine Social History: Global Trade and Local Transformation*, edited by Alfred W. McCoy and Ed. C de Jesus, 57–90. Quezon City: Ateneo de Manila University Press; Sydney: George Allen and Unwin Australia Pty. Ltd., 1982.

Melendy, Brett H. "California's Discrimination against Filipinos, 1927–1935." In *The Filipino Exclusion Movement, 1927–1935. Occasional Papers No. 1.* edited by Josefa M. Saniel, 3–10. Quezon City: Institute of Asian Studies, University of the Philippines, 1967.

Mercado, Leonardo N., SVD. *Christ in the Philippines*. Tacloban City: Divine Word University Publications, 1982.

Mesa, Jose M. de. "Holy Week and Popular Devotion." In *Morality, Religion and the Filipino*, edited by Rene B. Javellana, S.J., 220–33. Quezon City: Ateneo de Manila University Press, 1994.

*Minutes of the Katipunan*. Manila: National Historical Institute, 1978.

Mojares, Resil B. "Guillermo Tolentino's *Grupo de Filipinos Ilustre* and the Making of National Pantheon." *Philippine Studies* 58, nos. 1–2 (June 2010): 169–84.

Mori, Yasotaro."Hito Daitoryo no Nihon Homon wa Nani o Imisuruka" (What Does the Philippine President's Visit to Japan Signify). *Kokusai Panhuretto*, 11 August 1938, 1–30.

Moriya, Tadashi. *Firipin Sensen no Ningen Gunzo* (Human Images at the Philippine Battlefront). Tokyo: Keiso Shobo, 1977.

Murata, Shozo. *Murata Shozo Iko*: *Hito Nikki* (Posthumous Writings of Murata Shozo: Philippine Diary), edited by Fukushima Shintaro. Tokyo: Hara Shobo, 1969.

Naimusho, Keiho Kyoku (Home Ministry, Police Bureau), edited by *Gaiji Keisatsu Gaikyo* (Police Reports on Foreign Affairs). Vols. 1–4. Tokyo: Ryukei Shosha, 1980.

Nakamura, Koji. "Firipin Seifu no Yokogao" (Profile of the Philippine Government). In *Daitoa Senshi* (War History of Great East Asia), edited by Tamura Yoshio, 54–83. Tokyo: Fuji Shoen, 1953.

Nakano, Satoshi. "Firipin no Tainichi Kyoryoku Mondai to Amerika Gasshukoku," (Japanese Collaboration Issue in the Philippines and the U.S.A.) *Rekishigaku Kenkyu*, no. 600 (November 1989): 5–67.

———. *Firipin Dokuritsu Mondai-shi* (History of Philippine Independence Issues). Tokyo: Ryukei Shosha, 1997.

———. "The Politics of Mourning." In *Philippines-Japan Relations*, edited by S. Ikehata and L. N. Yu-Jose. Quezon City: Ateneo de Manila University Press, 2003.

Obo, Tadahiko. *Ah, Kusamakura* (Ah, Bivouac). Tokyo: Geibundo, 1992.

Ocampo, Ambeth R. *Rizal Without the Overcoat*. Manila: Anvil Publishing, Inc., 1990.

*Official Gazette. Commonwealth of the Philippines* 37, no. 100 (1937).

Ogawa, Tetsuro. *Shinbu Shudan Senki* (War History of the Shinbu Group) N.p., privately published, 1973.

Ohta, Kaneshiro. *Hito Dokuritsu no shishi, Rikarute Shogun Shoden* (A Short Biography of General Ricarte, a Zealous Fighter for the Philippine Independence). Tokyo: Firipin Tomono-kai, 1953.

———. *Kikoku* (Haunting Cries of Ghost). Tokyo: Firipin Kyokai, 1972.

Ohmori Sachiko. *Desu Bare* (Death Valley). Oita: Privately published, 1996.

Okada, Taihei. "Kankeisei no rekishigaku ni mukette: Amerika shokuminchiki firipinn no shokuminchi kyoiku o meguru seidoshi, shigakushi, shiseishi" (Toward the Relational History: Institutional History, Historiography and History of Mentality of Colonial Education during the American Colonial Period in the Philippines). PhD diss., Hitotsubashi University, 2008.

———. "School Strikes in the Philippines under U.S. Colonialism: With a Particular Focus on the 1930 High School Strike." *Tonan Ajia: Rekishi to Bunka* 40 (2011): 27–55.

Ozaki, Takuya. *Chomin Sakamoto Shiro* (Sakamoto Shiro). Tokyo: Chominkai, 1932.

Paredes, Ruby R. "The Origins of National Politics: Taft and the Partido Federal." In *Philippine Colonial Democracy*, edited by R. Paredes, 41–69. New Haven: Yale University Southeast Asia Studies, Yale Center for International and Area Studies, 1988.

———. "Introduction." In *Philippine Colonial Democracy*, edited by R. Paredes, 1–12. New Haven: Yale University Southeast Asia Studies, Yale Center for International and Area Studies, 1988.

Pastores, Elizabeth A. "Religious Leadership in the Lapiang Malaya: A Historical Note." In *Filipino Religious Psychology*, edited by Leonardo N. Mercado, 149–58. Tacloban City: Divine Word University, 1977.

Philippine Department of Labor. *Report of the Fact-Finding Survey of Rural Problems in the Philippines to the Secretary of Labor and to the President of the Philippines*. Manila, 1937.

Philippines, Supreme Court. "People vs Alvero." In *Philippine Report: Reports of Cases*

*Decided by the Supreme Court of the Philippines from April 1 to June 30, 1950.* Vol. 86: 58–103. Manila: Bureau of Printing, 1958.

Ponce, Mariano. *Cartas Sobre La Revolucion.* Manila: Bureau of Printing, 1932.

Quezon, Manuel L. *The Good Fight.* Manila: Cacho Hermanos, Inc., 1985.

Quibuyen, Floro C. *And Woman Will Prevail Over Man: Symbolic Sexual Inversion and Counter-Hegemonic Discourse in Mt. Banahaw, the Case of the Ciudad Mistica de Dios. Philippine Studies Occasional Paper No. 10.* Honolulu: Center for Philippine Studies, 1991.

———. *A Nation Aborted: Rizal, American Hegemony, and Philippine Nationalism.* Quezon City: Ateneo de Manila University Press, 1999 and 2008.

Rafael, Vicente. *Contracting Colonialism.* Quezon City: Ateneo de Manila University Press, 1988.

Ramos, Benigno. "Talsik ng Siglo XX." *Renacimiento Filipino*, 14 February to 21 May 1911.

———. *Pancho Villa, Maikling Kasaysayan ng Bantog at Kilabot na Taong Ito sa Mehiko.* Manila: Imprenta y Liberia de P. Sayo Vda. de Soriano, 1916.

———. *Maikling Balagtasan: Dalagang Bayan Laban sa Dalagang Bukid.* Manila: Alitaptap, 1930

———. *The American Government Does Not Like Peace in the Philippines.* Tokyo, Japan[?]: N.p., 1935.

———. "Firipin to Nippon" (The Philippines and Japan). *Kaizo*, May 1936, 42–51.

———. *Quezon is the Real Enemy of the Government in the Philippines.* Manila: N.p., n.d. (ca. 1937).

———. *Mga Patak ng Luha ng Bayang Api* (Teardrops of the Oppressed People). Manila: N.p., 1939.

———. *Syllabic Wealth of the Tagalog Dialect.* Manila: N.p. (Kalibapi[?]), 1943.

———. *Gumising Ka, Aking Bayan: Mga Piling Tula.* Compiled by Delfin Tolentino. Quezon City: Ateneo de Manila University Press, 1998.

Recto, Claro M. *Three Years of Enemy Occupation.* Manila: People's Publishers, 1946.

Reel, Frank. *The Case of General Yamashita.* Chicago: The University of Chicago Press, 1949.

"Remarks by Ambassador Ryuichi Yamazaki." http://ph.emb-japan.go.jp/pressand-speech/2006%20speeches/liberationofmanila.htm, 2006.

*Report of Cases Decided by the Supreme Court of the Philippines from April 1 to June 30, 1950.* Vol. 86. Manila: Bureau of Printing, 1953.

*Report of the United States High Commissioner to the Philippine Islands, Covering the Period from November 15, 1935 to December 31, 1936.* Washington, D.C.: United States Government Printing Office, 1937.

Retizos, Isidro L. "Why Sakdalistas Won in Laguna and Other Places." *Herald Mid-Week Magazine*, 27 June 1934, 6–9.

Ricarte, Artemio. *Sa mga Kabataan Filipino* (To the Filipino Youth). N.p., n.d. (ca. 1943–1944).

———. *Memoirs of General Artemio Ricarte.* Manila: National Heroes Commission, 1963.

Richardson, Jim. "The Genesis of the Philippine Communist Party." PhD diss., University of London, 1984.

———. "Hard Times: The Philippine Communist Party, 1933–35." 1995.

———. *Komunista.* Quezon City: Ateneo de Manila Univesity Press, 2011.

Rizal, Jose. *Political and Historical Writing by Jose Rizal (1884–1890).* Manila: National Historical Institute, 1976.

———. *Noli me tangere.* Translated by Ma. Soledad Lacson-Locsin. Manila: Bookmark, 1996.

————. *El Filibusterismo*. Translated by Ma Soledad Lacson-Locsin. Manila: Bookmark, 1997.

Robb, Walter. "Sakdals." *American Chamber of Commerce Journal* 15 (May 1935): 10–11.

————. "What Ho, the Guard." *American Chamber of Commerce Journal* 2 (February 1931): 3, 18, 25–26.

Royama, Masamichi, and Takeuchi Tatsuji. *The Philippine Polity: A Japanese View*. Translated by Takeuchi Tatusji, edited by Theodore Friend. New Heaven: Yale University, 1967.

Sada, Kojiro. *Nanyo Sosho: Hiripin-hen* (The South Sea Series: The Philippines). Tokyo: Toa Keizai Chosa Kyoku, 1939.

Saniel, Josefa. *Japan and the Philippines: 1868–1898*. Quezon City: University of the Philippines Press, 1969.

Santos, Angelito L. "Gleanings from a Cruel War." In *Under Japanese Rule*, edited by Renato Constantino, 5–63. Quezon City: Foundation for Nationalist Studies, Inc., 1994.

Santos, Epifanio de los. *The Revolutionists: Aguinaldo, Bonifacio, Jacinto*, edited by Teodoro A. Agoncillo. Manila: National Historical Commission, 1955.

Saulo, Alfredo B. *Communism in the Philippines: An Introduction*. Quezon City: Ateneo de Manila University Press, 1990.

Schumacher, John N., S.J. "Propagandists' Reconstruction of the Philippine Past." In *The Making of a Nation: Essays on Nineteen-Century Filipino Nationalism*, 102–18. Quezon City: Ateneo de Manila University Press, 1991.

————. "The Civic and Religious Ethic of Emilio Jacinto." In *Morality, Religion and the Filipino*, edited by Rene B. Javellana, S.J., 81–96. Quezon City: Ateneo de Manila University Press, 1994.

————. *The Creation of a Filipino Consciousness, the Making of the Revolution: The Propaganda Movement, 1880–1895*. Quezon City: Ateneo de Manila University Press, 1997.

————. "Rizal and Filipino Nationalism: A New Approach." *Philippine Studies* 48, no. 4 (2000): 549–71.

Scott, William Henry. "The Union Obrera Democratica, First Filipino Labor Union." *Social Science and Humanities Review* 47, nos. 1–4 (January–December 1983): 131–92.

————. *Ilocano Responses to American Aggression, 1900–1901*. Quezon City: New Day Publishers, 1986.

Shibutani, Tamotsu. *Improvised News: A Sociological Study of Rumor*. Indianapolis: Boobs-Merrill, 1966.

Shoesmith, Dennis. "The Glorious Religion of Jose Rizal: Radical Consciousness in a Contemporary Folk Religious Movement in the Southern Philippines." In *Peasant and Politics: Grassroots Reaction to Change in Asia*, edited by D. B. Miller, 149–202. Melbourne: Edward Arnold pty., Ltd., 1978.

Sijuco-Tan, Ma. Felisa. "Settling the Score: The Court Trials of the Filipino Informers and Paramilitary Collaborators (1945–1952)." PhD diss., University of the Philippines, 2009.

Sitoy, T. Valentino Jr. *Comity and Unity: Ardent Aspirations of Six Decades of Protestantism in the Philippines (1901–1961)*. Quezon City: National Council of Churches in the Philippines, 1989.

Sluimers, L. E. L. "Samurai, Pemuda und Sakdaslita: Die Japaner Und Der Radikalismus in Indonesien und den Philippinen, 1941–1945" (Samurai, Pemuda, and Sakdalista: Japan and Radicalism in Indonesia and in the Philippines, 1941–1945). 1972.

Stanley, Peter W. *A Nation in the Making: The Philippines and the United States, 1899–1921.* Cambridge, Massachusetts: Harvard University Press, 1974.

Steinberg, David Joel. *Philippine Collaboration in World War II.* Ann Arbor: The University of Michigan Press, 1967.

Stewart, Pamela, and Andrew Strathern. *Witchcraft, Sorcery, Rumors and Gossip.* Cambridge, UK: Cambridge University Press, 2004.

Stubbs, Roy Maning. "Philippine Radicalism: The Central Luzon Uprisings, 1925–1935." PhD diss., University of California, 1951.

Sturtevant, David R. *Popular Uprisings in the Philippines, 1840–1940.* Ithaca: Cornell University Press, 1976.

Taruc, Luis. *Born of the People.* New York: International Publishers, 1953.

Taylor, John R. M., comp. *The Philippine Insurrection against the United States: A Compilation and Introduction by John R. M .Taylor.* 5 vols. Pasay: Eugenio Lopez Foundation, 1971.

Terami-Wada, Motoe. "Cultural Front in the Philippines, 1942–1945: Japanese Propaganda and Filipino Resistance in Mass Media." MA thesis, University of the Philippines, 1984.

———. "The Japanese Propaganda Corps in the Philippines: Laying the Foundation." In *Japanese Cultural Policies in Southeast Asia during World War II,* edited by Grant K. Goodman, 173–211. New York: St. Martin's Press, 1991.

———. "Lt. Shigenobu Mochizuki and the New Philippine Cultural Institute." *Journal of Southeast Asian Studies* 27, no. 1 (March 1996): 104–23.

———. "Iglesia Sagrada ng Lahi: Upholding the Unfinished Revolution." In *The Philippine Revolution and Beyond,* edited by Elmer A. Ordoñez, 641–51. Manila: Philippine Centennial Commission and National Commission for Culture and the Arts, 1998.

———. "The Filipino Volunteer Armies." In *The Philippines under Japan: Occupation Policy and Reaction.* Eds. Ikehata, Setsuho, and Ricardo T. Jose, 59–98. Quezon City: Ateneo de Manila University Press, 1999.

———. "Cultivating Goodwill between Japan and the Philippines in the 1930s." In *Philippines-Japan Relations.* Eds. Ikehata, Setsuho, and Lydia N. Yu-Jose, 155–84. Quezon City: Ateneo de Manila University Press, 2003.

———. *The Japanese in the Philippines, 1880s–1980s.* Manila: National Historical Commission of the Philippines, 2010.

Tiongco-Enriquez, Carmen. "Revolt in the Grassroots." In *The Filipino Heritage.* Vol. 9 of *The Making of a Nation,* edited by Alfredo Roces, 2516–520. Metro Manila: Lahing Pilipino Publishing, Inc., 1978.

———. "Lapiang Sakdalista: Hibik ng Bayan Api" (The Sakdal Party: Supplication of the Oppressed People). Unpublished manuscript. N.d.

Tolentino, Delfin L., Jr. "Ang Panulaan ni Benigno Ramos." M.A. thesis, Ateneo de Manila University, 1980.

Tutay, Filemon. "Shadows in Nueva Ecija." *Philippines Free Press,* 14 November 1936, 10–11, 46.

*Unang Pagtitipon Espirituwal ng Kapatiran Pilipinas.* Manila: N.p., 1985.

United States of America, Commonwealth Government of the Philippines. *Court of Appeals: The People of the Philippines vs Fruto R. Santos et al. Criminal Case No. 5155* (Manila).

U.S. Bureau of the Census. *Sixteenth Census of the United States: 1940, Population, Characteristics of the Nonwhite Population by Race.* Washington, D.C.: Bureau of Printing, 1940.

U.S. Philippine Commission. *Annual Reports of the Philippine Commission*. Washington, D.C.: Government Printing Office, 1907–1910.

U.S. War Department. *Annual Reports of the Governor General of the Philippine Islands.* Washington, D.C.: United States Government Printing Office (for the years 1908–1935).

U.S. War Department. *Annual Reports of the United States High Commissioner to the Philippine Islands to the President and the Congress of the United States*. Washington, D.C.: United States Government Printing Office (for the years 1937–1930, June 1941).

Urgena, Cynthia B. "The Colorum Uprising in Pangasinan." M.A. thesis, University of the Philippines, 1960.

Valenzuela, Jesus Z. *History of Journalism in the Philippine Islands*. Manila: Privately published, 1933.

Veneracion, Jaime V. *Kasaysayan ng Bulakan* (History of Bulacan). Cologne, Germany: Bahay Saliksikan ng Kasaysayan (Historical Research Institute), 1986.

Ventura, E. V., and M. Mendez. *From Journalism to Diplomacy*. Quezon City: University of the Philippines Press, 1978.

Villamor, Blas. *Tayug en Colorums: Reseña Historica de la Conspiracion en Tayug en 1834, y de la Sedicion en 1931*. Bangued, Abra: N.p., March 1931.

Villanueva, Frisco D. "Sakdal Head Confesses." *Philippines Free Press*, 7 November 1936, 4, 30, 36.

———. "From the Mouths of the Sakdals." *Philippines Free Press*, 14 November 1936, 30–32.

Villareal, Bonifacio P. "Salaysay ni G. Olimpia Parafina (95 ang edad)" (The Narrative of Mrs. Olimpia Parafina [95 years of age]). Typescript. N.p. 1981.

Wada, Kota. *Jagaimo Jinsei* (Potato Life). Tokyo: Privately published, 1986.

Wagan, Venacio P. *Bathalismo, Inc. (Inang Mahiwaga)*. Manila ?: N.p., n.d.

Wallovits, Emily. "The Filipinos in California." MA thesis, University of Southern California, 1966.

Whittemore, Lewis Bliss. *Struggle for Freedom: History of the Philippine Independent Church*. Greenwich, Conn.: Seabury Press, 1961.

Wolters, O. W. *History, Culture and Religion in Southeast Asian Perspectives*. Ithaca, NY: Southeast Asia Program, Cornell University, 1999.

Woods, Robert G. "The Strange Story of the Colorum Sect." *Asia*, July–August 1932, 450–54, 459–60.

Yajima, Atsuo. "Gapan no Omoide" (Memory of Gapan [Nueva Ecija]). In *Hi to tsuchi to* (Sun and the Earth), edited by the Editorial Board of the *Hi to Tsuchi to*, 196–236. N.p.: Privately published, 1974.

"Zakken: Manira Hanto Dosei no Ken" (Miscellaneous: Movement of Manila Rebels). In *Nihon Gaiko Monjo* (Japanese Diplomatic Documents), 969–72. Tokyo: Ministry of Foreign Affairs, 1971.

## INTERVIEWS

### A. SAKDALISTAS/GANAPISTAS

Adan, Miguel. Atimonan, Quezon. 15 Dec. 1985; 24 Apr. 1986.

Adia, Jeremias. Cabuyao, Laguna. 20 Apr. 1985; 18 May 1985 ; 17 Aug. 1985; 5 Oct. 1985; 27 Nov. 1985; 29 Nov. 1986; 10 Jan. 1987; 24 Apr. 1987; 28 Mar. 1989.

Aguilar, Estanislao Cabuyao, Laguna 21 Nov. 1987.

Alatiit, Marcelo K. Biñan, Laguna 21 Nov. 1987.

Algabre, Dominador. Cabuyao, Laguna. 18 May 1985.

Amaba, Julio. Biñan, Laguna. 21 Nov. 1987.

Batitis, Arsenio. Santa Rosa, Laguna. 6 Dec. 1986; 10 Jan. 1987.

Bautista, Ruperto. Biñan, Laguna. 21 Nov. 1987.

Bernardo, Inocencio. Ugong, Pasig. 9 Aug. 1990.

Biscode, Ising. Silang, Cavite. 30 Nov. 1985.

Cayetano, Eligio S. Matungao, Bulacan, Bulacan. 27 Dec. 1987.

De los Santos, Tomas. Matungao, Bulacan, Bulacan. 27 Dec. 1986.

De Luna, Victor. Sariaya, Quezon 21 Nov. 1987.

Devoma, Gabriel. Cabuyao, Laguna. 23 Nov.1987.

Diego, Elladio Villa. Sariaya, Quezon. 28 Dec. 1987.

Esporlas, Perfecto. Alabang, Muntinlupa 21 Nov. 1987.

Esporlas, Ponciano. Alabang, Muntinlupa. 21 Nov. 1987.

Juares, Celestino. San Gabriel, Cavite 21 Nov. 1987.

Lagmay, Carlos. Biñan, Laguna 21 Nov. 1987.

Laguyan, Pastor. Biñan, Laguna 21 Nov. 1987.

Liwanag, Elias. Atimonan, Quezon. 24 Apr. 1986.

Marquez, Bernardo. Atimonan, Quezon 24 Apr. 1986.

Narvaja, Christina vda. de Factoriza. Santa Rosa, Laguna. 10 Aug. 1985.

Pamatmat, Mary. Quezon City, Metro Manila. 9 Sept.1997.

Patapat, Antonio. Santa Rosa, Laguna 5 May 1986.

Payad, Savina. Ulat, Silang, Cavite 30 Nov. 1985.

Perez, Vinancio. Sariaya, Quezon 28 Dec. 1987.

Potenciano, Dominador. Biñan, Laguna. 21 Nov. 1987.

Reymunda, Francisco. Palatiw, Pasig 25 Nov. 1987; 4 Sep. 1990.

Rosales, Ceferino. Sariaya, Quezon. 21 Nov.1987.

Salvador, Ismael. Rosario, Pasig 4 Sep. 1990.

Santos, Agustin. Rosario, Pasig 5 Aug. 1990.

Santos, Concepcion. Parang, Marikina 21 Nov.1987.

Tuazon-Ishita, Bibiana. Osaka, Japan 15 Apr.1989.

Tuazon, Gabino. Rosario, Pasig 5 Aug. 1990.

Zurbano, Cayetano P. Santa Rosa, Laguna 10 Aug.1985; 12 Aug. 1985.

Name Withheld (former Tanggulan member). Atimonan, Quezon 24 Apr. 1986.

Name Withheld (former Kaigun Jiyutai member). Zamboanga City. 23 Nov. 1998.

### B. FAMILIES OF THE SAKDALISTAS

Aguilar, Anna (daughter of Ricardo Aguilar, who was a Sakdalista in Santa Rosa, Laguna). Santa Rosa, Laguna. 10 Aug. 1985.

Generalla, Conrado, Liwayway Generalla, Luzviminda Generalla, and Virginia Generalla (children of Salud Algabre and Severo Generalla, both local leaders of the May 1935 uprising in Cabuyao). Quezon City, Metro Manila. 16 Dec. 1988.

Ramos, Amada (widow of Francisco Ramos, who is a younger brother of Benigno Ramos). Bambarig, Bulacan, Bulacan. 6 Aug. 1985.

Ramos-Uyboco, Leticia (daughter of Benigno Ramos). Alabang, Muntinlupa. 14 Apr. 1983.

Samonte, Lualhati (niece of Benigno Ramos, daughter of Enriqueta Ramos, sister of Benigno Ramos), and Amada Ramos (widow of Francisco, Ramos's brother). Taliptip, Bulacan, Bulacan. 23 Aug. 1985.

Tiongco-Enriquez, Carmen (granddaughter of Celerino Tiongco). Manila. 16 Dec. 1988.

*C. JAPANESE*
*They were all Japanese soldiers who either organized or led the Makapilis, unless otherwise indicated.*

Arita, Hiroshi. Sanda City, Hyogo, Japan. 29 Feb. 1991

Hayashi, Takashi. Tokyo, Japan. 11 Aug. 1991.

Hitomi, Jun'suke. Kyoto, Japan. 27 Feb. 1991; 7 May 1990.

Iwamura, Takashi. Kobe, Japan. 27 Feb. 1991; 6 Aug. 1991.

Maeda, Takuya. Himeji, Japan 6 Aug. 1991.

Matsunobu, Mikio Kawasaki City, Kanagawa, Japan. 3 July 1982.

Nakamura, Koji (correspondent sent to the Philippines). Tokyo, Japan. 5 July 1982.

Ueda, Shigeru. Kobe, Japan 25 Feb. 1991

Yajima, Atsuo. Nishinomiya, Japan. 23 July 1984

*D. OTHERS*

De la Rama, Atang (Mrs. Amado Hernandez, national artist, zarzuela singer). Manila. 19 Nov. 1987.

Dominguez, Minviluz (Maria Luisa Fleetwood, granddaughter of Gen. Artemio Ricarte). Fremont, California. 7 July 1995.

Lava, Jesus (member, Communist party of the Philippines). Mandaluyong. 23 Oct. 1985.

Maria Sinukuan (head of a religious organization). Arayat, Pampanga. 22 Feb. 1986.

Salazar, Lucila A. (Mrs. Aurelio Alvero). Quezon City. 9 Dec. 1992.

Taruc, Luis (leader, Hukbalahap, during the Japanese Occupation period and HMB till his surrender in 1954). Quezon City. 22 August 1986.

Tec, Carlos (local historian and a long-time resident of Pasig). 3 July 1988.

**CORRESPONDENCE**

Hayashi, Takashi (a member of Kenpeitai). 5 May 1991.

Hitomi, Junsuke (a member of Propaganda Corps during the Japanese Occupation period). 20 December 1990.

Ose, Shin'ichi (one of the organizers of Makapili). 11 November 1991.

Ueda, Shigeru. 20 and 23 January 1991.

Utsunomiya, Naokata (a member of the General Staff Office during the Japanese Occupation period). 7 October 1990.

# INDEX

Brummitt, Mabel, 13
Buencamino, Felipe, Jr., 120–21, 280n33
Bukal na Pananampalataya, 205, 206
Bulacan, 1, 3, 4, 8, 10, 13, 15, 25, 27, 41,
    43, 48, 61, 63, 66, 74, 77, 81, 83, 94,
    120, 128, 132, 138, 139, 147, 179,
    190, 193, 195, 204, 261n21, 286n17;
    Sakdalista movement, 65, 230n1,
    240n51, 242n66, 273n48, 288n32,
    289n35, 296n96, 309n113
Bumanlag, Francisco S., 132
Bureau of Education, 14
Butte, George C., 25, 241n55, 243n71,
    244n77, n81

Cabanatuan (Nueva Ecija), 13, 231n5,
    280n36; peasant unrest, 269n12
Cabiao (Nueva Ecija): peasant unrest,
    269n12
Cabuyao (Laguna): 2–4, 78, 81, 86, 119,
    203, 249n14; Sakdalista, 73, 77, 195,
    230n4, 231n5
Cailles, Juan, 3, 61, 260n10
Cajucom, Felino, 41, 138, 246n95, 251n29,
    246n95
Calendariong maanghang, 145
Calosa, Pedro (alias). *See* Tolosa, Pedro
Camarines Norte, 131, 133; Lapian
    members, 315n26
Camarines Sur, 203, 246n95; Lapian
    members, 315n26
Campomanes, Ciriaco V., 48, 64, 126, 130,
    138, 251n29, 259n107, 265n51,
    281n50, 300n32
Capa, Paulo V., 132, 251n29, 260n15,
    279n26, 281n50, 284n88
Capadocia, Guillermo, 130, 154, 193,
    283n77
Carriaga (Ricarte follower), 286n11
Castro, Amado, 274n55
Catholic Church, 57, 142, 144, 146, 149,
    161
Catholic Women's League, 273n51
Cavite, 3, 12, 48, 77, 84, 98, 100; Lapian
    members, 315n26; regional campaign
    committee, 255n64; Sakdalista

movement, 4, 41, 43, 54, 57, 65,
    75, 78, 85, 230n1, 272n38, n39,
    296n96
Cavite navy yard, 284n1
Cayetano, Eligio S., 242n65
Cayetano, Zurbano, 309n107
Cebu Sakdalistas, 41, 264n44
Cedula tax, 24–25, 40, 47, 70, 142, 171,
    217, 250n25, 251n30, 252n44
Centeno, Pio, 251n29
Christ the King Seminary, 184, 195,
    310n117
Christmas Eve Fiasco, 2, 5, 8, 84, 141,
    203, 260n11
Cifra, Paulino J., 252n41
City Laborers, 14, 26, 137, 143–44, 197
Civilian Emergency administration, 134,
    284n90
Cocheros, 13, 39, 62
Collaboration with Japanese Military,
    171–89
Colorum (organization), 6, 145–46, 205,
    208, 232n18, 256n71; in Catmon
    (Sta. Maria, Bulacan), 288n32;
    members, 19–20, 284n88
Comintern in Moscow, 93
Commonwealth government, 6, 21, 48,
    50, 60, 69–70, 78–80, 87, 92, 98,
    103, 105–6, 111, 114, 116, 118,
    154, 173–74, 190–92, 199, 225;
    first elections, 99; inauguration of,
    80
Commonwealth laws, 60, 79, 92, 103, 114
Communist Party of the Philippines,
    23, 26–28, 46, 67, 93–95, 98, 104,
    130, 203–4, 222, 234n26, 270n24,
    272n42, 280n33, n39, 284n88,
    313n17; illegal, 245n85
Concepcion, Ignacio, 280n33
Confessor, Tomas, 235n6
Congreso Obrera, 237n24, 287n25
Consejo Revolucionario de Filipinas, 139
Copra: export, 44; producers, 272n41
Cornejo, Miguel, 269n19
Coruña, Esteban, 251n29, 282n67
Covar, Prospero, 207

Laurel, Jose P. , 62, 147, 181, 182–83,
185–89, 192, 196, 200, 304n61,
306n75–76, n78–80; assassination,
304n63; donation to Ricarte's volun-
teer army, 306n76
Lauson, Felicisimo, 82, 85, 264n44,
279n29, 300n32
Lava, Jesus, 132
League, Jose E., 252n41
Legionario del Trabajo, 9
Lichauco, Faustino, 167
*Liwayway* (magazine), 237n28
Local belief system, 316n31
Longos (Laguna), 250n22
Lorenzo, Angel, 81, 263n35
Loyalty Day, 134
Lucban, Vicente, 298n15
Luna, Ladislao, 313n13
Luviminda, 193

Mabini, Apolinario, 14, 78, 95, 145, 168,
296n91–92
*Mabuhay* Journal, 62
Macapagal, Dionisio, 243n72, 309n113
Magbag, Evaristo (Tarlac), 251n29
Magno, Isabelo (Camarines Norte), 251n29
Magtanggol (military group), 10, 141,
286n14, 304n64
Majayjay (Laguna), 250n22
Makalinaw, Loreto, 130
Makapili organization, 185, 187, 193, 201,
207, 209, 212, 304n66; flag, 186,
306n80; formation of, 181, 184–89,
192; headquarters (Christ the King
Seminary), 195; members, 200–201,
203, 310n117; soldiers, 193–99; songs,
193; suicide squad, 194; victims of
Japanese Occupation, 229n1
Malabon Sugar Company, 240n52
Malayang Bayan (Sakdal) movement, 17–19,
22–24, 30, 32, 34, 242n61. *See also*
Sakdalista movement
*Malayang Tao*, 260n7
Malolos (Bulacan), 4; peasant unrest,
269n12
Manahan, Jacinto, 274n55

Manalatoc, Antonio C., 280n33
Mangampo, Venancio, 280n33
Manibo, Joaquin, 249n9
Manila: laborers, 287n25; municipal
meeting, 235n6; regional campaign
committee, 255n64; Sakdalista
movement, 296n96
*Manila Daily Bulletin*, 284n1
Manila Democrata, 270n20
Manila milling industry, 44
Manila North High School, 13, 15, 137,
149, 236n14
Manila Railroad Company, 240n52
Manley, F. W., 66
Manuel, Arsenio: on Rizal supporting the
1898 revolution, 295n85
Manuzon, Fernando, 98, 271n38, n39,
280n33
Mapagsumikap (endeavor), 285n7
Marco Polo Bridge, 115
Mariano, Patricio, 290n40
Marilao (Bulacan): peasant unrest,
269n12
Marinduque, 41, 43, 81; regional
campaign committee, 255n64
Martinez, Ignacio, 98, 257n87
Martinez, Tomas, 289n34
Martires, Martin, 290n41
Maruyama, Masao, 49, 253n52, 254n53
Masangkay, Guillermo, 16
Matsui, Iwane, 254n53, 278n19
Matsumoto, Kumpei, 49, 254n53
Matsuyama Butai (Matsuyama Unit),
178
May Uprising. *See* Sakdalista movement
Mayor, Dionisio C., 42, 251n29, 280n33
Members of Anti-Catholic Religious
Organizations, 144
*Memorial* (pamphlet), 51, 79, 96, 129
Mendoza, Alfonso, 23, 45, 76, 133, 17,
237n253
Mercado, Leonardo: folk Catholicism,
315n31
Metodistas en las Islas Filipinas
(Methodist Evangelical Church in
the Philippine Islands), 146